To,

Rev. Father J. Daly.

Valerie Pascal Delacorte

The Disciple
and His Devil

Sharon,
Ct.

Sept. 20/08

The Disciple

Gabriel Pascal

and His Devil

Bernard Shaw

By Valerie Pascal

AN AUTHORS GUILD BACKINPRINT.COM EDITION

The Disciple and His Devil
Gabriel Pascal Bernard Shaw

AN AUTHORS GUILD BACKINPRINT.COM EDITION
Published by iUniverse, Inc.

For information address:
iUniverse, Inc.
2021 Pine Lake Road, Suite 100
Lincoln, NE 68512
www.iuniverse.com

Originally published by McGraw Hill

Quotations from the letters and other writings of George
Bernard Shaw are reprinted with the permission of The
Society of Authors as Agent for the Shaw Estate.

Designed by Christine Aulicino

First Edition

ISBN: 0-595-33772-4

Printed in the United States of America

Gabriel Pascal is one of those extraordinary men who turn up occasionally—say once in a century—and may be called godsends in the arts to which they are devoted. Pascal is doing for the films what Diaghileff did for the Russian Ballet. Until he descended on me out of the clouds, I found nobody who wanted to do anything with my plays but mutilate them, murder them, give their cadavers to the nearest scrivener without a notion of how to tell the simplest story in dramatic action and instructed that there must be a new picture every ten seconds and that the duration of the whole feature must be forty-five minutes at the extreme outside. The result was to be presented to the public with my name attached and an assurance that nobody need fear that it had any Shavian quality whatever, and was real genuine Hollywood. Under such conditions I of course would not let my plays be filmed at all, though I quite realized their possibility in that medium. When Gabriel appeared out of the blue I just looked at him and handed him Pygmalion to experiment with. His studio was immediately infested with script writers and he thought that everything they did was wrong and that everything I did was right. Naturally I agreed with him. Pygmalion was an enormous success. . . . He shocks me by his utter indifference to the cost; but the result justifies him; and Hollywood, which always values a director in proportion to the money he throws away, is now at his feet; for he throws it away like water.

The man is a genius: that is all I have to say about him.

George Bernard Shaw

PART ONE

Chapter 1

Paris in Four Weeks

SEPTEMBER 20, 1946: a lazy autumn afternoon. I had met some friends in town, and when I returned to the modern apartment house where I lived, it was already twilight. In the sumptuous marble hall, a telegraph boy stood studying the tenants' names. I sensed that the white envelope in his hand was for me. Somehow I made my voice calm as I pronounced my name and asked, "Are you looking for me?"

He was. He handed me the cable. I caught sight of the "New York" on it, and my heart suddenly began to beat rapidly. I knew when I reached out for the envelope that it held my fate. I knew who the sender had to be and that after all these months and months he had not forgotten his promise. He had good news for me, otherwise he wouldn't have cabled. Yet with an almost masochistic delight I prolonged the expectation; instead of opening the telegram, I got into the elevator and pressed the seventh-floor button.

On the way up I studied my reflected face in the elevator mirrors. Was I playing the part correctly: a young woman on the verge of breaking the seal of a life-important message? What I was doing was the automatic self-checking of the actress, that double action which makes one simultaneously the player of a part and the observing public, something which an actress does so constantly that it becomes second nature even in private life. Indeed, my face often seemed to be something outside of me. I was used to seeing it smiling, crying, talking, while I sat in the audience watching my films. At times on the streets it laughed at me, blown up on billboards, and I would pass it by, detached. And now the mirrored elevator walls were casting back, multiplied and from every angle, that face, with eyes focused on the cable I had finally opened. It read: SPOKE WITH GABRIEL PASCAL WHO WILL BE IN PARIS RITZ HOTEL IN FOUR WEEKS TIME STOP WOULD LIKE TO MAKE TEST WITH YOU IF SUITABLE ENGAGE YOU FOR PICTURE HE IN-TENDS MAKING STOP CABLE HIM AMBASSADOR HOTEL NEW YORK WHETHER YOU CAN BE IN PARIS.

Gabriel Pascal, the world-renowned producer of the Bernard Shaw films! But how could I possibly get to Paris? I was in Buda-pest behind the fast-closing Iron Curtain. Paris in four weeks! I knew people who had been trying desperately to get out for months, people who had spent fortunes on well-connected law-yers.

The elevator stopped at the private floor of our penthouse apartment. I rang the bell, and Tibor opened the door.

"I'm going to Paris," I announced, handing him the cable. I re-alized it sounded idiotic and impossible, but I wanted to torment him as he had tormented me.

He read the cable carefully, then said, "Well, Little Rabbit, don't be disillusioned, but you know you'll never get out of here." He did not seem a bit hurt by my obvious desire for a new life and career. He walked with me to my room and patted my hand before going into the middle room occupied by my mother-in-law.

As he was closing the heavily curtained glass door in between, I could hear the impatient tapping of my mother-in-law's silver-headed ebony stick on the floor. I could visualize her sitting in her armchair, her severe black dress folded about her thin body, her iron-gray hair perfectly arranged, the narrow black ribbon hold-ing together the dried yellow wrinkles of her neck. Every inch an aristocrat, the ninety-two-year-old dowager sat there as if on a throne, commandingly erect; and, when she was displeased, her ebony stick tapped on the floor. In a low voice, Tibor said some-thing to her in German. They always spoke German to each other, a lifelong habit, yet it irked me. It was as if they thus built a wall around themselves and their private world. Then I heard Tibor going into his own room, next to his mother's.

The apartment house belonged to Tibor and was one of several properties he owned in the heart of the city. The penthouse, into which we had moved after our marriage in June, 1945, was built for a German baroness who had been Tibor's mistress for many years. But after the siege of Budapest, the baroness had married a French prisoner-of-war and left Hungary with him. Tibor moved into the penthouse after his own luxurious apartment was bombed.

Tibor belonged to the condemned class—the nobility. After the war, his huge estates in the country were confiscated, and the bones of his ancestors were thrown out of the old chapel in the park by the peasants who lived on the property. They must have bitterly resented the family, since for forty years Tibor's father had never visited his lands, leaving the welfare of the peasants to his bailiffs. He had preferred the life of Vienna, Paris, and London, spending his money and energy on beautiful women. As he lay dying, he called his sons around his deathbed and admonished them, "Sons, do not live for your penis alone as I did."

Tibor had taken no heed of his father's warning. He, too, possessed an insatiable lust for women. There was no heart involved in his conquests. He was charming and entertaining, always assuring his mistress of the moment that she was doing him a favor by accepting some large diamond ring or expensive furs. He would never force himself on her, but when he grew tired of her a valuable present would arrive with a poetic note about their lovely hours together. He never asked faithfulness, nor was he ever jealous. He never asked questions, but neither could questions be asked of him. He was a cynic, but a pleasant one. He had a sarcastic wit, and he had elegance. Tall and handsome, he was a little over fifty when we met—much too old for me, friends commented. I remember his hands distinctly. They were long and narrow—Renaissance hands with pale, elongated fingers. One could imagine them stroking deep purple velvet, fondling antiques smoothed by age, holding cards with the grace of a courtier, playing with precious stones and with the hair of his women.

After we were introduced, flowers and a thousand attentions were showered on me. I never felt the difference in our ages. He was amusing, and it was pleasant to have him as a beau. At the time of our meeting, World War II was at its midpoint and food was scarce; I welcomed the pheasants and the capons, fattened with nuts, from his estates.

Tibor said that he was in love with me, that I was the second love of his life. The first was the wife of his youth, a famous beauty named Marietta, who had divorced Picaver, a great tenor of the Vienna Opera, to marry Tibor, only to divorce him in turn after a year and a half. I knew about Tibor's mistress, the German baroness, but he assured me that their relationship had by then become nothing more than a friendship. He felt deeply responsible for her, he explained, as she had left her country for his sake and she had no means of support.

The war was all around us. Nineteen forty-four and the blood-flood broke over Hungary. From among the ruins and the dead we emerged into a changed world.

We decided to get married, but on my part there remained a question: would he have married me if his mistress had not eloped with someone else? He said he loved me, and I hoped his amorous adventures were in the past, but then came a remark. "You know," he said, "I am bored with jealous women and their possessiveness. I believe that a man was created polygamous. After a while he becomes incapable of making love to the same woman; he gets used to her. The way to keep a wife satisfied and a husband happy is to have other women in between. After them the wife will seem new and interesting again."

Later he was to swear that he had been faithful to me, but I never believed him, remembering the afternoons when he would disappear, offering vague excuses. And he found it barbaric to share the privacy of his room with a wife. He wanted to sleep alone.

We shared the penthouse with his mother. In ruined postwar Budapest, each person was allowed only one room. If the apartment one was lucky enough to have happened to be bigger, it had to be shared with other families; therefore, Tibor argued, his mother had to be with us so that we could hold the apartment.

But I knew that under no circumstances would he consider parting from "Mama Giza," as he called her. My own mother lived on another floor in the same building, as his guest.

Tibor's room had a hall and a private entrance. Mama Giza was settled between us, in the middle room, separated from me by a double glass door with thick curtains. Whenever I passed through her room to Tibor's, I could feel her cold amber eyes following me with disdain and suspicion.

Shortly after I married Tibor, I realized that he was as old-fashioned in his attitudes as his mother was. I found myself surrounded and overpowered by a world of old people—like Miss Mariella, a poor relative, who for years came every afternoon at three o'clock to play cards with the dowager. Mariella was an old maid and extremely ugly. Her heavy chignon, always disorganized, hung down her neck, making her large head look even larger. She had the expression of a sleepy toad. Twice a week she lunched with us officially, but the other days she came earlier than expected and stole into the kitchen to swallow quickly the remains of our luncheon. She would then go into the sitting room where my mother-in-law awaited her. Their conversation had the form of a ritual:

"*Küssen die Hand*, Auntie Giza."

"*Servus*. Again you are late."

"It is just three o'clock."

"Past three. You are unable to be punctual."

"On my watch . . ."

"Do not talk back to me. Bring the cards."

There would be the shuffling of the cards, accompanied by the peculiar sipping sound Mama Giza made. The rhythm of her sipping changed with her moods like a solo on a strange musical instrument. She was a cunning card player, and poor Mariella got on her nerves. "You ass," she would say sharply. "You will never learn the game. I can't understand that young man who asked for your hand eleven times. He couldn't have been mentally healthy. And on top of it you refused him."

This romantic event had occurred forty-five years before. Whenever Mama Giza mentiond it, Mariella would utter a faint "He, he, he." But Mariella was one of the clan, *their* clan, and she had turned openly against me, the newcomer.

One afternoon shortly after I had returned home from the hospital, where I had had a minor operation, I went to Tibor's room for a chat. He told me to go back and lie down, but I lingered on. There was a knock on his private entrance door. He rushed out, taking care to close the door behind him. In a second he was back and ushering me to my room; one of his business friends was outside, he said, and they had something important to discuss. His whole body emanated a lie. I went back to my room, Mama Giza watching me in silence as I trespassed on her territory. I went to the anteroom and looked out the peephole in the main door just in time to see Tibor motioning from his private door to a slim female figure. Knowing that I was sick in my room, he had arranged everything for a pleasant afternoon.

I told him that I could live with him no longer. He turned white with rage. Usually the perfect gentleman, he struck me, shouting, "Pack and go, together with your mother!" I could hear Mama Giza hissing from her room, "Let her go, my son, let her go," and Mariella, who was visiting, loudly agreed.

I moved into my mother's small apartment. After two days Tibor appeared, repentant. I couldn't bring myself to look at his face. Still convalescing, I lay in bed, trying to make plans. There was nowhere to go. The only thing I could do was act, and there was nowhere to act in the ruined city. My money had lost its value. What could I do?

Tibor came a second time. His face seemed narrower and he was pale. He said that he was very unhappy and that he had not been unfaithful. I felt sorry for him. I knew he suffered, but I also knew he was lying and that after I went back to him he would be the same as before. I looked at him as he sat, his tall, lean figure bent toward me, and at that moment I knew that he was not and never had been a part of me. I felt guilty. I avoided his eyes when I told him that I would come back to him.

Everything continued as before and the days passed, stretching like a long road between flat winter fields. Existence seemed meaningless with my career broken and my marriage a mistake. I had no ideals or beliefs to turn to. I did not doubt that there were such things as goodness and saintliness, and that somewhere possibly a God existed, but I did not love Him or desire Him. In an ambiguous way, I imagined Him as an energy which, having created us accidentally, had left us to our own devices, to become the victims of nature, paying for sins which weren't ours, and then to die.

I feared Him as one fears a capricious fate. As far as eternal life or the existence of the human soul was concerned, my beliefs were even more ephemeral. Life was short; before and beyond it was darkness. And now I was trapped. The Iron Curtain had closed; I could never leave Hungary.

The Russians seemed to have withdrawn from Budapest; one seldom saw them any more. The Russian soldiers who had lined the streets on the Feast of Saint Stephen, the first King of Hungary, when thousands of Hungarians had gathered to listen to Cardinal Mindszenty's fiery talk, were only a memory. The city administration had been taken over by Hungarians. The Communist Party had not yet come out into the open, but power was in its hands. People disappeared every day. Budapest was a city of fear, even though one no longer saw shivering citizens running through the streets in their underwear, stripped of their clothes by robbers. The shouting and clapping of hands in the dimly lit night— one of the early postwar peculiarities—was a thing of the past. Deserters from the Russian army would break into houses, robbing and killing the inhabitants, and Russian patrol cars would then spend the night searching for them. Since there were no telephones, it was impossible to advise the patrol in what part of the city the atrocities were taking place, so the tenants of an attacked house would crowd into the upper windows and onto the balconies. There, while the deserters ransacked the ground floor, they would clap their hands, clang pots together, and shout in a chorus the name of their street and house number. The next house would pick up the information, and in the same manner relay it to the neighboring houses. Sooner or later, this clamorous chain of sound would bring a patrol car to the scene. Fighting and shooting usually followed, while the people of the neighborhood watched from their windows. Once the deserters were subdued and handcuffed, the members of the patrol were rewarded with applause and bravos. Right and left they would bow to the upper-story audiences.

My mother never wanted me to become an actress. I came from a proud but impoverished family. The great wealth of my father's family had melted away, and although he worked hard he never went far on his own. He defied his industrious Dutch origin by being a most impractical dreamer. My mother was Hungarian. Because of an unhappy childhood, she distrusted happiness, suspecting that misfortune lurks ready to strike the moment one begins to feel comfortable. She was domineering, as she had to be with my dreaming father at her side. She was a good and ambitious mother who constantly sacrificed herself, and when she felt that my brother and I weren't grateful enough she reproached us. Her bad moods struck suddenly. But she had a quick, clear mind, vitality, and a sense of humor, and in moments of inspiration she revealed a deep wisdom and understanding.

My feelings about Mother were always to remain in confusion. She was the deep root of my existence, holding me at times an unwilling prisoner of that beloved root. In the foreign lands to which I was later to be swept along with her, she represented belonging, love, and home; lost childhood streets and the mother tongue; Christmas toys; the dead father and the warm, large-breasted aunts; the smell of acacia-honey, forest mushrooms, and of earth after a quick summer rain.

When I reached high-school age, Father was broke. Nevertheless, with a tremendous financial effort, Mother put me in one of the finest schools in Buda, a *gimnasium* conducted by nuns. I soon hated it. I felt inferior to the well-to-do girls, and at times I burned with humiliation. I neglected my studies, and the nuns had every reason to give me bad marks. With a few exceptions, I feared and disliked my teachers. They were strict, like Mother; they were so superior in their righteousness and piety that I was always in the wrong. Religion seemed to me nothing but long, boring doctrines which I was obliged to learn, together with a lot of don't-do-its. The more Mother and the nuns threatened me with hell fire or promised me an eternity in heaven with a God whose company I didn't want (I pictured Him like our long-bearded and rigorous school president), the more I turned away from religion, or rather from what I thought to be religion.

I scraped through the final exams of the *gimnasium* but Mother's plans for my future revolted me. No, I would never fit into that middle-class paradise, that unimaginative mediocrity that smelled of poverty. I would take my fate into my own hands: I would be an actress!

Together with a friend who had similar ambitions, I went to a movie studio to apply for a job as an extra. Certainly, I thought, the director would immediately recognize in me a new Garbo. The doorman refused to let us pass. My friend meekly left, but not I. "Look at me and remember me," I said to the doorman. "Some day I shall drive through this very gate, and you will run to open it for me. I shall be a star." And so it was to happen.

When I enrolled in the Royal Academy of Dramatic Arts, my father was already dead. Mother was shocked and deeply disappointed with my choice of a career, considering me a lost soul. My rise to stardom in the films and the theater was rapid and almost effortless. The fan letters, the limelight, I took as naturally as the admiration of men.

At the dinner table my eyes wandered over Tibor's face. If he was hurt because of my excitement over the cable from New York he covered it up well. Mama Giza, opposite her son, seemed sullen and exchanged only a few words with my mother, at her right. Absent-mindedly I watched our gay, round Austrian maid clear away the soup plates, but soon the maid and the plates and the faces around the table sank into a haze. *Be in Paris . . . in four weeks*—and I could meet Gabriel Pascal. I had just recently seen the revival of the film *Pygmalion*. It had first been shown in Budapest several years earlier, and the press was full of fantastic stories about Pascal, the producer, the poor Hungarian boy who had rocketed to world fame. At that time Gabriel Pascal was just a name to me, formless and faceless; and now suddenly he had burst into my life. I could meet him in Paris. *Paris . . .* each letter of the word was holiday red in my mind's eye, and the Paris landmarks, so well known to me from pictures, were misty backdrops.

I visualized myself strolling in front of them with Gabriel Pascal. We were talking, and he was saying wonderful things. The film test we had made, he was saying, was excellent, and I was his great new discovery. I listened eagerly, knowing how many stars he had created and that he was close to George Bernard Shaw.

It had all started six months ago. One afternoon Tibor had left home with his usual vague excuses, about which we had argued. I knew he had gone to meet another woman; he couldn't help himself. I was in my room, crying, when the phone rang. I didn't feel like answering, but the ringing sounded so insistent that I went into Tibor's room and picked up the receiver. The caller was an old friend of mine, a newspaperman, Adorjan Stella, "Dori" to his friends. He was at the Bristol Hotel bar, he said, with an American friend, Ben Blumenthal. "You must know his name," he insisted. I did. Ben Blumenthal had been the owner of one of the finest theaters in Budapest, the Vigszinhaz, of which I had been a member. It had been destroyed during the siege, and Blumenthal was now in Hungary seeking compensation from the government. He was also an influential man in Hollywood, Dori said, and as a Hungarian film star I ought to meet him.

"Then, too, I made a bet with him," he added. "Ben said that there are no more beautiful women in Budapest such as there were when he was young, so that's why I'm calling you to come and have a drink with us. Bring Tibor along."

I thought, why should I go? I wasn't interested in meeting Blumenthal. But on the other hand, if I went, Tibor wouldn't come home from his tryst to find me with reddened eyes.

"Tibor isn't home, but I'll be there in half an hour," I said into the receiver.

I left the house in a simple coat with a shawl over my head. No one dared dress up in postwar Budapest; besides, no one had anything to dress up in. The icy wind blew freely among the tumbled-down, burned-out buildings as I walked through the narrow streets of the Belváros to the Bristol.

The smoky, noisy bar was warm and crowded. Passing a mirror as I entered, I glanced at myself. With my red eyes and even redder nose I looked anything but a glamor girl. Adorjan was going to lose his bet, I smiled to myself.

I discovered my friend at a corner table. He jumped up and

rushed forward to greet me. And there was Ben Blumenthal, a thin, smallish, elderly man, smoking a big cigar. He had throat trouble and could speak only in a whisper, which did not seem strange, for in those days everyone whispered in Budapest. In a city where people simply disappeared from one day to the next, one whispered even when saying, "It's a nice day today."

Blumenthal looked at me with interest, and we talked about his theater. He said he was leaving for London the next morning. "Then back to New York," he added. "And then I have to fly to Hollywood." London . . . New York . . . Hollywood! Ben couldn't possibly have imagined the almost choking desire the mention of those places created in me. I visualized them as in a fairy tale, full of music, perfume, soft furs, bubbling life, skyscrapers burning with a thousand lights. For me I thought they would forever remain as distant as Mars.

I was aware of Ben's eyes studying my face. "You are very interesting," he said. "I'm sure you could be a success in Hollywood." He asked me to get some of my photographs to him so that he could take them when he left the next morning.

Three days later, an airmail letter arrived from London. Ben wrote that it was his honest opinion that I could have a career, and that he had already spoken about me to Alexander Korda and Gabriel Pascal, both famous producers in England and both of Hungarian origin.

Since that day I had been waiting. In the early summer there was another letter from Blumenthal, this time from Hollywood. He had shown my photographs to several people, but I wasn't there; and to transport an actress, unknown to them, all the way from Hungary—well! I feared I would never hear from him again, but I continued to harbor a secret hope. And this afternoon the cable came. By now its message was imprinted on my mind: SPOKE WITH GABRIEL PASCAL . . . IN FOUR WEEKS . . . WHETHER YOU CAN BE IN PARIS. Those words seemed to mock me now, promising a great opportunity—*if* in four weeks I could break through the Iron Curtain.

I sighed and reached for a cookie from the plate in the middle of the table. My eyes met Mama Giza's disapproving glance. I realized that that was to be my third cookie. My portion was two. After dinner those cookies would disappear into Mama Giza's closet, never to be seen again by me. I withdrew my hand fast. The longing to get away and go to Paris almost bit into my flesh. I have to try it, I told myself, I have to!

"It's impossible. No one could manage it in such a short time. You're an actress. Very well. First of all you have to get a clearance from the Actors Association proving you had no affiliation with the Nazis. Then with a clearance from your previous and present Police Districts, you must go to the Ministry of Culture, and there you have to get a permit to file an application for a passport . . ."

My head was spinning as I listened to a lawyer friend whom I had called up the first thing next morning. He went on, telling me that after I got the passport, which would take months, I wouldn't be through yet. I would have to get a French visa, and the French were not very keen on granting visas to Hungarians. I would also have to get a Swiss transit visa and a permit from the Allied Powers to cross Austria.

"Then comes the insurmountable." He took a deep breath. "You need a Russian permit to leave the country. To get that would cost you a fortune if you were lucky enough to find a middle-man. There's the risk, too, that you'd never see either your permit or your money again. Even if you were able to get all of your papers, it would take months and months. To be in Paris in four weeks! Don't make me laugh."

But I *had* to be in Paris in four weeks! I *had* to meet Gabriel Pascal!

Out of one office building and into another. Crowds waiting everywhere. Impatient official hands riffling through my innumerable identity papers and certificates. And in my handbag the cabled answer from Gabriel Pascal himself: COULD MEET YOU IN PARIS FROM OCTOBER 20 UNTIL END OF MONTH HOTEL RITZ PLACE VENDOME STOP AU REVOIR REGARDS PASCAL.

From behind desks, countless eyes looked at me discouragingly, shoulders shrugged. "Get out of here by October twentieth? It can't be done."

A little clerk sat typing in front of a large padded door leading to the inner sanctum of the Counsellor of the Ministry of Culture. I needed a permit from there before I could continue. My application, the little clerk informed me, had to wait for the consideration of the Counsellor, and hundreds of such applications were waiting.

"But I can't wait. I must be in Paris...."

The clerk looked up from his typewriter. His thick eyeglasses were too heavy for his weak nose; his hair, thinning and colorless, was greased close to his scalp. His eyes had the faithful, tail-wagging look of a sad spaniel. He smiled. "Leave your papers with me."

He looked even more spaniel-like the next morning when he handed me the permit. I could hardly believe it, but his boss, the Counsellor, had granted it right away! I thanked him for his help, and he said, "If you run into any trouble with the Russian permit, come back to me. I might be of some use."

How, I wondered as I thanked him, could such an insignificant clerk help me obtain a Russian permit?

The Passport Office was crowded, with policemen controlling the lines of people. I got a number and then spent days waiting from early morning until closing time. Less than three weeks remained until the twentieth of October. Finally the pressure of time made me brash. I swept past the line and the policemen. No one stopped me.

"You have to help me," I pleaded with the official behind the desk.

"Wait outside until your number is called."

"I can't. I have no time. None of those people outside have a fixed date. If I miss Gabriel Pascal in Paris, I will *never* meet him. My career depends on it. And *you* can help."

He was uneasy and looked away. "Even if I help you and rush your passport through—which I will try to do—you can never make it. You need visas and a Russian permit to leave the country. You won't get them in time."

What is this urge in me, I wondered, this power driving me with such mad stubbornness? My whole being became one powerful wish: to get to Paris. There was no other thought on my mind. I felt as if I were suspended on the hands of an enormous clock, disinterestedly ticking away the minutes, hours, and days, nearer and nearer to October 20.

Tibor watched me in silent apprehension. But he was sure I would never make it and that then my whim would pass.

On October 6 I received my passport! The vision of Paris grew clearer. I flew to the French Consulate, only to be told, "The application for a visa must first be sent to Paris. Then if it is approved there, it will be mailed back here. How long will it take? Six, eight weeks at best."

I called my friend Harriet, a beauty from an old aristocratic family, now hostess at the English Mission, a temporary administration of the foreign powers in Budapest. She arranged parties there, welcoming diplomats and foreign officers. She knew the French Consul, and made an appointment with him for me.

With Gallic charm and suavity, the Consul assured me that it was not possible.

"But I must be in Paris on October twentieth. I must!"

The Consul was fidgety. "I'll see," he said reluctantly, "if there is any possible way."

The next day the visa was approved without an application being sent to Paris. "Only in exceptional cases do I have such authority," the Consul explained.

The Swiss transit visa—no hope there either; it would take from one to two months to get the visa from Bern, said the Swiss representative. Could he grant me a visa without asking Bern? No, he had no such authority.

At home I went to my room, giving only a curt answer to Tibor's question. The calendar on the desk said October 10. All the rushing, all the struggle had been for nothing. I lay down on the bed, and closed my eyes . . . then I heard the telephone ringing in Tibor's room, and his steps approaching my door.

"It's for you."

I got up reluctantly and went to the phone. It was the Swiss representative. "I haven't had any rest since you left my office," he began. "The tragic look in your eyes still haunts me. There is a way out."

When I left the office of the Swiss Delegation, I could scarcely believe that I was holding the letter in my hand—a letter issued only to diplomats or commercial agents to enable them to pass through Switzerland. Suddenly I felt that there was something uncanny about this whole thing, as if a power beyond me were lifting me out of my old life and pushing me toward some unknown fate. Everything and everybody seemed to conspire to get me off to Paris.

Tibor was surprised by my success but said, half-hopefully, "You'll never get the Russian permit."

And he seemed to be right. A middle-man I had heard about named a staggering amount. And when would the permit be granted? "Who knows?" I had only eight days left. Suddenly I remembered the little clerk with the spaniel eyes and his offer to help. There he was, sitting and typing, his balding head over his papers. A light flickered across his face when he looked up and listened to my report.

"You really got all your papers! Unbelievable girl." He smiled. "Leave them with me, and in a few days I'll call you."

"But are you serious? I can't waste time."

"I can understand your doubts. I'm just a clerk—something between a receptionist and a doorman." There was no bitterness in his voice, only a slight mockery. "But you must *trust* me. I wouldn't play games with you."

"Well, let's speak frankly. I'm somewhat embarrassed and don't know how to put it. Would it cost much?"

Again the mocking tone. "Nothing."

Uneasily I left my papers in his care. Days passed without news. I began to accuse myself of being stupidly credulous. How could I imagine that a clerk could do what important people could not? But now it was too late. In a few days it would be October 20, and Gabriel Pascal would be waiting for me at the Ritz Hotel on the Place Vendôme...but I wouldn't come and he would go away, and we would never meet. I couldn't eat or sleep. I couldn't think of anything but Pascal and Paris.

The phone rang. "Come at once." The little clerk was brief and mysterious on the other end.

When I arrived, the anteroom was full of people. The clerk, typing at his desk, motioned me to be seated. I tried to catch his eye for a reassuring sign, but his glance swept over me with indifference. Finally the room emptied, and I stepped up to his desk. He opened a drawer and produced a sheet of cheap paper with a green diagonal line across it: the Russian permit. I couldn't say anything. I could only take his hand in silent gratitude.

"Well," he said, handing me the rest of my papers, "remember me sometimes."

"But how did you do it?"

"A little fellow out here might be more important than"—and he pointed to the big padded door—"the big fellow in there."

Who was this man? I made no attempt to find the answer; in the strange world of postwar Hungary one didn't ask many questions. There was one, however, that I had to ask.

"Why did you do all this for me?"

He opened the drawer again and took out a thick envelope.

"Take this with you, and when you have read it you will understand."

Tibor looked at the Russian permit, handed it back to me, walked slowly to the large glass door opening onto the terrace and, without turning, said in a colorless voice, "So you made it. I never thought you would. But why? Watching you these past weeks I've asked myself again and again—why? You frighten me. You behave like someone possessed. Why do you want to go so badly? Are you unhappy with me? I've talked stupidly in the past but believe me, Little Rabbit, I've had no other thought than you. I love you."

"Just think for a moment," I said. "You'll never make a living here. They've taken away your estates. If I get a good contract, you can sell everything you have left and leave Hungary. You can get a job too. Everybody is trying to get out. Things here are going to be worse than they are now." At that moment I seriously believed that my marriage could be salvaged and we could start a new life somewhere else.

"Don't believe that everything is honey out there," Tibor said. "And promise me one thing: that before you make your final decision, before you sign anything, you'll come back and we'll talk it over together. Your mother is here, too, remember," he warned.

"I promise. But I tell you, if there's a contract I'll sign it."

When Tibor left my room, I curled up on the sofa and opened the envelope the little clerk had given me. Inside were several poems and a letter, dated the day of our second meeting.

"I never thought the moment would come when I would meet

you face to face," the letter started. "And now that I have, I know that I shall never have another chance to tell you that since the day I saw you walking past me on the street, proud, beautiful, you have become the meaning of my life ... I know everything about you. Like a shadow I have followed you, sitting every night at the theater and in the movies, watching you a hundred times in your roles. But I never wanted to meet you—because only in this pre-Raphaelite vision, only in this pure, mystical ecstasy, could you ever be mine ... "

The poems were beautiful. It was getting late, and when I finished reading them darkness had crawled slowly into the room. The thought of the little man and his futile love filled me with sadness.

The Allied Forces Permit for the Austrian transit was granted without difficulty. A telegram arrived from Pascal: PLEASE WIRE ME GRESHAM HOTEL DUBLIN WHEN YOU ARE LEAVING FOR PARIS AND I WILL FLY THERE THE SAME DAY STOP BRING WITH YOU A REEL CUT TOGETHER OF BEST SCENES FROM YOUR FILMS STOP PLEASE MEET ME THE FIRST TIME WITHOUT MAKE-UP OR LIPSTICK AND DON'T WASTE YOUR ENERGY ON SOPHISTICATED DRESSES COME IN A BLACK SKIRT AND WHITE SHIRT-BLOUSE STOP YOU ARE WELCOME GOD BLESS YOU HAVE FAITH AND COURAGE BON VOYAGE ET A BIENTOT—PASCAL.

Miraculously I got a reservation on the Alberg Express, and I wired Pascal that I would meet him on October 25.

I stood with Tibor on the station platform beside the steaming train, and when the porters raised their signals and the engineer let out a full blast on the whistle, he took me into his arms. "Little Rabbit, I love you. Don't leave me. Come back. It will kill me if you don't."

In those feverish four weeks, I had all but forgotten his existence. I had never once thought, in that mad rush, of how he must be feeling. But his last words touched me. I was overwhelmed with shame at my own selfishness.

When the train reached the frontier, an army of officials, police, detectives, and armed soldiers swarmed aboard. Each piece of luggage was turned inside out; every person was examined. Hours passed before the inspection was finished and we could enter Austria. When we left Vienna, the conductor warned us to close the compartment door and not to go out into the corridor. Russian soldiers, he said, sometimes came aboard during the night.

I stretched out in my berth, but I couldn't sleep. My emotions in that moment—the triumph and the excitement—could only be understood by those who have also tasted the terror of war and of lost freedom, who have gone through the horrors of living in a bombed city with the ring of destruction closing tighter every day, of seeing the streets where one used to walk in normal day-by-day pursuits torn up. How many times death had threatened . . . I remembered the autumn of 1944. The streets of Pest were tumultuous with caravans of people, fleeing in the van of the Russian army, which was closing in from the north and east. Horse-carts and trucks were heaped with household objects, and sometimes peculiar things were among them: the bits and pieces which people grab in the unthinking hysteria of escape. Men, women, children, cows and dogs, push- and pull-carts, bundles towering above heads. Where they were going no one knew.

On the streetcar tracks of the once-lovely boulevards there was the chaotic confusion of trains filled with the withdrawing Germans and their munitions. I was rushing from Pest, where I had gone on an errand, to Buda, where I lived. At the bottleneck of the Franz Joseph Bridge, the commotion was dangerous. One could cross the bridge only step by step, passing, every few meters, weird structures, like huge bird-cages, hanging on the bridge railing. They contained dynamite. The Germans, who had placed them there, were planning to blow up the bridges when the Russians reached the city. Only a few days earlier, the Margit Bridge had been blown up, they said accidentally, burying in the Danube running refugees and their carts, pedestrians, streetcars and buses.

I was relieved to reach the other end of the Franz Joseph. I went to the Hotel Saint Gellert to see my friend Adorjan Stella, who was Jewish and hiding in a room at the hotel. We talked about different plans for him to escape the raging Nazi terror. When I left him, I decided to have lunch. I thought of going to the downstairs restaurant, then changed my mind for the first-floor dining room. The headwaiter, who knew me, apologized, saying that ten minutes earlier he would have been able to give me one of the tables by the picture windows, now all occupied by German officers. Instead he seated me near the large screen which concealed the kitchen entrance. I heard a plane above; then the whole building shook from the tremendous detonation of a bomb not far away on the Mount Saint Gellert.

I never heard the bomb that fell on the hotel. The last thing I saw were the huge chandeliers swinging before they crashed down. Then the screen folded over me, protecting me from the flying glass splinters of the huge windows where I would have sat had I arrived ten minutes earlier. The Germans at that table were all killed. Everybody died or was severely injured in the downstairs restaurant, where I didn't go.

Then the winter months of 1944. Germans and Russians, around and above the cellars where we were hiding, fought not only from house to house but from room to room. Months when one's ears were filled with the concerto of death: bursting bombs, the drumfire of machine guns, the solo of the "Stalin Organ" rolling through the sky like the grating gnash of infernal monsters. One sat hungry in the darkness where one's past seemed untrue and the future never to be; there was only the misery of an endless present. Then the war ended, only to close us in a new prison: the Iron Curtain.

But now that was past, all past, and I had escaped my prison, I told myself, stretching out with a relieved sigh as the train rushed me nearer to Paris, and to freedom. I fell asleep.

"Davai, davai . . ."

I was shocked awake by the dreaded Russian words—a command to give, to give anything and everything from a watch to a woman. The shouts and the banging on compartment doors drew nearer. My heart pounded as, amid drunken laughter and the metallic clank of guns, someone attempted to force open the compartment I was sharing with another woman. Then the thud of heavy boots on down the corridor, banging at another door— then silence.

The train stopped again. We had entered the Russian zone, and Russian officers were to examine our papers once more. I looked out the window. There was no station; we were in the midst of black fields. Farther away, in the uncertain glimmer, I could see the contours of some woods.

A flashlight blinded me. The heavy bodies of soldiers and the smell of tobacco and alcohol filled our compartment. The flashlight was turned on our papers, then on our faces. The men exchanged a few words in Russian, laughed, and left.

It was twilight the following day when we reached the clean whitewashed station at the Swiss frontier. No soldiers, machine guns, or secret police! No whispering any more. Freedom! There were long-forgotten objects on the pushcarts: bananas, oranges, grapefruit, chocolate, *Vogue,* and *Harper's Bazaar.* Crowding out of the train, we bought them in drunken joy.

In time the train moved on, bearing us through the mountains which at times seemed to close in above us. I thought of Gabriel Pascal, the stranger I was going to meet, and my throat felt tight.

Chapter 2

Seven O'clock, Place Vendôme

A Hungarian woman I had met on the train suggested a small hotel off the Champs Élysées. She would be staying there too, joining her husband who was already in Paris. On the long cab ride from the station, my eyes drank in the city through the October mist. I couldn't believe it; was it really me riding down the Champs Élysées?

The hotel was on a side street near the upper part of the Champs. The proprietress herself was seated behind the register: straw-blond ringlets, heavy make-up, a syrupy smile. The rhinestones on her fat hands glittered as she stroked an enormous red tomcat sitting beside her on the table. Brass bells at the cat's neck tinkled when he moved.

I didn't stay long in my room; I went out to walk on the boulevards. In contrast to the dead silence of demolished Budapest, the tumult, the clamorous river of traffic charged me with electric tension. It seemed to me that for the first time I was fully alive. Life had discovered me, my great moment was about to arrive, and my whole body was shaking with a longing and an energy it had never known before.

I awoke late the next morning, and for a few seconds the strange surroundings bewildered me. Then I remembered that I was in Paris; it was the twenty-fourth of October, and my appointment with Pascal was tomorrow.

After breakfast I walked aimlessly along the boulevard. In a shop window I saw a white blouse and remembered that Pascal had cabled: COME IN A WHITE BLOUSE. The one in the window was it—delicate, of weightless silk. I bought it.

After dinner, I suddenly decided that I had to go to the Place Vendôme and see the Ritz, the place where I was to meet Gabriel Pascal. Place Vendôme . . . I tasted the name on my tongue. Then I went to my Hungarian friend's room to ask directions. Her husband drew them for me with a red pencil on a piece of blue paper.

Strolling along the wide pavement of the Champs Élysées, I soon left behind the bright lights of the shops and the glassed-in fronts of the cafés. The crowd thinned out on the lower part of the avenue, where the park begins. The chilling, damp air of the October evening had a pungent taste. The street lamps, some half-hidden among the dark swinging branches, cast yellow circles through the mist. Here and there on the benches American soldiers sat in close embrace with thinly dressed French girls. Then the lights of the Place de la Concorde appeared, with the Tuileries in the background. Under a street lamp I studied the blue paper, and when I found the arches of the Rue de Rivoli I turned right. After a short walk, I entered the Rue de Castiglione. Toward the far end, where the dark throat of the street opened into the airy luminousness of a square, I could see the black shadow of a giant column, like an archaic phallic symbol. That's it, I thought, the Vendôme column.

At the end of the street I stopped. Before me lay the spacious Place Vendôme. Everything was silent, as if suspended in the eternity of a motionless moment. The lights of the Ritz threw a pink veil over the mist. A thrill swept over me: I thought of tomorrow and of Gabriel Pascal. And it seemed to me that he was not a stranger, that I had always known him, and that now we were to meet again.

When I called the Ritz in the morning, the desk clerk informed me that Monsieur Pascal was expected around five o'clock in the afternoon. I had an early lunch and tried to rest, but my mind was busy. How should I behave? Subtle or vivacious? If only I could be myself; but I was too nervous for that. And what would I talk about?

At five, I called the Ritz and was connected with Pascal's room at once. I heard a deep, strangely familiar "Hello." I introduced myself.

"I thought you hadn't arrived yet," Pascal said in Hungarian. "I reserved a room here for you but they have never heard of you. Where are you hiding?" Then he asked about my journey and added, "I am free to have dinner with you. Let's meet at seven o'clock here. I'll send a car to pick you up."

When the car arrived, I took a last look in the mirror. As Pascal's cable had instructed, I was wearing a black skirt with the new white blouse and no make-up. My long blond hair was tied at the back with a black velvet ribbon. I looked like a schoolgirl.

Passing shafts of light flooded the interior of the limousine as it retraced my route of yesterday. Soon I was going by the arcades of the Rue de Rivoli; then a sharp turn into the Rue de Castiglione, and finally the Vendôme column. I was trembling and my cheeks were burning. I was sorry for that; I wanted to look pale and interesting. The car drove around the Place and stopped in front of the hotel.

A doorman helped me out. As I started toward the entrance a familiar voice made me pause. I turned and met the eyes of a man: large, dark, luminous eyes. We stared at each other, then he said, "I was hoping for a Hungarian peasant girl to play Joan of Arc in my film, and here comes a princess!"

He escorted me down a long corridor to the dining room. Everything around me was in a haze. Colors and forms seemed to vibrate in the manner of the Impressionists, and the waiters' "*Comment allez-vous,* Monsieur Pascal?" sounded muffled. Only when we were sitting at a corner table beside a tall mirrored screen did I regain a clear view of my surroundings.

I looked at my companion. He seemed to be in his early forties. He was of stocky build, not tall, and his strong head sat upon broad shoulders; the shape of his skull suggested his Hungarian ancestors. Under the dense black eyebrows, his eyes were large and a bit slanting; he must have some *Kun* blood in him, I thought. His face was fascinating, proud and manly; it reminded

me of a lion's. Between his eyes were embossed deep wrinkles of
concentration ranging out above his eyebrows. A forehead with
wings, I thought, and the eyes of a seer and a dreamer; a despot's
bold nose. High cheekbones squared his face, but all the strength
dissolved into gentleness around the mouth. There was a deep
boyish dimple in his chin. His hair was thick, raven black, his
complexion a warm golden tan. Was he handsome? I couldn't tell.
It was the face of a man. Years later a woman friend of mine who
had seen him in a crowded lecture hall said of him, "Among all
those washed-out faces, there was only one man—Gabriel." There
was also something tragic about his strong and passionate face, the
face, I thought, of a fallen angel, yearning for a lost heaven.

As we sat down waiters surrounded the table. The headwaiter
stooped over Pascal with that servile curve of the spine which
only very important persons bring to those stiff backs. His anxious expression was mirrored on the faces of the waiters.

That was my first taste of Gabriel Pascal's grandeur. Though
he talked to people in an open and natural manner, he vibrated a
presence that made one feel he was somebody. His pleasantries
were bestowed like royal privileges. His bearing had an imperious
weight and an expectation of service which few could withstand.
Everywhere he went he was received with special attention, even
by absolute strangers.

The headwaiter's suggestions left Pascal dissatisfied. He sent
him to the chef with a detailed message in French on how our
dinner had to be prepared, adding in Italian, "But make it *con
amore.*" When his food wasn't just right, I was to discover, Pascal
would not eat it but would get up and leave. "This was made
heartlessly," he would say. "Food which has no love in it is poisonous."

I smiled to myself: the menu of the Paris Ritz wasn't good
enough . . . and I thought of the eternal noodle dinners of postwar Budapest.

I was feeling more relaxed. We spoke Hungarian, and I had
to answer many questions about the country he had left as a
boy.

Pascal smiled now and then, and I liked his open smile that re-

vealed strong white teeth contrasting with his tanned complexion.
It had something of a child's wonder at seeing a rainbow for the
first time. I remembered a summer afternoon in the country
when I was about fourteen. I had stopped to watch a gypsy caravan passing, a long row of covered wagons on the dusty highway.
On the end of the last cart sat a gypsy boy some years older than
I, half-nude, dangling his legs and chewing on a yellow corncob.
The warm wind ruffled his black hair, and the sun painted his
body gold. His white teeth glistened as he looked at me and
laughed with the freedom and joy of windswept open fields and
woods. I wanted then to sit beside the brown boy on the cart.

"You remind me of a gypsy boy," I told Pascal.

During dinner, Pascal announced that we were going to a party
at the home of a general, a close friend of De Gaulle.

"But I'm not dressed for it."

He waved my worry away. "You'll be more elegant than all the
old duchesses put together. And tomorrow," he continued, "I'll
send a car to move you over here. Your room is still reserved."

"Really, I can't accept..."

"You're my guest," he interrupted. "I invited you to Paris."

I thanked him for his kindness, and only then noticed that,
with his fork, he was picking the food from *my* plate. He had finished his own and seemed to find it most natural, while I was
talking, to continue with mine, pawing at my food like a gluttonous but benevolent bear. I swallowed what was left of my *foie gras*
in a gulp. He laughed.

The party was in a mansion on the Avenue Gabriel. In the entrance hall the butler helped me off with my coat, politely con-
cealing his surprise at the sight of my simply clad figure. He
opened the wing of a tall, heavily gilded door, and I found myself
at the top of softly carpeted stairs leading down to the crowded
drawing room. We were announced. The deep décolletages and
bejewelled arms stiffened and the white dress shirts straightened
up. It seemed to me that the world stopped as everybody stared
at the thin, short-skirted girl who had forgotten her make-up.

It's a dream anyhow, I told myself, what does it matter...

As the host hurried to greet us, Pascal's big voice broke in.
"Here she is, my new discovery. She is going to be a great star—
the Hungarian peasant-princess."

The noise resumed. Men surrounded me. I was a success because I was different.

My eyes followed Pascal as he passed flamboyantly from one group to another, always the center of attention. I felt myself fighting against the mesmeric power he seemed to exercise over everybody. He isn't my type at all, I thought, trying not to look at him—but I had to. I didn't know that I was experiencing something which Bernard Shaw used to call Pascal's "Cagliostro charm," nor did I know that Shaw had written that Pascal was one of "those extraordinary men who turn up occasionally—say once in a century."

We left the party early. Pascal suggested that we go back to the Ritz for a half hour or so; then he would take me back to my hotel. I hesitated for a second, then assured myself that this was business and that I shouldn't think of him as a man. I was an actress, he was a producer, and I had come all the way to Paris to talk with him.

We went up to his suite. He offered a drink, which I declined. He said he would like to arrange a test for me in one of the studios and hoped that I had come prepared for it. When all this was said, our conversation began to falter. It was time for me to go to my hotel. I got up.

Our kiss came as naturally as between Adam and Eve. He withdrew slowly. "I didn't want to kiss you. I didn't ask you here for that. I'm not that kind of man . . . also you are married."

Married. Reality returned. Tibor's face seemed to appear against the heavy velvet curtains. I'm in Paris, I thought, kissing a strange man—but it's only a wild dream.

The kiss was not repeated, and Pascal took me back to my hotel, sitting away from me in the car. All he said was that I had to move next day to the Ritz, where my room was still waiting for me.

I couldn't sleep that night. In the morning red roses arrived, the card signed "Gabor," Hungarian for Gabriel.

At the Ritz, Pascal was waiting for me near the reception desk. Lights played in his eyes as he smiled at me. We lunched with the writer Marcel Pagnol, who had just been elected to the Académie Française. Dinner was at the Ritz, at the table we had had the night before—"our table," we now called it. We ate in silence. The very spoons and forks felt tense as I touched them. The commotion of the dining room seemed far removed.

Then we were again in the sitting room of his suite. He ordered cognac for me. "I never drink, except some wine occasionally," he said in answer to my question. "There was a time when I began to drink too much; then I made a vow to the Madonna . . . and since then I don't drink." From a long wooden cigar box on which was printed "Especially selected for G.P." he took a thick greenish Havana and, freeing it from its jacket, snipped its end. He lit it with rolled-up paper and, after inhaling the first smoke, leaned back in his armchair. I sat across the room, warming the large cognac glass between my palms.

Pascal talked again about my acting and the need to improve my English. I was only half-listening. I had met him just yesterday, yet I felt as if I had always known him. I was trying to remember of whom he reminded me: someone so close, so deeply familiar. Even his voice, that soft baritone—I would recognize it anywhere. He finished his cigar as I did my cognac, and I got up to leave. We stood at the doorway, my hand on the knob. We mumbled a few sentences, and a moment later we were holding each other close. *Run,* I told myself, *run.* But I didn't.

"You know," he began, "last night I couldn't sleep. I felt like a student—a boy again. My reason tells me I'm too old to fall in love at first sight. I don't know what it is, all I know is I want to be with you. There's something uncanny about it, too. Last spring in London, when Ben Blumenthal showed me your picture, it was as if something turned inside me, as if some faint instinct told me you were going to play a part in my life. All these past months you've been in my mind like a faraway echo—that Hungarian girl behind the Iron Curtain. When I met Ben again in New York this September he said, 'You ought to see that girl.' I told him I didn't want to be bothered with you. He insisted and that faint instinct returned, and then I knew that I *must* meet you."

I recalled my own efforts to get to Paris.

"Then," he continued, "I was worried for fear you wouldn't come, and yet I wished you wouldn't. I felt I was in for trouble. And you're married."

I sat silent, looking at his brown hands holding mine with boyish awkwardness.

He turned toward me, wrinkling his forehead into the worried frown of a dachshund. "The day before yesterday, sitting in front of the fireplace at my farm in England, I thought about you and about our date in Paris and I suddenly felt a great joy."

"What time did that happen?" I asked.

"Between nine and ten in the evening."

"That was when I was standing at the corner of the Place Vendôme and the Rue de Castiglione and felt the same joy!"

There was a deep peace in me, as if suddenly everything in my life had found meaning. It was natural and simple for us to be together, and beyond that nothing else mattered.

He went on in a low voice, as if talking to himself. "Then, while I was flying here yesterday, that strange feeling returned, but it wasn't conscious until I saw you coming toward me on the Place Vendôme."

He got up and went toward the window. "Last night I couldn't sleep," he repeated. "I was thinking of you. I'm disturbed. I'm afraid. I don't want to get involved. You came here for your career . . . and you're married . . . it wouldn't be right."

My eyes embraced him. I lost all sense of time or place, past or future. There was only *now,* the glorious, joyous present.

And I said, "I love you."

Next morning, a sunny, cool Sunday, we drove to Fontainebleau and walked through the woods. Many-colored autumn was etched against a pale blue sky. Dry leaves swirled among old tree trunks. Hand in hand, we walked in the moment's fulfillment.

"Once," Gabriel said, "I planned to make a film of a book called *Forever,* by Mildred Cram. It's a strange, mystical story of an eternal love, a love even death couldn't destroy. Last night I thought of that book."

"Forever." I repeated the English word. It can't be true that we met only two days ago, I thought. "Time can only measure ordinary days," I said. "When you first kissed me, I realized that you were the one I was waiting for; therefore it doesn't matter that we met only two days ago."

"I have always known you and loved you. This isn't the first time that we've met." So he had the same feeling that I had: of finding someone he had known before.

The castle of Fontainebleau was like a pastel in the faint autumn sun. We walked to a restaurant opposite. A fire was burning in the dining room. Gabriel ordered the meal with his usual care. After we had finished eating and were drinking strong black coffee, I suddenly fell out of my timeless joy. "Do you know that we have only seven and a half days left?" I asked him. "According to my Russian permit, I have to return to Hungary after that or I can never go back there again."

"I can't lose you," he answered.

I looked at him as he sat there with the shadows deepening the strong lines of his face. He seemed nobly beautiful and tragic—a fallen angel, Lucifer. His long cigar box lay empty on the table: he was finishing the last one. I reached for the box and opened it, inhaling its delicate scent.

"I will keep this for the memory of today," I said. "I want to enclose this moment into myself, to see you always as you're sitting here, in that wine-colored waistcoat with the brass buttons, to remember the way you move your hand as you smoke your cigar, to remember its fragrance, and your face against those gray curtains, as you're looking at me now."

He reached for my hand. "You can't go back. We must think over what has happened to us. Everything was so sudden . . . First I must know what you really want: to have a career, to stay with your husband, or to follow me? You came here because of your career. I can help you, and you'll owe me nothing. If you want to get Tibor out of Hungary, I can help you there, too. But if you really love me, then we must be honest and telephone Tibor and tell him everything and ask him to set you free."

"No, I can't tell him over the phone."

"That means you want to go back."

"I must. I can't just walk out like this. When I get back I'll tell him everything. He'll be shaken but I know that he has never really loved me."

"Yet I feel very bad about him," Gabriel said. "I feel like a thief. I really think it's better that you go back, but how can you get new permits to get out again?"

"I'm sure a contract from you could get me a six-months' permit. And now it would be easier; I know everybody who can help me. In a short time I can be here again."

"I want to marry you," Gabriel said slowly. Then, frightened by his own words, he told me how many times he had escaped marriage. He loved his freedom, he said; he would make the worst possible husband. He looked just like a worried little boy.

I couldn't help laughing. "How silly you are."

"You've bewitched me," he complained. "If someone had told me three days ago that I would ask a woman to marry me—I, who hate the very idea of marriage! How Bernard Shaw would laugh at me now."

"But you don't need to marry me. You mustn't feel it's your duty."

"And it even seems unfair for me to marry you," he continued, disregarding my remark. "You don't know anything about me and my hobo life. I could never belong. I'm not a conformist and I don't understand bourgeois morality. My morality comes from my heart. Nobody taught it to me, only nature and the inspiration of the Madonna, who has been my Mother since my childhood. I was a foundling. I don't belong to any caste or nation. I'm not practical and shrewd enough for this life. I'm like Puck in *A Midsummer Night's Dream:* more intelligent than the human beings whose cleverness I don't understand."

"Probably that's why I love you," I told him. "I've also always felt left out of the games, as if the others knew something and I could never learn their secret, though I pretended I did. Yet at the same time I felt another kind of knowledge hidden in my heart which was incommunicable to them. I was an alien everywhere and always until now . . . until I met you."

The days rolled on like multicolored marbles. We wandered through the streets, lost ourselves in the Louvre, strolled enraptured through the Rodin Museum. Then evenings at the Opéra or at the Comédie Française, where the statue of Voltaire in the corridor looked down on our love with a sarcastic grin. In the theaters, we sat with clasped hands in the red velvet stalls.

We often dined with Gabriel's friend Marcel Pagnol and his

current wife, a lovely blonde. I met General Corniglion Molinier, a good friend of General de Gaulle and the head of the Gaumont Theatres. We had dinner with Jean-Louis Barrault, who was thinking about accepting the role of the Dauphin in the film version of Shaw's *Saint Joan,* a future Pascal production. And there was Christian Bérard, the stage designer for the Théâtre Marigny, a chubby-faced, bearded genius, called Bébé by his friends. He had inspired Christian Dior's "New Look."

One afternoon Gabriel left me alone for hours. An illogical, almost insane fear came over me: he would never return. Again I felt the sensation that he was far away, unreachable.

But he did return, and in my joy I nearly thanked him for it. He carried two hatboxes from which he produced two masterpieces: one hat of ash-gray, light-pink, and powder-blue gauze, the other of bird-of-paradise feathers, pale yellow and black. Gabriel had designed them himself.

"Only a man knows about hats and dresses," he bragged. "Women have no taste. Bébé Bérard ought to paint you in the nude, wearing only these hats."

At that moment the phone rang and Gabriel answered. He motioned to me: "It's Budapest."

Tibor's voice came from a forgotten world. With a sudden shame, I realized that in the space of a few days I had almost forgotten him. His voice was hoarse with ill-concealed jealousy. He had called several times, he said, but my room never answered.

"Give me the receiver," Gabriel commanded. "I must talk to him!"

But I held onto the phone. As we struggled silently, I had to keep talking to Tibor, but Gabriel became so forceful that I had to hang up.

"Why didn't you let me talk to him?" Gabriel shouted, his face distorted. "I'm going to call him right back. Give me your number in Budapest. How I hate you! How could you talk to him like that, in that sweet lying voice? What kind of a woman are you? 'Rabbit this, Rabbit that'—you should have heard your false voice. How I despise you!"

"But he's my husband," I protested. "I'm very fond of him, and I never denied it to you. How could I tell him on the phone? How could I? Or let you talk to him?"

He wouldn't be pacified. "You're dishonest if you don't tell him the truth. Perhaps you still love him and are only deluding yourself and me. No, you don't love me! And you're lying to him! You're lying to both of us! Go back to him at once. Go back to-morrow. I'll arrange for your tickets."

He ran out, slamming the door behind him.

It was already dark. I sat motionless in an armchair in my room. My eyes were swollen, and my body ached as though I had been beaten. I couldn't move; I was drained, empty, and lonely. The noises of Paris came in through the windows; the street lights made patterns on the walls. How could I go back to Tibor and continue my life with him as before?

I jumped up as the phone rang; then my hand paused in mid-air. But at the third ring, I couldn't hold myself back any longer. Gabriel's voice was low and lifeless. "Come down. Have dinner with me."

We sat at "our table" in the dining room. He was silent, his face masklike and unsmiling. Then he began to speak in a grave tone. He had not ordered the tickets after all, he said. He realized I had come to Paris for my career, and he wished, without any personal interest, to help me. As matters stood, he didn't know whether I had talent or not, so after dinner I must play some scenes for him.

Upstairs he sank into a deep armchair. I stood before the tall window, clutched the heavy gray velvet curtain and, throwing it passionately aside, recited Juliet's soliloquy. When I finished I went into the other room. With my hair in a braid, a shawl about my shoulders, and carrying a small book, I returned. Kneeling before an imaginary statue of the Blessed Virgin, I recited Gretchen's prayer from *Faust*.

Gabriel sat without a word. When I finished, he said, "What I did to you was selfish and foolish. You are a real actress. You went through hell to get here to build a career. That is your birthright. I threw you off balance, mixed you up. Forget me! I'll make a great star out of you. But from now on you must concentrate on work. Forget me, forget Tibor. First you will learn correct English speech, then I will put you into the Royal Academy of Dramatic Arts in London."

"Forget you!" I cried. "How can I? Not even for a career!"

We told ourselves over and over: there was no use ... we could not fight against it. I would return to Hungary, we decided, and explain it all gently to Tibor. If only we could stay a few more days together here in Paris! That night, Gabriel would not let me go, grasping my hand forcefully. "Don't ever leave me," he mumbled, half-asleep, "don't ever let go of my hand ... or I'll crash."

In the morning we went to the Hungarian Consulate to try to extend my permit, but I was refused.

"Only two or three months," I told Gabriel, "and we'll be together again." I was trying to reassure myself, but I feared I was going to lose him. As I listened to him talking on the phone, carrying on film negotiations with London, Dublin, Hollywood, Rome, New York, his plans dizzied me. And there was his restless past in different countries. Once I left, how could the memory of our ten days survive?

With only three days left, our talk became subdued. The calls from Budapest were more frequent and more pleading. "I'm powerless," Gabriel said. "I would like to shout, to beg you not to go, but I agree that you have to clear the situation with Tibor personally. But will you ever come back to me?"

One afternoon Gabriel took me to the Church of Saint Étienne. He knelt down, and I followed his example. The stained-glass windows filtered the outer light into peacefulness. Steps sounded, their echoes losing themselves among high arches. I felt Gabriel reaching for my hand.

"Do you really love me? Are you sure? Think before you answer. Look into your heart," he asked.

"I love you."

"Were you married in church?"

"No, we never wanted it."

"Then you're free. Could you love me forever?"

"I love you forever."

"Then here, before the altar, I solemnly bind my soul to yours forever because you are my soul. I promise to make you happy. From this moment you are my wife, and I put our future into the hand of God. Come now," he whispered, "I will take you to my Mother."

He took me to the altar of the Blessed Lady. We lit two candles side by side, one for him and one for me.

Outside the church Gabriel said, "When you are free and back again in Paris, we are going to have our marriage blessed in this church."

Our last evening. We ate without appetite. Would we, would we ever meet again?

Leaving the restaurant, we walked around the Place Vendôme. I showed Gabriel the corner of the Rue de Castiglione where I had stood the night before he came. It hurt now to think about it; it was already in the past, even as our steps were turning one by one into yesterdays.

It was late when we returned to the hotel. The heavy velvet curtains closed out the world and only a thin streak of light came through and imprisoned itself in the mirror. I stared at it. Tomorrow, I thought, when this light appears again in the mirror, I will be on the train.

It was on that night, when I finally fell asleep, that I dreamed the same dream which in infinite variations I was to dream throughout the coming years: a strange town but in the dream well known to me, surrounded by high walls. A hostile bridge across a noiselessly flowing black river. The town is asleep. I run through deserted streets searching for my lost love. He is Gabriel but he has another name . . . and I can't remember. We are to meet somewhere but where I can't remember. Dark shadows approach, soldiers. They are chasing me. The pain for my lost lover is unbearable, and I run and run . . .

The next morning Gabriel said, "Let's say goodbye here. I don't want to go with you to the Gare de Lyon."

I agreed. While I was packing Tibor phoned again. As I talked to him, giving the time of my arrival, Gabriel, feigning disinterest, sat in an armchair with his back half-turned toward me. His right fist was clenched on the arm of the chair and the knuckles showed white. He was jealous, and the fact that he was in the wrong made it even worse. After I finished talking he went out, saying that we should meet later in his suite.

My packing done, I went to his suite to find him sitting at the desk, surrounded by crumpled sheets of letter paper.

"I have to write to Tibor. I have to tell him the truth."

"But why don't you let me handle this?" I argued. "I know how to do it because I know Tibor. If you want to write to him, why not just tell him about my career?"

"But aren't you going to divorce him?"

"Yes, later on, but it would be less painful for his vanity if I left him for a career rather than for another man."

"But if we get married, will you want your career, too?" He looked at me sharply.

"Why not?" I asked. "I'm an actress. Can't I have both, you and a career?"

He didn't answer but, bending over the desk, continued to write.

After tea he said he would go back to his farm in England and postpone his negotiations with Hollywood until I could come. We would meet again here in Paris, get married, then fly to the United States. He talked about his place in England, Mumford's Farm, which he was going to sell. He had no future in England, he said, because of intrigues in connection with his latest film, Bernard Shaw's *Caesar and Cleopatra*. Bitterness crept into his voice. I knew then that he loved England and his farm. He said we would live in Hollywood and in Ireland. He was negotiating with United Artists in Hollywood about the filming of *The Devil's Disciple,* and his dearest wish, to have his own studios, seemed about to be realized in Ireland: the Irish government was ready to build studios in Dublin for the filming of the Bernard Shaw plays.

After my luggage had been placed in the car, Gabriel decided to come to the station, no matter how painful it might be. We stood at the entrance of the Ritz, almost on the same spot where I had first seen him ten days before. The lights of the Place Vendôme were scattered through the gray chiffon of the late twilight. The column rose like a warning finger. Our hands clung together and my every heartbeat seemed to repeat, "You fool, turn back to love, to life, to freedom!"

At the station the suitcases were put into my compartment. I was traveling alone, as it was a direct car to Budapest, and who else would be going there? Fifteen more minutes . . . we assured each other that it would be only two months. Divorce was fast and easy in Hungary, and I would arrange quickly for my visas and permits. But something inside me cried, "It isn't so. You won't be here in two months. You're going to lose him. Don't go. Run for the porter, get your luggage out, run, run . . ."

Gabriel looked at his watch. "Only ten more minutes. Don't go. Let's get your luggage." He echoed my thoughts. "This whole thing is a crazy lie. You're doing wrong, you can't go back."

When the conductor signaled, I threw myself into Gabriel's arms. Our hands were parted by the slow starting motion of the train. I looked back at Gabriel standing in the dim light of the platform, steam enveloping his figure, his right arm stretched out toward the departing train.

Chapter 3

Budapest, Andrassy Ut 60

TIBOR followed me into my room, which he had decorated with flowers, and took me in his arms. "Little Rabbit," he said, "I'll never let you go again."

"Let's not talk about it now."

"You belong to me," he continued, trying to look into my eyes, "and this is your home. Don't believe in big promises. You don't know how cruel the world is."

"Well, if you insist on talking about it now, here's a letter from Pascal to you." I handed him the letter Gabriel had written the day I left Paris.

"You mean Mr. Pascal took the trouble to write to me? How very considerate of him."

He drew up an armchair and tore open the gray envelope with the Ritz letterhead. Soon he turned to me with a snort. "I don't know what Mr. Pascal means by these lines," he said, reading from the letter: " 'Valerie played several scenes from different plays for me. I am convinced that she is talented. We both feel, however, that she must go back to Budapest and talk over all our problems honestly with you. I am ready to send her a contract— but you should both consider, in harmony, what is best to be done. Because if you can't find a solution between you, it will create unhappiness for all three of us.' "

Tibor tossed the letter to the floor and stood up. "You're not going back! It was utterly foolish of me to let you go in the first place. I don't want to hear another word about it!"

I jumped up. "You have no right to steal my life. I *want* to go, I'm unhappy here!"

"And you want to be happy with Mr. Pascal!" He gripped my wrist. "Is that it?"

I screamed as he moved as if to strike me. But he freed my wrist and left the room.

I sat down on my bed and wept. I liked Tibor and I was sorry for him, but I was in love with Gabriel and I couldn't live without him.

The next three days Tibor was almost always out. We met only at lunch and dinner, and our conversation was short and impersonal. On Sunday the phone rang, and Tibor, his face expressionless, came into my room to tell me that London was calling. I passed through the sitting room, feeling Mama Giza's gaze on my back, and closed the door of Tibor's room behind me. There was a chaos of voices on the buzzing wires: "*Hallo Budapest . . . Ja, Fräulein, geben Sie mir Budapest . . . Hallo London . . .*" Then Gabriel's rich deep voice speaking from Mumford's Farm. But his tone and words were so reserved that I was miserable for the rest of the day.

A few days later Tibor sent a large basket of flowers and smiled faintly when I thanked him. He was more talkative at lunch. I felt Mama Giza watching us, even forgetting to scold Mariella about the gulping noise she always made while she ate her soup. Mother sat silent too. My Paris adventure had left her bewildered. I ate absent-mindedly, thinking of Gabriel's first letter, which I had received through Adorjan Stella, my newspaper friend; I had given his address to Gabriel so he could write to me there. The letter was written after the phone call which had disturbed me so much.

"A few hours ago I talked to you in a cold, businesslike way. Yet I wanted to shout into the receiver that ever since we parted I have been dead. My soul is gone . . . I am maimed. What magic charmed our Paris meeting? That ecstasy could not be just a mood. The flame of our love sprang from elementary forces, and I feel that in the future those flames, purified, will ascend to Heaven. I thank God that I found you. Nothing can ever part our souls. You must find a place where I can call you freely and tell you that I love you even more than I confessed to myself in Paris. I don't know how you are going to solve the problem with Tibor, but be good and generous—there should be no shadow on our new happiness."

The only person other than Adorjan who knew about my love was my friend Harriet, who had a charming apartment in the English Mission building, where she worked as a hostess. She offered me the use of her place, saying that Gabriel could call me there any afternoon.

With pounding heart, as if I were going to a forbidden tryst, I slipped away to Harriet's and waited for the phone to ring. When the call came through, we talked in tormented joy. Gabriel said he was preparing a contract, and that when I received it I should take action at once on my visas, as he had to leave soon for Hollywood. Again he urged me to talk sincerely to Tibor.

One dark evening when I was leaving the English Mission building after one of our long conversations, I found Tibor standing in the shadows of the entrance. His eyes narrowed and the muscles of his face tightened as he asked, "What do you do here in the afternoon?"

"I visit Harriet," I replied.

"Almost every afternoon? Why this sudden deep friendship?"

I moved to the offensive. "Aren't you ashamed of yourself, spying on me?"

"Aren't *you* ashamed yourself, doing things behind my back?"

"I come here to wait for Gabriel's calls from England."

"I guessed as much. And how is Mr. Pascal, the very correct gentleman who enjoys stealing another man's wife?"

"You're right! He *is* correct! He's more than correct. He has a soul and a heart, he is real, he has vision, he's an artist, he can fly! He's a man who has made his own life; he's a man and not a sex machine like you. I always knew there must be someone like him somewhere."

Tibor sighed contemptuously. "And now on top of all those virtues he offers you a career too?" Without sarcasm, he added, "I don't blame him. I would probably do the same if I were in his place. I'd give anything to keep you, but what can I offer? I have nothing left, and I even doubt my heart."

"I'm sorry," I said tearfully and sincerely.

The softness of my voice seemed to give him hope. "Little Rabbit, I can't lose you. Why do you want to ruin our lives?"

Cold wind whistled through the dark, deserted streets. The few lamps on the corners threw only small circles of light.

"It's dangerous for you to be out alone at this time of day," Tibor continued. "I don't think Mr. Pascal realizes that this city is still teeming with riffraff. If there is anything he wants to tell you, he should call you at home."

Budapest came to life again in a desperate effort to recapture her once-famous charm. Her dead lay buried under the ugly tombstones of destroyed buildings, but the odor of their decay, which had ridden the winds the year before, was gone, making it easier to forget them. Shops opened up among the ruins. Hats and dresses appeared in the windows. One could buy French perfume and American nylons. Social life began with a slow swing. The first cocktail party since the siege was given by a lawyer friend of ours. To be sure, one had to be an acrobat to reach his apartment in a bombed-out building. A corner of the drawing room was missing, the furniture was decorated with machine-gun holes, and the guests engaged in a polite but ravenous fight around the buffet. More parties followed, given for the most part by the English and American legations. Astute Hungarians came with paper bags in their pockets, snaring a snack or two for the next day.

The famously beautiful Hungarian women were lovelier than ever, although lighter by several pounds. They were the cleverest girls in the world. Making the most of a small piece of silk or a dress which had miraculously survived Tolbukhin's Third Army, they looked as if they had just stepped out of *Vogue*.

Restaurants opened. Gypsy music struck up softly, and jazz drums beat a new rhythm. Some members of the old aristocracy and the upper classes mingled with the new rich, or at least with those they considered housebroken. The British and American officers on hand were lionized by the loveliest society girls. Foreign businessmen and promoters began to descend on us to enjoy the resurrected gaiety that seemed like a *danse macabre.*

All but a few of the Russian soldiers had vanished from the streets. The Communist Party was hidden in the background. I remember a reception given by Bela Zsedenyi, the naively optimistic lawyer who had been elected the temporary head of Hungary. At the party were a number of foreign diplomats and Hungarian politicians, as well as members of the society that had grown up in postwar Budapest. Far off in a corner a man with a round, bald head and sickly moon face sat watching the fawning group around Zsedenyi from under half-closed eyelids, and smiled to himself. It was a smile to make one shiver. The man was Matyas Rakosi, a one-time Communist fugitive from Hungary to Moscow who had returned with the Russian army. For the next ten years he was to be the terror of Saint Stephen's country. Now he sat watchful and smiling, as if he knew that in due time his host was going to die in the darkness of an underground cell.

I hardly noticed what was going on around me. My only happy moments came when I heard Gabriel's voice from Mumford's Farm or when his letters arrived. Then I would shut myself into my room and write to him: "You are the miracle which happens once in a lifetime; you are right, this is our fate. Yes, I am sorry for Tibor. I am fond of him, and it is difficult to cut this chain but I must come to you . . ."

Torn between two sentiments, I was miserable. A thousand times I asked myself how much a desire for the big world and a career was weighting the scales in Gabriel's favor and boredom and hopelessness were tipping them against Tibor. Would I follow Gabriel if he were a plumber?

The contract arrived and, since I needed an extension of my passport before I could ask for visas, I went to the Passport Office. It presented the usual picture of many people in long lines. But this time I couldn't get through out of turn. Days passed before my number was called. When I handed the clerk my passport and a photostat of my contract, he said, "We are very busy. Come to inquire next week." When I returned, it was still not ready. "Next week," the clerk said.

Gabriel's letters and phone calls betrayed his confusion. Was it right to buy our happiness at the expense of another man? "We must end the sufferings of all three of us," he wrote. "How many letters have I started, saying that we might be making a mistake if you were to leave him? Also that I am too old for you. Also those ten days in Paris could not give you a realistic picture of me and my life. I do not know how many things I have counted against our love—but I cannot live without you. Only you can inspire me, only with you can I create again and open my wings and fly again."

He decided to wait for me in Italy, stopping in Paris on the way. He wrote that he was going to visit the Church of Saint Étienne, "where you became my wife," and ask the Madonna for help. But when his letter arrived, with a picture postcard of Saint Étienne enclosed, the note on it was desperate: "Coming back from the church, I suddenly saw clearly how wrong this whole thing is. Into what a terrible situation I have put you. You still have a strong feeling about Tibor, you said it yourself. You have known me only ten days. We must try to think soberly."

I telephoned Paris from Harriet's apartment and reached Gabriel in his hotel room. He had been trying to get me all day. "I even canceled my flight to Rome because I had to talk to you," he said.

"I've just gotten your letter with the postcard," I told him. "Do you really want me to stay with Tibor?"

"I don't know any longer what I want."

"Did Tibor write you?"

"He did. He wrote very nobly, and . . ."

"I guessed it. That's why he's been so calm lately. I won't let him ruin my life. He has had his. He was never faithful to me, any other woman would do. I'm not going to sacrifice my love, my future . . ."

He interrupted me. "Your future? You mean your career?"

"Don't you understand? I want you! You, and not the career. You and our children."

There was a short silence at the other end, and when he spoke there was joy in his voice. "Then that's it. We can't live without each other."

That was our last conversation for a long time. We couldn't get calls through any more. Preoccupied with my problems, I hadn't noticed the changes that were occurring in Budapest: the new people in important positions, the sharpened tone of the newspapers. When I thought about it afterwards, I realized that our last call must have been monitored.

Returning once again to the Passport Office, I noticed that the desk where I had left my papers was occupied by a different clerk. A familiar face greeted me with a malevolent smile. "Well, well," said its owner. "Aren't we old friends?"

. . . March, 1945. Mother and I returned home from the last of the eight different places to which the siege had swept us. The house had been bombed, but our apartment, although looted and windowless, remained in one piece. We fixed up one livable room, nailing up the windows with lumber we had gathered, and shared it with two couples: it was an unwritten law to share. One of our guests, an old man, walked around with a hat of mine he had found in the debris. Since the locks were gone, we barricaded the entrance door in the evening. One morning our barricade was pushed in to the accompaniment of much shouting of "*Davai!*" Some Russian secret police officers, a civilian, and three machine-gunners stood there. We looked at them with the least possible interest; we had witnessed so much horror that we had become immune.

The civilian, a Hungarian, asked rapid questions. When the old man answered somewhat sleepily, the civilian slapped his face with such force that our guest spat out his two front teeth.

Now the man at the desk in the Passport Office was watching me, the grin widening on his face. "Of course you remember me," he said. He had been the civilian, a member of the secret police. With mockery in his eyes he handed back my papers. "We can't do a thing about your passport. Next case, please."

"But talk to me, tell me, what should I do?"

He waved toward a smallish blue-eyed man who took my arm and pushed me out, muttering, "Move on. Shut up and move on."

The lawyer I found said he would try to help, but his promise sounded thin. Leaving his office, I wondered if I would ever get out of Hungary again. Why had I ever come back into this trap? I could have been with Gabriel in Italy—happy days together, now all lost and never to return.

I had nearly reached home when I became aware of someone following me—or was I imagining it?

A few days had passed when, after another fruitless visit to the lawyer's office, I came home to find Tibor ashen-faced. "You've had a phone call from the secret police," he told me. "They're going to call again. It must be something connected with that damned Paris business."

When the call came, a clipped voice commanded me to appear at nine o'clock next morning at Andrassy Ut 60. *Andrassy Ut 60*—a dreaded address, first as the headquarters of the terrorist Hungarian Nazi Party, later of the Communist secret police. Entering the place at five minutes before nine the next day, I couldn't help wondering if I would ever come out again. Those who were summoned seldom did.

I soon found the room number. Through a mist of fear I saw an officer seated behind a desk, and another standing nearby. They asked me to sit down and offered me a cigarette, which I refused.

"Perhaps a glass of champagne would be more to her taste. Those capitalist beauties like champagne." The shrill voice belonged to an ugly little man I hadn't noticed before. My tensions eased; the word "capitalist" had revived my sense of humor. I thought of Tibor in the mornings, diligently cutting sugar cubes into quarters and doling them out for breakfast, and of our endless noodle dinners.

"I am all ears," I said.

"Aren't you too smart? Don't you know where you are?"

"I know, but I have a clear conscience."

"We don't bother here with clear consciences."

"Why waste time with me then?"

"She's right," said the shrill voice from the back of the room. "Let's make her sing and get it over with."

I felt angry, but I realized that they wanted me to lose my temper. So in a honeyed voice I inquired, "Who is the delightful gentleman in the corner?"

"Shut up, you dirty whore!" He jumped toward me, his eyes full of hatred. "You perfumed whore, with your pale face and white neck!" And he reached for my throat with crooked fingers.

The officer grabbed his collar and pushed him toward the door. "Out with you, Pista. Any time there is a good-looking bitch, he gets out of his trousers."

"Forgive his manners," said the other man behind the desk. "He isn't a bad sort, just over-nervous."

I sat still, waiting for the attack.

"Well, let's see." The man at the desk opened a file and looked through it. "You are accused of an anti-nationalistic deed."

"I was always bad at riddles," I answered, "and I hate all this secrecy. Why don't you tell me openly what you have against me?"

"We are the ones who ask the questions here," he growled.

"I'm only too willing to answer."

"What were you doing in Paris?"

"I went there to meet Mr. Gabriel Pascal."

"What were you doing besides that?"

"That was all I was doing."

"For two weeks?"

"No, for exactly ten days."

"Where did you stay?"

"First at a small hotel, later at the Ritz."

"The Ritz? How could you get that much money out?"

"Mr. Pascal was taking care of my expenses."

"In other words, for ten days in Paris you were just seeing Mr. Pascal."

"He promised a film contract."

"Did he change his mind?"

"Certainly not."

"Then why did you come back?"

"This is my home. I had to come back."

"You've requested an extension of your passport. Why?"

Why, why, why . . . questions, cross-questions, impertinent questions. Suddenly both of them went out, and I was given permission to go to the ladies' room. Apparently this particular comfort station was only for those who were being investigated. A woman detective guarded the door. Inside, a young schoolgirl, covered with blood, lay moaning on the floor. An elderly woman leaned dazed against the blood-spattered wall. What crimes had they committed? But there was no way to find out; conversation was forbidden.

When I returned to the first room, two new policemen came to question me. Perhaps they had counted on that scene in the ladies' room to soften me up, but I had nothing to confess. The only thing which worried me was what lay behind all this: some influential person who wanted to prevent my leaving Hungary must have denounced me. The secret police must have known perfectly well that I was not a spy and they were just amusing themselves with the questioning under the cloak of duty. So finally I was dismissed.

Tibor let me in when I returned. "Thank God you are home. I was absolutely helpless. I didn't know what to do, where to go, whom to ask."

"They were trying to prove that I was a spy in Paris," I said, "and they couldn't understand why I came back here if I had a contract."

"If you're not going to stay with me, I really don't understand either. Why *did* you come back?"

"To talk to you. I just couldn't go off like that."

"This whole thing is wrong. Tell me honestly, are you in love with him, or do you just want a career and are using him for that?"

It was the moment to tell the truth. I couldn't lie to him.

"Yes, I am in love with him. I can't help it. I'm so sorry."

"Do you intend to marry him?"

"Yes."

"So you want a divorce?"

"Yes," I answered in tears.

He walked out of my room without saying another word.

It was a denunciation, my lawyer said, and my situation was serious; my passport could be held up unless I could prove my innocence. He was going to try another angle, he told me, but I would have to be silent about my plans for leaving Hungary.

New Year's, 1947. Gabriel was in Hollywood; he couldn't wait for me in Europe any longer. His letters came: "I am like a monk who is leaving his monastery. I have never yet lived like others. I have been running after fantasies like a somnambulist ever since my youth. Only when I held you in my arms did I learn that I am a human being too. Throwing away my mask and jester's cap, with you I could be my real self. I have found my mate. *Anima mia.*"

Then other letters: he was seeing his old friend Charlie Chaplin often, and his fear about the age difference between us eased. "Young Oona and Charlie are so happy that he has become a changed man." Chaplin had shown him parts of his new film, *Monsieur Verdoux,* and Gabriel thought it great. He sent me a photo of Chaplin with an inscription wishing me happiness with Gabriel and adding, "We are all waiting for you in Hollywood."

Another letter described the baptism of a baby boy, which made Gabriel think of the child "God would give us." He was also looking for a house to rent. The Santa Monica house of Monty Banks and Gracie Fields was for rent, with an option to buy; should we buy it? In Paris, he had told me about the great plans he and Bernard Shaw had made to build studios financed by the Irish government. But, Gabriel wrote, even after the studios were built, he *should* make one film a year in Hollywood. He liked the climate and had many friends there. "If only Shaw didn't hate Hollywood so much . . . anyhow Gracie's house would be big enough for half a-dozen wild boys and girls. Our children. How would they look, blond like you?"

It seemed he had had some difficulties with Shaw but now, Gabriel informed me, the "old man" had finally agreed and the contracts for *The Devil's Disciple* had been signed with Mary Pickford. He was to start preparations at once, and I should come straight to Hollywood. To expedite my permit to leave Hungary, he arranged a contract for me with United Artists to play the lead in *One Touch of Venus.*

When I showed the contract to my lawyer, he said, "Hide it, and don't breathe a word about it to anyone."

March came. I didn't write Gabriel about my difficulties; I simply said that I had to wait a bit longer for my permits than I had anticipated. But he was just as silent about his own troubles. He did not explain why he was suddenly on his way back to Europe;

all I knew was that he had to see Shaw. He was hoping to meet me in Paris. His letters, written every day aboard the *Queen Elizabeth,* arrived together in a big bundle.

"Only a few weeks more," he wrote. "You would have laughed when the London newspapers called me on the ship today, asking if the rumors were true that I was going to marry a beautiful Hungarian star. I had to give a vague answer on account of Bernard Shaw. He would be upset to hear it first through the papers, even though he always told me if I ever went mad and wanted to get married, I should only marry a Hungarian."

Other letters were written at night in the quiet of his cabin: "You are my first real love, the only true one . . . You are the first woman with whom I want to settle down and raise a family . . . I wish nothing more for myself than your happiness . . . I pray God help me keep my heart pure and strong for our marriage."

It was April; and still no word of my passport. But one day the lawyer called to say that he had succeeded in getting it. A jubilant letter went to Gabriel: I was coming soon. I was glad that we were to meet in Paris again; and after that, I thought, we would sail for America, taking Mother with us. It never occurred to me to leave Mother behind. My divorce case was coming up soon, too.

To make my happiness even greater, the ban on foreign calls was temporarily lifted, and once more there was Gabriel's rich baritone from faraway Mumford's Farm. I was so happy and relieved that at first I refused to notice that something had changed in his voice. His enthusiasm over my coming seemed somewhat restrained, as if he wasn't sure any more.

Tibor was calmer now. Our approaching divorce no longer seemed to upset him. Once more the gay little feathers appeared in the band of his hat and he looked at women, smiling to himself, as he paced through Vacy Ucca with long, lazy steps.

By this time my American visa had been promised, but to obtain it I needed a certificate proving that I had no political affiliations. Once more it seemed that I had come up against an insuperable obstacle: a clerk in the police department informed me that my record showed there was an unfinished case against me. It was the "spy case"; though the secret police had dropped it, I had never been officially cleared. Only by bringing my case to the People's Court, said my lawyer, could I be cleared. That meant at least a year's delay. The lawyer also explained the source of my troubles: a very influential actress who envied my Hollywood contract. The lawyer hoped to make a contact to counteract the actress, but meanwhile I could do nothing but wait in silence. There was no way to advise Gabriel; even letters going abroad were opened in those days.

The lawyer made the contact: no less than a top officer in the secret police. At our meeting he wore civilian clothes. I told him the whole truth about my love and he advised me to tell the story to the American Vice-Consul, who had the power to issue me a visa without the certificate.

"You can tell him who I am and that I am acquainted with your file," said the police officer, "and I am ready to support you with my word of honor to the American Vice-Consul that politically you are clear."

The irony of those days! I needed a Communist secret police officer to bear witness that I was not an anti-Communist spy—in order to get a visa for the United States!

"Arrange a meeting if it's necessary between me and the Vice-Consul," he continued, "and I can show him your file with the false denunciation. But don't say anything to him on the phone, only in person, and if you call me at Headquarters, do it from a phone booth, not from your home."

The Vice-Consul said the secret police officer should meet him at his home, as the officer was unwilling to come to the American Consulate. When I told the officer this, he laughed without gaiety. "Tell him," he said, "that everyone who goes in or out of his door is photographed. It is a strange world. But this is just the purging process."

"But why do you help me at all?"

"Because I don't approve of charges such as the one against you. I don't like injustices. If you were really guilty there would be no pity in me for you."

At long last I was cleared, and the American visa was entered in my passport. A Swiss transit visa and a French visa to Paris were easily granted. The Russian permit took longer, but it eventually came.

Meanwhile, my divorce was granted. I returned to our apart-

ment from the courtoom on Tibor's arm, crying. I continued to
live in the apartment. Where else could I go?

By now it was May. Though that was the month when Gabriel
was supposed to start *The Devil's Disciple* in Hollywood, he
was still in England. I knew nothing about his complications
with Bernard Shaw over the picture. He didn't write about that,
or about Hollywood, or about my contract, or about the house in
Santa Monica; now our home was to be a castle near Dublin,
where the studios would be built.

When I received my Russian permit and wired him that I
could come, he phoned me. His voice was lifeless. He told me
that Hollywood was definitely off and that so far the Irish could
not furnish the necessary money. "I have to try in Italy with another Shaw film," he said. "I've written you a long letter. Think
it over and answer me."

When the letter arrived, I went to my room to read it. For
nights he could not sleep, he wrote, and finally he had to tell me
the truth. But the letter did not explain what had happened; it
only said that he, as a British subject, was under Treasury control. "You cannot imagine my panic," he wrote, "when I visualize
you and your mother arriving at the Paris station while I myself
have to count every shilling until I can start to work in Rome.

"But now comes what I really want to say. Do not deceive yourself, because our happiness depends on it. When I told you on the
phone that my Hollywood film had been cancelled, you asked in a
disillusioned voice, but still with half a hope, whether or not we
would go to Hollywood later so you could start your career—and
you seemed to be sad when I told you that your contract for *One
Touch of Venus* was also off. At that moment I realized I had forgotten that you were a full-blooded actress, that I had promised
you a career. But under the present circumstance I cannot help
you. I will need all my strength and concentration to save my
own career.

"If your love is real," the letter went on, "and if you embraced
me in Paris out of that deep love and not for other reasons, then
now, before you burn your bridges, stop and think—*what is it
you really want?* . . . I have a suggestion: come to me alone, with-

out your mother, and be with me in Italy for a few months so you can get to know me and my way of living. Then you can decide whether you want to marry me, or leave me and work on your career, or go back to Tibor, for whom you still seem to care deeply. Show him this letter. He will agree with me. I would be the happiest man on earth if after a few weeks in Italy you would say to me: 'You are my life. Do not decide now, only answer whether you agree with me. I do hope that between these lines you feel my tender and endless love for you. I want us to look into each other's eyes before we join hands for the long road from which there is no return or looking back."

I wired him only three words: I LOVE YOU.

May was beautiful as the moment of our meeting drew nearer. I didn't give much thought to Gabriel's worries; I didn't understand them. The only thing on my mind was that finally I could go. The full moon promised a summer in Italy with Neapolitan songs echoing among ancient ruins where I would be with my lover.

One thing I remembered: the lawyer's repeated warnings to keep my departure a secret. My enemies, he said, had the power to take me off the train. I hinted everywhere that I had changed my mind and was going to stay with Tibor. Tibor kept quiet, too.

One afternoon, only a few days before I left, Tibor and I had tea in a small café. Gabriel's suggestion of a three-months' waiting period had given Tibor new hope; he was sure that I would come back to him. We sat at a corner table. A pianist was playing "*J'attendrai toujours.*" We were melancholy. The past I was about to leave still had a strong hold on me.

"*J'attendrai toujours,*" Tibor sighed. "Don't forget that I'll wait for you. Don't take this hope away from me. Soon I'll have to take you to the station. Do you know what it will feel like to come home to the empty apartment, to your room, looking at the chair where you won't sit any more, the pillows of the bed where your blond head won't rest again? But I know you'll come back to me. That other man doesn't love you as I do."

There were tears in my eyes. And Tibor was drying his eyes too as the waitress approached with the tea tray. She was young and dark, and she wore a tight, low-cut blouse with no brassiere. Her breasts bounced over the teacups as she bent across the table.

"I know you'll come back to me and then—" Tibor stopped, his gaze caught and held by the décolletage above him. "And perhaps in September, when you are back again..." His voice trailed off. His eyes, lazily summing up the girl, focused again on her breasts. He smiled. He didn't finish what he was saying to me, but in a different, almost flirtatious tone, he spoke to the girl. "Thank you, my dear. Do you always work here?" His glance ran down to her ankles.

"No," she answered with a coquettish smile, "only every other day, from four till ten."

My tears dried. I laughed and imitated the transformation of his voice and face. Nonetheless there was the same old stab of jealousy as I added, "You certainly made a mental note about every other day, didn't you?"

The last day came, and I tearfully waved goodbye to Tibor from the window of the Alberg Express. On the second evening I was sitting in the dining car and thinking of the dark eight months behind me and of arriving in Paris the following morning. Gabriel would be waiting for me at the station, the same station which on that foggy November evening had seen our goodbye. I hoped to have a good night's rest and to look my best in the morning. Thus occupied with my thoughts, I was only absent-mindedly aware of a sudden commotion in the dining car.

"Why all this excitement?" asked my table companion, a fat Hungarian.

The conductor stopped at our table.

"Madame, Monsieur—bad news. There's a train strike in France. We won't be able to cross the French border. We don't know how long it will last, but it won't break in the next forty-eight hours, because of the weekend."

The dining car buzzed. "Please be calm," the conductor pleaded. "We'll know more when we get to Basel."

I was trying to think. With a feeling of panic I realized that in my last hurried telephone conversation with Gabriel I had forgotten to ask him at which hotel he would be staying. He had mentioned that he couldn't get a reservation at the Ritz, but then we talked about something else, leaving it that he would wait for me at the station. But he would be waiting in vain. I was allowed to take only fifty dollars out of Hungary. If I could get a bus or a plane to Paris from Basel, where would I go? How could I find him? I didn't know the city well; I had no friends there, and my French was poor.

When the train pulled into Basel we were not allowed to get off. Everyone stood at the windows, waiting for news. On the platform, border officers and policemen were talking to the conductors and supervisors. Finally our conductor climbed back onto the train and announced that only those passengers holding Swiss visas would be allowed to get off. Hungarian citizens holding only transit visas would have to return to Hungary.

Noise billowed around me. I was frantic, but others were as desperate as I. Many of them had paid fortunes for permits to leave Hungary. "Let's form a committee," my neighbor said. "The authorities here must be made to understand what it means for us to be sent back."

So a committee was formed, and the officials listened to our arguments. They had to get instructions from higher sources, they told us, and they left us for hours. Finally they returned. In view of the fact that we would be endangered by going back, they told us, we could leave the train, but only to spend the night at the hotel opposite the station. Tomorrow morning we must leave Switzerland.

The hotel was a cheap place. We passed through the crowded dining room and its mess of beer bottles and glasses. The air was thick with smoke and the gay sounds of yodeling and harmonicas. Only two rooms were available, so we divided them between the sexes. There were nine of us in the women's room. Still, it was better than going back.

I rushed to the phone, a public one in a narrow corridor between the noisy dining room and the men's toilet, and called the long-distance operator. A pleasant, intelligent-sounding girl answered. I asked for her patience, and told her everything that had happened.

"*Mon Dieu!*" she exclaimed. "What a story! But don't worry, I'll call all the big hotels in Paris. We'll find him. Go to your room and rest. I'll call you if I need you."

I went back to the room. Three women were lying on the bed, and all the chairs were occupied. I put my coat on the floor and

stretched out. The scene reminded me of a crowded shelter during the siege of Budapest. They had started to dance downstairs,
and the yelling and thudding, mixed with the smell of pipes and
stale beer, filled our room. I thought of Gabriel asleep in his unknown hotel. He would get up early in the morning, to be at the
Gare at nine.

I dozed off, for what seemed just a moment, only to be awakened by a knock on the door. I was called to the phone.

"Madame, I am sorry," the operator said, "I've called all the
best hotels, but Mr. Pascal is not registered at any of them."

"The Scribe?" I asked in a panic, remembering that he had
stayed there once.

"I called it."

"The Crillon, the Georges Cinq?" I was trying to remember
names.

"Yes, I called them. All of them, Madame."

"What shall I do? Even if I get to Paris, how can I find him? I
have only fifty dollars."

"Don't worry yet. Stay on the phone. I have the Paris phone
book; I'll go through all the hotels alphabetically. Let's see:
Athénée ... *Allô, Allô!"* I heard the purring noise of the wires.
*"Allô, Mademoiselle, ici Bâle ... ici Bâle, donnez-moi Paris ...
Paris? Merci beaucoup. Donnez moi, s'il vous plaît, Kléber 7 ..."*

The phone was ringing at the faraway Hotel Athénée. A sleepy
voice answered, *"Allô."*

"Allô, ici Bâle. Is a Monsieur Pascal registered there?"

"Who?"

"Pascal. P-A-S-C-A-L."

"Un moment." Then, *"Inconnu."*

"Allô ... ici Bâle, donnez-moi, s'il vous plaît, Elysée 2315."

"Allô ... ici Hôtel Bristol."

"Monsieur Pascal, s'il vous plaît ..."

"Inconnu."

Then came the hotels starting with C, D, and E, but always
with the same answer: *"Inconnu ... inconnu ... inconnu."*

"Madame, don't worry; go back to your room. I'll call some
other hotels. But wait—what is his number in England?"

"Gerards Cross 3613. But that's no use. He told me he was
going to close the house because we were to go to Italy together."

"No one is there?"

"The gardener and the bailiff. But they don't live in the main house."

"You go back now. Everything will be all right."

"God bless you for what you are doing for me."

"I'm a woman, too. Go and rest. I'll find him."

Dawn was breaking. The noise downstairs had stopped. A rooster crowed far away, then another one nearby. The three women on the bed were snoring and those in the chairs sat with nodding heads. I lay with my open eyes aching and burning. What would I do if she didn't find him? Should I go on to Paris and call from hotel to hotel, as long as my fifty dollars lasted?

"Madame, telephone."

I rushed down and picked up the receiver.

"Good news. I've found where he is."

"How? Where?"

"I went on calling the hotels, but in the meantime I kept ringing the Gerards Cross number. I am a stubborn Swiss girl." She giggled. "At five A.M. the cook answered. She said she had intended to leave the house yesterday, but something had detained her. When she found she couldn't sleep because of a headache, she left the servants' cottage and went over to the main house to get a glass of beer and an aspirin. Just at that moment, I rang again. She says Mr. Pascal is at the Prince de Galles Hotel. She knows because she overheard him say so on the phone. Funny! Among all the hotels, I never thought of that one. If we had continued alphabetically we would have found him. Stay on the line, I'm calling him now. My word of honor, I have palpitations of the heart myself, I'm so excited! *Allô . . . Allô, Paris . . .*"

"*Ici Hôtel Prince de Galles.*"

"*Monsieur Pascal, s'il vous plaît.*"

"*Un moment.*"

Tense, excited silence. Then his "Hallo."

My beloved operator remained on the line, and we both thanked her.

"With pleasure," she said, "and much, much happiness to you both."

With every jolt of the bus, the large, blue-veiled hat bent closer to the gold-trimmed shoulders of the elderly French officer. In turn, his shakoed head folded over the hat, rippling its veil with a windy snore. Many hours earlier those two had embarked at Basel on the emergency bus for Paris and had taken the seat in front of me. For a time the blue-veiled hat and shako sat straight, but the long hours of jerking, tugging, and clanking had shaken the strange ingredients of the human cocktail into the togetherness of a mutually shared uncomfortable fate. As the night wore on everybody told his neighbor his life story, his philosophical concepts, or his ailments. Everyone was bored stiff with everyone else and with the cursed train strike.

The bus reached the suburbs of Paris. I was back in the city of my dreams. In the lobby of the Prince de Galles Hotel a tall mirror reflected me, gray with dust and weariness, my dress dirty and creased. The Paris hat, Gabriel's present, balanced clownishly on top of my head. I had developed a gastric disturbance that protested loud and deep in my stomach, and I was fighting nausea.

It was about four in the morning.

"Monsieur Pascal is waiting for you," the sleepy desk clerk informed me. "He calls down every fifteen minutes. He was expecting you at dinnertime."

The elevator started up. In a few seconds everything I had fought for and dreamed about would be mine. I tried to think about the greatness of the moment, but all I could feel was increasing nausea. The porter showed me to the door. A light knock and I entered the paradise I had longed for. Gabriel rose from a chair, with his boyish smile and his black silk dressing gown open at the neck. This was the moment I had visualized thousands of times: me ravishing in a lovely dress, enveloped in a vapor of perfume; his eyes caressing me before we fell into each other's embrace.

Now I stood, awkward, unkempt, sticky, my hands hanging clumsily, my noisy stomach more audible than my greeting. If only I could cease to exist, I thought.

And so we stood, embarrassed, opposite each other. The table was set for dinner—a bottle of champagne in a dark pool of melted ice, and withered red roses hanging their heads in the gray dawn.

Chapter 4

The Gypsy

I knew nothing about the past of the man whose future I was going to share. Gabriel Pascal's origin was shrouded in a mystery which, I often suspected, he enjoyed thickening with contradictory remarks. When people tried to probe into his past, he had a tailor-made answer for each inquirer. In moments of grandeur, he liked to hint that he was either the illegitimate great-great-grandson of someone like Talleyrand or the kidnaped child of a princely family. In that he was like his master, George Bernard Shaw, who insisted that he had sprung from Macduff.

Once in Paris when I mentioned my mother his face clouded. "I hate family ties," he said.

"What about your parents?" I asked.

"I had none." He seemed to set the sentence about himself like an impenetrable wall.

Somewhat later he began to talk. "Whether I was an orphan or a foundling, I never knew. I was tossed from one place to another, unwanted. I don't know whether I dreamed it or not, but I faintly remember a burning house and being afraid of the flames and the heat . . . and the cries of a woman, a woman who seemed warm and soft, like a mother. She was crying for help: 'Save Gabor, come save him!'" The next thing Gabriel remembered, he was among the gypsies. Later I wondered whether this part of the story grew out of his irresistible urge to dramatize.

"How I got among the gypsies," he said, "I don't know. There were the mountains of Transylvania, shepherds and dogs. The gypsies taught me to do acrobatic tricks and to beg and steal. I was a great pupil, self-supporting by the age of four."

Then somebody took him away from the gypsies. He recalled being on a train. "I remember I was crying," he continued. "To quiet me they gave me a little drum. It was bright red. The first toy I ever had. I shall never forget the joy of owning it. I hugged it, I kissed it. Then I was told we were going to my mother. That reminded me of the soft, warm one and her cry, 'Save Gabor,' and of the flames. I held my drum tightly all through that journey. Then we entered a house. In the half-darkness, a woman got up and approached me. 'Here is your mother,' I was told. I stretched out my hand and said, 'Mama,' as I had heard other children say. She pushed my hand away. 'I am not your mother,' she said. A blond boy, about my age, was playing nearby. Later the woman took my drum and gave it to that boy."

Sometimes I got the impression that Gabriel was really born at the age of seventeen, as the stories he told of his life from then on lost some of their fairy-tale vagueness. At seventeen, he was in a military school in Holics, Hungary, placed there by a mysterious patron, a Jesuit priest. He was in his *Sturm und Drang*, his energies freed but not yet channeled. Like many young men of that age, all he could do was rebel against accepted values and social forms and call them "bourgeois." The difference from other young men would show up only in his later years: while others would fold into the herd, Gabriel's rebellion would never end. He remained forever the outsider, the fiery, impatient romantic, the impractical chaser of visions, always suffering with the deep, wild suffering of youth.

One thing soon became obvious: Gabriel was not made for an army career. He had one burning desire: to become an actor. He was an avid reader of plays, and the theater was more real to him than life. His own complex self puzzled him. He tried to find himself in characters like Peer Gynt, Faust, or Til Eulenspiegel.

He felt within himself the confusion of Byron's Manfred, who

... hath all the energy which would have made
A goodly frame of glorious elements,
Had they been wisely mingled; as it is,
It is an awful chaos—light and darkness,
And mind and dust, and passions and pure thoughts,
Mix'd, and contending without end or order,
All dormant or destructive. He will perish ...

So he bid goodbye to the military school and Hungary and went to study acting in a stock company in Hamburg. The great tragedienne Francesca Ellmenreich advised him to continue his studies at the Academy of the Hofburg Theatre in Vienna. Once in Vienna, he wanted to become a member of the Hofburg Theatre right away. That this was impossible never occurred to him. He believed superstitiously in his "star of destiny" that was leading him to reach his "vision"—a word that summed up all his aspirations to find himself and his mission in life. He never doubted that God had a definite plan for him.

His "destiny" helped him to get an appointment with the Secretary of the Theatre. "I want an audition arranged for me," young Gabriel said to him in his commanding tone, "so all the directors of the Theatre can see me. I want to become a member."

The Secretary, in his gray redingote and stiff high collar, was so outraged that he couldn't find words. He straightened his gold-rimmed monocle to give himself a better view of the madman in front of him. Then his hand moved toward a large brass bell to summon a lackey to throw out the intruder.

"I am Gabriel Pascal," said the young man. He paused to give the Secretary time to digest the importance of the name which he had recently chosen as his stage name. "And I give you a week," he continued. "Meanwhile, I shall be here every morning to remind you that if by the seventh day you haven't arranged my audition you will be fired."

Before the Secretary could gather himself together sufficiently to reach the bell, the young man had left the room with unhurried steps. Though he was thin as a dancer and short in stature, he walked larger than himself.

He was back at ten o'clock the next morning, and the next, and the next. Each time, lifting his arm in a silent warning to the Secretary, he indicated with his extended fingers how many days were left; and each time he disappeared before he could be seized and thrown out. Not until the sixth day did he speak, saying to the Secretary: "One more day. See about my audition tomorrow —or you will be fired." By this time, the Secretary's mind had begun to work. Somebody, he decided, must be behind this boy, somebody very important—a cabinet minister or even higher. When Gabriel appeared the following morning, the audition was arranged.

News of the madman had spread throughout the theater, and everybody was curious to see him. Even Baron Bergner, the executive producer, was present at the audition. The directors, actors, and actresses all made ready for a good laugh. But when the young man stepped onto the empty, half-lit stage and began the "To be or not to be" soliloquy from *Hamlet,* following it with selections from other roles, silence fell on the listeners. Only real artists can appreciate another artist. Thus young Gabriel became a member of the Imperial Hofburg Theatre. He was the first member of the Theatre, he remembered, who did not believe in the old declamatory school: "At times I even *whispered* on the stage." As an actor, he said, he was "like a flame, a beautiful blue flame."

It was at this time, too, that he became a Shaw enthusiast. He read everything Shaw ever wrote. His favorite play was *The Devil's Disciple.*

At vacation time Gabriel hiked in the Tyrolean mountains. An episode of that time is as symbolic of his character as it was to be of his future career. Early one morning, he set out to see the wild goats and chamois grazing on a high plateau not far from the village where he had spent the night. In the cool of the morning the climb was easy, and he soon reached the plateau. The snow-capped peak above it seemed an easy leap from where he stood, shimmering in the sun like a vision of the Mont Salvatch of the Holy Grail legend. Gabriel decided to scale it. He felt light and happy. To be even more one with nature, he took off his clothes and laid them on a rock. Then he began to climb. A sense of divinity gave wings to his body. The sun rose higher, the wind grew stronger. His naked body began to burn and his feet hurt. Exaltation left him. The mountaintop seemed no closer than it was at the beginning of his climb. He knew that it was time to turn back, yet he stubbornly pursued his goal: the top. He reached the snow. His eyes blinded, his feet a mass of bruises, on he went. He could not remember just when he lost consciousness, but it was late afternoon when he came to. He felt deathly ill, but he had to gather all his strength and get down to the plateau before nightfall: without food or clothing he would have no chance of survival. As it grew colder in the fading sun, he forced himself to get up, but he had lost his way; he could not see the plateau any more. Frantic, he began to descend, falling from time to time, his body one bleeding wound. It seemed like an eternity of slipping and sliding until suddenly in the twilight the plateau appeared far below him. Miniature figures were moving on it: a shepherd and his flock.

The shepherd's campfire became the beacon leading Gabriel down. When he appeared naked in the firelight the old man covered him with a blanket and gave him wine. Gabriel told him what had happened, ending his story with the words: "First, I only wished to see the wild goats, but then the desire for the heights overtook me."

The old shepherd's deep, peaceful eyes were full of pity as he said, *"Manneschla, das heist Gott versuchen."* (Little man, you were tempting God.)

Gabriel, who couldn't kill an animal, soon found himself in the middle of World War I, an officer in a Hussar cavalry regiment. Two of his dachshunds and a large mongrel accompanied him to the Italian front. Dogs and horses appear in the stories he told of those times, wearing almost human faces and of equal importance with his human friends.

In a small Italian border town came his first collision with sex. The women of his youthful dreams had been women of legends and poems, virginal and far away. His ideal of womanhood was embodied in the image of the Madonna, to whom he had a special devotion his whole life. This devotion gave rise to a sharp conflict: from his youth he had felt that sex was incompatible with his spiritual aspiration. At times he even dreamed of becoming a monk.

One day his Hussar comrades, never suspecting that he was still chaste, inveigled him into going with them to a bordello. When Gabriel found himself alone with a woman undressing, perspiration broke out all over him, but he could not leave and become the laughingstock of the regiment. He stayed. From then on, he continued to visit the house with his comrades. Only the woman knew that, behind her closed door, the young man would take a book from his pocket and read plays to her.

When World War I ended with the collapse of the Austro-Hungarian monarchy, the Hofburg Theatre folded and Gabriel sought work in Berlin, but in vain. His money gone, he was finally forced to sleep on a bench in the park of the Tiergarten.

Awakening after the second night on the bench, he saw a lovely young woman passing by. Embarrassed by her sweeping glance, he sat up. She quickened her pace, only to stop suddenly as though disturbed by something in the hungry-looking young man's eyes. She reached for her purse, and so began what was to be a lifelong friendship. Her name was Hedwig Brugge, and at the time she was a promising young actress. Gabriel's restless life was soon to sweep them apart, but the friendship never lessened.

After a year of misery in Berlin, Gabriel gave up the theater and, with the help of the same mysterious Jesuit priest who in Hungary had placed him in the military school, he entered an agricultural academy in Copenhagen. On his first summer vacation, he took a job caring for horses on a farm. In this unlikely setting his theory that destiny finds you and leads you, no matter where you are, was to be proven again.

Every morning at the farm, he took the horses to the river for a scrub. Then, after taking a swim himself, naked, he would tie the horses together, jump on the back of the lead horse and, still naked, gallop back to the stables through a forest. One day as he rode out of the forest into the open fields, he noticed a commotion. A movie company was filming a scene in the field. Asta Nielsen, the Swedish film star, was playing the lead, and her husband was the director. Gabriel and his dripping horses galloped straight into the scene. The director, enchanted, made him repeat the performance. And presently, Gabriel took the horses back, said goodbye to the farmer, and joined the movie-makers, who were going to Italy. He learned the techniques of film-making, and fell in love with Asta Nielsen.

Soon on his own, he started his film career as a director in Italy. He made pictures and sold them in Germany. With Robert Reinert of the UFA Studios in Berlin, he directed the film *Populi Morituri,* in which he also played the lead. The picture made him famous in Europe. Then he tried his hand as a producer, built up distributing companies, and bought movie theaters. Money cascaded in. He moved into a luxurious villa in Rome and met Nuchy, the daughter of an old Roman family that excommunicated her for loving and living with Gabriel.

Then Gabriel went bankrupt. His explanation was that some "Machiavellian" scheme he had worked out proved to be too complicated. He was always fond of his so-called Machiavellian schemes; the only trouble with them was that he never was a Machiavelli himself. In this instance, everything he had was auctioned, including all the furniture in the marble villa except one mattress, which, according to Italian law, could not be taken away. When the noise of the auctioneers died down, a dark-faced Gabriel sat on the mattress with Nuchy crying by his side. She cried even more at the station when the train took Gabriel away toward new dreams.

The time was the mid-twenties. On a blue-gold summer morning Gabriel was walking alone along the sandy beach at Cap d'Antibes on the French Riviera, where he had just arrived for a short rest. Behind him was a fairly successful film he had made in Paris, and now he was looking forward to a new venture in Berlin.

"Life is a divine poem," Gabriel thought. This was a sentence he liked to repeat to himself when he was in a good mood, sometimes adding, "and it is our own fault if we recite it badly." He walked buoyantly down to the water, his past misfortunes forgotten. "As I looked at the horizon," he related many times later, "a strange presentiment came over me. I felt something was in the works for me, that something important was going to happen."

Far out in the water, a red buoy caught his eye. Bouncing invitingly among the waves, it struck him as a good goal for a swim. Since the only way Gabriel enjoyed swimming was in the nude, and since the beach was abandoned, he took off his shirt and shorts and plunged in. He was soon nearing the red buoy, now appearing, now hiding among the waves. Only when he was almost there did he notice that a body was attached to the buoy by a long, thin arm. Drawing nearer, he saw a white head with a white beard floating in front of it, and beyond the beard a thin, elongated body rocking contentedly upon the waves. Gabriel saw blue eyes contemplating a pair of big toes sticking out of the water. "Where have I seen this face?" he wondered. Then he remembered. Overwhelmed, he seized the buoy, thus upsetting the balance of the white beard. The Beard looked at the intruder with disgust, but Gabriel merely radiated his mesmeric smile, revealing white teeth in his sun-tanned face.

The White-Bearded One, it seemed, also believed in swimming in the raw, and this created a ground of conversation. Seeking a more comfortable position, Gabriel turned on his stomach. As he moved, the green veil of the water was pulled aside for a second from his emerging rear and the rays of the sun were mirrored on its wet golden-brown.

The Beard took in the view and lifted a quizzical white eyebrow. "Of course," he remarked, "that cannot be sun tan, not on that part. What is your nationality, young man?"

"I am Hungarian," Gabriel announced.

"I could perhaps be wrong, but you struck me more as a gypsy," said the old man, shaking the water from his beard.

". . . and an ex-Hussar," Gabriel continued, adding with mock pathos, "who is still fighting under the banner of Beauty and Truth with the Hussar sword of artistic integrity." Then he continued in a more serious tone, "It is a rather hopeless fight, though, as I am in the stinking *métier* of producing films."

They became friends then and there. The White Beard, of course, was George Bernard Shaw.

Gabriel, with his magic wand, could conjure scenes before his listeners, and he was among the very few who could make Shaw a listener. He talked of his artistic dreams and great future plans with his own special vibrant enthusiasm and naive faith. Displaying his great knowledge of the Shaw plays, he projected filmed versions of them over the Mediterranean blue of the waters.

Shaw was amused.

When at last Gabriel swam away, Shaw called after him. "If one day," he said, "you are finally driven to the conclusion that you are utterly broke, and there is no doubt that you will be, come and call on me. Maybe then I will let you make one of my plays into a film."

Many rivers would empty into the Mediterranean before Shaw was to fulfill his reckless promise.

Berlin was a complete flop, but Gabriel did not give up. When he could no longer afford his hotel, he moved to a rooming house. The house had a sympathetic landlady, who had an even more sympathetic young sister, Elsie.

Gabriel became seriously ill and one night, as he lay shivering in his bed with a high fever, sleep brought mixed-up dreams. There was a boy in his dream, with large dark eyes and shaggy black hair—himself, Gabriel suddenly realized, at the age of six. Then the dream took a turn and now he was outside of the boy, looking at him; and the boy was his son. A proud, warm, protective feeling came over him: my son! The door opened slowly, and he saw the landlady's sister, Elsie, approaching, with a hot drink in her hand. Dream and reality became one in Gabriel's feverish mind. My son, he thought, wants to be born. He wants to be born from this woman.

Nine months later, Peter, Gabriel's only child, was born.

Gabriel was in Holland at the time. He had never been in love with Elsie and, as much as he loved his son, he would not bind himself in marriage. It never occurred to him that he did wrong to Elsie: on the contrary, according to his unusual logic, Elsie was rewarded by a beautiful baby boy, and should have been greatly pleased. Gabriel wanted to take care of the child, but so far he couldn't take care of himself.

In Holland he had met Sir Basil Zaharoff, the mysterious munitions maker. Sir Basil seemed willing to back Gabriel's films —provided he made them in China. Gabriel could have millions in Chinese money at his disposal for any film he wished, Zaharoff explained to him, so long as he made friends there with a General Seeckt. Gabriel was to watch the General's doings a bit and keep Sir Basil informed.

By the time Gabriel discovered the hook in the bait of Zaharoff's artistic interest, some months had passed. Gabriel was living comfortably in Amsterdam at Zaharoff's expense. "But I wasn't ready to be mutilated as a spy in China," Gabriel later said. He refused China, and Sir Basil refused the hotel bills. Gabriel became a prisoner in his room until one night, with the help of the room waiter, he escaped, leaving his trunks behind. During the lean years, such exits from hotels developed into a useful pattern; in time, hotels all over the world were holding his trunks.

Misfortune, however, did not discourage him; there was always a next day. In England, where he journeyed next, he mended his fortunes by producing a film with Pola Negri, *The Street of the Lost Souls*. Next on to Paris once more; but no luck there in business, and a short, unhappy love affair with a French girl, which left him distressed. Then a new friendship: he met Pauline, a highly educated, charming, and creative Hungarian woman, who for the next eight years greatly influenced his life. Pauline followed him to Berlin when Gabriel, in partnership with Max Reinhardt, began to make films for the UFA Studios. Those pictures, especially *Fredericka*, by Franz Lehár, were highly successful. This film established Gabriel's name among the top producers of Germany. His lovely villa became an artists' meeting place, with Pauline the gracious hostess.

Now was the time to get Peter, his son. Elsie was still unmarried and was willing to give him up. Pauline and Gabriel took Peter to their house and grew very fond of him. The six-year-old boy was the carbon copy of his father. Gabriel started action to adopt him, but before the legal complications could be ironed out, Elsie got married and claimed him. She was German and was now married to a German, while Gabriel, as a foreigner, had no chance in the Nazi courts.

Germany was undergoing a profound change, and Gabriel was too outspoken in his criticism. Soon he was advised to get out of Germany, leaving behind his villa, his rare book collection, and his career, as well as his hopes to have Peter. All through the years, Gabriel was to make attempts to recover him and at one point, when Gabriel's fame as the producer of *Pygmalion* reached Germany, Elsie finally agreed. But then World War II broke out. When the war was over, Gabriel rushed to Germany to search for Peter, but he was listed among the missing *Hitler Jugend*. Elsie and her husband had been killed by a bomb.

After Berlin, Gabriel's life with Pauline broke up, and later she married someone else. Gabriel's years following his flight from Germany were a modern version of Marco Polo's adventures. First, invited by a Paramount executive, he went to Hollywood. The deal fell through when he refused to work with the famous star on whose name the backing depended, and insisted there was only one girl to play the part, an unknown actress, Jean Arthur. A sad period of hatching great plans followed while he hid at the New York Athletic Club. It was 1933. Unexpectedly Gabriel turned up once more in Hollywood. He sounded mysterious to his friend, the writer Hy Kraft. Gabriel told Hy that he had worked with Carl Volmuller, the author of *The Miracle,* on a story about the seven stages of reincarnation. "We have unlimited financing for it," Gabriel continued, "and I want you to write the script." Not even listening to Hy's protest that he was busy at Metro and did not believe in reincarnation, Gabriel added, "But first you have to meet my master, Shri Meher Baba."

Shri Meher Baba was a celebrated holy man in India. He called himself the "Awakener," and was believed by his numerous disciples to be a "Perfect Master," or *Avatar,* a divine incarnation on earth. Baba never spoke. When he had embarked on his Avatar career in 1925 he made a vow of silence, communicating thereafter in faultless English on his alphabet board. But all his disciples knew that the day would come when Baba would speak once again. At that time he would utter just one word, but that word, coming in the last moment of a world catastrophe, would change the fate of mankind. Several times already his disciples had heralded the "word," but so far Baba had remained silent.

Gabriel had met Baba several years earlier in Switzerland. Baba was then staying in a hotel in Zurich, and Gabriel, eternally fascinated by the mysterious East, naturally looked him up. He found

Baba sitting motionless on a tiger skin, clad as always in white garments, his long, dark hair touching his shoulders, his silent lips buried between mustache and beard. On the floor, around the master's feet, women sobbed and groaned. Gabriel walked up to Baba, pushing away the women on the floor. "I came to see *you,*" he said to Baba, "and have your answers, but this room smells from the pee of hysterical women. Send them out and then I can listen to you *if* you have anything to say."

Baba opened his eyes and laughed. His laughter was soft and melodious as a woman's. From then on he was to be an enigmatic influence in Gabriel's life. On his alphabet board, Baba called Gabriel his Phoenix, the mythical bird which forever rises reborn from its ashes.

In 1933 Baba had come to the United States to spread his "message," and stayed in a house in the Hollywood hills. It was there that Hy Kraft, finally persuaded by Gabriel, met Baba. Kraft had a strong prejudice against phony mystics and he suspected Baba of being one.

Instead he was shaken by his meeting with Baba. "There was a tremendous power emanating from that man," Hy told me later. He couldn't say "no" to Baba and was engaged to write the script for the film on reincarnation. But when the time came to leave for India with Baba and Gabriel, he shook himself awake from the "Eastern maze" and refused to go.

Nothing came of the reincarnation film and Gabriel was stranded in India. A more realistic man would have despaired, but Gabriel welcomed the opportunity. He put on pilgrim garb and accompanied Baba along the dusty roads of India, visiting the holy places.

Though at times Gabriel talked about Baba as the "sweet charlatan," he regarded him with awe and was convinced of his great occult powers. Gabriel was raised as a Roman Catholic, but he never became a dogmatic one. His inherent deep spirituality was undisciplined, and his restless imagination could never be channeled into any religion. He picked up appealing ideas from different religious philosophies and, even though they were often contradictory, they coexisted peacefully in his mind, together with his own brand of Catholicism. He was a poet and not a logician. And mysticism, real or phony, attracted him immensely.

The pilgrimage in India and then his stay in Baba's *Ashrama* was an experience Gabriel remembered with nostalgia.

"For the first time in my life I was really free," he told me. "I was poor and my poverty was pure, as I desired nothing."

In time desires returned, and about a year later Gabriel reappeared in the Western world, though he never gave up the thought that one day he would return to India and become a monk. His farewell gift from Baba was a pair of sandals, once worn by the master himself. The sandals and a small weather-beaten suitcase were all the luggage Gabriel had when he was put ashore in San Francisco by a sea captain he had befriended in Bombay.

Gabriel went to the St. Francis Hotel, where he knew the Italian manager. It took some time for the manager to recognize his old customer in the bearded Hindu. Gabriel, as always, chose the best room.

As a man of intuition, Gabriel sensed that soon a great change was to come in his life—but where and how? He decided to try Hollywood again.

The manager of the hotel was firm. Gabriel must leave his one and only suitcase in lieu of unpaid bills. He offered Baba's sandals in settlement.

"You have to realize," Gabriel said, "that those sandals are worth millions of dollars. They belonged to a seer in India. I tell you they will bring luck and you are fortunate to have them for my stinky little hotel bill." And as he talked, his dark eyes above his black beard vibrated with the power of the Yogis.

Overwhelmed by the magic sandals, the manager, being Italian and superstitious too, let Gabriel go.

When, years later, Gabriel came back to the St. Francis with plenty of money to collect his sandals, the manager was no longer there. Having become a multimillionaire shareholder in a big company, he kept the lucky sandals in a safe-deposit box. He refused Gabriel's money but permitted him to see the sandals once more. The butler brought them in. The worn, cowhide sandals, the work of an Indian village cobbler, were lying on a solid gold platter.

In Hollywood, Gabriel needed transportation to get around to the studios, and a certain car dealer in Beverly Hills told me years later that he would never forget the day when a man with a black beard walked majestically into his shop and announced, "I am Gabriel Pascal."

When the dealer said that he had never heard the name, the man assured him, "You will." Then he looked at the cars and chose the finest one. "This car I shall *borrow* from you and when I have money I'll pay for it."

The words were pronounced in such a way that the dealer couldn't protest. But soon both Gabriel and the car were back. He had finally realized where his intimation of a great change should lead him.

"I have to go to England," he explained to the dealer, "to look up George Bernard Shaw. I am going to produce his plays."

Ever since the Shavian shadow had fallen across his vagrant path, Gabriel had never forgotten the words from the red buoy: "If one day you are broke . . . come and call on me." And at this point, nobody could be more broke than he was.

Gabriel assured the dealer that he would settle the rental of the car on his return, but just before leaving he tried out the biggest and newest Packard convertible in the shop. He liked it and said he would buy it on his return if some alterations were made. He wanted an azure blue top to match the California sky, azure blue seats, and a steering wheel inlaid with ivory. He also wanted his initials in gold on the door.

Then he left for New York, hiding in the toilet of the train.

Chapter 5

The Half-a-Crown Deal

I T seemed that Shaw, after years of stripteasing with the film world, was never to be reached, but Hollywood tried and tried. Blanche Patch, Shaw's secretary, wrote that the film moguls were "forever angling for one of his plays."

Not that Shaw didn't want to see his plays filmed; but he rightly suspected that the screened versions would not be his plays any more. Shaw was not a writer who wrote to amuse and distract minds, but a playwright-Socrates who through his plays tried to induce his audience to think and accept his message. Every word, every sentence was measured with that in mind, and Shaw did not trust Hollywood not to sell him out for cheap box-office effects. He said that he could not find anybody who would not "mutilate" his plays, "murder" them, and then "give their cadavers to the nearest scrivener . . . The result was to be presented to the public with my name attached, and an assurance that nobody need fear that it had any Shavian quality whatever, and it was real genuine Hollywood."

Shaw, as was well known, was fond of money; and Hollywood offered big money. Shaw couldn't help but be pleased. "I have already an offer of a million dollars for the cinema rights to all my plays," he wrote in the early twenties. But he would not sell his soul.

There was a parade of the greats to Shaw's threshold, from
Harry Warner, Alexander Korda, Louis B. Mayer, and Sam Goldwyn down to some lesser lights, and even some abortive dealings
with RKO about *The Devil's Disciple*. Finally, Shaw thought
that he had found his man in Cecil Lewis, a screenwriter and producer, who agreed that "the films produced under this Agreement
shall be faithful reproductions of the Play."

They were and the result was a disaster. The Shaw plays Lewis
filmed in the thirties, *How He Lied to Her Husband* and *Arms
and the Man,* were such flops that a critic remarked of one of
them, "No more dismal film has ever been shown to the public."

After this Shaw grew allergic to movie offers. He swore he
would not touch movie-making unless through some miracle he
found the man designed for him, a Shavian man, independent,
who would not sell his soul, and "a producer who also knows his
job." And just about that time a man who believed it was his
"destiny" to interpret Shaw to the public through films was approaching British shores on a cargo boat.

"A Dutch cargo boat was cutting its way through the heavy fog
over the Channel," starts Gabriel's own description of his pursuit
of George Bernard Shaw. The year was 1935. He was sitting on
deck on top of his small suitcase and so deep in thought that he
even refused the cup of coffee offered him by a kindly sailor.

"I was reflecting," he wrote, "whether Shaw would remember
me and our meeting in Cap d'Antibes and his parting remark:
'One day when you are broke and have nothing left in the world
but your imagination, which is your talent, then come and see
me. Maybe I will let you film one of my plays.'

"Who could be poorer than I?" reflected Gabriel. "The few
coins I have on me would not even make a Dutch gulden."

"The hours passed slowly on the cargo boat," Gabriel's memory
of the day continued. "It was drizzling. I do not remember which
part of the ship I slept in overnight. Early in the morning we arrived at London Bridge. I thanked the Captain for his hospitality.
One of the sailors put my suitcase on shore. I offered him a tip.
He refused it. He had more than I did."

From London Bridge, Gabriel walked to Bayswater and took

lodgings in a cheap hotel. Such earthly considerations as how he was going to pay his bill never bothered him; fate always brought along something—though, to be sure, his "destiny" had been neglecting him lately.

"Then I remembered," he wrote, "that there was a Hungarian, a brother of a friend of mine, working at Chappel & Co., on fashionable Bond Street. The man's name was Lucas." Gabriel walked to Bond Street and, looking like a hungry wolf, nose pointing forward and flanks flattened, confronted Lucas. The man made a feeble attempt to duck, but it was too late: he was caught in the web of Gabriel's mesmeric smile.

In the good old days Gabriel had never been a small borrower, but this morning he was possessed by strange thoughts. "Ten pounds," he began, but then, looking at the glassy eyes of his compatriot, he amended, "Five. Just five pounds. It will bring millions. By the way," he added, "call up George Bernard Shaw for me; I want to make an appointment with him."

By then the compatriot was convinced that his attacker was raving mad, with his "unshaven face and strange attitude," and to get rid of him fast, he gave him a one-pound note. He felt he had escaped cheap when Gabriel folded the pound majestically and said, "Now I am going to see Shaw to get his film rights."

Gabriel was still sporting his Yogi beard from India. "I could not appear with my beard before Shaw," he wrote. "He would have thought I was competing with him." An Italian barber friend from the better days shaved him for nothing, and part of the one-pound note was spent in no less a place than the Savoy Hotel on a "fantastic rich breakfast, which was a real feast after fasting for one and a half days on the cargo boat."

An Italian tailor, also from the better days, pressed his trousers for nothing. And now "I was ready to leave for GBS's home," Gabriel wrote, "but then I discovered that I had left my gloves in the hotel in Amsterdam" (no doubt together with an unpaid bill). "At that time," he continued, "I had the same conception as Gandhi did when he first went as a young man to England, that without a pair of gloves a man was not a gentleman. How could I dare to go see the greatest living dramatist and not look like a gentleman? I went and bought another pair of gloves on a newly opened account at Robert Douglas."

Then, just like Eliza Doolittle going to see Professor Higgins, Gabriel took a taxi to Shaw's. "And after giving the elevator man sixpence for taking me up to GBS, I was left with two and a half shillings," he wrote.

It was well known that it was easier to see the King of England than George Bernard Shaw. When Gabriel rang the bell, the maid informed him that Mr. Shaw wasn't seeing anybody.

"You go and tell your master," Gabriel commanded with his customary authority, "that the film producer from Rome, whom he met in Cap d'Antibes about twelve years ago, is here." Then he added, "Tell him the young man with the brown buttocks."

Within two minutes, Gabriel Pascal was facing Bernard Shaw.

"Twelve years ago," Gabriel began, "you called after me from a red buoy that when I was utterly broke you would give me one of your plays. So we have a gentlemen's agreement . . ."

"Young man," Shaw broke in, "I am an Irishman and not a gentleman."

Gabriel went on. "I've just come back from India, where I was searching my way to become a mystic. But I feel I have yet to go on in this incarnation to experience life as a creative artist and use the talent God has given me." He flashed a boyish grin as he added convincingly, "You know, in India my guru told me that I am chosen by fate to make your works and message more widely known through films. So here I am. Your man, the man you were waiting for. I think we could start with *The Devil's Disciple*. Since my boyhood I have wanted to direct and play *The Devil's Disciple*. I am Richard Dudgeon—I am that dark, tragic, Gemini character."

For the first time in his life Shaw found himself speechless, and just stared at the stranger. A black-haired, tan-skinned stranger, with eyes large and luminous as black diamonds. And those black eyes were focused intensely on Shaw's blue ones.

"*The Devil's Disciple,* indeed." Shaw was finding his voice.

"Or, if you think that would be a heavy beginning, we could start with your Cinderella story, *Pygmalion*." And Gabriel smiled that wide smile his contemporaries described as irresistible.

Shaw must have had an eerie feeling that the man facing him couldn't be real. He was an incarnate figment of his own brain, a type of character only he could invent. To subdue the feeling, he

asked ironically, "Is that all you want?"—reminding himself that
he had just recently refused another fantastic offer from Sam
Goldwyn. "And may I ask you, young man, how are your
finances?"

"I have all the money one needs to make a start—provided one
has talent as well—which I have limitless," answered Gabriel.
He plunged his hand into his pocket with a self-assured smile, as
if he were about to produce the hugest diamond of India, and
threw on the table his two and a half shillings.

"This is all I have on earth," he declared, "and even this was a
loan."

Really, the man belonged in a Shaw play. Could there be anything more Shavian than that answer? Maybe this was indeed the
man and the producer Shaw was waiting for, a man oblivious of
money, with the soul of Dubedat.

Legend says that Gabriel left with not only the *Pygmalion* contract in his pocket but also some money, which Dubedat-like he
had borrowed from Shaw. One thing is sure: Shaw did ask Gabriel to come back to see him again. But he was a far cry from a
contract.

Shaw took his time to study his man. Gabriel succeeded in getting some money on an old deal and took a small room on Duke
Street. He kept visiting Shaw. Each time he was asked back, but
not another word was said about *Pygmalion;* instead, Shaw let his
man talk and talk. And Gabriel could talk. A vibrant raconteur
and an exhibitionist like Shaw himself, he was greatly preoccupied with his own complex *"I."* He had obviously lived the
Shavian leitmotiv to the full: "Never stagnate. Life is a constant
becoming: all stages lead to the beginnings of others." And he
had come to Shaw from many becomings: from the orphan among
the gypsies, to the self-supporting street urchin, to the cadet,
actor, cavalry officer, then the movie tycoon and later the partner
of Max Reinhardt, to the penniless pilgrim in India. He told
Shaw about his inner struggles, his attempts to discover what his
"mission" was, his search for expression as a creative artist.

Shaw listened, a very unusual thing for him. Blanche Patch recorded: "GBS never met a man who entertained him more." He
had found another spellbinder like himself, and a man whose soul
was not for sale.

But the waiting for Shaw to decide about *Pygmalion* could go on forever. Gabriel's money was gone, and he had to do something. He had a vague offer to produce a film in China and a Chinese financier's letter to Thomas Cook & Sons to book a passage to Shanghai. In desperation, he arranged to sail from Liverpool to China on December 15. He was booked on a train to Liverpool on Friday the thirteenth. On December 8, he went to Shaw and told him if he did not make up his mind about the *Pygmalion* film rights by the thirteenth, he was off to China.

"Shaw said to me," Gabriel remembered, " 'What? Is this an ultimatum?' And then he smiled with that unforgettable smile of his, which was half Mephistophelian and half the smile of a saint: 'But I hope you will come and see us before you leave.' "

That last sentence did not leave much hope. "When I left Shaw," Gabriel wrote, "I went back to my small flat in Duke Street. At that time, I was in love with a lady from India, one of those Anglo-Indians, half princess and half offspring of a British civil servant, which is the most unfortunate mixture in the world. She was to go back to her country and she prayed that GBS would not give me the license for *Pygmalion* and we could travel together to the Orient. I did not hear from GBS and now it was Friday, the thirteenth of December, the day I was to leave for Liverpool."

Gabriel and the Indian lady had a silent lunch together in his Duke Street flat. After lunch she said triumphantly, "You had better start packing now, your GBS has let you down."

Gabriel was reluctant to pack: he was still hoping. The train was to depart at five-thirty, but to get to the station they had to leave the flat not much later than four o'clock.

"I waited," wrote Gabriel. "It was quarter past three . . . it was half past three . . . it was three-forty-five . . . still no telephone call, no contract. My lady friend, who was burning incense all this time in front of her Kali statue to insure that GBS would not give me the contract and that she would have me, sat now in quiet meditation in front of her shrine. There was silence and only the red glow of the incense and the blue spiralling smoke seemed alive in the rapidly darkening room. A few minutes were left before four o'clock when I made the attempt to pack my toothbrush and the top half of my pyjamas. As I never used the bottom part, I had not much more to pack anyway.

"Suddenly I heard Big Ben striking. At the stroke of four, my doorbell rang and a little cockney boy in a messenger's uniform stood there. He asked: 'Are you Mr. Pascal? I have a package for you.' And he handed me an enormous envelope."

Gabriel tore the envelope open. Inside was a photograph of Shaw, inscribed "To Gabriel Pascal in commemoration of Friday, the 13th of December, 1935. Auspicious Day—from G. Bernard Shaw." In a separate envelope was the signed contract for filming *Pygmalion,* and a letter:

Dear Mr. Pascal:

I enclose the agreement in duplicate. I have put in an additional clause to safeguard you against the possibility of G. P. Films supplanting you with another producer. It gives you a personal hold on the film which you may find necessary.

Here was the first sign of that fatherlike protective attitude which Shaw was to maintain toward his somewhat unbusinesslike new producer.

"Shaw timed it as a great producer would: the package to be delivered to me when Big Ben strikes four, everything to the minute," wrote the relieved Gabriel. "My Hindustani friend was heartbroken but I was the happiest man in the world. I did not realize that this contract would be the source not only of great glory for me but the beginning of a horrifying Calvary of humiliations and endless sufferings." Jubilant, he wrote to Shaw, "I promise I will make you even more famous and very rich."

His destiny apparently fulfilled, Gabriel said, "GBS entrusted me with the magic flute of his art, which he knew I could play." But nobody else seemed to believe it. The financiers did not rush to put money into a Shaw movie. Millions had been offered before for Shaw film licenses provided the studios could change the sacred texts and add some cinematic touches. But nobody wanted unadulterated Shaw.

Two miserable years followed. Gabriel was told that Shaw's

name had been box-office poison ever since the miserable flop of his two filmed plays; that he was too highbrow for the public; that his plays, with a minimum of action and a maximum of dialogue, were unsuitable for films without major changes; and that *Pygmalion* was the deadliest play of all since it did not have enough action for a two-reel short, and worse, it did not have a happy ending. As a matter of fact, it had no ending at all: it left the audience and Eliza Doolittle in the air.

So nobody would touch *Pygmalion,* and Gabriel was rejected by every studio. The movie executives gave orders to their secretaries to get rid of the "madman" who kept insisting that there were "millions in *Pygmalion.*" But there still remained the great Alexander Korda, head of British Lion, who for years had tried to get the Shaw rights, to no avail. Reluctantly, Gabriel went to see his Hungarian compatriot. Korda was still anxious to have Shaw —but without Pascal. He turned Gabriel down. Gabriel had reached the depth of his humiliation: he had to walk back all the way from Denham Studios to London, as he did not have sixpence for the train. "I was too proud to ask for a loan from Korda," Gabriel wrote, which was indeed unusual of him.

Gabriel was looking shabbier and shabbier when he finally seemed to have found his man through a Hungarian friend, the writer Geza Herczeg. He flew to California to meet the would-be financier. Geza drove Gabriel to a breakfast meeting at the financier's house, begging him to keep his mouth shut, behave, and listen.

The table on the financier's terrace looked especially lovely because there was a big bowl of cherries on it, and Gabriel loved fresh cherries. But he took an instant dislike to his host. He never had patience with people he disliked; nonetheless, faithful to his promise to Geza, he listened. But his disgust was growing and, to conquer his rising temper, he concentrated on the cherries. The host was now explaining how he was to improve on the Shaw play. Gabriel's mouth was full of cherries when the host suggested that *Pygmalion* lacked sex, and, if he was to back it, "plenty of sex" had to be thrown into the picture. With perfect aim Gabriel shot the cherry pits into the would-be financier's face; then he rose, grabbed a handful of cherries, and walked out. He had kept his promise: he never said a word.

But it was indeed Gabriel's destiny to make *Pygmalion*. Not long after the cherry-spitting episode, miracles began to happen. Gabriel met the head of Pinewood Studios, Richard Norton, later Lord Grantley, the first movie executive he encountered to see the possibilities in *Pygmalion*. Together they formed Pascal Films, and Norton used his vast influence to round up backers. Financing was promised, the movie was cast, and production was scheduled to begin. But some of the financiers were slow to deliver their checks, and to prod them into paying Norton gave a much-publicized party at the studio, ostensibly to celebrate the first day of shooting. Society people and show-business notables, along with a mass of newspapermen, gathered to watch Leslie Howard and Wendy Hiller play a short scene. Only three people in the elegant gathering knew that the first day of shooting might be the last. These three were Shaw, Gabriel, and Norton.

Gabriel was, in fact, so discouraged that he was tempted to get up and tell everybody, "Go home, the whole thing is a joke. We haven't got a cent to continue," when he felt a pull on his coat. He looked up. Shaw winked at him and slipped a piece of paper into his pocket: the check had just arrived from the dilatory financiers.

Shaw stood up, raised his glass, made a toast "To George Bernard Shaw, the young Irish playwright," drank the wine, then bowed to himself, saying, "Thank you, Shaw," and walked out. The event made headlines.

At the launching of *Pygmalion,* Shaw was in his eighties, but he started on his new career with the exuberance of a young man, concerning himself with every detail, accepting mostly, but at times rejecting, Gabriel's ideas. "No; I must have two policemen," he argued with Gabriel on April 16, 1938, "one aged forty and the other aged twenty, and two scenes, because I must produce the impression of the two lovers having run at least as far as Cavendish Square from the first policeman. It seems the merest trifle, but it makes a lot of difference." Later Shaw wrote, "I approve of Miss Jean Cadell only if she plays Mrs. Pearce. Her salary would be wasted on the other parts." Or again: "Who is going to play the Ambassadress who received the guests? Surely Violet Van-

brugh would be ideal for that. Why waste her on a walk-on? It is
a real part and a dignified one, small as it is. And she isn't like
the Queen of Rumania. Why not, by the way, a black princess,
talking Hottentot (all clicks), with Higgins following her and taking down the clicks frantically in his notebook?"

The real miracle which left the theatrical and movie world gasping was that Gabriel succeeded where everyone else had failed: at
making Shaw change his sacred text. Blanche Patch wrote in her
memoirs that what Gabriel did "was to persuade Shaw to make
the play presentable in the new medium. It was the biggest con-
cession Shaw ever made to anyone . . . Gabby now had GBS well
under control."

How did Gabriel do it? Shaw was not a man easily hypnotized;
he must have been convinced that his producer indeed "knew his
business." Or perhaps those flops in the thirties made him realize
that a movie needs to be more than a photographed stage show.
Or maybe in Gabriel he finally found his equal, a fighter like
himself, with a violent temperament. Gabriel wrote, "I went to
GBS, and told him I needed several changes. He smiled and
started his Irish fight; and I started my Hungarian fight; and I
think the Hungarian is more effective than the Irish—because I
won."

Among the many new scenes added to the picture was the one
in which Mrs. Pearce, the housekeeper, gives the screaming Eliza
her first bath; the scenes with the love-struck Freddy forever waiting in front of Eliza's house; the sequence between Freddy and
Eliza on the street; and the later scene at Covent Garden when
Eliza realizes there is no way back for her.

Shaw also added a reception scene. Gabriel elaborated it into
the Embassy Ball, the sequence where the film reached its crescen-
do, where Wendy Hiller as Eliza was literally transformed into
a princess in front of the audience. Gabriel let himself fly into
the world of Cinderella, making Eliza dance with a crown prince.
Earlier, Shaw had suggested making the Queen the Queen of Rumania, but Gabriel was too much of a Hungarian for that; his
Queen and Crown Prince had to be from his own native land,
Transylvania, and Eliza, at the height of her female charm, had to
be suspected of *Hungarian* royal origin. Shaw was only too glad to
oblige his Magyar friend by having Karpathy say about Eliza,

"Only the Magyar race can produce that air of divine right, those resolute eyes . . ."

Karpathy, incidentally, was a new creature of Shaw's. He had given the name Nepomuck to this hairy and bombastic Hungarian ex-pupil of Higgins, but Gabriel changed it to the more Hungarian-sounding Karpathy.

Because the basis for *Pygmalion* was a miracle of metamorphosis performed by phonetics, Gabriel felt that the most important scenes in the movie should be the ones where Higgins teaches Eliza. He worked out those scenes in great detail, and it was he who introduced the famous phonetic exercises: "The rain in Spain stays mainly in the plain," and "In Hartford, Hereford, and Hampshire, hurricanes hardly ever happen."

It was Gabriel who discovered the movie's Eliza. At the Malvern Shaw Festival he found the then-unknown Wendy Hiller, who became his perfect Eliza. "This is your fate," he told her, "and I will make you famous." He was true to his word.

Shaw was unhappy about Gabriel's choice of Leslie Howard for Professor Higgins. He felt that Higgins shouldn't be a matinee idol but a "heavy." He thought that Cecil Trauncer, who played the Policeman, would have been a better Higgins. "The best heavy lead on the English stage is Trauncer," Shaw wrote to Gabriel. "It is amazing how hopelessly wrong Leslie is. He ought to change part with Trauncer." And Shaw was aghast that Higgins was made into a nonchalantly elegant figure. "Higgins is fatally wrong," he wrote Gabriel. "He should have a topper (cylinder hat) badly in want of brushing, stuck on the back of his head, and a professional black frock coat and black overcoat, very unvaleted." But he admitted, "However, the public will like him and probably want him to marry Eliza, which is just what *I* don't want."

On that one point Shaw was adamant: there would not be a "Hollywoodish" ending. "I have given my mind to the *Pygmalion* film seriously," Shaw wrote on February 24, 1938, "and I have no doubt at all as to how to handle the end of it." In his screenplay Shaw married off Eliza to Freddy, explaining that she would never marry Higgins: "Galatea never does quite like Pygmalion; his relation to her is too god-like to be altogether agreeable." Eliza and Higgins were to part forever in the drawing room but it should be a pretty parting, as Shaw continued in his letter to Gabriel: "Will you impress on Lawrence Irving [the set designer] that the end of the play will depend on him? Not only must the drawing room be pretty and the landscape, and the river if possible, visible through the windows with the suggestion of a perfect day outside, but the final scene on the embankment at Cheyne Walk must be a really beautiful picture. Its spaciousness must come out when the car is driven off. Irving must eclipse Whistler in this."

And what then would be the epilogue of the story of Eliza Doolittle? Shaw not only married her to Freddy but put the couple in a flower shop, financed by a loan from Colonel Pickering. He sent the scene with a letter to Gabriel: "I am sorry, I have to stick in the flower shop, but it need not cost more than it is worth and you will save by getting rid of the wedding-rubbish. It is not a Bond Street shop but a South Kensington one: half florist's, half greengrocer's and fruiterer's with a fine bunch of property grapes for Freddy to weigh for a lady customer."

That the battle cry during the filming of *Pygmalion* was economy, which was a strong side of Shaw anyhow, is obvious from the continuation of the letter: "The counters can be made for a few pounds; scales can be hired; and the building can be faked out of any old junk. Everything unsightly can be covered in flowers."

Gabriel made no comment. But at the sneak preview of *Pygmalion,* a very nervous Gabriel was tightly holding Charlotte Shaw's hand. Mrs. Shaw and "Gabe," as she called him, were great friends. Beside them, Shaw's white beard seemed to be fluorescent in the darkness. Gabriel was sure that the white beard would soon be ruffled with anger, for Shaw had not been told that Eliza was *not* going to marry Freddy, and there was *not* going to be a flower shop. Instead, the rebellious Galatea would return to her Pygmalion. And entering Higgins' study, she would have a moment of complete victory; she would see her tormentor in the loneliness of his room, head bowed, listening to her recorded voice from the cockney past. The sight would stir the eternal female in Eliza; she would turn off the machine and finish the recorded sentence softly: "I washed my face and hands before I come. I did."

But now the victory would belong to Higgins: the creature was subdued and returned to her master, and he knew that their future relationship depended on his behavior at that moment. He leaned back in his chair, stretching his legs comfortably, and then, as if it were the crown of a newly anointed king, he pushed up his hat triumphantly, asking in the words of the master:

"Confound it, Eliza—where the devil are my slippers?"

Thus the movie ended, leaving the public assured that Eliza would be running for those slippers to the end of her days. That was not how George Bernard Shaw ever let his women behave—but that was how Gabriel Pascal wanted *his* women to behave.

When the preview was over, Shaw did not say a word, but there was a faint smile above the white beard. Mrs. Shaw turned to Gabriel. "This," she said, "is the finest presentation of my husband's work."

After the sneak preview Shaw proudly wrote to Gabriel, "An all-British film, made by British methods without interference by American script writers, no spurious dialogue, but every word by the author, a revolution in the presentation of drama in the film. In short, English *über alles.*"

Shaw was therefore aghast when he found that Gabriel had submitted the script to the Hays Office in Hollywood for the approval without which it could not be shown in the United States. "I did not know," wrote Shaw, "that you intended to send the script to the American amateur censors, who have no legal status whatever. If I had known I should have locked you up until the film was finished . . . it is entirely impossible for any serious dramatist to work under the M.P.P. regulations or subject to the lists of words as compiled by the Catholic Action for the guidance of their office boys. There is only one course for you if you want to do serious work in the film drama, and that is to make your film and let M.P.P. attempt to boycott it if they dare. They won't dare."

Pygmalion broke box-office records. Overnight Gabriel Pascal and his discovery, Wendy Hiller, became world-famous. And Shaw? The box-office poison? "You are a greater box-office star here," wrote Gabriel to Shaw from Hollywood, "than their Greta Garbo." And the newspapers commented that "a man with a long, white beard is writing a new chapter in motion-picture history," adding that Shaw became known "among millions of people who had never heard of him before."

Shaw stormed, "I suppose Hollywood has now heard of me for the first time." But when the movie earned the Academy Award, Shaw put his Oscar above the mantlepiece. At the 1938 Venice Film Festival *Pygmalion* won the Volpi Cup. "The German Minister asked me to send a print of *Pygmalion* to the Führer," Gabriel reported to Shaw from Venice. "He will see it this week. Mussolini's son asked me to send a print to the Duce . . . so this will help the income tremendously in Italy and Germany."

The success of *Pygmalion* had far-reaching consequences in the film industry. According to the critics, it had lifted movie-making from "illiteracy" to "literacy," thus compelling Hollywood, at long last, to take on real writers. As for Pascal, the critics dug into their thesauri in trying to describe his personality. He was called "the cosmopolitan, dynamic ex-Hussar" who had "swept like a comet to world fame," upsetting "all conventional ideas of what makes a successful film." Reporters described his "majestic air," called him a man "who has vision" and who leaves people "spellbound with his personality." *Time* placed Pascal, together with the Pope and Adolf Hitler, on its list of the ten most famous men of 1938.

For many, the success of *Pygmalion* was hard to bear. Jealousy flared up like brushfire around Gabriel. Malign rumors started right away and the ripples of hostility were to spread wide in the coming years. Some claimed that the success of *Pygmalion* was due entirely to them. But Shaw knew the truth. He wrote to Gabriel, "You have a tremendous triumph on which I congratulate you and myself. Also, I congratulate several other gentlemen who would have spoiled the film if you had not prevented them but are in the bills as presiding geniuses of the production."

With the worldwide fame of *Pygmalion,* the "enigma" grew in proportion: why did Shaw, who had refused the great and rich, give *Pygmalion* to the unknown, penniless Gabriel Pascal? Why had Shaw, who thought so much about English phonetics, chosen Pascal, a "very foreign foreigner," to film the very play whose plot revolved around correct English pronunciation?

Shaw's own explanation was simple. "Gabriel Pascal," he wrote, "is one of those extraordinary men who turn up occasionally—say once in a century—and may be called godsends in the arts to which they are devoted . . . Until he descended on me out of the clouds, I found nobody who wanted to do anything with my plays on the screen but mutilate them . . .

"When Gabriel appeared out of the blue," Shaw continued, "I just looked at him and handed him *Pygmalion* to experiment with . . . The man is a genius: that is all I have to say about him."

To be called a genius by Bernard Shaw was no small compliment. But it was a compliment that was hard to live with, as Gabriel was soon to find out.

Chapter 6

The Rock and the Whirlwind

EVERYBODY involved in *Pygmalion* made big money—except Gabriel. He was bankrupt. In order even to finish the film he had to raise more and more money, each time giving up his own shares against the loans. In the end he hadn't one share left.

In 1939 he went to Hollywood to arrange further distribution deals for the film. Famous, but poor as ever, he managed to make the crossing in luxury on the *Normandie*. On the same ship was a group of Metro executives with their new film, *Goodbye, Mr. Chips,* in the can, and their star, Greer Garson, with whom, to complicate his life, Gabriel was madly in love.

In New York the loan he was hoping for did not materialize, so he wired a friend, the writer Mercedes de Acosta, in Hollywood: MEET ME WITH YOUR CAR IN PASADENA STOP PRESS WAITING LOS ANGELES STATION STOP CANNOT APPEAR WITHOUT LUGGAGE. The Sherry-Netherland Hotel in New York was holding his trunks.

In Hollywood he stayed with Mercedes de Acosta, who provided not only lodging but loans for flowers for Greer Garson. Meanwhile, the Hollywood papers reported that everywhere Gabriel Pascal went he was "hailed reverently" and that "he could write his own ticket." The Shaw-Pascal-*Pygmalion* combination had Hollywood on its knees. Questions buzzed: what would be the next Shaw film? *The Doctor's Dilemma,* perhaps? Whatever it was, every studio wanted it.

Shaw became alarmed. He did not want his discovery to be kidnaped by Hollywood. PRESS CAMPAIGN AFOOT HERE, he cabled on January 3, 1939, TO REPRESENT DILEMMA AS AMERICAN FILM WITH HOLLYWOOD STARS AND HOLLYWOOD DIRECTORS STOP OUR AGREEMENT MUST BAR ALL AMERICAN COLLABORATION STOP YOU MUST BE SOLE DIRECTOR.

"You must be sole director" was an indispensable condition of any agreement Shaw ever gave Gabriel after *Pygmalion.* All through the years, Gabriel was accused of vanity because he insisted not only on producing but on directing his pictures. But Shaw would not change this condition. He trusted no one but Gabriel, and always warned that if Gabriel was not to be the sole artistic director a contract was to "fall through." So people called Gabriel, as S. N. Behrman did in *The Suspended Drawing Room,* a "megalomaniac." He was convinced, Behrman writes, that he was a great director, better than anybody else, and "this delusion of Pascal's proved ultimately tragic for him." Alexander Korda, Behrman remembered, had told him once that Pascal could have been a very rich man and achieved a respected position in the British film world had he been content to produce and to engage competent people to direct. His own directing, according to Korda, "threw shooting schedules way out of kilter."

But in 1939 the way to Hollywood was open to Gabriel; all he had to do was say the word. Against the Hollywood temptation, however, he had to set the constant warnings of Shaw, who wrote, "Now is the time to be careful—extraordinarily careful. The success of the *Pygmalion* film will set all Hollywood rushing to get the rake-off on the next Shaw film. Where the carcass is, there will the eagles gather. No American feels safe until he has at least five other Americans raking off him, most of them contributing nothing except their entirely undesirable company. They get so settled in that way of doing business that they do not understand how a European with a cast-iron monopoly under his hat can play his game singlehanded. So again, I say be careful, or the film will make a million yet leave you with a deficit."

That Gabriel had the "cast-iron monopoly under his hat" proved to be his greatest hindrance in this moment of decision.

Obviously Shaw would never accept any Hollywood offer: "Do not consider shooting in America. We must keep all-British." And he warned Gabriel again that it would be his end "being annexed to Hollywood," adding, "Let our slogan be: Shaw is British; Pascal's address is the world."

Hollywood wanted Gabriel Pascal with or without Shaw. All the major companies were offering fabulous sums to have him as their producer. To make matters more complicated, Gabriel was contemplating marriage with Greer Garson, his "red-headed Circe," as he called her; and this would have meant that he had to stay in Hollywood, since she had a long contract with Metro. But how could he leave Shaw, who now had entered into partnership with him for the filming of all his plays? Looking forward to the adventures of film-making had given Shaw a new lease on life. "Take care of yourself," he wrote to Gabriel, "my film career depends on you." How could he tell Shaw that it was all over, that he was going to settle in Hollywood after all? That he did tell his partner something of his problem is shown in a letter from Shaw dated July 24, 1939: "Now that you have shifted the artistic center of gravity of the film industry from Hollywood to Middlesex, I hope you will shift your nationality in the same direction ... You have your choice of all the world except the place where you were born. The operations of Herr Hitler have closed that to you. The next best place for you is the British Empire with residence in London. It would be a calamity for British films and for me and for yourself if you chose California. England is the place for you: your work and all the employment it gives are there; and the new departure you have made so successfully in film drama would have been impossible in America. Besides, you will be far more at home with us. California is not suited to a Magyar *de la vieille souche.*"

By that time, Shaw had given Gabriel agreement letters for *The Devil's Disciple, The Doctor's Dilemma,* and *Caesar and Cleopatra.* As the negotiations for *The Devil's Disciple,* with Clark Gable, were bogged down for the time being, Shaw suggested *Major Barbara* as the next venture and he was eager for further discussions: "And now what is the next film after *Barbara* to be? I want to know before I begin a new play."

Gabriel was at the crossroads. He made the inevitable decision:

"I answered them [a major studio]," he wrote Shaw from Hollywood, "that I would not sign up for ten times that amount. All I want now is to turn your plays into movies."

And that was the end of Hollywood and his marriage plans.

Shaw endured Gabriel's almost filial devotion to his "dear Maestro" and returned it with fatherly scoldings: "Incorrigible, thousand times incorrigible." And Gabriel would answer with indignation, "I am not incorrigible; on the contrary, since my fourth year, when I started my independent life as an orphan, I have corrected myself every day and every hour, and the result is not so horrifying as you try to make me believe."

Shaw, who liked to cover up the fact that he too possessed a heart, and that in fact he was very fond of Gabriel, sometimes let himself go at the end of a severe business letter by signing it *"Sempre a te caro Gabriello,"* or just *"Sempre, sempre,"* or *"Sempre astuto ed infidele,"* or at times "Hardheadedly yours." If Gabriel stayed away too long on his trips, Shaw would cable: AWAITING YOUR RETURN IMPATIENTLY . . .

During those lean war years, Gabriel never came back to England empty-handed. Shaw and his wife were very grateful. "Just a line to say," he would write, "how glad we were to see you again, so robustly yourself after your adventures, and thank you for all the good things you brought. The whole household is gobbling them up with great enjoyment."

Shaw couldn't help being impressed by Gabriel's "dare to live," by his boiling energy and his complete disregard for the cherished values of society. He would watch with amazement as Gabriel, negotiating all over the world, appeared and disappeared. And he would complain, "You, in your abandoning energy and reckless disregard of costs, persist in making plans for me on the assumption that I am 35; but actually speaking I am a dead man; and a grasshopper is a burden . . . I discovered you ten years too late."

Gabriel's restless drive worried Shaw, who predicted his early demise—"I will yet survive you"—and, when RKO was discussing the financing of a Shaw-Pascal film, he wrote to Gabriel, "RKO should insure your life heavily so that they could replace their money if you started again in another world; but I could not replace you. So be good."

What dismayed Shaw and Mrs. Shaw most was Gabriel's smoking. "You must not smoke big cigars," Shaw wrote on the thirty-first of October, 1940. He brought up the story of Mario, a famous tenor of his childhood. Years later he had heard him again in Dublin, but by then "his voice had dried up into a broken-down baritone, utterly without tone . . . My mother's voice at the same age preserved its purity of tone so perfectly that she said it made an old woman ridiculous and would not sing in public . . . What then happened to Mario? He smoked cigars, smoked and smoked until his voice dried up and became the voice of a mummy. If you lose your voice you will lose all your authority in the studio. Your charm will be gone forever; and my plays will vanish from the screen."

Thanks to Shaw, Gabriel became a British subject about the time the war broke out. "You were naturalized just in time," Shaw rejoiced. "That was a piece of luck to begin with. All I fear now is that officers who can really command are so valuable that you will be conscripted."

To bind himself to his new country, Gabriel bought a home, Mumford's Farm in Buckinghamshire. "In my whole life," he wrote to Shaw, "I was driven from one place to the other like a cursed Ahasuerus. I was born an outcast and stayed an outcast. Now I am going to challenge my fate." He was planning to build a dramatic art center around the old Tudor house, a plan which would remain in the form of rolled-up blueprints in the bottom of his closet.

One thing that Gabriel never wanted was a Mrs. Pascal at Mumford's Farm. He was in complete agreement with Shaw's saying that "the greatest sacrifice in marriage is the sacrifice of the adventurous attitude towards life . . . Those who are born tired may crave that settlement; but for the fresher and stronger spirits it is a form of suicide." When in an interview in 1943 Gabriel said, "I shall never get married," Bernard Shaw's reply was, "That's right. He is wed to my plays."

It was never easy for Gabriel to find backers for the Shaw projects, because of the unorthodox way Shaw conducted his business affairs. He would never sell the rights to his plays for any amount of cash; he would only license them for a five-year period with renewable option rights. Gabriel held so-called letters of agreement for almost all the Shaw plays, but Shaw licensed one play at a time, and only when Gabriel had found solid backing. This practice led to a vicious circle: to get solid backing Gabriel had to show a solid contract, but Shaw would give no contract without the solid backing. And when Gabriel finally found backers, Shaw would issue the license not in Gabriel's name but in the name of the financing company. The license would nevertheless have a clause making Gabriel the absolute artistic director and producer; without Gabriel the contract would be annulled.

Another difficulty arose from Shaw's insistence that he himself be paid with 10 per cent of the gross receipts, a clause for which he required the strongest guarantees, usually the underwriting of a bank. Shaw never believed in profit-sharing deals. "It may cost a lawsuit," he wrote, "to determine what the profits are, whereas the receipts are absolutely ascertainable."

Those financiers who braved this stipulation were then confronted with Shaw's self-drawn contracts. "Mysterious documents," Richard Norton called them, "which had nothing whatever to do with the law. They would fill our legal advisers with horror and dismay." He also recalled Shaw's "alarming obstinacy" regarding these homemade documents.

To Gabriel's pleading, Shaw answered, "I hope I did not seem too impossible on Saturday; but I had given that agreement long and careful consideration and made up my mind like granite. If I give away an inch, you give away a foot, and everyone gives way or grabs all over the place until the whole business goes to pieces. There must be a rock somewhere in the shifting sands; and I have decided to be that rock."

Shaw urged Gabriel to make the same 10 per cent gross deal for himself: "Have a personal contract with the distributors as I have," he advised, "with a salary and a deferred royalty on the receipts, profits or no profits." If Gabriel didn't listen, Shaw predicted, he would end up in the poorhouse.

Gabriel would never know when his partner would take a deep breath and blow the whole shaky structure of his production plans apart by such notes as: "Three companies and one superfluous director to share the plunder! . . . Oh, if you were only a schoolboy! Unfortunately, you are a genius, and the whole gang of speculators is out to pick your bones. They shan't pick mine."

Not only were Gabriel's negotiations hampered by these practices of Shaw's; Gabriel himself was deeply hurt by them. That Shaw would not issue a contract to his producer in advance and in his own name created, in Gabriel's words, "a very weak and ambiguous situation." "I really don't understand," he wrote to Shaw, "why the contracts should not be in my name. When you gave me the contract in my name for *Pygmalion,* I had two and a half shillings from a borrowed pound in my pocket. And I managed not only the artistic but the business side of the picture very well. . . If I wanted to enrich myself through your contracts, which apparently is what you fear, I had ample opportunity to do so before the war, when I could have stayed in Hollywood where I had fairy-tale-like propositions from Metro and others."

"You say very truly," Shaw replied, "that money is nothing to you. So much the better from the artistic point of view; but it throws on me a moral obligation to prevent you from ruining yourself. On every agreement I give you, you can raise, say £50,000 per play. But there is no limit to what you may spend on each play. You are generous and reckless instead of having, as you need to have in this business, a heart like the nether millstone. And you have mad fancies for introducing Chinamen in color which you cannot photograph, into all British films. If I give you contracts for nine plays, you will raise £450,000 on them, and spend it all on a single Chinaman. Then, having nothing left for the other films, you will have to borrow at 50 per cent from hysterical serpents and others who will bleed you white. I shall get nothing; and you will get worse than nothing. That is, ruin, bankruptcy, disgrace, despair and suicide . . . Now, there is only one way in which I can make you set a limit to your expenditures on each play; and this is to give you one agreement at a time . . . I want you to have those successes without utterly ruining you. Hence my obstinacy . . . Your adamant G. Bernard Shaw."

Shaw called himself the "Rock of Gibraltar" when it came to business, and it was obvious to him that his "whirlwind" producer was anything but a businessman. To Shaw's scoldings, Gabriel answered cheerfully, "Nothing could be more natural than business agreements between the Rock and the Whirlwind."

Gabriel often said that his luck had been to be an orphan, so that he grew up in freedom and his "wings were never cut." And now in his middle years he found himself with a protective father who was constantly rebuking him. No wonder at times he rebelled. "Let us cooperate without dictatorship," he wrote to Shaw, "and without knocking my head whenever I try to lift it up to justify to God, to you, and to the world my talent, courage, and artistic integrity . . . You cannot treat me as the Inquisitors treated your Saint Joan: signing a letter and then taking my freedom away. My freedom, my spiritual freedom is my life! I am not compromising any more—not even with you, G.B.S.! God has given me inspiration, as He gave it to your shepherd girl, and I will follow it through. If you like what I am doing I shall be happy to continue, but if you feel that I am not the right man for you, it would be better to tell me so, and I will take the consequences."

But whenever Gabriel decided to free himself from the "yoke of the Old Man" there came the siren song from the Rock: "Take care of yourself; for if you go, I know not where to turn for your successor."

The usual difficulties arose when Gabriel sought financial backing for *Major Barbara*, the next Shaw play to be filmed. The invasion of Holland and Belgium in 1940 froze the finances, and Gabriel was advised to postpone the picture. He sought help in Hollywood, but Shaw was not about to give up: "Is it really necessary to trouble Messrs. Whitney [John Hay Whitney] and Selznick? Why not ask your British bankers to back you on the strength of *Pygmalion's succès éclatant?* Failing with them, there are lunatics in London who, excited by the press notices, will back anything filmable to any amount if it has our names attached. We must show the Hollywood distributors that we are independent of them as far as capital is concerned."

When after much tugging and pulling Gabriel had arranged the financing of the film, the setup was received with suspicion by Shaw: "The supplementary agreement puzzles me. I want to know who is providing the capital. . . . How does Korda have a finger in this pie? They are all to be paid first, but where do I come in? As for you, you will be left with nothing, though you are in complete command of the situation. You should have a prior claim to at least £24,000, win, lose or draw."

Hardly was the money question finally settled when trouble

started anew, for Shaw balked at signing the bank's agreements. "Agreement a booby trap. I will not sign," he threatened. When Gabriel begged, he answered, "Do not let your time be wasted by attempts to get the agreement [Shaw's] altered and the affair put on the old Hollywood basis. There will be no alteration and no side lines of any sort: they must take it or leave it as it is."

The bankers gave in, and Shaw wrote with glee to Gabriel, "Let me remind you that I make no further concessions to the financiers. . . . You can receive any threat to cut off supplies with the thumb to your nose. Only, the more you spend the less will be left for everybody except the author, who, being a ruthless shark, takes care to come in on the receipts and not on the profits."

But Gabriel had to admit to Shaw, "I am ashamed to tell you . . . to save the continuity of production I was obliged to give up the remaining half of my salary for the picture . . . But, believe me, I will make this picture such a masterpiece that these parasites of the City will not be good enough to polish our shoes." Shaw threw up his hands in despair: "I cannot protect you against yourself . . . when you are eager to work you will sign anything, promise anything, do anything."

Shaw had begun to work on the *Barbara* script in the middle of 1939. The opening of the film, Gabriel wrote to Shaw, was worrying him "day and night." The opening scene as it stood was a "disaster." There should be a short introductory scene between Barbara and Cusins. "I remember a speech," Gabriel wrote, "that I heard last year in New York, when I went to see Katharine Cornell and later walked outside the theater onto the corner of Forty-fourth Street and Broadway." And he quoted the speech, which he suggested that Major Barbara make with Cusins listening to it: "Amid all the noise and hurry of this street it is still true that God is in this place. We do not need a temple, built by hands of men, in which to worship Him. Here on this street corner, beneath God's open sky, we can draw near to Him. Some of you feel Him near you, even now, and feel too how much you need Him. Won't you let Him come into your life tonight? You want His guidance, His strength, His comfort—you need His forgiveness and friendship. Is there anyone who has courage enough to raise his hand as a sign that he would like us to pray for him? Make a decision now—in your need and loneliness, God can meet with you. (She pauses and looks around the audience.) Someone feels that he should raise his hand, but it isn't easy. You feel too shy, perhaps? . . . I can feel someone wants to raise his hand . . . Shall we bow our heads in prayer, and pray specially for him who should decide tonight?" And here, Gabriel suggested, Cusins, carried away by the fire and beauty of Barbara, would raise his hand.

Gabriel was persuasive: "You would certainly need to rewrite this in your own way, but believe me, my dearest Maestro, I have an unfailing instinct for pictures . . . and I believe that a prologue of this kind is needed badly, to introduce the relationship between Barbara and Cusins . . . It would not cost a penny in supplementary money, so I ask you, as your Undershaft asks Cusins: 'Be reasonable!' " Then, dismissing any further argument on Shaw's part, Gabriel ended the letter, "I will send my driver on Monday morning for this suggested prologue scene."

The sequence was ready by Monday, written as Gabriel suggested, and became the most moving scene in the film.

But Shaw wasn't always in agreement with his producer's suggestions: "I have read the Undershaft-Sardanapalus scenes, you . . . must have got frightfully drunk in Hollywood to conceive such a thing. Stephen and Cusins playing baccarat and Undershaft living like a second lieutenant just come into legacy, with nautch girls all complete, is beyond the wildest dreams of Sam Goldwyn. I cannot put on paper the imprecations with which I hurled it into the waste paper basket."

Soon the usual fights began. Gabriel was proposing cuts of the sacred text. He begged Shaw, "Please, leave it to me without going into polemics. I promise to keep my faithfulness to you as an artist," but he *had* to cut "when that is demanded by the iron law of movement in cinema . . . Have faith in my judgment where to cut . . . I only do it in extreme necessity."

Shaw gave as much attention to the music of his films as he did to the scripts, stating that music was just as important as dialogue. Originally, Shaw and Pascal hoped to get Arturo Toscanini, and Shaw had worked on the great musical scene of *Major Barbara* with him in mind.

The *yes* came slowly from Toscanini, and Shaw began to give him up: "No use waiting for Tosca: I cut no ice with him . . . as you are handling the affair with consummate ability, I just don't think about it."

Toscanini or not, Shaw attacked the task. "I left undone," he wrote to Gabriel, "an important bit of *Barbara:* the words for the Rossini quartette. I have now done them and will send you a fair copy . . . It has been a horrid job. Nothing would have been easier than to write a few pretty verses; but to fit them to Rossini's notes and accents, and to provide open vowels for the big recurring portamento was the very devil; and the result is queer but singable. I almost drove my wife mad bellowing it over and over on Sunday night."

But it was Sir William Walton who finally wrote the musical score for *Major Barbara.* Shaw advised Gabriel to ask Sir William "to try the effect of a single trombone sounding G flat quite quietly after the others have stopped, Undershaft pretending to play it. It ought to have the effect of a question mark."

What music did to Shaw became evident when *Major Barbara* was finally under way. During the shooting of the big Salvation Army revival meeting in Albert Hall, with its hundreds of extras, Shaw stood among the technicians watching the scene develop, with the band playing and all the participants singing and waving. Unexpectedly, he broke away from among the onlookers and, before anybody could stop him, joined the actors, singing and waving along with them.

Next day, sobered and embarrassed, he sent a note to Gabriel: "My apologies for interfering on Friday. I tried to keep quiet; but suddenly felt twenty years younger, and couldn't."

When it came to casting the film it seemed only natural that Wendy Hiller should play Barbara. But it soon became obvious that she wasn't Eliza Doolittle any more, but a princess, a star, and Gabriel's Professor Higgins approach just did not work. "Ungrateful," Gabriel raged, reporting their wrangles. Shaw had to interfere: "It would be the height of folly to quarrel with her after we have made her a star of the first magnitude. Somebody else will get her and exploit the work you have done with her." But soon he too showed disappointment in her performance. "I doubt whether Wendy understands Barbara," he wrote while

watching the rehearsals. "As Eliza, whom she did understand, her
face changed marvelously with every wave of feeling. In *Barbara,*
her face never changes at all. But to tell her so would only discourage her. If she is a heathen, like all those young people, you
cannot convert her at rehearsals."

Among the other players in *Major Barbara* was a young actress
whom Gabriel had discovered one day when he was discussing the
casting of *Major Barbara* with Richard Norton over lunch at the
Savoy Hotel. When the question of the small but important part
of a young Salvation Army girl came up, Dicky suggested a certain actress.

"She is a bitch," Gabriel replied curtly. "I want somebody
pure, with a spiritual face, an innocent girl."

"Difficult," said Dicky.

Not far away a young girl sat lunching with another woman.
"Look, Dicky," Gabriel said, "look at that face." Getting up, he
made straight for the table where she sat and placed a patronizing
hand on her shoulder. "Are you a virgin?" he inquired, and before the blushing girl could answer, he continued, "My name is
Gabriel Pascal and I need the face of an innocent girl for my next
film. I have a feeling you can act. Why don't you come out in the
lobby after lunch and recite for me something, anything."

It turned out that the girl was a dancer in the Sadler's Wells
Ballet, with dreams of becoming an actress. She never finished her
lunch, but rushed with her friend into the ladies' room to rehearse a monologue which she knew from the Spanish play *Cradle
Song;* and later, in a quiet corner of the lobby, she spoke the first
lines of the monologue. Then Gabriel asked her if she knew the
Lord's Prayer. She did, and she said it so beautifully that when
she finished Gabriel's eyes were moist.

"You are the girl," he said.

And thus, with the Lord's Prayer, the career of Deborah Kerr
began.

Shaw enjoyed nothing more than watching the shooting of a
film. A consummate actor, he made keen observations, as his rehearsal notes on the filming of *Major Barbara* show. Watching
Rex Harrison as Cusins, Shaw wrote, "Cusins thinks that when an
actor is unfortunate enough to have to speak old-fashioned verse,
he should be as colloquial as possible, so as to make it sound like

cup-and-saucer small talk. This, of course, only throws the verse away. When I write verse, it must be deliberately declaimed as such—I mentioned this to Rex."

The popular belief presents Shaw as an atheist (which he definitely was not) or at best an agnostic. But in his rehearsal notes he wrote, "Nobody seems to have been brought up religiously. Such passages as the two ways to salvation (from the Church Catechism) and 'the peace that passeth all understanding' are slurred over because nobody recognizes nor understands them. The two ways—baptism and the Supper of Our Lord—in their contrast to money and gunpowder, go for nothing."

Then, while observing Gabriel sweating with an actor, Shaw scribbled a note to him: "Don't waste time trying to coach him. You will only worry him and drive yourself mad. You might as well try to teach the differential calculus to an umbrella stand."

Ironically, Shaw's peace play was shot during the air raids. Bombs were constantly exploding around the studio, and Shaw wrote to Gabriel, "I was surprised when I learned that Denham gets so large a share of bombing. The truth seems to be that the German pilots, flying blind and trusting to their instruments, are convinced that they are bombing Whitehall."

Bombs were exploding even on the day when Shaw made a new contribution to his film career: that of actor. He played himself in the preface he had written for the film. In the middle of his speech came the air-raid alarm and the noise of planes overhead. Gabriel leaped forward to save him, but he remained undisturbed. He looked up, as if waiting for a bomb to drop, and improvised, "Let me get this word in before it happens." Then, inquiringly, to the audience, "Do I discern an expression of hope at the possibility?"

Shaw made fun of his star billing. "If the picture is a failure with *me* on the bill," he said to Gabriel, "you can go out in a redingote and a sandwich board with the legend: 'That Irishman ruined me!' *Any* Englishman will give you a shilling."

Gabriel's perfectionism began to wear Shaw out. *Major Barbara* wasn't finished when it was supposed to be, and the financiers grew impatient. Though Shaw wrote earlier that it would pay to "out-do Korda in extravagance," now he got cold feet. On July 6, 1940, he wrote:

My dear Gabriel,

As I feared, you have made a worse financial mess of *Barbara* than you did of *Pygmalion*. Things have now come to a crisis at which the film has already cost twice what it should. Yet it is still unfinished. The financiers won't go on; the cast is exhausted and sulky; and you have lost your head . . .

Now here are my instructions, which you must obey like a lamb. You will finish screening the script *without a single retake,* until you have it complete. When it is finished, and not until then, you will go through the rushes and be satisfied with what is good enough, no matter how much better you could make it if you had another hundred thousand pounds and another six months . . . You must finish, finish, finish at all sacrifice until *a* Barbara film is ready for release, no matter how far it may fall short of *the* film of which you dream . . . If you would like to come to Ayot St. Lawrence on Sunday at 12:30, so that we can have an hour before lunch for a glorious row, do so; for I can stand up to you and none of the rest can. Your thoroughly alarmed and now iron-jawed GBS.

Of course, Gabriel could have argued with Shaw that the main fault for his running out of time, and consequently money, lay with Hitler. The bomb count in the vicinity of the studio was around 125, and whenever the sets were ready and lighted and actors and camera were poised to start, the air-raid alarm would sound. At other times, the noise of the planes overhead made shooting impossible, and once, when the crew returned to a location, all the houses had been bombed out; they could only throw the takes of the previous days' work away.

Major Barbara was finally released and had a grand opening in Nassau under the aegis of the Duke and Duchess of Windsor. Gabriel escorted Katharine Hepburn to the opening; at the time he was considering her for the lead in *The Millionairess*. Though some critics claimed that *Major Barbara* was artistically superior to *Pygmalion,* it never had the same box-office success. The story itself lacked *Pygmalion's* Cinderella charm, and without that the Shavian sentences were too much meat for commonplace stomachs. Financially, Gabriel fared no better with *Major Barbara* than he had done with *Pygmalion,* and he was still in debt. He literally worked for nothing, and it became even more obvious to Shaw that his producer would never grow rich from film-making.

Shaw's greatest worry was what to do about his film rights. He was on the horns of a dilemma. He wanted "to protect" Gabriel against the Public Trustee, the executors of his estate ("when Charlotte and I die as we may any day ... you will be in the hands of the Public Trustee"), and also against "your indifference to money." But because of the latter he was reluctant to transfer his film rights irrevocably to Gabriel. The only solution, Shaw felt, would be to create a company with solid backing and with Gabriel as its artistic head; he then could transfer all his film rights to competent hands.

This idea of a Shaw-Pascal film organization with its own studios was to crop up in the coming years, starting with an offer from Axel Wenner-Gren in 1939 to build studios in Nassau in the Bahamas. Shaw was excited: "The development of Nassau into a second Los Angeles would be a tremendous score for the Treasury," he wrote to Gabriel, "... and you are unquestionably the man to carry through with my plays to begin with." Shaw even considered moving to Nassau with Mrs. Shaw.

World War II destroyed this plan, and Wenner-Gren himself was under suspicion as a German sympathizer.

In the war and postwar period filming became extremely difficult in Europe, and Shaw began to have second thoughts about Hollywood. He and Gabriel discussed possibilities for American productions: *Arms and the Man* with the Lunts; *Candida* with Katharine Cornell; *The Millionairess* with Marlene Dietrich ("the foreign touch would suit *The Millionairess* very well," Shaw thought, "if she can act"); *The Devil's Disciple* with any one of a number of stars, including Clark Gable and Cary Grant. Actual negotiations with RKO for *Arms and the Man* with Ginger Rogers got to an advanced stage. The RKO bigwigs had an idea, to which Shaw answered, "The suggestion of changing the location of *Arms and the Man* from Bulgaria ... will not bear examination. The population of Bulgaria is 6 million, the theatre-going portion of which is negligible. Their feelings may be disregarded."

More suggestions, and Shaw thundered, "To change *Arms and the Man* into The Chocolate Soldier ... with a dance and plenty of laughs for Miss Rogers—that would suit Hollywood to perfection ... Tell Miss Rogers that Raina is the star part ... if she suggests that the part of Louka might be made that star part... do not argue with her; just throw her out of the window and tell her not to come back."

But soon there was no necessity for Gabriel to argue with "Hollywood." His desperate letter went to Shaw: "When your contract arrived and you were not willing to change a syllable, RKO, just as so many other companies before, tore your agreement to pieces."

In 1943, J. Arthur Rank expressed interest in a partnership with Shaw and Pascal. Shaw, who had learned about Rank's extensive financial holdings, got excited and wrote to Gabriel, "We can discuss the situation with him on Saturday. Meanwhile make no contracts until you have mine. I may die this year (87 this month) and then where would you be?"

When Saturday came, and Gabriel arrived in Ayot with Arthur Rank, the old man surveyed him with great curiosity. "Isn't it a bluff," he finally asked Rank, "that you have all that money? Confess to us that you are a pauper, like Gabby and myself, then we will treat you as one of us."

Arthur Rank was definitely interested in a partnership, to begin with three films. Shaw was agreeable, provided Rank would secure Gabriel's 10 per cent interest from the gross earnings.

"I am very grateful," Gabriel wrote on July 7, 1943, a few days after the meeting, "for your kind and valuable help in discussing my financial situation with Arthur Rank... you have the proof now that A.R. intends to back me 100%... All the budgeting will be done by his people, so I am not responsible for it, and I can concentrate exclusively on my creative work, which was always your desire." He went on to tell Shaw how happy Arthur Rank was after their meeting, ending, "He certainly went away inspired, and promised me that he will take care to protect my financial interest in the spirit you wish it to be done."

Gabriel was not telling the whole truth. Much later he admitted that "Arthur Rank persuaded me in the car coming from your place to change the agreement [to give Pascal 10 per cent of the gross receipts]; otherwise he would not finance the picture." And when Shaw found out about it, Gabriel complained, "You rubbed it under my nose on each occasion that I betrayed you and myself... so as my nose is long enough, I do not want any rubbing any more."

But Gabriel was more worried about those ambiguous Shaw agreements: "The contract question should be cleared up as soon as possible . . . I remind you again that you called yourself once my Rock of Gibraltar, which I believe you are . . . but I beg you, in these few years while you are still with us, try to help me with your understanding, so I can continue your work for years to come."

The partnership with Rank was formed for the production of three films: *Caesar and Cleopatra, Saint Joan,* and *The Doctor's Dilemma.* The first picture was to be *Saint Joan,* the filming of which was most eagerly awaited by Shaw. Even before he met Gabriel, he had written a scenario for Elisabeth Bergner which was to be produced by her husband, Paul Czinner. But that scenario, Shaw wrote to Gabriel, was "obsolete."

"It was written," Shaw continued, "when Czinner was dreaming of locations and afraid of too much talk and too little change of scene . . . I had not then seen what you could do with a stage version. . . . Your genius is independent and can do better with the play as it stands."

Gabriel, like Czinner before him, feared censorship because of Shaw's unorthodox presentation of the Maid and decided to confer in Rome with a Monsignor. Shaw retorted, "As to conciliating the Vatican, that is utter nonsense. I make it an absolute condition that the Catholic Action shall be entirely ignored, and the film made in complete disregard of these understrappers of the Church. Really responsible Catholics will not object to the film; but it is not fair to consult them about it, as it is one thing to welcome a film and quite another to guarantee it as orthodox. When the play is filmed it will be irresistible."

Gabriel disagreed with Shaw and insisted on talking with his friend the Monsignor. Shaw warned that he should not approach him; "but if you happen to meet him you can explain to him the utterly silly and impossible objections, grossly insulting to me, which were made in America, and say that the play led to great hopes in England among Catholics of my conversion to the Faith . . . But whatever you do, do not ask him for any official expression of approval. Say that nobody, not even the Pope, could be made answerable for Shaw."

In Shaw's garden stood a makeshift cabin where he did his writing. The cabin was so narrow inside that it seemed anyone who was trying to write at the desk had to sit edgewise. It was in that sanctuary—visits were allowed only to a few chosen ones—that Shaw was working on the new scenario of *Saint Joan.* His letters to Gabriel were filled with ideas, quips, and explanations of his characters: "We never discussed Cauchon, the fantastic Churchman, nor Stogumber (a terrific acting part never half touched yet) nor Warwick . . ."

"Rex H. [Harrison]," Shaw's answer came to Gabriel's suggestion, "as the Dauphin would be a Zweiter Leibhaber instead of a gargoyle on a Gothic building. Rex must play Dunois."

The decisive question, of course, was who could play Joan. From 1938 almost until Shaw's death, he and Gabriel never ceased to search for their "perfect Joan." They rejected many actresses in their letter exchange: "Her face is rigid . . . she isn't spiritual enough . . . there is a cold air about that one; a saint and a martyr, as you know, must be full of warmth and burning flames . . . she played Joan on the stage as if she was a milkmaid who stole money to keep her illegitimate child and was punished for it."

The greatest of the stars fared no better: "Elisabeth Bergner persists in wanting to play the part on the stage . . . She wants to make a Pitoeff success by leaving out everything except crying. I have told her finally that I dread nothing more than a success on these lines, and that she must *lasciar ogni speranza.* I hope Hepburn is not a cry-baby."

The suggestion of Katharine Hepburn shows how Shaw must have mellowed toward Hollywood. Only a few years earlier, when Gabriel had come up with the name of Greta Garbo, Shaw stormed, "Garbo is quite out of the question. We must stick to English films and English stars and never let a Hollywood sex-appealer within two thousand miles of the studio." The suggestion of Garbo for his Joan was so "Hollywoodish," Shaw continued, that he was convinced "if the heroine of the play were the Blessed Virgin, they would probably have suggested Miss Mae West."

After Wendy Hiller's success as Eliza Doolittle, Shaw and Gabriel had been convinced that she was their "perfect Joan." But in 1940, seeing her play the role at Malvern, Shaw was disappointed. "Wendy did not make much impression in it," he wrote to Gabriel. "I thought this was the fault of the producer, who made the fatal mistake of slowing down her last speech, which ought to be a blaze of fury . . . but after Barbara, and your confirmation of my suspicion that she does not feel religious parts . . . I am doubtful about her being right for Joan."

The "little girl" who played Jenny in *Major Barbara,* Deborah Kerr, was growing up into a big star. She had the "spiritual face" Gabriel was looking for, but Shaw felt that she wasn't "thick enough" yet for the part.

Sometime earlier, Gabriel had begun discussions with Ingrid Bergman. When Shaw saw her photo, he became enthusiastic: here, without doubt, was their Joan. But then Ingrid decided to play Maxwell Anderson's version of the story on the stage. Shaw was undaunted. "What a stupendous stroke of good luck!" he exclaimed to Gabriel. "Anderson, without stepping on my grass, has given us a film advertisement that will make America rush to see Ingrid as the real and only possible St. Joan. She now cannot do without us nor we without her; so let her know at once that we must have her . . ."

If Shaw was an eternal Professor Higgins, so was Gabriel: they both loved Pygmalion-like experiments. Accordingly, in the early stage of their search for Joan, they had thought of picking an unknown girl from a convent. She should be a girl, Higgins-Shaw and Higgins-Pascal agreed, "who has never been before the camera and who would never face it again after St. Joan."

Gabriel embarked on the mission during a visit to Canada. He actually possessed letters from a church dignitary to several Mother Superiors, asking them to allow him to look among those novices who had not yet taken the veil. But, alas, the local bishop was on his guard. Before the dashing Pascal arrived, the Mother Superiors were all alerted and warned that "the cinema is immoral and any direct or indirect contact with it would be a sin."

The long series of would-be Joans was briefly interrupted during the war by a most unlikely candidate. The British Office of Information felt that now would be the most injudicious time to make a film about St. Joan and remind their French allies of England's little mistake of burning their saint. But a "no" could never stop Gabriel. The case of *St. Joan* was tossed from one government office to another, with a stubborn Hungarian ex-Hussar pursuing the vibrant shadow of the Maid. Finally, it was agreed that *if* the French government, then in England, would agree . . .

Gabriel put all his magnetism into his interview with General de Gaulle and gave his own performance of *Saint Joan*. Carried away, de Gaulle gave his enthusiastic consent, remarking that he himself had sometimes felt that his mission was similar to Joan of Arc's, as it was his destiny to liberate France. "The thought struck me then," Pascal reported to Shaw, "that, instead of Garbo, de Gaulle wanted to play the Saint himself."

Because of all the difficulties with *Saint Joan, Caesar and Cleopatra* seemed to be more suitable as the first Shaw film with the Rank organization, and Shaw once more plunged into the preparation for the production.

"Caesar must not be a *primo amoroso*," he warned, so he was happy when Gabriel got Claude Rains for Caesar. Vivien Leigh was to play Cleopatra.

"Vivien's shyness does not matter," Shaw assured Gabriel, "I can knock all that out of her and get going in a half a jiffy." Shaw still loved to rehearse with his actors.

But he did not like Gabriel's choice for Septimius: "He looks ten years older than Caesar instead of at least ten years younger . . . fat and overfed. Such a creature could no more cut off Pompey's head than he could win a hundred yards' sprint. Septimius must be under forty, in Roman military uniform, an athlete and a swordsman without an ounce of fat on him, swift and disciplined in movement, crisp and hard in speech, as unlike Caesar as possible, and as like Hitler (barring the moustache)."

Then about direction: "Caesar couldn't possibly have his wreath in the Pharos scene. He won't want to when he gets into the spirit of the scene, the main bit of acting in which is the change from the old baldheaded discouraged futile disillusioning superannuated dugout before lunch to the ebullient impetuous steel-nerved Caesar after it. That will play out Claude's whole gamut as an actor."

Shaw, though much older now, still enjoyed watching the work in the studio and posing flamboyantly for pictures in a Roman helmet. But at one point, his enthusiasm was shaken by his strong sense of economy. "On Thursday," he wrote to Gabriel, "there were hundreds of men in the studio; and only twelve at most had anything to do but take snapshots and pick up scraps of my conversation. Most of them did not even do that much. Were they all on the payroll?"

Then he added, "And the retakes! With Vivien Leigh gabbling tonelessly such sounds as *cummineecho* and *oaljentlemin!* Does she always go on like that, or should I have had her here to drill her into the diction of the part?"

During the casting Gabriel, searching for a very young girl to play the harpist slave girl, went to a dancing school at Golders Green in London. There among a roomful of girls he saw a fourteen-year-old with a sharp but delicate face. "Girls," he said to all the others, "you are witnessing the birth of a star." He advised the fourteen-year-old to say goodbye to her friends: "You will be a star one day." The girl's name was Jean Simmons.

As always, the music-conscious Shaw wanted to be sure of the right composer. "Choose Bliss without hesitation," he wrote to Gabriel. "The more leading composers you give a chance to, the better for your prestige." But no composer should make the trip to Ayot. "No need to show them to me," Shaw wrote, "I cannot tell what a man's music will be by looking at him."

But finally it was Georges Auric, the French composer, who wrote the score for the film.

While Caesar was fighting his 2,000-year-old battle of Alexandria in a British studio, Hitler was fighting his battles in the reality of the present. Only a few days after Gabriel started shooting the film, the new German weapon, the V2, began the systematic destruction of London. Gabriel wrote to Shaw, "The French windows in my sitting room were blown completely in and the ceiling in my bedroom was cracked, so I am having the same gay start on the picture as I had with *Major Barbara* during the blitz."

Caesar and Cleopatra was shot from beginning to end under adverse circumstances. Gabriel's good star of destiny began to change. "That cursed gypsy woman, Cleopatra," Gabriel sighed to Shaw, "never brought luck to anybody."

As if the German bombing weren't enough to slow down production, it turned out that though Vivien Leigh had assured the company that she wasn't pregnant, she was. Hardly was the shooting schedule rearranged to give priority to all her scenes, when she suffered a miscarriage and was sick for months. Once more the schedule had to be changed, mostly to do the location scenes. Now the sun turned against Gabriel, refusing to shine for weeks on end. Expenses rocketed. Worst of all, some of the leading actors had to be brought back from their other engagements. Finally, bombs and no sun forced an expensive and desperate step: the production moved to Egypt, carrying its own papier-mâché Sphinx.

Here was a marvelous opportunity for the hostile press to pounce on Gabriel: it made a good story to ridicule the man who carried an English-made Sphinx into the land of the Sphinx. Rumors were added that he had even transported loads of sand to the desert. It was no concern of the press that the small Sphinx with which scenes had already been shot had no counterpart in Egypt.

The sun was shining in Egypt, all right, but the natives somehow got access to the props, found the glue of the papier-mâché shields nourishing, and ate them up. Over three hundred new shields had to be made and shipped: another expense and delay.

Back in England, the now utterly frustrated Gabriel ran headlong into trouble with the trade unions and handled it in his usual go-to-hell manner. Even Shaw did not sympathize with him: "As to the dispute with the trade union. If Independent Producers, instead of sticking to its business of producing, is going to engage in the class war with its extras, and make friction when it should be making films, then I shall rule it out of my future arrangements. I prefer oil to sand in my bearings. Extras who do not belong to a union and will not join in are, in the lump, stupid, disloyal, selfish, undisciplined vagabonds. Those who belong to a union are steady, sensible, provident, punctual, and can be disciplined by their union if they behave unreasonably. The war between employers and trade unionists is a hundred years out of date."

That the security of belonging to a big organization was a mixed blessing soon became evident, for the independence of the Shaw-Pascal team was now limited by "advisers." Shaw certainly must have gotten indigestion from some of their propositions, as this letter to Gabriel shows: "What!!! Cut out the first act!! ...

This is not mere ignorance of the job. There are plenty of people who would like to see Arthur [Rank] ruined and get rid of us. Some of them have got into the studio and are making suggestions with this in view. Shoot them out of it, since it would be unlawful to shoot them in it."

Shaw's suspicion seemed to be well-founded: jealousy and intrigues surrounded Gabriel during production. And he could not function in the midst of ill will. "I was surrounded by saboteurs," he complained later to Shaw, "and I made the picture without joy and inspiration." His "Cagliostro charm," as Shaw used to call his effect on people, was wearing off. His success had made his faults unforgivable. His temper tantrums were no longer looked upon as the outbursts of a genius. His heavy accent and Genghis Khan features made him appear more and more like a "very foreign foreigner," an intruder into the British film world. His "majestic air" now seemed to many just sheer arrogance. And the camp of his enemies grew to outnumber his friends.

Shaw saw the danger with the press and tried to keep Gabriel quiet, asking him to "be prudent"; but to check either his anger or his enthusiasm was equally hopeless. His enthusiasm was as volcanic as his anger. When an idea occurred to him, he would rush headlong into action. That infuriated Shaw. "I have had to give you away completely," he wrote to Gabriel on one occasion, "as there is no possible excuse for the announcement. I have told them that you have done the same thing to me every week for years, and that when you spot a promising talent or think of a new film you immediately announce it as your next venture without asking anyone's leave, and that nothing ever restrains you."

That was true. A promise for Gabriel was as good as gold in the bank. He no sooner had a promise or a verbal agreement for a film than he put in motion the whole involved machinery, from the distributors on, promising in his turn jobs and careers. And then, if the plans collapsed, more and more people would be disappointed and would spread rumors about Pascal's unreliability. But Gabriel tried hard to keep his promises alive with further promises, building up in the process a time-consuming correspondence. "I'm only trying to make people happy," he would say. "If I can't fulfill my promise, at least I have given them hope and faith in themselves."

As things worsened with the press, Shaw was angered. He blamed Gabriel for letting newsmen into the studio: "This Press foolishness must stop absolutely . . . In future, unless our proceedings are treated as sacredly private, I will take no part in them. A report on what passes at rehearsal or production is worse than betrayal of a confession . . . Get rid of all your Press people; they damage you every time."

Even before the film was finished, malignant rumors were spread that Shaw was dissatisfied with it. But in fact he was very pleased when he saw the first reels. "You have surpassed yourself in this production already in one scene," he wrote to Gabriel. "When it is all finished, it will lick creation."

One thing Shaw would not do was help to promote his films. A small booklet was published about the filming of *Caesar and Cleopatra;* it included some of Shaw's letters and a lot of photographs. When Gabriel asked him to autograph a few copies for some important people to help launch the film, Shaw answered, "You have gone quite mad. You ask me to take this illustrated prospectus of my goods round to celebrated people . . . as if I were a commercial traveler selling vacuum cleaners. I am to bribe the Press with my autograph to boost my sausages. You really made me ill and had given me a bad night. I loathe those books, and have, with great difficulty, refrained from tearing them to pieces. My plays do not need nursing."

Shaw always felt that advertising was beneath the dignity of the Shaw-Pascal team: "A Pascal-Shaw film either succeeds or fails: the silly little tricks by which they push their trash on the exhibitors have no place in our business. I send no messages and make no appearances at trade shows: I remain majestically aloof, a Mahatma in the mountains of Thibet." When Gabriel begged to differ he got another angry letter: "If you go on . . . piling up expenses for publicity which we have already got you will end by getting deeper into debt instead of making thousands out of your monopoly and forcing me to break up our partnership by refusing to endorse your entanglements."

By then the general animosity was mounting. Gabriel was ridiculed and criticized at every step by the newspapers and by a word-of-mouth campaign. "There was definitely a plot to kill him off," somebody told me later. The waves of criticism even reached

Parliament, where an M.P. made a speech asking for restriction on the expenditures of *Caesar and Cleopatra.*

Nevertheless, opening night was a great society event. Queen Mary and the Court attended, and the newspapers reported that the opening caused the biggest traffic congestion since V-J Day. Gabriel himself couldn't get through the traffic around the Odeon Theatre near the Marble Arch in time to greet the Queen.

By a strange coincidence, the opening was on December 13, 1945—exactly ten years after the "auspicious day" when Shaw had inscribed his photo "in commemoration of Friday, the thirteenth of December, 1935," the day he had given Gabriel the *Pygmalion* contract. Later it seemed that the magic circle of good luck in the Shaw-Pascal relationship, which had started on a December 13, also closed on a December 13.

At first, *Caesar and Cleopatra* was a success, but the newspaper attacks continued. Articles turned public opinion against the "foreigner" who had squandered British money in wartime and had occupied the studio too long, thus robbing others of space (Gabriel retorted, "I was the only man who had the guts to shoot a film in Denham during the blitz"). And to finish him forever in the British film industry, Gabriel was censured by the General Council of the Association of Cine-Technicians, which ruled that he could work again in any British studio only under severe restriction.

As yet another blow, Arthur Rank, making the excuse that he was transferring his interests to Hollywood, had bowed out from the Shaw-Pascal team, thus breaking his contract for the two other films they were to do. Though Shaw had grown uneasy about Rank well before the completion of *Caesar and Cleopatra,* he did not want to hold Rank responsible for a breach of contract: "We must play fair with Rank. We must not spend a penny of his money . . . outside the completion of the *Caesar* film. *The Doctor's Dilemma* scheme must be dropped at once. We go into the market with *Arms and the Man* and *Saint Joan.* Why Rank, having gone so far with us, has thrown away these two plays which were just what was necessary to finish the Rank-Shaw-Pascal scheme, is beyond any possible explanation except that he has gone completely Hollywood, where they are still twenty years out of date in the illiterate movie period . . . and must rule him out of our operations as an Americanized anti-Shavian." He added, "It is a pity for he financed us very handsomely."

That *Caesar and Cleopatra* had some very good reviews in America did not help Gabriel in England. By now there were even speculations about who would inherit Shaw from Pascal. Alexander Korda seemed to be the most likely successor. Korda, soon to be knighted, was not only greatly talented as an artist but was all that Gabriel wasn't: smooth, diplomatic, and a marvelous businessman. There was always a secret rivalry between the two famous Hungarians. Gabriel once remarked to Korda jokingly, "Two gypsy primas cannot fiddle in the same pub."

That he was now ousted from the "pub" finally dawned on Gabriel when 1945 and 1946 brought a series of futile negotiations. Toward the middle of 1946 he had to confess to Shaw, "My dearest G.B.S. . . . we have come to a crucial point . . . I have no studio space any longer at my disposal in England."

Gabriel, betrayed by everybody, stood as alone as he had been when the Dutch cargo boat landed him a decade before at London Bridge. Everybody had forsaken him except one man: George Bernard Shaw. "In our next venture," wrote Shaw, remembering the one-time offer of Wenner-Gren, "we must try to secure an up-to-date Studio reserved (perhaps built) for our use exclusively, and lettable only during your holidays . . ."

Though Shaw's suggestion of an organization and studio for the Shaw-Pascal films at this point seemed like wild fantasy, Gabriel was a man of fantasies and the idea began to take root. Soon came a thought that was bold but very logical: why not give the "Irish Pope" back to the Irish? With his usual "do-it-at-once" enthusiasm, Gabriel flew to Ireland and in a few days he had Eire buzzing: THE SHAW FILMS TO BE MADE IN IRELAND; BERNARD SHAW RETURNS TO EIRE, the headlines proclaimed.

Nothing could have appealed more to Shaw or to the Irish, and the Irish venture started under a lucky star. Gabriel showed *Caesar and Cleopatra* to Eamon de Valera, who was enchanted with the film. He wrote to Shaw and invited Gabriel back to Dublin for further discussions. On his return, Gabriel had meetings with de Valera and a number of politicians and ministers. They were open to the idea of building studios and starting an organization to produce Shaw films. Ireland wanted its son back!

When Gabriel reported all this in Ayot St. Lawrence, Shaw's eyes "became veiled with joy."

Arthur Cox, a Dublin attorney, worked out a detailed memorandum, and Irish national pride flared up in a unique effort to raise the necessary capital. Grounds for the studios were chosen at Shanganah, an estate near Dublin. Gabriel was sure that he could purchase the necessary equipment in the United States with the help of his old friend Henry Wallace.

And Gabriel's luck elsewhere seemed to be turning once more. Mary Pickford made an offer for *The Devil's Disciple* and *The Shewing Up of Blanco Posnet*. Shaw had always agreed that his "two American plays" should be filmed in the United States and, as the Irish studios were a far cry yet, Gabriel started negotiations with Miss Pickford, leaving for Hollywood at the end of August, 1946.

From Shannon airport, he wrote to Eamon de Valera and thanked him for his kindness in spending so many hours discussing the Shaw-Pascal productions in Ireland. The project, he wrote, would be "for the advancement of both: of my artistic mission inspired by G.B.S. and your great work for a greater Ireland."

Another letter went from the airport to Bernard Shaw: "Somehow, now I feel that all the trouble I had in England was all for the good . . . my predestination as an artist maybe is that I should work in Ireland. You were right when you told me that the Irish race suits my Hungarian temperament." Gabriel went on to say that Mary Pickford's interest in the two "American plays" was a "wonderful stroke of luck until we have the Irish studios . . . However sad it is that I must miss our weekly meetings, it is perhaps better that I should make the next pictures in America, and come to see you in between pictures." At the end of the letter he pleaded once more, "I would like you to consider the whole position and decide finally that the time has come to establish our program in a legally written form without which I cannot go on with these ventures . . . Once you believed that I had a special gift to film your plays. Do not spoil that gift!"

There was no reaction from Shaw to those last sentences.

In New York, at the Ambassador bar, Gabriel ran into Ben Blumenthal. It was September, 1946, and Gabriel was on his way back to Europe for a conference with Shaw before the final arrangements with Mary Pickford.

"Did you ever do anything about that Hungarian actress?" Ben asked him over a drink. Gabriel had a faint recollection of a photo of mine Ben had showed him some months before in London. "Why don't you see her now on your return?" Ben suggested.

The hell with it, Gabriel thought and told Ben he had other worries than Hungarian actresses; besides, "she can't get out anyhow."

"Give her a chance," Ben insisted. "There's star material there, I think."

The premonition was as light as a breeze but as insistent as Ben. "All right," Gabriel said finally, "cable her to be in Paris in about four weeks' time." And that was how we came to meet at the Place Vendôme.

When Gabriel, sometime after our meeting in Paris, returned to Hollywood, he informed Shaw of the details of Mary Pickford's offer in a five-hundred-word cable—an extravagance which must have curdled Shaw's blood. Shaw promptly cabled back collect: AGREED FOR DISCIPLE ON MY PART. Acting on that cable, Gabriel signed a preliminary contract with Miss Pickford. He should have known better and remembered earlier warnings from Ayot: "And no matter what agreements you make or how many, the last word is with me . . . and ICH LIEGE UND BESITZE."

For when it came time to sign his part of the agreement, Shaw found fault with it. He wanted the Bank of America, which had already given the completion guarantee for the film, to guarantee his 10 per cent of the gross as well. Mary Pickford's guarantee would not do, he explained, because his long friendship with Mary should not be mixed up with business.

The bank, after receiving Shaw's "indispensable" wish for their guarantee, went as far as agreeing to take the Shaw contract in trusteeship and sent a draft agreement. Shaw did not like it and made up his own instead. "I can suggest only," he wrote, "that the Bank shall sign *my* draft on the dotted line, trusting my many years of experience . . . or else withdraw from the transaction as outside of its scope."

The bank refused to sign Shaw's homemade draft agreement, and a compromising third draft was drawn. After reading it, Shaw answered that it was "so absurdly incompetent that I am telling him [the lawyer] high-handedly that as neither he nor the Bank understands the case, they must sign my draft, which they have ignored, on the dotted line, or cry off the transaction . . . They simply do not know what they are about; and I do. I must, therefore, dictate the terms: take them or leave them."

The bank left them. Somewhat subdued, Shaw wrote to Gabriel, "The enclosed cuts out the Bank. Do we give up Hollywood?"

It was then that Gabriel left Hollywood and, without explaining anything in his letters to me in Hungary, rushed to see Shaw in a last desperate effort, taking him his own preliminary contract. "I read through your agreement and marked 20 places where it needed alteration," Shaw informed him. "When I came to the end I found that you had signed it. It is too late now to do anything but leave you to your fate . . . you are incorrigible."

Gabriel was still hoping to remedy the situation when the final blow fell: without advising Gabriel, Shaw had written Mary Pickford that he had decided after all to postpone *The Devil's Disciple* for two years. This letter had a bomblike effect on United Artists, which had widely publicized the forthcoming production. Their ire fell on Gabriel, whom they threatened with a lawsuit. Shaw only shrugged his shoulders: "I have made no contract with them." Of course my contract for *One Touch of Venus* was automatically canceled too.

Shaw seemed to be relieved that Hollywood was out. He never liked the idea of losing sight of his producer, and he would have missed those weekly meetings. He set his heart on Eire and *Saint Joan*. He had no time to wait; he wanted *Joan* on the screen before he started "on the long pilgrimage." And Gabriel? He could only try to adjust himself to the new situation

The Sunday Express in London broke the story of the Irish venture, emphasizing Gabriel Pascal's role in the setup. Shaw blamed Gabriel for indiscretion and raged like a Gaelic god. He sent the article to Gabriel with a letter dated May 15, 1947:

"The enclosed may make a frightful mischief. Our business is to start an enterprise which is above all Irish, Irish, Irish. And here comes a Hungarian from Arthur Rank's camp who is to buy the whole affair without a single Irishman or a penny of Irish capital in it. You must write to the *Sunday Express* contradicting the whole article and declaring that you will own nothing in Ireland but your artistic talent; that the capital will be Irish, the shareholders Irish, the chief author Irish, the financial and political control Irish, and no foreigner concerned in the project (an Irish project) except your humble self, chosen for your peculiar job by a famous Irishman. Nothing short of this will undo the mischief and turn it into an advertisement."

It soon became evident that there was no money immediately available in Dublin to start *Saint Joan,* much less to build the studios. Though Arthur Cox, the lawyer, assured Shaw that he would be able to raise the money for *Saint Joan* eventually, Shaw did not want to wait. He remembered Gabriel's earlier suggestion: to film *Androcles and the Lion* in Italy. But the offer from Rome for *Androcles* had come before the Pickford deal, and by now the lines of contact were broken. Shaw wired Gabriel: "I have promised to hold up *Joan* for Irish pictures . . . Meanwhile go on with *Androcles* as an Italian picture."

It would have been bad enough for Gabriel to start a new wild-goose chase to Italy all alone, but I was in the picture now too, divorced for his sake and on my way to join him.

We were waiting at the Paris airport to leave for Italy. I was looking at the hill of our luggage which we had carried to our second Paris meeting as separate luggage: his and mine. From now on it would be put together as *our* luggage—not only the dresses and suits from the times when we hadn't yet met, but also our stories, habits, experiences, and wounds. And like so many other couples, we did not worry about our dangerous luggage, as we believed that *our* love was different, that it would work the miracle: to make one whole from the fragments of two lives.

PART TWO

Chapter 1

Il Fuoco della Morte

ROME. The Grand Hotel on the Piazza dell' Esedra. Foaming fountains and string quartets from the cafés. We stood amid our luggage in the lobby, and my happiness reached out to take in the wine-colored carpets, the wide staircases, the milling people, the hotel staff greeting Gabriel with an enthusiastic "*Come sta,* Signor Pascal?"

I wanted to be happy. I wanted to erase that "second Paris" from my memory. Something had gone wrong; Paris didn't have the same ecstatic taste it had had the first time. We had made a pilgrimage to the Place Vendôme, sat at "our" table at the Ritz, talked feverishly about our love, but at times Gabriel's eyes looked far away, and it seemed to me as if he wasn't really there.

One evening I had been bitter. We were in a café off the Champs Elysées with Christian Bérard—"Bébé"—the painter, Louis Jouvet, the great French actor, and an actress whose name I don't remember. Gabriel had admired a recent performance of hers and said that maybe she could play *Saint Joan.* It was late and the café was almost empty. The three men's attention focused on the actress's lovely face as Gabriel formed a medieval peasant headgear out of a napkin and fastened it on her head. Her strong Breton face became like the Maid's. She said a few lines from *Saint Joan* in French. Rapt, the men watched her, and I could see how Gabriel, his eyes and face aglow, took in her loveliness. I might as well not have been there. It was as if I had ceased to exist as a person, an actress, a woman—I, who used to be the center of attention.

Back at the hotel, I burst out. He wasn't the same since I had returned to him, I said, and began to cry. He left the room without a word. We made up later, but that first misunderstanding drew a mist over my happiness.

But now, in Rome, the horses' hooves clapping on the stones of the Pincio talked of happiness once more. And the cool, fragrant night around our *carozzella,* the softness of the hazy sulphur waters in the swimming pools of Acqua Albule, the smell of the *trattoria* in the harbor of Porto d'Anzio and the salty taste of the *zuppa di vongole*—all that was happiness. A cat with curved back balancing on a Pompeian-red vase under our window in Fregene —that was happiness, too.

We drove north. We were getting acquainted. He was a man, a real man, I thought, a master I could look up to. I also found him an odd mixture of gentle boyishness and rough strength. There was something barbarous about him. His laughter came easily, thundering free without inhibition, and so did his anger. No rules bound him. He walked through social taboos and formalities, throwing them over with impatient shoves. He went where he pleased, said what he pleased, and talked only with whom he pleased.

Venice. Mornings in rowboats, then dives into the iridescent greenness. Loafing on ancient, crooked streets, hunchbacked bridges. Sometimes Gabriel, in an exuberant mood, would joke with the people lazing on weatherbeaten steps, or perform magician's tricks for children with his cane, or slap the backside of a fat woman passing by. At fruit stands he would poke into the boxes for a cherry or a strawberry. Again his hands reminded me of the paws of a gluttonous bear. The fruit vendors weren't angry at him. He took the fruit as naturally as if it belonged to him, grinning impishly at the vendors, who would grin back.

I noted again the exceptional attention with which he was received everywhere: in shops, hotels, restaurants. How the chefs would rush to prepare something "special" for him and the waiters would gather electrified, as if awakened from a sleep. When he was in a good humor he would go to other tables, offering a taste from his own food with a big smile. "Don't eat that stuff; let me order for you." The place could be the Champagne Room at El Morocco or a peasant *trattoria* on the roadside; it was all the same to Gabriel.

The way people reacted to him was once well described in a write-up about him: "As an individual Pascal is so singular that at first meeting he is little short of startling . . . A dynamic enthusiasm dominates his personality." And he could be enthusiastic on diverse subjects. Once at a dinner party in New York he was describing with fervor the talent of his Italian shoemaker. "He is an artist, a great artist," he said, and with that he raised his leg above the table so that everybody could admire his shoe. "These are not shoes," he added, "these are wings."

Once more we talked as we did the first time in Paris. Gabriel said he believed that God creates a mate for each soul and the two are drawn together through the ages to be one again. Other loves are searchings for the real one. And only with one's true mate can one better oneself and climb the ladder of reincarnation, finally to be purified and then together to be one with God.

"With your help," he said, "I will be able to subdue that other Gabriel in me, that cursed, unhappy, self-destructive me. You don't know that other side because ever since I met you everything is lightness, purity, and sunshine: the miracle of finding my way back to myself, to the boy I was in the mountains of Transylvania . . . after that I was never myself. I had to wear masks. I had to pretend. With you, I don't need any mask. You aren't like the others, you are not really a human being, as I never was one. You are a nymph, an innocent, pure, forest nymph, akin to the animals . . ."

I told him that even so he wasn't sure about us; after all, he had given me a three-month option to decide. He said that was because of his changed financial situation, and also because "I was always a hobo. Do I have the right to marry someone? Can I be loved at all?"

Gabriel never showed me the postcard he had received from Shaw a few days before our second meeting in Paris. It was dated

June 4, 1947, and it read: "... I have also wired Cox that unless at least a quarter million Irish money is on the table on Friday I withdraw. Do not engage yourself to the Italians until the Irish question is settled. If the Irish money is forthcoming Rome is only a location job."

The "quarter million" had not been "on the table" on the appointed Friday, but Mr. Cox was convinced that if Gabriel could find studio space and half of the backing in Italy, he could raise the other half in Ireland. The Italian group Gabriel had found was not, however, interested in *Saint Joan* or *Androcles and the Lion* but did have partial Vatican backing for a film about Saint Francis of Assisi. The Irish felt that they should join the Italian group on the filming of Saint Francis; if they made money with it, the second project could be *Joan,* about which Shaw had written earlier, "I will not let it be made anywhere except in Eire."

Could Shaw perhaps work on the Francis scenario?

"I do not see," came Shaw's answer, "how I can collaborate with the Italian authors of the St. Francis scenario. I have strong views as to the character of St. Francis, who was an apostle of Holy Poverty, whereas my doctrine is that poverty is a social crime and root of all evil ... In any version made by me the saint would appear, not altogether as a hero, but as a well-intended but dangerously mistaken enemy of the Vatican ... the result would be a film which the Church might find hard to sponsor."

We went to Montecatini to take the cure and "clean our bodies" of all the poisonous food one eats, as Gabriel said. He was constantly exorcising the "poisons" with mineral waters, baths, colonic irrigations, herbs, and such, as if punishing it for its gluttonous appetite. We drove to the springs in a cab, and Gabriel would inevitably shout to the driver, "To the Palazzo di Cacarilla," which order the cabby would receive with a wide Italian grin. Each morning we went to the same table in a quiet corner of the spacious, open Hellenistic portico. While drinking his daily eight glasses, Gabriel read books about Saint Francis of Assisi to prepare for the planned movie.

One morning, as we sat quietly in the sunshine, Gabriel seemed deeply absorbed in his book. Suddenly his hand, which had been reaching regularly for his glass, stopped, and he sat motionless. I looked up from my book. He wasn't reading. A strange, faraway expression widened his eyes, and his face was almost translucent.

"I want to be a monk," he said gravely.

I wasn't alarmed. I knew that in the past, when he felt himself too much entangled with a woman and wanted his freedom back, the urge to become a monk arose in him.

"Francis was right," he continued. "He found the way, and it should be my way, too. I felt that instinctively when I was in India, but then I was still self-seeking. Yet I knew that I had a mission from God. I thought it was making films in the service of art. But more and more I wonder if I was not mistaken. If only I could leave all that business dirt behind and be a monk."

I teased him gently. "But haven't you also said that I am your eternal mate, the female created for you, the soul of your soul? How could you be a monk then?"

"Why not? There is a higher love than sex, and it is not sex which I love in you. Even if the sexual part of our love should cease one day, I could never share my life with any other woman. But if someday you should leave me, I would go on alone and search for that perfection of Saint Francis. I would go to India, to Shri Meher Baba. To achieve a higher perfection, one should have no attachments. One can still love, and that love would then be as of the angels. Look at Saint Clare. I think she was the eternal pure mate of Francis in a mystical sense. They were united in the love of God, yet they never touched one another."

"I'm not a likely candidate for a Saint Clare," I said, laughing. "When I was a child I put pebbles in my shoes so that I would suffer and become a saint, and all I got was holes in my stockings. I gave up sainthood fast enough. I worship a god of my own, the god of joy, beauty, and gaiety. I am a pagan. My prayer is the pleasure of the sun on my skin, the joy of swimming in the water, the dew on flowers, and good food in lovely surroundings. I can pray in the meadows better than in churches."

Bowels cleaned, the rest of the poison had to be sweated out, Gabriel said, and for that there were the volcanic steam baths of the nearby Montsummano. We arrived there in the morning hours, and at lunchtime Giovanni Papini and his wife drove over from Florence to visit Gabriel. The controversial author of the *Life of Christ*, a convert to Catholicism, was already an old man. His wife, a gentle white-haired lady, was the seeing eyes of her huge-framed man: Papini was blind.

When they left, we had an early dinner, then sat on the terrace in front of our rooms. Somewhere in the garden flowers sent up their perfume. A light breeze arose, and an enormous moon, orange-yellow and full, was born in the dark lap of the mountains.

"Let's go for a walk," Gabriel suggested.

A dusty, steep path wound among the vineyards. Gabriel walked in front of me and soon disappeared around the turn of the road. I passed a bush heavy with white flowers, and picked a twig from it. The fragrance was lustful yet sad—the tortured kiss of parting lovers.

The moon rose higher, and in its light I saw my shadow on the sandy path before me: the short tunic-like skirt, the narrow waistline, the hair covering my shoulders, the flowering twig in my hand. Looking at my shadow, I was caught by a memory like a whirlwind... and I felt as though I were falling through time, away from the present. I, the girl with the flower, and my beloved going before me. I knew this path... and my lover, the young boy... I remembered, but what? The vague feeling vanished, then returned. Gabriel and the young boy were one in a dim, misty memory of something past, strangely mingled with the present.

Gabriel, high on a ridge, had stopped to wait for me. As I climbed upward, I saw him standing under a sycamore tree, looking very young in the play of shadows and silvery light. The vague memory returned, sharper now: I had seen him like this once before, standing under a sycamore tree.

I reached for his hand. Then we sat down on a rock. Opposite us, the volcanic mountain arose, hostile and monstrous in the moonlight. The dim memory was trying to free itself from my subconscious. I knew this mountain... suddenly I recognized it.

"The volcano... I'm afraid... we're going to die," I stammered to Gabriel, not looking at him but sensing again that he was the young boy. "I saw my own shadow on the road when you walked before me," I told him, "and the volcano—they reminded me of something, but I don't know of what."

"I felt the same. When you were coming up the road with the flowering twig in your hand it seemed to me I had seen you like that once before."

"And when you stood under the sycamore tree, I saw you young as you were then ..."

"Then? When?"

"I don't know."

I stood up. My body felt light. The moon seemed near enough to touch. The silence was like a dream of eternity, as if life and death were one in that moment.

"There is a joy and pain in me," I said. "I am so happy and so sad, I want to dance."

My body felt weightless. "I can leap over the mountains and fly into the sky," I said, and began to dance.

Back at the hotel, I put the flowering twig into a vase on my night table. When I awakened in the morning, Gabriel had already gone to the steam bath.

As I was dressing, the maid came in with the mail. She glanced at the twig in the vase. "Throw that out, Signora," she said. "It's bad luck."

"Why should I throw it out? It's pretty."

"It's bad luck," she insisted, rolling her eyes in fear. "This is the flower of death, they say. They call it *il fuoco della morte*. There is an old legend about it and two young lovers."

Il fuoco della morte: the fire of death. What a strange name for a flower. The white blossoms among the dark leaves seemed so pure and innocent. I buried my face in them.

We returned to Rome. In spite of Shaw's blunt refusal, Gabriel had no other choice if he wanted to save the Irish deal but to continue negotiations for the St. Francis film. This time we stayed in the newly opened Hotel Hassler. One hot evening, as we sat on our balcony, we saw a young woman undressing in the house opposite us. She stooped over to wash her naked breasts.

Gabriel watched her. "Like a French painting," he said. "How marvelous. The little attic room, red geraniums on the window sill, the pink contours of a woman, and the way the breeze blows the curtains. . . ."

"And here beside you," I laughed, annoyed, "sits the woman for whom you waited eight months, your 'eternal love.' Only a few weeks ago we started our new life together, and now you have only to see the contours of a fat young woman, not even her face, and . . . oh, you're no better than Tibor!"

"But that's exactly what intrigues a man's imagination, that I can't see her face. And the difference between me and Tibor is that I was interested in her only for that one moment when she started to wash herself, bending over the basin. Tibor would try to meet her and make love to her."

"And you wouldn't?"

"No. But if I were a painter I would be inspired to paint that moment, or if I were a poet I would write a few verses about it, but being only a film-worm I might use it in a scene."

"I think you've been quite a Don Juan too."

"The difference between me and the Don Juans is that they chase women for their own pleasure's sake. I despise sex just for the sake of sex, and I never chase women. I can do without them. I think I am more Peer Gynt than Don Juan, and maybe your sad fate is to be my Solveig."

"Don't call me Solveig again—it's a ghastly part!"

I smiled, but my smile was forced. I was worried. Since our return to Rome, Gabriel had left me alone not only during the daytime, but also on several evenings, to go to business meetings and dinners. I knew that he was working hard to find a basis for our future, yet whenever he left, a frightful loneliness descended upon me.

By the end of July, Rome was suffocating. The populace grew noisier, if that was possible. It seemed to me that Italians never slept. The sirocco, which lingered on, was hard on me, and Gabriel accepted an invitation from Nuchy to visit her country place. Nuchy was the Italian love of Gabriel's youth, the girl he had left at the station in Rome. They were still good friends. She had never married. She was no longer young, but she was still lovely, with her fresh face, bright blue eyes, and honey-colored hair worn in a simple knot. She had a hearty laugh and smelled of garlic.

Her place was near the little hilltop town of Lanuvio, among olive groves and vineyards. Her villa had been destroyed during the war, and she was now living in the gardener's cottage. The bombing had revealed the foundation of an antique villa said to have belonged to Roscius, an actor of Nero's time.

Nothing had changed in Lanuvio since the days of the Caesars. On the winding road leading up to town one could see women sitting erect on donkeys, balancing baskets and water jugs on their heads, and down at the bottom of the hill was the old well where a time-blackened, broken Priapus dreamed forgotten.

Nuchy's cottage was small but comfortable, with a large wide terrace. A torso of Aphrodite stood there, striped white by pigeon droppings. The statue had been found among the ruins of Roscius' villa. Round about were many antique fragments, heads of columns carved in marble and mosaic pieces. Roscius was as near as yesterday, and the peasants talked about him as if he were a rich uncle who had died not too long before.

One evening Nuchy and I were sitting on the terrace, waiting for Gabriel. A young boy who had been sent to watch for his car came running up shouting, "*Il Signore!*" Nuchy disappeared into the kitchen, rattling commands in Italian. When she came out, we started along the dirt road to meet the car. Soon we saw two approaching headlights. The car limped up the uneven narrow road. When Gabriel got out, we took him between us, arm in arm. He was exhausted by work and the sirocco, but happy to be here.

On the terrace, the table was already set. There stood a large green bottle of Orvieto in its plaited straw basket, many-colored fruits in fragrant maturity on a deep bronze plate, and hot garlic bread folded into white napkins. The boy lit the candles of a tall, rusted wrought-iron candelabra. "Inherited from Uncle Roscius," Nuchy said, smiling at me. "It was unearthed by the bombing."

Dinner finished, Gabriel leaned back in his chair and lit a cigar. Mischievously he looked from Nuchy to me and back. When he was in a good mood, he loved the "harem" atmosphere: women around, serving and flattering him as women always did. He brought out a mixed mother-and-slave complex in them.

"You were an idiotic bitch," he said to Nuchy, but with such a smile that she melted. "But you always cooked well, and how beautiful you were, Nuchy, like young Venus herself."

"Oh, Gabriele, *mio ragazzuccio.*"

"Only," Gabriel added, "you talked too much, starting at six in the morning: trrararara, tra, tra, tra. It went on and on, till you fell asleep at night. And you were always jealous—like her." He gestured toward me. "Women have no brains. Why are they all jealous? That was one of the reasons I left you, and ran off to the station that day, do you remember? And I never came back. I told you I wouldn't. But the main reason was that I was utterly broke. Do you remember, Nuchy, when they auctioned the furnishings of the villa that cold winter day?" Gabriel turned to me. "Only a mattress was left on the marble floor, which was like a block of ice, and poor Nuchy cried that she was freezing to death as the cold penetrated through the mattress. So I offered to let her lie on top of me to keep warm." This last sentence, pronounced with a child's innocence, sounded more than funny, yet he hadn't meant it to be. He was only describing their misery in the darkest colors he could find—not to mention his own spontaneous self-sacrifice.

It was getting late, and Gabriel, yawning frequently, said he wanted to sleep on the terrace. We brought him a mattress, put it under the torso of Aphrodite, and hung the hook of a mosquito net around the statue's neck. We used the fragments of Roscius' villa as weights to hold down the net.

Late the next morning, when I got up, Gabriel was still snoring under the net. Nuchy was kneeling beside him, her red-gold hair shining in the sun. There were love and tears in her eyes as she looked at him. She smiled at me when I kissed her good morning.

"*Ecco,*" she whispered, pointing at him. "*Ecco,* the great romance of my youth. How I loved him. Take care of him, *cara,* but don't lose your heart too much. He is dangerous, with the innocence of charming, poisonous flowers. Well, he is old enough now, and you are young and lovely, and he is madly in love with you. Perhaps you will do what no woman could ever do: hold him."

The news from Hungary disquieted me because my mother was still there. Tibor, waiting and hoping, wrote long, touching letters. Only two months of the three-months' "option" time had passed, but I felt that Gabriel and I must talk over our future, mainly because of my mother. She had her papers and was ready to leave Hungary, and I was fearful that any delay would be dangerous. When I brought up the matter, Gabriel said, "The best thing we can do is for you to go to Paris alone and wait for your mother there. I have to fly to England to see Bernard Shaw. Then I have to go to Dublin, to talk over the Italian situation. I've neglected you in the past few weeks, but I had to. I am desperate to start my work and everything will be different when my affairs are straightened out. It will be good for you to be alone in Paris and talk everything over with your mother. And if you are sure that it is the right thing to do and I am really your man, then join me in England and we'll get married."

When Gabriel left for England Nuchy and I stood together at the Rome airport and watched his plane disappear.

"He left me like this too," Nuchy said, drying her eyes. "But then he went on the train."

Paris made me unhappy. Mother arrived with Tobias, our pet squirrel, both bewildered by the change. August was long and hot, and Gabriel didn't fly over to see me and meet Mother. Later he would say, "I left you alone so that without my influence you could decide before taking the big step," but at the time, he simply said he was too busy with his film negotiations. He could find time, I thought, *if* he really cared.

Did he feel that he was trapped by his love for me? And that now he had to go through with marriage against his better judgment?

Many years later he was to write a letter to a friend referring to a theater evening during that August of 1947. "You remember," the letter said, "when we saw that horrifying Sartre play *No Exit* together? I sensed already then that my own marriage with Valerie was destined to be like that—hell on earth."

Mother received her visa for England and I called Gabriel.

"What have you decided?" he asked, and I sensed uncertainty in his voice.

"Do you really want me?" I asked.

"I love you."

"Then yes, I will marry you."

"And Tibor?"

"I am sure I can never go back to him."

There was another short silence and then: "And your career?"

"You are my career," I answered. But deep in my heart I was afraid of marrying him. Those summer months together had revealed a great similarity in our way of thinking, in our tastes and reactions, but they had also warned me of the enormous patience and even physical strength I would need to stay in rhythm with his energies. I felt confused and tired. He said that if his current deal went through, "we will sell Mumford's Farm and live in Italy." That was the third place he had planned to live since I had known him: first Hollywood, then Ireland, now Italy. I didn't realize then how much I yearned for stability.

Something else disturbed my thoughts. From the beginning, a sentence recurred in Gabriel's letters: "You should choose to share my life only if you blindly believe in me." Later I understood this. It meant not to show doubts, not to advise, correct, or worry—because he believed that he could be successful only if he was untouched by other influences. And now, through the daze of my love, it dawned on me that during our two months together I had been nothing. Will, thought, wish—all were Gabriel's. He had taken possession of my mind, spirit, and soul as naturally as he always took anything he wanted. Though it thrilled me to have my man strong and masterful, I was aware of a resentment within me. Then again, could I trust him? He had left every other woman in his life. Yet I was packing, ready to go to England. There was no life for me without him.

"My dear love," Gabriel wrote, "only two more days and you will be here. Our Calvary of waiting is finished, our new life begins. For this I prayed today in church, asking the Blessed Mother to help us on our way together. All the bitterness and disillusion that my profession brings day after day cannot touch me any more . . . the curse on me now will be lifted through your love . . ."

Another letter was enclosed in the same envelope.

"There is a deep sadness in my heart tonight: I cannot live without you! I felt it stronger than ever before. Suddenly, it is clear to me that if one day in the future you cease to love me, my spirit will be crippled and finished. I am not so much sad as frightened that one day I shall lose you ... Come, come fast so that feeling your living breath and biting into your flesh will convince me that our love is the only reality on this strange planet where I have lost my way in my wanderings ..."

Chapter 2

The Miracle

THE silence was such that even the beating of my heart sounded noisy as I turned restlessly in the large antique bed. I heard the moisture dripping from the old trees outside, and the bitter smell of early September fog slipped in through the window. I was at Mumford's Farm. Tomorrow at twelve o'clock I would be Gabriel's wife. There would be no publicity; everything was to be kept secret. There would be a quiet ceremony at the Registrar's Office in Amersham, not far from Mumford's Farm; then later, on our way to Italy, the church wedding in Paris at Saint Étienne.

Mrs. Gabriel Pascal, I asked myself, are you going to be happy? . . . My thoughts wandered to our first serious quarrel. The innocent cause of it was Tobias, the squirrel. It had been wrong of me to smuggle him into England, but I had never expected such a violent reaction from the man I loved. Gabriel had waited for Mother and me at Dover, but I had not told him that Tobias was hiding in my beach-bag until we were seated on the Golden Arrow. Dark silence followed my words. He broke out only as his chauffeur drove us away from Victoria Station.

"How could you do such a thing?" he stormed. "What if they had caught you? Tomorrow the newspapers would have been full of it: 'Pascal's wife-to-be smuggles in a squirrel.' I have had enough bad publicity lately. I explained to you on the phone that you must leave the animal behind with a vet and we could pick him up on our way to Italy. I told you about the quarantine."

"But how could I? No vet was willing to take him. The only other thing would have been to put him to sleep. Poor little helpless animal, he went through the whole siege of Budapest with us. I just couldn't . . ."

Until then, I had not experienced Gabriel's anger. It was terrible. He became more and more excited; he shouted, he hurt me. Mother sat in the car numb with horror: was this the man her daughter was going to marry? It did not occur to me that the squirrel incident was a result of his realizing at last that he would soon lose his bachelorhood. All the beautiful love-thoughts were shocked out of him when he faced me and his future mother-in-law at Dover.

I entered the door of Mumford's Farm with tears in my eyes.

The somber charm of Mumford's Farm enthralled me. The hilly landscape was sweet-sad in the autumn mist. The black pond at the edge of the fields was noisy with ducks and geese, and the courtyard with chickens. Far off in the meadows the grazing Jersey cows were slowly moving shadows. I liked the dark-beamed Tudor stables which Gabriel had converted into a large guest cottage with oak-paneled walls, flint-glass windows, real Gothic fireplaces, and linen-fold oak doors. The servants' cottage was attached to the main house, yet separated by a massive brick wall embraced by ivy branches, thick and pale with age. We also had a ghost, but our old and elegant chauffeur, who had degraded himself by accepting a position in the household of foreigners and who spoke Oxford English, didn't think too much of it: he thought it was a commoner. At Earl So-and-So's, whose household he had graced before, the ghost, called the Gray Man, was a beheaded duke.

Every morning, at the crack of dawn, Gabriel was awakened by Giuseppe, the Italian gardener, singing as he passed under the bedroom windows on his way to the garden. His tenor flew high and stretched wide over the morning fog. While Gabriel breakfasted, Giuseppe stationed himself in sight of the dining room windows, singing and digging ferociously. He toiled around the gate as Gabriel got into the car to drive to London, but as soon as the car disappeared Giuseppe became invisible, to be found breaking his back and sweating again on the master's return.

My scattered thoughts projected another picture: a blue gypsy caravan decorated with flower motifs. It stood in the fields not far from the house Gabriel had adorned with rare paintings and *objets d'art*—that many ropes to tie him to stability. He had found the caravan somewhere and on a nostalgic whim had transported it to his farm; and now its bulky body, like a fat gypsy woman in gaudy shawls, squatted patiently outside, its two windows—two large gypsy eyes—gazing at the house, a quiet reproach to the renegade within. And her silence said, "The roads are waiting, do not tarry long . . ."

I shuddered, feeling suddenly cold, and pulled the brocade eiderdown higher. It must have been late, around three or four in the morning. I should get some sleep for my wedding day. I thought of taking an aspirin. On my way to the bathroom I noticed that a light was shining through from the sitting room. I opened the door to switch it off and stopped in surprise. Gabriel was sitting beside the gray, ash-filled fireplace, a half-bottle of cognac in front of him, staring sadly at nothing. He looked up, astonished.

"I couldn't sleep," he said. "This is the last night of my freedom. It is a terrifying thought. I will be a married man by this time tomorrow."

His voice was tragic and his eyes pleaded for help. I sat beside him and took his hand and said to him that he didn't need to marry me.

"I want to marry you—yet I'm afraid. There is a question I am asking myself tonight as I have so many times since I met you. I'm searching within myself for the answer. Do I have the right to marry at all? Am I capable of making you happy?"

"No one else can."

"I am not made for marriage. Can I be a husband? How I hate the word 'husband'—*me* a husband!"

"Then don't be one."

"I'm so much older than you. You want a social life, which I hate. Also, you will be sorry for giving up your career. I'm not the romantic lover you possibly have imagined me to be. I'm a hard-working man. And now that my career is in danger, I have to fight even harder. Only God knows if this Irish-Italian deal will come through. I have to be careful with money until I can start to work. It won't be easy being my wife, you have to realize that. You are still free to decide . . . are you sure, are you sure? Do I have the right to take you?"

"I'm not afraid of hardship as long as we fight together. And in my heart, my own career is forgotten."

"Is it really? I promised you great things. I still hope to give you all of them, but if I cannot, if I should be a failure . . . How strange. I never before thought of failing. I've walked through life like a dreamer, with easy steps, and succeeded. And now I'm afraid. I love you too much. I have to prove myself again and again or I might lose you. One day you might leave me."

"Never."

"That's too big a word to say. How can you know it now?" And he reached with his brown, boyish hands for the cognac bottle.

Things hadn't seemed so gloomy for him earlier that afternoon —at least, not in the letter he had sent to Bernard Shaw. "I am getting married finally," he had written, "tomorrow morning in Amersham. I am certain that I am not making a mistake, but starting a new, more human life." There was no doubt, he went on, that Shaw would approve his choice: an obedient, sweet woman, a real homebody with a simple heart, someone "who will bring the coffee in the morning to my bed . . ." Indeed, an Eliza Doolittle with the slippers!

Next morning we set out for Amersham with a married couple, Gabriel's friends, as our witnesses. The wife was very pregnant. Gabriel wore a checkered suit and with it a hangdog expression. He remarked to the husband, a professor, "I have always hated this suit and had a foreboding that something awful would happen to me while I was wearing it."

The smile of the professor, himself not long married, had a tinge describable only by the German expression *Schadenfreude*.

Gabriel, who was clutching my hand, mumbled, "It still isn't too late. A miracle can still happen. The Madonna will not let me down."

We all laughed, yet I knew he wasn't joking. He was pale and the skin of his forehead was like twisted ropes. I whispered, "Let's run away and not get married."

Finally, we reached the old town of Amersham and the car stopped in front of the Registrar's Office. Two officials, wearing their ribbons, were waiting for us inside. Our witnesses took their positions behind us and one of the officials started the ceremony. He asked the customary questions, then began to read the marriage text. Suddenly a man burst in, shouting, "A car in front of the door is on fire!" The official, thinking it was his car, threw the book down and ran out, his colleague after him; and after *him* went Gabriel, roaring like a lion whose cage door has suddenly flown open: "The miracle . . . the Madonna . . ." Later he explained that, at the moment, his only thought was to be "helpful" with the car.

The professor's wife started to moan, "Help, help, I'm having my pains!" The professor turned pale and fled, shouting, "For heaven's sake, where can I find a doctor here?"

I, the bride, stood all alone in the middle of the room. The officials returned, reporting, "It was only Mr. Pascal's car, the chauffeur making a lot of smoke with his pipe."

My pregnant witness stopped moaning and said to the professor as he returned, "False alarm, darling."

Minutes passed, and more minutes—still no sign of Gabriel. The officials became uneasy. They straightened their ribbons and cleared their throats. One of them turned to the professor. "Will you kindly remind the bridegroom that we are waiting?"

The professor found Gabriel at the pub opposite. "The miracle was performed," Gabriel told him, after which he meekly followed the professor back.

The officials stood up again and everybody took his place. The taller official once more began reading the text, but had gotten only as far as he did the first time when the door burst open again and a nearsighted man with a beard and a weathered doctor's kit rushed in. "Where is the childbirth, please?"

Somehow we got married and Gabriel's eyes were moist as he embraced me, whispering, "My wife!"

While we were getting married, Czinka, Gabriel's Old English sheep dog, whelped several puppies. My husband found this and the fact that we had a pregnant witness the best of omens. "We shall have at least ten children," he announced.

On my bedroom table was a note. He must have put it there before the wedding. It said: "I have two prayers in my heart today: to make you happy and to work again. To create again, to be able to say aloud all that is shining in my soul."

Next day a postcard arrived from George Bernard Shaw: "Too late now, Gabriel. You've done it."

I signed my new name for the first time on the register at the hotel in Folkestone, by the seashore. Gabriel seemed carefree and happy and did not mention a write-up about the Irish venture in the *Daily Mirror* and the ensuing letter from Shaw:

My dear Gabriel,
    You must positively stop telling the newspapers that you own my film rights, or that you are the director of the new company, or have any interest or control beyond that of my choice of you as art expert in the studio.

    Do you not see that the first condition of the enterprise is that it is to be Irish through and through, and the fact that you are a very foreign foreigner must be kept in the background until the films are actually on the screen with your name on the titles.

    If you persist in claiming rights that you do not possess, I shall be forced to contradict you publicly, which is the worst that could possibly happen to both of us.

Nothing infuriated Shaw more than those constant newspaper references to Gabriel Pascal as "the man who has all the Shaw film rights." Shaw never sold his rights; as he said, "My invariable practice is to issue licenses for performances and publications, retaining all my rights intact." In vain Gabriel protested to Shaw that he was not responsible for newspaper articles, which of course were not concerned with the legal difference between actual ownership of film rights and those letters of agreement that Shaw gave to his producer. The fact was that Gabriel at one time or another held such option letters for practically all the Shaw plays, with the understanding that "your share in all our enterprises [is] secured by a clause in my licenses naming you as artistic director as of the essence of the contract."

Shaw never fulfilled his threat that "I shall be forced to contradict you publicly," but somebody else did: F. E. Lowenstein, Shaw's bibliographer. What Shaw did not want to do to his producer, Lowenstein set out to do on his own.

Shaw was apologetic. "Already I find," he wrote, "that Lowenstein has told the *Daily Mail* interviewer that the statement that you hold my rights is a mistake."

The cup of humiliation for Gabriel was full. He appeared a liar after all those years of faithfulness to Shaw. Lowenstein's statement, he realized, could hurt his pending lawsuit with Mary Pickford's United Artists, as well as the Irish deal and any future projects. But Shaw washed his hands: "I have done the utmost for you in making you indispensable . . ."

Yes, *if* the Irish Screen Art project came through, Gabriel was safe, but the idea of co-financing the Saint Francis film with the Italian concern irritated Shaw. "I will not touch *St. Francis*," he wrote again. "All I have to say about saints is in *St. Joan*. Of course, they would like me to go on repeating myself like Jannings and the Green Goddess man whose familiar name I forget (I forget everything) or like Priestly and Coward; but I WON'T . . . We must go straight on with *Androcles*. Then *Arms and the Man,* Cary or no Cary [meaning Cary Grant]. He is not indispensable; nor is he growing younger."

On our return from Folkestone, we flew to Dublin. I met the members of Irish Screen Art: Arthur Cox, the attorney, a thin man with reddish hair; and an Irish national hero, Dan Breen, who had led the "Flying Column" of young Irishmen from Tipperary against the British in Ireland's war of independence. There was also a Grecoesque Franciscan monk, whose connection with Irish Screen Art is not quite clear in my mind, but I only hoped that he had no knowledge of the postcard Gabriel had just received from Shaw: "I think we both left St. Francis alone. You don't care a rap about him: and my view of him and of Savonarola and of Jesus is that their propaganda of Holy Poverty and amateur Communism was mischievous and ignorant."

The Dublin trip was inconclusive. On the plane going home I noticed Gabriel's changed expression: his eyes were narrowed and yellowish, his nose rapacious. The look made him resemble the bust Jacob Epstein made of him.

"You have that lupine nose again," I said.

"I'm afraid the Irish are bluffing to gain time," Gabriel said, disregarding my remark. "They aren't serious about *The Bicycle Thief,* either."

In Rome we had met Vittorio de Sica—a shy man, who talked little during dinner and looked upon Gabriel with great reverence. But the after-dinner de Sica was a different man. He was transformed as he told a story of the Italian slums, poverty, tearful humor, and a bicycle thief. Gabriel was enthusiastic, shouting in Italian that de Sica was a genius. They embraced each other.

The Bicycle Thief, Gabriel was convinced, was the perfect vehicle for all of them: de Sica, the Irish, and himself. It could be made inexpensively in Italy in no time; on the money it would bring they could go on with the more involved Shaw projects. Time proved Gabriel's instinct right: *The Bicycle Thief* grossed a fortune—but not for Irish Screen Art. The Irish could see Saint Francis, but saw no world market in such a typically Italian story as *Bicycle Thief.*

The chastised Gabriel wrote to Shaw, "Somehow, whenever I try to be unfaithful to you and do any other picture than yours, I have no luck . . . maybe you are my destiny. Anyhow, my Irish partners agree with me that, as our Company is founded on your name, we should start definitely with one of your plays."

Back at the farm Gabriel's nervous haste to get to his morning appointments in London began again. His business affairs grew more and more complicated as he sought to involve three countries in the upcoming film of *Androcles and the Lion:* the company in Ireland, the distribution in England, and the studios in Italy.

Gabriel was a man who pushed twice as much work into one minute as it could hold. He did everything with a killing energy, driving himself and others mercilessly and flying into a rage at the smallest imperfection. In his office, amid constantly ringing telephones, he would dictate in four languages to four secretaries, and wear the girls out as rapidly as they came.

Every morning he trembled with irritation as he gulped down his breakfast while two secretaries ran in and out searching for files, which were constantly being misplaced. He would give me a hurried kiss, saying that he would call from town; then his car would disappear down the sloping, narrow farm road. I had the whole lonely day ahead of me. There was no use doing much about the house, as we would soon be leaving for Italy. Gabriel's Irish secretary ordered the food and paid the bills, just as she did before I came. "You don't know how to order," Gabriel said, "and don't know where to order, and you don't know English money, and right now I have no time to explain. You can run the house in Italy."

"I have no time to explain" was Gabriel's nervous, rushing answer to everything.

The shortening fall afternoons were dreary. Mother and I had our dinners alone at the Queen Anne dining room table. Behind the low windows, the garden was black. We ate in silence. There was only the noise of dripping moisture outside and the crackling of the logs in the fireplace. The room was hazy with wood smoke. Everything around me was alien. I felt the two secretaries and the household help looked at me and my mother with a secret aversion. I did not know then that I was suffering from the emigrant disease: the pangs of beginning a new life in a new country where one feels oneself surrounded by disinterest or downright hostility. The food has no taste; dreams are nightmares; the trees, the grass are strangers; the air smells different; and the people speak a secret language.

The nights were long as I waited for the noise of the returning car. I would listen to Gabriel's steps on the stairs and then in the corridor as they moved toward his room . . . and my yearning for him would dissolve in tears.

By then, we were both bleeding from the wounds of many fights. One among the many was caused by the visit of a woman friend of Gabriel's, someone who had once worked for him and had never ceased to love him. She was no longer young, and the kindness of her expression escaped my attention. We had tea and I felt assured and triumphant in my youth, but that feeling left me as soon as she and Gabriel became immersed in conversation. They talked old-friend talk, sharing memories and laughing together. After she had left Mumford's Farm, I said that if she ever returned, trying to take the position she had had before our marriage, I would leave.

Hardly had that storm passed when came the incident at the opera. Gabriel had asked me to take an Italian business friend of his to Covent Garden; he would pick us up after the performance, as he himself could not come because of a previous engagement. When he gave me the two tickets, I noticed that he kept two others. At the opera, I couldn't concentrate. Why couldn't he cancel his engagement? He took me to town so seldom.

During the second intermission, I left the Italian; I wanted to be alone. I wandered upstairs to the boxes. When the bell rang, I started back to my seat, only to find myself face to face with Gabriel and a woman I had never seen before. I stood there speechless. Gabriel tried to say something, but I was gone before he could do so.

Back at the farm, he defended himself: "If I had anything to hide, would I have gone to the opera?"

"If you were sincere," I said, "why couldn't all four of us have gone together? You said you had a dinner engagement . . . and why didn't you come with her, if you had nothing to hide, to my seat, during the first intermission?"

"I was going to greet you, but we met some friends. And we couldn't go to the opera together because it was only after dinner that we decided to go."

"You're lying. I saw you put those two tickets back in your pocket. You knew very well *then* that you would go. You thought that I would never find out, since your box was on the other side."

"I am a decent man," he shouted, "and you make a liar and cheat out of me . . . oh, why did I ever marry!"

It was at this time that Tibor began to call from Budapest. He obviously thought my marriage wouldn't last. It was good to hear from him. His voice was the voice of the home and the country I had left, and suddenly I didn't feel so lonely. Sometimes the calls came when Gabriel was present. He would leave the room, just as Tibor had done in the past, his lips pressed tight.

Mother's living with us added to the tension. Her presence in the house, although usually invisible, was a constant aggravation to Gabriel. For him, who had never had a family life, to acquire a mother-in-law in addition to a wife was too much. Mother was never easy to live with and now, suddenly torn from her old life, she became even more difficult. She didn't speak English, and would have been lost alone. There was no solution for her but to live with us. She felt she was a stumbling block, useless, unloved, and unwanted. Without meaning to, she used me as her only outlet, thus unwittingly making my own adjustment more difficult.

To make matters worse, this period was a decisive one in Gabriel's career. Fanatically single-minded, he couldn't help but feel that he was being intruded upon by two women who hadn't the slightest conception of the fight he was waging or of the world in which he lived. I realize now that I behaved most immaturely at times.

Many years later, Gabriel would remember, "Sometimes, in those days, I walked the streets of London for hours and hours in the evenings and was too hurt to go home: there was an invisible conspiracy against me." Even Bernard Shaw seemed to be against him. For the first time he called off their weekly meetings: "I do not want to see you. I do not want to see anybody . . . Keep away, Gabriel, keep away, everybody. Come only when there is the most pressing necessity unless you want to kill me."

The Irish business partners arrived at Mumford's Farm in the midst of the tension between Gabriel and me. The executive secretary, a handsome, dark-haired, American-Italian girl who had worked for Gabriel in America, came with them from Dublin. She ignored me, moving about with an air of authority and giving orders to the help. One day I found her in my room, turning a drawer inside out. She was looking for some papers, she said, which Mr. Pascal had kept there before he was married.

One evening, after dinner, she stayed to take some letters. She set up the typewriter on the dining room table and when the maid came in to remove the damask tablecloth, Gabriel sent her away, telling her to do it after he had finished dictation.

I went up to my room. Again, a lonely evening: Gabriel was going to London. He came up to kiss me goodbye and then drove off. The maid had already left for her room when I remembered the tablecloth. I went to the dining room, where the secretary was still working at the table. When I proposed to remove the cloth, she flared up with such hostility that I became numb.

Next morning after breakfast Gabriel came to my room. His eyes were blazing. "You offended my secretary," he said; "you were rude to her."

"She offended me and in my own house," I said. "She hates me. All I wanted was to remove the tablecloth. She herself should have had sense enough not to work on it. Why didn't she use the office anyhow? This whole house is a madhouse. Wherever I go there is a stranger, a stranger in every room. I have no place here. You treat me like an enemy. I have no word here."

"You had no right to interfere with her," he shouted. "She had some urgent letters to type. Many things depend on those letters and on her faithfulness to me. She is in a key position in Dublin; she could harm me. Instead of helping me as a wife should, you make my life even more difficult. All I get from you is irritation. You bother me with things like that tablecloth, then the household money, then the servants. I need my brain to get us out of a dangerous situation, but you don't understand me or care to. Life is cruel, the fight is ruthless, and I cannot allow myself to be sentimental. One needs a cool brain, a Machiavellian cleverness, and peace at home; otherwise failure is sure."

I did not understand my own self. "What is wrong with me?" I wondered. "Why can't I act intelligently? Why can't I simply reach out for his hand?"

I remember coming downstairs one afternoon, my hand gliding on the banister. The voices of Gabriel's Irish guests and his own baritone filtered from the dining room on the left, the clatter of typewriters from the office on the right, the clang of dishes from the kitchen. I stopped short on the staircase. What am I doing here? I asked myself. A stranger . . . a stranger . . . I don't belong here . . . I am not loved here . . . nobody cares about me and I have nobody except that old woman sitting bewildered upstairs in her room, with the red squirrel Tobias.

At that moment Gabriel, smiling, stepped out of the dining room to cross through the hall to the office. He saw me and his smile faded. My heart turned over. "I want to go home!" It burst out of me against my wish. Gabriel, stunned, would have spoken, but I ran out.

Fog was descending when I returned to Mumford's Farm. The lights breaking through the dining room windows were yellow wheat sheaves on the black lawn. I hesitated. Through the low windows, the flames in the fireplace and the table set for dinner looked like home, but a home I hated now with the painful yearning of unhappy love. Gabriel was sitting alone at the table, his face grave as he stared at an empty plate. I slipped upstairs to my room.

My mother said next morning, "Last night I heard your husband through the walls of my room. He was sobbing aloud like a little boy, as if his heart was breaking."

That evening, when Gabriel returned late, he came to my room, stopping shyly at the door. I put down the English grammar I was studying and stretched out my hand to him.

A few days later Gabriel said, "I must fly with the Irish to Italy." He said I couldn't accompany him because it was a business trip. "But even more," he added, "there is the trouble with the frozen pound. As a British subject I am under the control of the Bank of England, and I have already used almost everything I was allowed for this year."

It would be the time of the first anniversary of our meeting at the Place Vendôme, and we would be apart. I was deeply disappointed.

Everything went well, nevertheless, until the last few days before his departure, when I found out by coincidence that the daughter of one of his business associates was going on the trip as his guest, notwithstanding the problem of the frozen pound. He tried to explain that she was almost forced on him and that all of his future plans depended greatly on her father, an important Irish politician. The secretary who disliked me was also going, "at the company's expense." What company, I wondered. So far as I knew, only Gabriel was footing the bills.

The explosion came as I drove with him to the airport. He gave orders to the chauffeur that, during his absence, the car should be put in the garage for a checkup. "So I am to be a prisoner of the farm," I burst out. Not at all, said Gabriel, I could take the farm car or a bus to London. That made me wild. For his secretaries, he would always send the car with the chauffeur, but I should take the farm car or the bus!

"You twist my words, my actions," he shouted. "You deliberately make a monster out of me. You talk to me as if I were a stranger. Always, before I was married, when I went away, I put my car in for a checkup."

Alienated, we parted at the airport, where Gabriel was joined by his gay Irish travel party.

The farm to which I returned was sunk in a gray fog. The black yawn of the fireplace was like the coming days. My thoughts in confusion, I wandered about the empty house. What was happening to me—to us? Was it my fault? After the commotion of the previous weeks, the silence was frightening. I sat down in Gabriel's room; it was still filled with the smell of his cigar and cologne. It hurt.

He called me the minute the plane landed in Rome. "Forgive me, forgive me . . . I didn't mean to hurt you."

Now the love we couldn't express at home was poured into letters.

"You ask me if you can make me happy?" I wrote. "No one else can. You taught me those words: happiness and unhappiness. This mad, selfish, unbridled passion with which I love you is causing my sufferings. Because I want you. The whole of you. I am hungry and thirsty for you—my dear husband . . ."

Writing from Rome, he blamed himself: "I have not enough time to give you, for I am swimming against the tide, and until I have a secure basis, I can't have peace. My fear for your future is stronger and deeper than you understand . . . Give me back my faith in myself and the faith in our love—without it I am not worth anything. Give me back my smile: without it you cannot love me and I cannot work. Take my hand again and my heart which is strong and courageous to fight for you. Let us have faith in the dream of the Place Vendôme. I must meet you in Paris again and I know that there we shall regain our vision."

So we met at the Ritz again, on the Place Vendôme. Our candles burnt once more on the altar of the Blessed Mother at Saint Étienne. But I didn't say that I wanted to have our marriage blessed there. We never again spoke about a church marriage. Gabriel's face, taking on a closed look, did not express his suspicion that I was avoiding a church marriage because I wasn't sure. Years would pass before this would come into the open.

There would be many more visits to Paris, but never again would he take me to Saint Étienne.

Chapter 3

Shaw's Corner

THE car made a circular turn and stopped in front of "Shaw's Corner" at Ayot St. Lawrence. It was four o'clock sharp on a misty late autumn afternoon. Returning from Paris, Gabriel had found a letter from G.B.S., its last sentence reading, "I shall be glad to see your lady when you return."

My heart was beating fast as I looked at the modest red brick building half-hidden among trees. I knew that Shaw did not approve of our marriage, as he had declared many times that a man like Gabriel should stay unattached.

Mrs. Laden, the Scottish housekeeper from Aberdeen, opened the door. She gave me a fast, appraising look and smiled at Gabriel. "I will tell Mr. Shaw that you and Mrs. Pascal have arrived," she said, giving me a second glance. "Isn't she young?" she added a bit disapprovingly.

We were led into the sitting room. I felt like a schoolgirl about to take an important exam. George Bernard Shaw was a legend I had been brought up to respect, and now I was going to see the legend in the flesh. What could I say to him? Already my thoughts were stumbling; and what about my weakness in English?

Gabriel laughed. "Just sit gracefully and be yourself," he suggested. "You don't need to talk."

For sitting gracefully I thought the best background would be the armchair beside the fireplace. It was covered with a pinkish material.

"Please don't sit there," said Mrs. Laden as I headed toward it. "That has been Mr. Shaw's place for years."

I settled opposite the fireplace, facing a pastel portrait of Charlotte, the late Mrs. Shaw.

Soon Shaw entered, coming in from his walk, a faded loden cloak about his shoulders. He kept himself erect. His white-bearded head seemed to have a separate life, his body serving only one purpose: to support it, like a long stem holding up a large flower. He smiled at me as Gabriel introduced us. Then we had tea, Shaw and Gabriel immersed in conversation.

As we prepared to leave and Gabriel was helping me with my coat, I noticed that Shaw was playing flirtatiously with his moustache and looking hard at my clinging knitted dress. There was a twinkle in his eyes. Noting that I had caught his glance, he shifted it to Gabriel.

"Gabby," he said, "this wife of yours should be in the films." With his hands he drew in the air the outlines of a well-developed female form. "She, you know, has a good figure."

Gabriel mumbled something about old Don Giovannis, which prompted Shaw to hearty laughter.

My husband's face was shining as we waved goodbye to Shaw, who had accompanied us to the gate and kept waving back to us as the car pulled out. "He liked you very much. I never saw him so melted. I told you that if you kept your mouth shut he would be mad about you."

After dinner that evening we were sitting in front of the fireplace. Gabriel was enjoying his pale green Havana. "While Mrs. Shaw was alive," he said, "I had an easier understanding with the Old Man. She liked me and sold all my ideas to him."

"How did Shaw feel when she died?" I asked. "He is always mocking sentiment and emotion."

"When it happened, I was in America," Gabriel said. "You know how psychic I am at times. One night I dreamed of seeing her as a young woman with flowers in her hair, which according to an old gypsy belief means death. The news came soon that she had taken ill and died. I got back too late for the funeral. At that time, they still had the London flat and I went straight there. I was informed that Mr. Shaw was alone in the sitting room, but he didn't answer my knock. I heard the piano through the door. When I entered I saw him sitting with his back to me at the little piano, playing and humming old Irish love songs, the songs Charlotte had liked.

"He played one song after the other. When the last chords died away, he remained as he was for a second, with his hands motionless on the keys and his back bent. Then he closed the piano and turned and noticed me. I was embarrassed; I felt almost as though he had caught me eavesdropping. I expressed my sympathy. He lifted his eyebrows and said, 'You know, Gabby, I feel like a man who has carried a chest heavy with precious jewelry on his back for long decades, and then, one day, finally, he finds that he can put it down and relax.' The old cynic, he would rather have died than admit to whom he was playing those love songs."

By the middle of November, 1947, Gabriel and I were settled in a rented villa on the Via Cassia, in Rome. Gabriel was in a happy mood. His trip with his Irish partners to Italy had been successful and they had definitely decided to start with *Androcles and the Lion.* The board meeting of Irish Screen Arts in Dublin had accepted the budget of £250,000, the amount necessary to start production and purchase some equipment.

The villa Gabriel had rented to surprise me was a veritable palazzo in the hilly outskirts of Rome: the famous Villa Manzoni, where Hitler and Mussolini had signed their pact. It had marble columns, frescoes, niches with shivering marble statues, and a view of Rome framed by dark cypresses. I was much too overwhelmed even to notice Gabriel's proud smile as he showed me around. To my worried question, he answered, "You'll see, in the long run it will be cheaper than the Hassler."

We had a marble bath and dressing room with columns, too beautiful to describe. In it, I had to wear a winter coat while I put on my make-up. Bath? Well.

We had a butler ("cheaper in the long run") who in a blinding white uniform served breakfast on the terrace in the winter sun. In my memory, the sight of potted orange and lemon trees on the terrace mingles sensually with the smell of coffee and red-hot brioches.

Gabriel worked with killing energy, dictating again in four languages (and quarreling in a fifth, Hungarian, with me), taking and making long-distance calls, and rapidly wearing out four secretaries. I recall thinking that being his secretary must be almost as difficult as being his wife.

I was learning the world. I had a masterful teacher in Gabriel, who enjoyed and suffered life to the full. Each day for him was a new challenge, a gamble. Living with him was like holding highly explosive matter in one's hands. I often thought that extraordinary people like him are magnets in that they not only draw to themselves extraordinary situations and people but also extraordinary objects. Life was a constant surprise with him.

There were no leisure hours for Gabriel in Rome, and he would say, "Be patient. Once I have put a strong foundation under our future, then I'll give all my time to you. Meanwhile, be patient."

I wanted to believe in his success, but the nights brought confused dreams that betrayed my hidden fright, and I would toss in the huge baroque Venetian bed, under a fresco of angry bearded gods and pink, naked goddesses.

Then out of the blue came the news that Shaw had terminated the Irish venture. On November 30, 1947, Shaw wrote to Arthur Cox:

Dear Mr. Cox,

I have read your letter, and also the minutes of the Board Meeting. It is now beyond all reasonable doubt that nothing approaching the necessary capital can be raised in Ireland for Screen Art. It must be wound up, and my contract cancelled. We have tried and failed; and we must face it sensibly and promptly.

£41,000 is ridiculous. A quarter of a million would vanish like a puff of smoke and leave behind one film, probably unfinished. A million and a half should be within sight, and most of it in cash at the bank . . .

Meanwhile, I cannot afford to wait any longer. I must get on with *Androcles* in Italy quite independently.

It is a disappointment; but I knew all through how unlikely it was. I am not at all sure that it is not the highbrow terror of my

name that has defeated you. You may have better luck when you
are rid of me.

Shaw also advised Gabriel of the change, adding, "I am sending
a line to Mary [Mary Pickford] to say that the Irish project is off,
and that the American plays must be filmed in Hollywood after
all."

But Mary Pickford was not interested any more, and the threatened lawsuit against Gabriel had been filed.

Arthur Cox's answer to Shaw shows a deep personal hurt. "We
were never quite so foolish as to imagine the £41,000 would suf-
fice," he wrote. "I therefore do not understand how you should
say 'it is now beyond all doubt that . . . the necessary
capital . . . cannot be raised in Ireland.'" When they received the
budget for *Androcles*, about £250,000, the Board assured Pascal
that "the sum would be immediately available as required . . . We
quite definitely understood that these funds would fully answer
what was needed . . . A capital such as a million and a half was
never mentioned or dreamed of . . . It was, therefore, a very great
and unexpected shock to us to receive your letter . . . We under-
took this burden—and it was a real burden—not with a view to
personal profit but because we did not want you, the greatest
Irishman since Saint Patrick (who was not an Irishman at all), to
think that Ireland wholly failed to respond when you made your
generous call."

Christmas was sad in the Villa Manzoni. The jewel Gabriel
wanted to buy for me went back to Bulgari and we sat around the
lighted tree in silence. To "get on with *Androcles* in Italy quite
independently," as Shaw wrote to Cox, wasn't quite that simple.
Gabriel accused Shaw of ruining everything again by writing letters without consulting him, as he had done in the Pickford case.
Now he had to start his negotiations all over again. To make
things worse, there were rumors that Metro was contemplating a
multimillion-dollar production of *Quo Vadis* in Rome, the pomp
and expense of which the production of *Androcles* could not possibly match. Naturally, then, nobody would finance *Androcles* in
Italy.

Anyhow, Gabriel was right when he said that to be an independent producer, even without the glorious handicap of George

Bernard Shaw, called for the skills of a magician. Of necessity, such a producer had to be Machiavellian to put together all the pieces of that jigsaw puzzle known as an independent production. Money was scarce in the postwar years. Shaw did not understand how times had changed when somewhat earlier he had written to Gabriel, "We have only to sit tight and when the time comes hold up our finger. If you go begging and bargaining . . . getting deeper into debt instead of making thousands out of your monopoly . . ."

But the "iron monopoly" which Shaw so many times mentioned was anything but "iron." Shaw still refused to make out his licenses directly to Gabriel or to the "Pascal enterprises" or give more than one letter of agreement at a time, but insisted on the security of a strong financing group. One cannot blame Shaw, but one can also understand the tragic situation of a man who had built all his life around that "monopoly," who had wound his emotions around the father-image of the aging playwright. The older Shaw got, the more difficult he became. His unexpected behavior in the Pickford and the Irish deals put Gabriel's negotiating power into a very dubious position. "Don't leave me in a vacuum," he wrote to Shaw. "I have refused every offer to do pictures other than yours. I refused honor, money, security . . . to stick to you. I kept to my last healthy drop of blood my faith in you—isn't it your turn now to say something?"

By the end of January, 1948, it became obvious that there was no money immediately available in Italy for *Androcles*. We took a plane back to England. "I had the strangest dream," I told Gabriel on the plane, remembering my last night in the big baroque bed of the Villa Manzoni. "I dreamt of Gandhi, of all things, and it was a kind of nightmare. Why would I dream of Gandhi?" I asked, still astonished, as I had never given one thought to the Mahatma.

"Gandhi." Gabriel became pensive. "Strange that I never talked to you about him. He has deeply influenced me ever since I read Romain Rolland's book about him. If I ever free myself from the Old Man's yoke, I want to do a film about Gandhi."

We landed at London Airport and lined up at Customs. The

officer who looked at our bags suddenly turned to us: "Did you hear the news? Mahatma Gandhi has been assassinated in India!"

We had sublet a small furnished house after our return from Rome, as Gabriel's daily commuting from Mumford's Farm had become impossible. I had been more than pleased, thinking that now I could stay in London with him during the week and see more of him. But it had not happened that way. Gabriel kept excusing himself, saying that he was too busy, that I could join him next week, and then again next week.

One Sunday I told him that I would like to drive with him in the morning to London and stay a couple of days. He made his usual excuses, but in an unfriendly tone. Then I made a biting remark and he became furious. On and on he went. I ran out of the house, down to where the farm road joined the Oxford highway. The passing cars lit up the roadside evergreens, vivid against the black wall of the night. Was there any solution to my life? Where should I go? What should I do? Gabriel's voice still hammered in my ears: "I want my freedom back. I hate marriage."

Yes, I thought, I must leave him if I want to survive. He is devouring me. I cannot obey him blindly. I have my own mind, my own will, my own life; he cannot make a shadow out of me. Then those "surprise attacks"! At times, he provokes me to say something he can turn and twist into something monstrous so that he can discharge his anger against it. And when the storm passes, he humbly repents like a sorry little boy: "Help me, please, help me. I know something is terribly wrong with me." Then I melt with compassion, which only puts me back where I was . . .

Behind me, the farm lay in darkness. I hated it now because it represented him. I began to shiver; it was cold and I was wearing only my dressing gown. I couldn't go back and face him. I thought of the cow barns. The warm breath of the animals welcomed me. Blowing the air noisily through their nostrils, they smelled me over and put their soft, moist muzzles against me.

"Vally . . . Vally!" I heard his distant cry. I sat up in the hay. His voice drew nearer, then died away. Some time passed before I heard his steps approaching the barn. He stopped at the door. His voice was soft as he asked, "Are you there?" He pushed the door open. I held my breath. In the gray of the open door I could see his shadow. He entered, closing the door quietly.

"Where are you?" he asked. "I can't see you." I kept silent. "I know you are here, I feel you."

With uncertain steps he came toward me. His outstretched hand touched my hair. "Why don't you talk?"

"Tomorrow I am leaving you forever!"

"Don't, don't cry." His hand awkwardly stroked my hair. "I'm sorry. And you're right to leave me ... I can never make you happy because I am so unhappy myself. Help me to overcome myself and let us not kill the beauty in each other's hearts."

Once more I reached out silently for his hand.

Soon Gabriel flew to Italy again, for a new group was interested in financing *Androcles*. He asked me to go with him, but I refused: I was busy getting ready for a screen test which Alexander Korda had offered while Gabriel and I were having lunch with him. I had accepted eagerly. Gabriel's reaction was silence. He did not say a word when I ordered the gown for the test or when I refused to go to Italy with him. Too late, my friend, I thought with satisfaction; there was a time when I begged you to take me on your trips; but now I am the stronger.

I was electrified at the prospect of a new career. Gabriel's young discoveries, fluttering about him, were thorns in my flesh. He put them through dramatic school, gave them tests, introduced them to important people, and placed them in productions. That Korda was interested in me was a great victory, and I knew that Gabriel felt doubly hurt because of the secret rivalry between them.

"Your voice on the phone," he wrote from Rome, "sounded remote; perhaps you do not love me any more. I feel as lonely as if I were no longer on this earth. You don't need me; you devote all your strength to freeing yourself from me. I have nothing more to do here." He spoke of difficulties and intrigues, saying that his negotiations were getting more and more involved. "Everything is so phony here that even Tobias, the squirrel, when he looks

down from heaven, is sorry for me ..." (Tobias had died suddenly and was buried under a tree at the farm.)

When Gabriel returned from Italy, a short happy interlude
followed—because I bowed to his passive resistance, canceled my
screen test, and assured him, once again, that he was my only career.

So went our stormy marriage. In time I learned to keep silent
—and developed gall-bladder disorders. Living in a self-made
hell, we lost the natural approach to each other. The shyness and
the tension grew, each feeding upon the other. Yet we were
bound to each other, and by an inexplicable contradiction: we
could rest and relax *only* in each other's company. In our depths,
we were inseparable, and we knew it.

I stood at the airport, once more waiting for Gabriel's plane
from Italy. Mumford's Farm was ready to be closed down. "Everything is sunshine and smiles," he had written, "because I can start
to work: but only if you love me can I be successful ..."

There was no smile on his face when he got off the plane. He
looked worn. I didn't ask anything while he was getting through
Customs, nor in the car driving to the farm. Gabriel was silent,
too. But back home, looking at the packed cases and the question
mark on my face, he had to tell me.

"That jackass banker and his group!" he said. "After asking me
back urgently to Italy, it turned out they weren't interested in
Androcles at all. All they wanted was to buy my name for some
vulgar sex movie with the banker's big-titted whore in the lead.
They kept putting checks under my nose. I suspect that the
checks weren't even real, but they were big, and as they kept tick-
ling my nose with those checks, I stood up at the meeting and
said, 'Gentlemen, you can all kiss my ass.' And I left."

New deals, more rushed trips, and more letters to Mumford's
Farm: "Do not panic. I am strong and still young enough and
filled with an endless talent to live. But you must agree with my
vision, which is the price you must pay for following a mad
dreamer like me."

But I did panic, and not alone: Bernard Shaw grew uneasy too. "Troppo vecchio," he wrote on a postcard to Gabriel, mimicking the trembling handwriting of a very old person and interrupting his lines with ink blots. "Will be retiring by the time we get to work. Kein Zukunft. An amiable friend: sonst nichts."

Chapter 4

Mont Salvatch

WE had come to Paris to be unfaithful to Shaw. Not too unfaithful, just to make some money by going into partnership with Jean Dalrymple for a Sartre play, *Les Mains sales,* to be produced on Broadway. Jean, the famed producer of the New York City Center, was an old friend of Gabriel's. Jed Harris, who was to direct the play for Jean, was in Paris too.

By day Paris wore the greens of May and early June, and at night she glittered with her floodlighted fountains and buildings. Many nights the four of us—Jean, Jed, Gabriel, and I— wandered in the streets in sheer delight. Once at two o'clock in the morning Jean stood on the Place de la Concorde, the cascading white waters of the fountain behind her and a full moon among white clouds above her, singing, arms outstretched and tears in her eyes, "Paris . . . Paris"—the song of her dead friend, Grace Moore.

As the Grand Prix at Longchamp had filled up all the hotels, Paul-Louis Weiller, the multimillionaire art connoisseur and a friend of Gabriel's, invited us to stay at his house on the Rue de la Faisanderie, where one had the experience of sleeping in a bedroom surrounded by Bouchers. Soon we were swimming in the life of Paris society: the Grand Prix with the Maharaja and Ma-

harani of Baroda, a luncheon party at our host's Versailles villa
for the Duke and Duchess of Windsor, parties every day. I was
eating up Paris like a rich dessert which I knew would be gone
before it could give me a stomach ache.

There was only one thing which kept me in terror: I never
knew what my husband would do or say when he was with people. He spoke five languages fluently and was well versed in the
unprintable shadow words of every one of them; and he used
those unwashed urchin words especially in priggish company. But
they were simply tools he availed himself of to emphasize his
viewpoint; he took no delight in filth and therefore never
sounded offensive. He preferred the four-letter words only because of their brevity.

The Sartre venture was a big flop on Broadway, and with it
went Gabriel's hope to turn the play into a movie. Back to Me-
thuselah he went.

"My dear G.B.S.," he wrote, "two days ago, I saw Ralph Rich-
ardson and he was very impressed with your message . . . For
Bluntschli I am waiting news from Cary Grant and Rex
Harrison . . . *Arms and the Man* could be followed with
Androcles . . . I met in France the great comic, Cantinflas, who is
the Mexican Charlie Chaplin. He would make a superb
Androcles . . . "

We were back from Paris at our "Heartbreak Farm," as Gabriel
called Mumford's Farm. He loved the place, the only home he
ever had, but we would have to sell it soon; we could not afford
the upkeep much longer. We entertained constantly. Weekends,
we had guests drop in for lunch, tea, or dinner. "Dicky," Lord
Grantley, the head of Pinewood Studios, who had helped assem-
ble the financing of *Pygmalion,* came often, speaking his Oxford
English, swallowing his words to such an extent that I was constantly wondering what he was talking about. In cold weather he
would wear an old camel's-hair coat tied together with a piece of
rope, giving him the appearance of a monk of some strange order.
He would sit sunk in a deep armchair, looking wistful with his
hunchback and his round, sprightly eyes and monocle. He seemed

to watch everything, attentive but slightly bored, like someone who had seen too much.

Another weekend visitor was the actor Robert Newton. His countenance benevolently savage, he exuded the sadness of an outcast and the smell of liquor. And liquor was what caused his untimely death. Gabriel always thought he was one of the great actors.

Many others came from the London theater and art worlds and society, from Benjamin Britten and Jean Simmons to Sir Kenneth and Lady Clark. The Maharaja of Baroda, whose estates were nearby, served us Indian curry on heavy golden plates; in return, he had our Hungarian goulash on clay plates. Ingrid Bergman drove out with her husband, Peter Lindstrom, and their little daughter Pia. There seemed to be a well-balanced, healthy happiness about her. Nothing suggested the coming earthquake of Stromboli and Roberto Rossellini.

Romola Nijinsky often had tea with us. She came to discuss the possibility of a film about Nijinsky. As I listened to her quick, nervous talk, I tried to visualize her as she once had been: the lovely daughter of a great Hungarian actress who, one fateful day, had seen the touring Russian ballet's performance in the Budapest Opera House and had then followed Nijinsky. She sat with us now, old and broken, and I felt about her the tragic shadow of Nijinsky, once the living spirit of the dance, whose genius was too great for his body and who for long years had been immersed in darkness. They lived at Virginia Water in a weird house, its doors and windows always closed, a house where a heavy old man danced day after day in a huge room from which all furniture had been removed, his movements awkward, his legs refusing to obey. "I am flying," he would shout, "look, I am flying."

Fillippo Del Giudice's fabulous Sheepcote Farm was not far from our place. Del Giudice, an Italian, was the third famous foreigner in the English film industry at that time, the others being, of course, Korda and Pascal. Sheepcote was the scene of tremendous parties attended by the great in politics, art, and society. But Del Giudice's star in England had begun to decline. In the theater and film world one knows only in retrospect when such a decline sets in, and the last one to notice it is the sufferer himself.

Del Giudice was soon to lose Sheepcote, his yacht, his money. He would be a deeply disturbed and bitter man when we met him later in Rome. He invited us to his elegant suite at the Excelsior and explained that we were to have dinner there, as he hadn't one lira to take us out but still had credit in the hotel. He talked feverishly, and with more gesticulations than ever, about a film he was to make, and his cheeks burned with two red circles. I thought of Gabriel's unsuccessful attempts and wondered, shivering, if we were headed toward the same end.

It was in those days, too, that I finally met Pauline. Gabriel had talked a lot about her and their time together in Berlin. She was now married to a famous man and had long since forgiven Gabriel. He corresponded with her just as faithfully as he did with Hedwig Brugge, the first love of his youth. I never met Hedwig, but Pauline and I became friends. She lived in New York but often visited England. I found her enchanting.

In a magazine one day I saw a picture of a boy about six years old who was playing the lead in a film called *The Boy with Green Hair*. As a child, Gabriel must have looked like him. If I had a son, he would probably be like this—large, dark eyes, shaggy black hair, and a winning smile. I showed Gabriel the magazine.

"My son Peter," he said, looking at the picture. "He looked like this boy, and I suppose you are right; I probably did too, at that age."

"And you, my poor darling, you also had green hair and you still do. Always different from the rest," I said, and then, putting my cheek against his hand, I said, "You are my Green-haired Boy. And today when I saw this picture, I thought again that we should have a son. I must have him."

I felt the muscles tighten in his arm. He pulled his hand away.

"No," he said. "Till we know where we are, I hope God will not give us a child. My worries are strangling. But my turn will come this year . . . we shall live in Italy and have a dozen green-haired boys and blond girls."

After that conversation, he frequently signed his letters to me, "Your green-haired son."

Around that time I discovered the Moral Re-Armament movement and was introduced to Frank Buchman, its founder, who invited me to their headquarters in Berkeley Square.

I went, to return more and more often. Outside, the house looked like all the houses on a London square; inside, there was the new-found warmth of friendship and smiling faces.

The people there seemed to come from every walk of life and from every country, and all age-groups were represented. They all enjoyed talking about their conversions. There were stories of promiscuity, alcoholism, hate, aimlessness, and despair—and then the drastic "change" which happened after they found Moral Re-Armament. They were Christians, taking the Gospel as the basis of the "change" but welcoming any faith, so they had no commonly shared theological beliefs. The "change" could come to anyone honestly striving to find God through a moral life, free from selfish aims. The changed one then had to go out and change others, and the living, continuous chain of change would finally alter the world.

Daily they observed a "quiet hour" in which they prayed and waited for an inspiration, which they wrote down and regarded as their "guidance." The thoughts that occurred during the quiet hour were inspired, they felt, by the voice of God within the soul and thus had to be obeyed. But I got a bit shaken when I complimented one of the ladies on her dress and she answered in all earnestness that her "guidance" had advised her about the shop where she would find it.

These people seemed to be sharing their material goods. The women cooked sumptuous dinners which were served by young girls whose only make-up was their angelic smiles. My mother came once, curious to meet my "saints," as I enthusiastically called them. After dinner, she had only one short comment: "They are eating too well to be saints."

But Mother's remark could not spoil my happiness on Berkeley Square. My zeal carried Gabriel with me. He was unbelievably entertaining; the young people sat around him, listening to his stories.

Buchman invited Gabriel, my mother, and me for after Christmas to Caux-sur-Montreux in the Swiss Alps, the headquarters of
the movement. The main reason for the invitation was to get Gabriel interested in a Moral Re-Armament play. Buchman realized
the importance of theater and movies in his aim to reach souls.
Thus Gabriel seemed like a great catch for the Buchmanites; and
at this point, for his own reasons, he did not mind being caught.
Probably, he said, God had led him to Moral Re-Armament.
There were some great Swiss financing houses behind the movement, and Gabriel thought it possible that Shaw would give the
Buchman group the same deal he had been ready to give the
Irish. A partnership for the filming of certain Shaw plays would
bring money and prestige to the movement, and to Gabriel the
fulfillment of his "vision."

"Imagine," he said to me, "I could start with *Saint Joan,* then
Androcles and the Lion, and later we could produce plays with a
spiritual message. That is what I always wanted: to speak Truth
through Beauty."

On the blindingly white mountaintop of Caux, our friends
were waiting for us at the funicular station, Frank Buchman
among them. Their kind faces, red from the crisp air, were
smiling—that smile which had captured me the first time I met
them, which seemed to set them apart from the rest of the human
race. Their headquarters was a large edifice, once a hotel and now
the scene of the Moral Re-Armament Assemblies. Only a part of
it was open for the small group of Buchman's inner circle who
came to meet us.

New Year's Eve of 1949. The people in the room were dark and
still shadows by the candlelight of the tall Christmas tree. In the
center I could see the strong profile and balding head of Frank
Buchman bowed in silent prayer. There was something wonderful in that silence, so different from the silence of terror, of fear,
or of passion, or the silence of dullness and slumber—an active silence, filled with good will: the silence of *Caritas.* The candles
slowly burned out, one after the other. The starry night outside
became visible through the windows, and eleven hundred meters
below the lights of Montreux gleamed.

After New Year's Gabriel went to Zurich and Bern with the
group's lawyer to negotiate about the possibility of filming a

Moral Re-Armament play and, at a later date, the two Shaw plays with a religious theme.

By then it was obvious that, in a subtle way, the Buchmanites were out to convert us. Right after our arrival in Caux, Buchman had walked us over to a spacious chalet on the grounds and offered it to us as a permanent home, in a fair exchange, it seemed, for our farm in England. The offer was a vague one and was never repeated. We soon found out that those who joined the movement usually gave over not only their private property but also their bank accounts for communal use. So far Gabriel and I had not committed ourselves, but in no way were we pushed. Our friends just smiled and waited and watched us.

I felt a growing uneasiness. The people around me were as kind as always, but their constant smiles began to wear me down. Living among them, I awakened to the fact that I was not among my brothers and sisters, not even among friends: I was left out. They had meetings with closed doors and often, when I entered the large living room, their conversation suddenly stopped. They all smiled at me, but now their smiles struck me as so many screens they pulled about themselves. Maybe I was not worthy of them? I felt hurt.

Mother contracted flu, and a doctor in the group ordered her to bed. She was still in bed with a high temperature when Gabriel returned from Zurich. It was quite late and he said that he could not make out just where the negotiations stood; the discussions had been vague.

Next morning we breakfasted, as usual, at Frank Buchman's table. Afterwards, Gabriel was asked to a conference. He looked stunned when he returned to our room. "Pack," he said, "we are leaving at once." He was told at the meeting that Dr. Buchman, on the advice of his morning "guidance," had changed his mind about doing any films in the near future. Also they were about to close the house, and we would have to leave as soon as possible. Not a word was said about wanting to see us again, or being worried about our souls any more.

But what about Mother, in bed with a high fever? The doctor's opinion of yesterday was that she should stay in bed. If we were to leave at once, there was the walk to the funicular station and train changes before Geneva; at Mother's age, that could be serious. Could I stay, I asked my smiling friends, for just a few more days? Terribly sorry, they shook their heads, but they had no coal to heat the house. I couldn't bring myself to tell them that I had seen trucks delivering loads of coal in the back yard. Was there any other place in Caux where I could stay with Mother until she got better? There was none and, they added, the doctor's opinion was that she could travel safely. God would take care of her.

We left next morning. They must have forgotten that they had invited us, because they presented us with a large bill. Dr. Buchman and the group walked us to the funicular station. They waved and smiled . . . kind, red faces against the snow-capped mountains.

The Caux incident was followed by weeks in a clinic in Lausanne: I had a gall bladder attack. Gabriel, on his way to Rome to continue negotiations for *Androcles,* had placed Mother in a convent nearby, and me under the care of a specialist at the clinic. If he was upset about the Buchman people, he did not show it. "They are only human," he said. "And you should not judge religion unfavorably because of your disillusion. There are a lot of fine people among them who are sincere."

When Gabriel was gone and I was left alone in my hospital room, I did not like to close my eyes because the boundaries between sleep and waking would begin to wash away. Then, as on a large and surrealistic canvas, the faces of my lost friends would appear. I would see their eyes smiling at me and their voices would resound in my mind: "Change . . . change . . . find God." Then the eyes would turn cold: "You have to leave us, we are closing the house."

I do not remember any fear like the fear I felt in that hospital in Lausanne. The fear of the siege and bombing of Budapest was a natural, physical fear of death which, paradoxically, had given me extra strength, a feeling of well-being and tremendous will to survive. This fear was so elusive that it was hard even to pinpoint it. It was like cancer in its first stage, not detectable but eating into the marrow of one's life. I did not know what I feared; I only had the sensation of some unknown horror.

The doctor usually visited me in the evenings. He would stand tall and handsome in the middle of my room, studying the nurse's report. Then he would sit down to talk. He began to stay longer and longer.

When he had first examined me, he asked a strange question: "How is your sex life?" I blushed and told him that his question was not only rather impertinent but irrelevant.

He had only a shadow of a smile for my outburst. "Basically," he said, "there is nothing wrong with you. There is a slight inflammation of the gall bladder, but that is not the cause, that is only the effect of your mental state. Your face is tense, your eyes are restless, you are skin and bones, and there is no doubt in my mind that you are unhappy. So, once more, how is your married life?"

Reluctantly, I told him about Gabriel's endless traveling, of his everlasting rush when he was at home, and no time for ourselves. He only nodded.

When I had informed Gabriel that, beside the physical trouble and being too skinny, I was lovelorn, he became meditative. "It's my fault," he said. "When I have worries, I forget to be a husband. My poor darling, what an awful life you have with me."

Gabriel had arranged to stay four more days in Switzerland before placing me in the clinic. The Gabriel of those four days had been the Gabriel of the long-ago Paris. At the end of them I took him out to the airport.

Gabriel was in Rome now and my longing for him grew as painful as hunger. I waited for the mornings when the nurse would come in with a letter from him. He would write: "I love you truly and if a man loves truly and he is sincere with God and with himself, the problems will straighten out . . . a great miracle is still waiting for us . . . How I would like to give all the money to you to buy everything. If only I could do like Liliom, steal a star for you from Heaven. Maybe I will one day when I am dead . . ."

Suddenly on his way to London he paid a surprise visit to the clinic. We flew into each other's arms. Not much later, pale and shivering, we faced each other in a spiteful quarrel. There was a sulking luncheon in town. On our way back to the clinic we passed the Church of Saint Francis of Assisi. Hesitatingly, Gabriel turned toward it and I followed. Inside, in the faint light of our two candles at the altar of the Blessed Mother, his face mellowed.

"In church," he wrote later from London, "I was asking the Madonna for her help and thought of a legend about a Knight of the Holy Grail who wandered on a pilgrimage for ten years searching for his lost wife. Then Our Lady took pity on him and led him back to her . . . maybe one day she will bring your heart and soul back to me."

I left the clinic, though I still had to return for treatments, and moved into the convent where my mother was. The Maison de Repos, on the outskirts of Lausanne, was a lovely home for elderly people, run by French nuns. The spacious house, adorned with turrets in the style of the *fin de siècle,* was surrounded by a large garden with walks and ancient trees. At the end of the garden, the good sisters had put up one of those popular shrines of Lourdes, so innocently ugly in their attempt to translate into reality the luminous mystery of the Grotto.

Once one entered the house, one became conscious of that something so typical of convents or homes run by nuns—the atmosphere of a sanctuary, sheltered from the evil, the foolishness, and the dust of the outside. There was the sensation of cool, clean air, the smell of freshly polished floors, and a tinge of incense. The shades were always half-pulled, so that the sun would not ruin the furniture or fade the curtains more than they were already faded from too much washing and starching.

The furniture, old-fashioned without being antique, consisted of never-matching pieces, standing straight in disciplined rigidity. They were obviously the discarded pieces of families who must have said in their moments of charity, "Nobody would buy *that* . . . why not give it to the Sisters, providing they pick it up." On the backs and arms of the overstuffed sofas and armchairs were the inevitable white, hand-crocheted coverlets, made by the nuns during their recreation hour while they listened to the monotonous voice of one of the sisters reading some meditations or the life of a saint.

The nuns at the Maison de Repos were in no way different from those of my youth. Then I had wanted to get away from them and their discipline, not realizing that in later life I would be overcome by nostalgia whenever I entered a convent. The nuns of the Maison de Repos would adjust their veils with the same delicate movement of chaste white fingers as did those I knew in my childhood. And they listened the same way, like attentive birds, their heads slightly cocked and their hands hidden in their wide black sleeves.

The Maison de Repos was the end chapter of many interesting lives. The old lady guests often pointed at a tall, thin woman in her eighties, dressed in severe black, walking erect and alone in the garden. She was, they said, a Russian Grand Duchess. Another one—and the old ladies exclaimed her name excitedly—had been a famous actress. The two boarders I was interested in were the "bird ladies." Everybody in Lausanne had heard of them and everybody who found an injured bird would make a trip to the Maison de Repos.

The bird ladies lived on the top floor where an ancient oak stretched its arms in front of their windows, always open for bird guests.

When I was leaving for Rome to meet Gabriel, the bird ladies became agitated: "Oh, the Roman fever . . . this time of year . . . and please don't go to the Catacombs; they're filled with robbers!"

I simply looked at them as they sat there shaking their heads, their parchment-colored hands trembling on their laps and the nineteenth century frozen about them.

"*Voilà le Simplon,*" my porter announced, as the train broke through the white, early-morning fog. I had boarded the train with a tight throat: the trip to Rome had been preceded by a feverish exchange of letters, and time seemed to malinger. But today, at midnight, I was to be with him . . .

A happy weekend among softly flowering mimosas and wind-blown palm trees at Monte Circeo by the sea. Then five more days in Rome together. Five days of short, hurried breakfasts; then Gabriel disappearing for the rest of the day. Business meetings, business luncheons, and business dinners. I was hurt and I was mean. One terrible, devastating quarrel, with words we did not mean, and cold silence for the rest of the days. Then back to

the train station: time for me to return to Lausanne for further
treatments and for him to fly to Paris for yet another business
meeting.

We stood by the steaming train. Gabriel's expression was dark
as he said, "Forgive me that I have no talent for happiness."

He wrote me at once from the Ritz in Paris: "Here I am again
where our Calvary or our eternal salvation started. I greeted the
Place Vendôme and fell on the bed. It was not so much the long
stormy flight that tired me out as the mental agony: is our road
together leading to happiness or to disaster? As I told you in
Rome, everything is in your hands: the miracle, the salvation, or
the damnation. I often think that God will yet take pity on us but
the price of that will be a true self-sacrifice. True love is self-
sacrifice . . .

"Somewhere we left our real selves and since then we have ram-
bled dazzled in space, and only sometimes in a kiss we remember
that we belong forever, and that through long times we searched
for each other . . . But here I am ready again and again to start
anew with you—but I am afraid that in the deepness of your soul
you don't see any happy future in my poor, sad love. You said it
yourself and your eyes were cold. Answer me if all this self-tor-
ment of mine is without basis. Write to me as you would write to
your own soul—perhaps I am your true soul and in some future
life through my heart and blood my spirit will lead you to
truth . . .

"Here is my cart with the two old gypsy horses waiting for you
on the dusty road. But if you forgive me and get on it again I will
drive it—and not you! But perhaps you don't trust in my peasant
cart any more and are dreaming about princely coaches?"

I called him in Paris to assure him that I preferred his gypsy
wagon. He answered at once. "Everything will work out now because I have regained my vitality and will power since you said
on the phone that you really love me and that I had misunderstood you in Rome. The sun is shining again . . ."

Life was simple in the Swiss mountains. Early in the mornings,
I would set out for excursions. There was an emptiness at my side
where Gabriel should have walked, eaten, and slept, and the pain

of unshared beauty: budding trees born orphan because he never saw them with me as they glanced at their innocent green in the mirror of the lake.

On my walks, I passed a chapel hidden among the pines. I went in sometimes. It was silent in the dark pews, and the red flame in front of the altar breathed peace.

In those days I was reading again about Saint Francis of Assisi. Since the time Gabriel had given me books about him, my fascination with Francis had been unquenchable. We had talked a lot about Francis in the days when Gabriel was planning a film about him. "What these books don't make clear," I remember saying to Gabriel, "is the reason for Francis' sudden change. What turned a lustful, fun-loving young man overnight into an entirely different person?"

"He realized God," was Gabriel's rather halting reply, "and thus he found his real identity."

I had told Gabriel of certain childhood experiences, of times when I too had longed for God. Each time, I recalled, it had been a sensation at once painful and sweet—and vague. Once I had been so overpowered by it that I had stopped still on a meadow, opening my arms toward the sky.

"All that passed later," I added, "though beauty can still bring back to me that nostalgic, sweet pain. Now I am neither spiritual nor religious, but I don't doubt the existence of God—though I can't see that realizing it is ever going to change me in the least."

"That is not the realization of God," Gabriel said. "It is reasoning with your common sense. Your faith has no wings and no love; it isn't alive. But one day it will be. You say you are not spiritual? You're mistaken. All that is not formed in you yet, but the seeds are there. I knew this the very first moment I looked into your eyes."

"And what about you? Have you realized God?"

"If I had, I would be a saint. I do have moments of light when I know what those sages and saints were talking about, and sometimes I am miserable not doing what I should do—which is to search only for God"; and he sighed.

In the mountain chapel, thinking of those talks with Gabriel, I pondered about Francis and the saints. What had made them alien to the world they loved and desired with a normal human

hunger? What was their secret? A long-forgotten word—grace—
came into my mind; but it remained only a word. I tried to think
of God. My thoughts remained empty and cold. Around my con-
viction, I felt an impenetrable wall. Those who had changed must
have known more. Their faith was intoxicated. As if possessed by
the power of some tremendous knowledge, they jumped over that
wall into an unknown land—to a land of whose magnetic existence even I had some faint perception. What was that impenetrable wall which hid it from me? Suddenly I knew: it was myself. I
looked at the altar. "Are you calling me, too?" I asked. The red
light above the sanctuary shimmered in silence. A feeling of resentment seized me. I got up and left.

More letters from Gabriel—worrisome letters. "I am only fighting to secure your future," he wrote, "and when this is done I
will not be worried if your Green-haired Boy is called to another
school—you will be safe. Sometimes I ponder what a bad pupil I
was here." He was now negotiating with Warner Brothers and at
the same time carrying on talks with a Paris banking house about
the possibility of filming Shaw's *Candida* with Deborah Kerr;
and of course *Androcles* was still in the air.

What if these deals fell through as so many others had? But
why? His words hurt me: "Everybody is planning here, everybody
is working—only I am left behind in the dust of the road, forgotten."

Days passed evenly in the small mountain hotel. I was getting
stronger by the day, developing a ravenous appetite. When on
some mornings the proprietor left early, his fishing equipment
dangling on his shoulders, I knew that there was to be a trout
dinner, served with the fresh, bitter leaves of dandelion in vine-
gar and oil. I used to see the proprietor's children gathering the
small young plants on the sunny slopes where the snow had receded.

My visits to the chapel increased. I was trying to pray for Gabriel. God, help him, help him . . .

When one morning the proprietor handed me an especially
thick letter, I had the sensation of falling. By then, I knew that
thick letters were the bearers of bad news. Both pending deals

were off, Gabriel wrote, and he felt very sick. I wrote to him to come to Switzerland for the Easter holidays. Prices were more than reasonable where I was staying; the hotel charming; and he needed a rest. Then we would return together to Mumford's Farm. He wired back that he was coming.

My longing for him grew even more painful as I counted the days and hours before I would see him. It was almost as if I had a fever. At night, I tossed sleeplessly, and during the day, walking on the now-familiar roads, I could only think that soon he would be walking next to me. Every bend of the road, every rock or distant mountaintop became alive because soon I was to show it to him.

Finally one crisp morning he arrived on the funicular. He stepped out of the cabin, pale and worn and worried-looking. For the first time I noticed a few gray streaks in his black hair. He walked heavily back to the hotel, fell on the bed, and awakened fourteen hours later.

Two more days of rest and the color in his cheeks and his optimism returned. Sunset was near one afternoon when we finished tea in the wood-smoky room of a timber coffeehouse and took a path between pine trees rocking in the spring wind. Reaching a clearing, we sat down on some sun-warmed rocks.

"Look," said Gabriel, pointing at a snowy peak among white clouds. "Isn't it like Mont Salvatch in the legend, the dream peak with the cloud fortress where the ghosts of mighty knights live and descend to earth to fight for justice and truth? And down here, we all dream of one day reaching those peaks of peace and beauty."

"And having reached them, one discovers they are only vapor and the real Mont Salvatch is still beyond." Though my answer sounded pessimistic, the futility of human aspirations didn't disturb my pleasure in the clear spring wind, the smell of fresh grass, and the sight of two brown eagles ascending the blue heights.

"Where is the simple peasant boy I was?" asked Gabriel, gazing at the horizon. "The boy building dreams from clouds. I stretched out my hands and seemed to touch mountaintops . . . Ever since, I've been running, trying to reach that peak, only to find it withdrawing farther and farther. Where did I lose my faith— and myself? As a man I've done nothing but play parts. When

I'm disgusted I put aside one mask, only to put on another. Sometimes I look into myself, and I wonder—is there any real face left? You who love me, you must know the real me."

"Yes, I do," I replied. "I know you. You are the green-haired one who came down from his Transylvanian mountains to cope with the inhabitants of the lowlands. To hide the green-haired you, you created a new identity and called it Gabriel Pascal, which isn't even your real name. Since then, you've been shouting to the world in a ceaseless effort to remind it and yourself of that assumed identity. You would do anything to keep your false ego alive. But then, aren't we all playing parts, to some degree?"

The end of our mountain vacation was nearing. One afternoon I felt tired and Gabriel set out alone for a walk. At dusk he still wasn't back, and I began to worry. The lights went on in the hotel and blackness had settled over the mountains before he finally returned, sweat frozen on his shirt from the evening cold. Paying no attention to my worry, he announced proudly that he had gone down to the village in the valley and climbed back again. "It would have been enough even for a twenty-year-old."

"What a child you are," I chided, "always overdoing to prove yourself. You shouldn't overtax your body by climbing for hours in these heights."

"I thought you would be proud of me." His face fell as he left me to go to the bathroom. He was gone a long while. Worried, I went after him. He didn't answer my knock and when I opened the door he was wiping the floor with a wet towel. The towel was red.

"What happened?" My breath stopped.

He hung his head as if he were ashamed of himself. "Please, darling," he said, "go out."

"But what happened? Was it your nose? Tell me at once!"

He looked at me strangely. "I've been bleeding at the rectum for quite a while," he said. "I've just had a terrible attack."

The bathroom turned about me. "Since when have you been bleeding, for heaven's sake?"

"I don't know exactly. It was hardly anything at the beginning."

Against my will, I shrieked, "Cancer . . . my God!"

He tried to calm me. A Harley Street doctor had seen him and assured him it was only a hemorrhage; and anyway he had been much better lately. He was certain that the climb up the mountain had brought on the bleeding.

I was not reassured. "We should go at once to a hospital in Geneva," I insisted, "and have you examined."

"But I'm so happy here now," he protested, "and we have only a few days left anyhow. Don't get your hopes up, darling, I have no intention of making you a widow."

Chapter 5

"Maybe God Will Give Us Another Chance..."

G ABRIEL turned and looked back, then lifted his cane toward Mumford's Farm in a jesting salute. But the "who the hell cares" gesture ended like the flapping of a bird's broken wing. The corners of his mouth were deepened and his eyes clouded. Another chapter of his restless life was closed. The place he had hopefully called "home," where he had spent his few good years and where he had planned to grow old, had been sold.

He turned away from the house and got quickly into the car. He was late for his plane to New York.

"The fairy tale of my strange life is to begin again," he wrote en route. Then more letters, to me and to Shaw. Shaw's growing impatience made Gabriel feed him with hope, and Shaw wanted to believe. "It leaves open the question," he wrote at the age of ninety-three, "of what plays we shall begin: 3 before the end of 1950, and 2 per year after that."

But negotiations for *The Devil's Disciple* with Associated British Films and an American distribution company came to nothing, and Gabriel had to report to Shaw: "They tried to dictate such conditions—to change the script even after you approved it —that I told them 'go to hell.' Then I remembered, dear G.B.S., our last conversation and it kept ringing in my ears what you said: that you felt that we should go on with *Androcles and the Lion,* as we originally planned, with my Roman friends, followed by *Arms and the Man . . .* Also, you said we should postpone *The Doctor's Dilemma . . .*"

At the same time Gabriel was postponing his own dilemma with the doctors. He had been bleeding when he left for New York. He had refused to be examined in Switzerland and had had no time for doctors in London. He promised me solemnly to see a specialist in New York; but once there, he kept putting off an examination. He was much better, he wrote me, thanks to a "miracle cream" sold to him as a sure cure. Gabriel's faith in quackery was stupendous. He was a ready victim for charlatans and food fads. The more sinister the "doctor" and the more mysterious and illogical the "medicine" sounded, the more he was convinced of their sorcery. He loved to exchange notes on the subject with Shaw, who at one time seemed to be sold on a live hormone cure, though he was not in favor of a raw-carrot regimen as the sole solution for Gabriel.

It was alien to Gabriel's character not to see a doctor about his bleeding. He enjoyed doctors, chiropractors, chiropodists, masseurs, barbers, tailors, and shoemakers fussing over him. He was everlastingly "curing" himself with mineral waters, herbs, laxatives, colonic irrigations, hormones, vitamins. He had a hellish dread of old age, infirmity, and the loss of his creative talents, and was constantly out to discover the Fountain of Youth. And now he did not go to see a doctor!

The month of May was beautiful at the farm, but the new owners walked and planned in the garden on weekends and my plants greeted them in the greenhouse. The tiring task of selecting, discarding, and packing was almost completed, but the most painful was still ahead: the placing of the animals. The flat we had rented in London was at an exclusive Mayfair address, South Street 51, which had irked Bernard Shaw, with his puritanical thriftiness, into writing to Gabriel: "The Connaught and South Street are needlessly expensive and are for the idle rich. NW, SW, would have given you more and better accommodations for less than half the money . . . However, as you seem to have unlimited millions always at your command, it does not matter."

The two Old English sheep dogs, Czinka and Graucho, were lucky: the owners of a charming little hotel in Kent had adopted them. I had to give them up; they were farm dogs, never house- and leash-broken.

The two dogs gone, the horse, the three cows, and the calf were the first to sense that something was wrong. One afternoon when I was walking back to the fields with Mother, they stopped grazing and came toward us, silently pressing close to us as if for protection, the horse even forgetting to search my hand for sugar. The small, deerlike Jersey calf was trembling on her delicate legs. They had been nervous ever since the dealers had come to look them over.

Then the trucks came for them. The cows and the calf were nudged and pushed up a wooden plank into the dark depths of the truck. Their bellowing was soon muffled. But the horse refused to go, kicking in every direction. He turned around, noticed me, and stopped: I was there to save him. But I just stood like Judas Iscariot, and the men started to push him inside. Once more he looked back at me, his eyes wild with fear and astonishment.

The commotion made by the large animals heralded the coming disaster to the barnyard. There was much nervous cackling, answered by the chorus of ducks and geese on the pond. They had been happy birds, so far never disturbed by mysterious disappearances of their fellows: we never ate them. But now the hens were up for sale.

Our ducks looked like mallards because of a migrating mallard group which had rested a short while on our pond. Hoping that their looks might save them from human cannibals, I packed them into large boxes and drove them to Saint James's Park in London. The keeper looked at them with a bit of surprise: they were larger, he said, than most mallards. But he promised not to eat them, and let them free on the lake.

The geese were sold, except for my orphans: a gander and a goose I had brought up. They used to follow us like dogs and in the early mornings they would cackle under our windows. I put a long advertisement in the paper, addressed to geese-lovers, not geese-eaters. There was only one answer, from a retired major. He drove to the farm and he had kind eyes and did not look hungry and swore not to eat them.

Now the pond was empty, the barnyard silent, the cowsheds abandoned, and I would never again be awakened on summer nights by the pounding of the horse's hooves outside. I would never again look out the window and see his ghostlike form in the moonlight, running around in the dewy grass, neighing with the sheer joy of being alive, his mane flying after him, his legs high in the misty air.

And out in the woods, under a pine tree, lay buried Tobias, the Hungarian red squirrel. He would remain there. And the gaily painted gypsy caravan would remain, too—the only reminder of a short episode in the long story of Mumford's Farm, when a dark-haired, flamboyant foreigner donned there for a while the mask of a British squire.

One afternoon a day or two before I moved to London a call came from New York. I sat next to the phone, waiting with pounding heart to hear Gabriel's voice. Never more than now, severing my only roots in a strange country by leaving Mumford's Farm, did I need the security of that voice. When he finally came through, something in his "hello" sent a chill through me.

"Listen carefully," he said calmly, "and please don't get excited. I have cancer. I am talking from the office of Dr. Henry Cave and he wants to speak to you now."

The doctor asked me to persuade Gabriel to undergo without delay what he called a colostomy, an operation involving the excision and closing of the rectum, followed by the provision of an opening in the abdomen for elimination. Otherwise, the doctor said, he could not guarantee Gabriel's life. Gabriel's reaction had been to threaten to jump from the office window. The doctor wanted me to calm him.

Gabriel took over the phone. "I can't let him do it . . . I can't," he said in Hungarian. "That would be the end of me. I don't wish to live so . . . like a walking toilet . . . you wouldn't love me any more but . . . you'd be disgusted . . . better to die . . ." His voice broke.

I don't know what I said. When the call was disconnected, I
wanted to get up, but I couldn't.

Several days of silence followed the New York call, then a letter
from Hollywood: "Once more my old fighting spirit returned,
and any sort of criticism as to where I will finish cannot touch
me: I shall finish where I belong—in God. I was born of inspiration and only of inspiration can I live." Not a word about cancer,
nor any reaction to my urgings to go to a hospital at once.

Gabriel was in Hollywood discussing Deborah Kerr's dates for
her to play Lavinia in *Androcles and the Lion*. He wrote to Shaw,
"Also I have seen a wonderful actor, José Ferrer, when in New
York. I am working on a contract with his manager here for the
part of Androcles."

Gabriel assured Shaw of an imminent production and me that
he couldn't have cancer. But the bleeding recurred and on his
way back to New York he stopped at the Mayo Clinic in Rochester, Minnesota. His letter from the plane tried to minimize his
fear; he would yet live a long life and would finally learn how to
make me happy: "As in a vision I see your Venus body and I the
poor faun bring flowers to adorn you. Flowers are your real jewels: you should never wear man-made ornaments. In a near-hys-
teria I realize how much you have grown into me. You say you
love me. I am not lovable . . ."

I moved to London and waited tensely for the result of the examination at Mayo's. Finally it came. "My heart," the letter said,
"I am sorry for the bad news. It is cancer. I have to be operated
on at once . . . I am only sorry for you, not for myself. Life with
me has given you only grief. Personally, I deserve the punishment
and I take that terrible verdict from God humbly. I was vain, arrogant, conceited, and became superficial. Such an elementary
blow had to come to save my soul and get me back to my senses. I
only hope that you will be strong and not sorry for me. I do not
deserve either pity or help. I played with life arrogantly, not listening to the inspiration of my heart. I am a sinner. I left the simple life and my real self behind. How right I was when I felt the
danger of money! I became obstinate in ill-success, not willing to
bend, but running like a madman after luck, pulling you with

me. Everything was an impotent grasping. One cannot force Fate
... Come at once, my Heart. In the coming weeks, my only happiness will be to be with you again. I never wanted to wrong you.
Forgive me if I ever hurt you. Perhaps God will give us another
chance."

The July heat hadn't yet subsided when I left the hospital late
at night. Before Gabriel fell asleep from the drugs he tried to
make me smile. "You'll see that after the operation tomorrow,
you will get back a brand-new husband. That old morose one is
going to be kicked out; he wasn't worth anything, anyhow."

"I liked him just the same," I said, sitting next to his bed and
holding his hand.

"When I am cured, we shall start a new life," Gabriel continued, getting drowsy. He said that ever since the ill-fated *Caesar
and Cleopatra* he had been a failure in everything. "That cursed
picture," he sighed, "broke my body and spirit. I was a broken
man when I married you and I had no right to get married. Yet
in the depth of my soul I belong to you and I wish you would
stay with me—not only in this life but in the eternal one as well."
He fell asleep.

Out on the deserted streets of Rochester the heat was suffocating. As I walked to the hotel the terror returned with a choking
force: suppose he dies tomorrow—and if he survives, will he be
cured? "Only colostomy could save him," Dr. Cave had said, and
the Mayo doctors had also recommended it. Gabriel refused. The
doctors then agreed on a local operation, cutting out only the malignant tissue instead of the whole rectum.

A few days later I was making chicken soup in the kitchen of
an Italian tailor who had pressed Gabriel's suits before he went to
the hospital and had fallen victim to his charm. It was to be Gabriel's first meal after the operation. He told the nurse, "Now
that I have a brand new rectum, I am not going to offend it with
the luke-warm piss you call soup. I want my wife to make me a
soup with fresh vegetables, fresh meat, and love." Then he said to
me, "The first food I eat coming back from the shadow of death
should be yours."

He was getting stronger daily, but still putting off an answer to Shaw's last letter. He had kept the news of his operation from Shaw as long as he could, but just before the surgery, on July 16, 1949, he had cabled to Ayot St. Lawrence: FORGIVE MY LONG SILENCE. TRIED TO AVOID LETTING YOU KNOW I AM AT THE MAYO CLINIC. AN OPERATION NEXT MONDAY INDISPENSABLE, BUT NOT DANGEROUS. OUR NEXT PICTURES, ANDROCLES AND ARMS AND THE MAN ALL FINANCED AND AMERICAN DISTRIBUTION FIXED. CAN START WORK IN A FEW WEEKS AS SOON AS RELEASED FROM CLINIC. EXPLANATORY AND ALSO DOCTOR'S LETTER FORWARDED TODAY.

Gabriel never confessed the malignancy to Shaw. And there was no backing for *Androcles* and the other film, only a portfolio full of empty promises.

Shaw's handwritten answer came to the Clinic:

> 27th July 1949
> (I was 93 yesterday)

My dear Gabriel:
Whenever I see the word operation, especially trifling operation, I at once write off the patient as dead, and begin to consider how to replace him. In your case, this will be so difficult that I am deferring it on the off chance of your achieving the Miracle of Resurrection and popping in here one afternoon alive and hearty. Meanwhile, what else can I say?
Absolutely nothing.
G. B. S.

Though Shaw tried to sound heartless, and though in the last few years his partnership with Gabriel had brought him nothing but disappointments, his loyalty still stood like the Rock of Gibraltar, as he proved during Gabriel's sickness. The British producer Sydney Box made him a tempting offer, to which he answered on July 21, 1949:

"Many thanks for your proposal and its quite satisfactory terms but filming of *The Devil's Disciple* is engaged to Gabriel Pascal.

"He is at present in the U.S.A. in bed after an operation; so I shall bear you in mind in case—??? G. Bernard Shaw"

Box replied:

Dear Mr. Shaw,
I cannot wait for Gabriel Pascal to die; he is extremely tough

and, if he takes care of himself one half as well as you do, will live to be 105. (Whether he will make *The Devil's Disciple* before then is a matter of conjecture.)

How about *The Doctor's Dilemma* on similar terms to those set out in my letter of July 20th? . . .

Shaw answered on July 26, 1949:

"No. Gabriel has the whole boodle as long as he is alive and efficient. But he may be dead; the operation was a serious one."

Cable from Gabriel to Shaw: I AM SORRY NOT TO BE ABLE TO GIVE YOU THE JOY OF OUTLIVING ME. MY DOCTOR DECLARED TODAY THAT I AM COMPLETELY CURED AND WILL RELEASE ME FROM THE CLINIC WEDNESDAY. SEMPRE, GABRIEL.

One morning I found Gabriel reading in bed as usual among towers of books but with that translucent expression on his face I knew well.

"Here is the Archangel again." I said, pointing at the book. "Is it Saint Francis?"

"Now I know why God has given me another chance," he said. "I *must* do a film about Gandhi. The world has never needed his message more. His example is the real evolution of the human spirit, the evolution which began with Christ. This would be my task: to spread Gandhi's teaching of non-violence through the medium of film. Here is the *only* answer to the atomic bomb, to race prejudice. Only self-sacrifice through non-violence can overcome evil. We will go to India."

With this new inspiration on his mind Gabriel felt chained to the bed. His impatience was growing. But he knew that Gandhi had to wait: his loyalty belonged to Shaw and he had to do *Androcles* first. Once more the mad drive began: letters and more letters and tantrums with a secretary, long distance calls, and finally, a scenario writer flown all the way from Hollywood to work on the *Androcles* script, only to be thrown out on the third day. "The greatest ass I ever met," said Gabriel. "That nincompoop tried to improve on Shaw's dialogue."

Then he had a relapse. For the first time in his life, he realized that he wasn't indestructible and he had to take it easy.

The Kahler Hotel, where I spent my sweaty nights (before air conditioning), stood tall and ugly on a sun-drenched street in the middle of Rochester. It was my first encounter with that torturous invention, the transom. You close it first in the vain hope of shutting out the noise in the corridor; then, properly suffocated, you open it again to let in the illusion of a draft. The noise outside bites into your earplugs. Up again, this time in the dark so as not to drive away sleep, bumping into everything while you feel for the pull of the transom. And so on till the morning.

The Kahler had a large dining room, the entrance roped to keep the hungry sick in order, and a hostess armed with green menu-cards guarding the opening. The waitresses uniformly wore round, dark sweat-stains under their armpits and, as they rushed from table to table, they carried with them small clouds of the smell of sweat and of Irish stew.

Liver, kidney, gall bladder, stomach ulcer, and arthritis at every table. From every direction, in an endless vesper, the names of the doctors were incanted and the white-coated spirits of the demi-gods hovered over every table: "*My* doctor said . . ."

I was in another world—an outsider in the exclusive club of the sick. I caught myself making excuses: "I actually have had a gall bladder disorder."

When Gabriel first came to the Mayo Clinic, he had struck up a friendship with Dr. Charles Mayo and his family.

Not far from town was Mayo-Wood Farm, the spacious family home, overlooking a lake. Once admitted among the Mayos, you were caught by their friendly, informal spirit. No dark, tragic shadows, but the sunshine of a big family and a meaningful, well-spent life seemed to emanate even from the furniture.

The Mayo who stands out clearest in my memory is Muff, the oldest daughter. About twenty then, Muff had honey-blond hair and the graceful body of a young goddess; her wide gray eyes gazed detached at the world, and there were freckles on her turned-up nose. Still a tomboy, she was utterly unconscious of her beauty. She had a quality of innocence that seemed to set her apart from the world. Those who did not know her well enough, and it was not easy to know her, thought she was simple-minded. She was just different. She was a forest elf, who understood animals better than humans. It was only natural that she became our friend. She was akin to Gabriel's puckish faun spirit and as, according to Gabriel, I was a water nymph myself, we made a happy trio.

For Gabriel's convalescence a cottage in the woods of Mayo-Wood Farm had been kindly loaned to us by Mrs. Mayo. Muff decided that it needed redecoration. "It's dull," she said. "How about painting one wall pink and the other blue? I could paint a few horses on them, too. That would cheer up Gabriel."

When we were living among the pink and blue walls of the cottage and Gabriel felt strong enough for a canoe ride on the lake, we found a family of mice in one of the canoes. They were a heart-breaking sight, with Mother Mouse trying desperately to get herself and her naked children out of the slippery aluminum cavity of the canoe. How did she ever get there for her delivery? That Gabriel was a fake faun and I was a phony water nymph was proved by the fact that, though we wanted to help the mouse family, the horror of touching them was greater. Muff wasn't around, and all we could do was go back to the cottage and get some cheese and a dust rug to cover them, for the September days were turning cold.

Muff, when she came, handled the situation like a *real* forest elf. In no time the whole family was in a comfortable straw nest at the bottom of a large jar. Muff said that it was too cold for the newborns to live outdoors, and there was sadness in her eyes as she headed with the jar toward our cottage, but she wanted to be fair.

"They are *your* mice," she said. "After all, you found them."

Gabriel was never so magnanimous in his life: Muff could have them all.

"What are you going to do with them?" I asked, shuddering.

"Why," Muff said, "I'll just let them free in our house. Mother will never know the difference."

Gabriel enjoyed our canoe rides on the lake. We discovered a narrow passage leading to the Zumbro River. Its gray-green waters curved quietly among shallow banks through the woods. The canoe, sliding noiselessly, left behind small earth banks thick with reeds from which birds were flushed, their cries echoing back from the depth of the woods.

"Cranes, look at the cranes!" Gabriel would cry. "Since my boyhood in Transylvania I haven't seen those birds."

In the evenings, we ate in the garden. Gabriel barbecued chickens and steaks while I fixed the vegetables and salads and set the table with a red-checkered cloth, glass-covered candles, and wild flowers. With our meals, we drank light wine. Gabriel finally seemed to understand that to get well he had to relax. His tantrums eased; and maybe I was more understanding, too. Our problems evaporated and our bitter quarrels in the past seemed like attacks of insanity.

Here, for the first time in our marriage, we lived in each other, free from the pain of separateness. The doctor's prohibition of married life for the time being also helped, easing that undercurrent of tension and that painful timidity which had built up after the quarrelsome beginning of our marriage and had trapped our sexual relationship into an increasingly vicious web. At Mayo-Wood Farm I had only the warm feeling of being close to him, the delight of washing away the sweat of his fever, of massaging his back, of cooking for him, feeding him.

And then, finally, we talked and talked, as we sat in the dark coolness of the nights with the charcoal glowing in the burner. "The ways of God are strange," Gabriel said. "I had to be seriously sick to find you again and to realize that you are a true-hearted girl. Many times in the past, when you talked to me as if I was a stranger or even an enemy, I wondered if you had a heart at all. I think all our troubles started with your mistrust of me that night at the opera in London. Ever since that night you've doubted me. Maybe it was your experience with Tibor which ruined your trust in men, but I've never been like Tibor. I've kept my body and my soul clean."

"I may have doubted you," I said, "but I've always loved you."

"But you still fear for the insecurity of our lives. Even if you don't talk about it, your fear projects from you and frightens me. I've never feared life before, and you must remember that the smallest doubt has an effect on me like a shout on a somnambulist. And level-headed as you are, can you live with a sleepwalker like me? My responsibility toward you weighs on me. How I'd like to give you security, to find happiness with you, how I long for work and a pure, simple life together. How happy we are here."

The burning coals grayed to ashes. I became aware of something missing: Gabriel's inevitable cigar. I offered to bring his cigar box.

"Do you remember the big cigar I had the evening before my operation?" he asked. "I smoked it down to the very end because it was the last one. The cigars belonged to the lie of prosperity. 'Selected especially for G.P. in Havana,' initials printed on the boxes—the image of the successful producer. But I got accustomed to their taste. When we went to the chapel before I entered the hospital, I suddenly got worried: what would become of you if I died the next day? Then I put you under the protection of the Madonna and gave up the cigars as a small sacrifice. Shaw will be happy when he hears that!"

He never smoked again, and there was no further mention of cigars.

On one of our walks, a kitten with gray stripes followed us back to the cottage. Next morning I found her on the mat at the front door. There was so much pleading in her wide eyes that from then on, we had a cat. I began weaving plans of smuggling the cat into England. The kitten took our love humbly and gracefully. I had heard there was a ferocious Doberman dog in the neighborhood, so I let her out only when we were around.

One Sunday, we were expecting an old friend of Gabriel's, the painter Oskar Kokoschka. At that time he was living in nearby St. Paul–Minneapolis and Gabriel invited him for a Hungarian-goulash dinner. Muff was excited, as Kokoschka was one of her idols.

Early in the afternoon I began to make the dinner and Gabriel moved out to the garden with a book and the kitten. After a while, he came in to lie down.

"Are you bringing the cat in?" I asked him through the kitchen door.

"What a silly thing to bring the cat in. I just cannot stand this any longer!" he exploded. "She needs fresh air. You make an idiot out of everybody. She is a free animal."

"Will you stop shouting and bring the cat in. My hands are wet."

In a minute we were in our first quarrel since his operation. As he stood at the kitchen door with blazing eyes, he harangued at the top of his voice.

"My God, how happy I was as a bachelor; a happy, free animal I was before you came into my life ... I was just like that cat ... Caught, caught by you ... why did I ever let myself ... I want my freedom back ... Oh, go ... go and leave me ..."

A piercing cry from outside interrupted his monologue. A big black dog was tearing the kitten to pieces before our eyes. Gabriel ran out with a stick and fought the dog off. The dog dropped his victim: a blood-soaked bundle of pain. I carried her back to the cottage and called Muff to get a vet, but we couldn't find anybody. Even Dr. Mayo was away; there was nobody to help the cat.

When Oskar Kokoschka arrived, the cat was still alive. By then she had hidden under the bed and her agony filled the house. Muff's suggestion to put her out of her dying pain made Kokoschka's face gray, but there was nothing else to do. Muff's brothers came and took the cat into the woods, but not far enough for us not to hear the dull rifle shot. Kokoschka jumped up and rushed to the bathroom and soon left, never tasting my goulash.

Gabriel avoided my eyes the whole evening. In the morning he was subdued. "Forgive me," he said. "Like everything else, the cat was my fault, too. *I* killed her, not the dog. I should have taken her in just as you asked. From now on, I promise I will always listen to you."

Soon we were off to Hollywood. On the way to the station, we passed over the bridge above the lake and I saw two cranes flying toward the mouth of the Zumbro River—Gabriel's cranes. But he did not see them. His forehead contracted, he was looking far away.

Chapter 6

The Disciple and His Devil

THEY talk about the "odor of sanctity"—a state which I do not doubt has a quality almost smellable to the sensitive—but if anything has an "odor" it is failure. And nowhere does failure smell so loud as in Hollywood. The nose of the movie industry is a most sensitive organ at detecting failure. Though the person involved may still be basking in the rays of his own importance, he is a dead body, fast decaying, and the long feelers of the studios are pulled back from him in disgust. His carcass is left to the smaller carnivores to chew to non-existence in the columns of Louella Parsons and the like.

Though outwardly Gabriel's spell-binding personality would never show defeat, and he seemed to be filled with bouncing confidence, I could not help sensing that "odor of failure" about us. His unsuccessful business attempts on the other side of the ocean had had a long echo in Hollywood. Louella's column did not welcome Gabriel to town. Maybe she was irked by his press announcement that Rex Harrison was his only choice for the part of the Emperor in *Androcles and the Lion*. Just then Rex Harrison's name was a bad word in Hollywood; a suicide story was circulating and Louella blamed "Sexy Rexy" for his part in it.

The Hollywood of that time was enveloped in a thin, bluish veil called "smog," and it was as far from my vision of Hollywood

as truth is from daydreams Maybe we stayed at the wrong place.
The Hollywood Athletic Club, midway downtown on Sunset
Boulevard, was handy and economical, but it certainly wasn't
glamorous. It did not help to build an image of success either.
Gabriel used to stay there in his wonder-boy days, but then,
under the shining halo of his *Pygmalion* success, he could well afford to.

The Hollywood trip was summed up in the words of Mike Cur-
tiz, the director and our fellow Hungarian. We had lunch with
him in his studio where he was directing a picture against his best
judgment. "Don't try to hit your head against the wall, Gabby,"
he said, "you will only break it. You cannot be an independent
producer in this town. And leave Shaw; he is old hat. Then you
may still have a chance."

Back to New York we went, I to sail on the *Caronia* for England, Gabriel to stay and look into new possibilities. By then it
was evident that I had not gotten back a "brand new husband instead of the old morose one," as Gabriel had promised me before
his operation. Neither did he get back a more understanding and
patient wife. "Charity understands, charity is patient," Saint Paul
had written, and my love lacked that charity. Gabriel had every
reason to be difficult; he was sick, he was worried. He was burning with creative desire and each time he was about to reach his
goal, it was snatched away from him.

I remember one afternoon at the Plaza Hotel. We had said all
we could to hurt each other and I ran out across the street into
Central Park. I wandered around, ending up on a bench by a
small lake. Slowly emerging from my distress, I looked around.
New York filled me with aversion—or was it some kind of fear?
Everything seemed to be so different from all the other cities I
knew. There was, I felt, something so unnatural, even foreboding,
about the skyscrapers, something so terrifyingly un-homelike and
impersonal, as if Aldous Huxley's *Brave New World* were coming
true here, and as if the children, sailing toy boats on the lake in
the late autumn sunshine, were the forebears of those future
monsters of human evolution.

The sun was setting when I went back to the hotel. If only I
could run away from Gabriel, forget him forever. Maybe he
missed me, maybe he was worried where I had been all this time.

And how I wanted to see him worried, sitting in our room waiting for me. Anxiously, I turned the key in the lock. The room was empty. It was I who waited for him, worried and without dinner late into the night.

The boat moved slowly away from the dock and the waving figures of Gabriel and Jean Dalrymple became smaller and smaller. Jean had taken us to the boat, turning discreetly away when Gabriel enclosed me in his arms. "Forgive me," he said.

His letter was waiting for me in the new flat, South Street 51.

"How I need you," he wrote. "But do you want me still? Me, who so far have been a disappointment to you with all my sins, sorrows and fantasies. Why should you love me? Why should you live your young years with an impossible man like me? My body isn't worth anything any more and my soul nearly flew away. Only your nymph eyes and the cranes of the Zumbro River called it back."

One day, after a thick manila envelope had arrived from Gabriel at our London flat, I reached hesitantly for the telephone and asked the operator for Codicote 218. I heard the ringing and a Scottish accent answering.

"Please, Mrs. Laden," I said. "Would you tell Mr. Shaw that I have to see him? I've received a very important communication from Mr. Pascal and I'd like to bring it out to him."

I waited on the phone for quite a while. Then Mrs. Laden picked up the receiver again: "Mr. Shaw is expecting you for tea tomorrow afternoon at four o'clock."

Gabriel's letter had informed me of a new, great hope. In New York, he had met again with Cantinflas, the Mexican comedian, who was now definitely interested in playing the part of Androcles. Cantinflas suggested the Mexican studios: modern, cheap, and where he had the power of a king. He was then, and still is, the most popular man, actor and comic bullfighter in Mexico. Gabriel had brought the whole matter to his friend, Floyd Odlum, of the Atlas Investment Corporation. Odlum was interested; he even discussed future cooperation on more Shaw films to be made in Mexico. But the experience with the Pickford deal made Gabriel wary, and before going any further with Atlas, Cantinflas, and Mexico, he wanted Shaw's written consent.

"I want you to deliver to him personally the material and my letter," he wrote to me. "I have faith in you as a go-between. Shaw likes you. You can melt even the hearts of the Wall Street financiers, that is, if they have such organs in their bodies."

The countryside was still aflame with the reds and yellows of late October as I drove out to Ayot Saint Lawrence. I was concentrating nervously on what I was to say to Shaw. A million small knots pulled my insides tighter and tighter as I was ushered into the living room. I gave a fleeting glance to the old-fashioned coat-rack in the right corner of the dark, small entrance hall. As always, it held a display of Shaw's headgear, from Tyrolean hats to sombreros. Proud hats they must be, I thought, covering the Century's Most Famous Brain. Even hats have destiny.

The room was empty, for I was a bit ahead of time. Tea was brought in by the Irish maid, with her ready smile and constant blushing. Then Shaw returned from his walk, wearing a faded cloak and knickers. His cheeks had a pinkish glow from the crisp air, and I noticed the vigor of his sharp blue eyes. Throwing off his cloak, he settled in the pink armchair, next to the fireplace above which hung the pastel of Charlotte Shaw.

Shaw's first question was about Gabriel's health. I handed him the report of the Mayo Clinic doctors which Gabriel, with his usual foresight, had included in the manila envelope. He knew Shaw too well. He had warned me not to mention the necessity of the periodic check-ups at the clinic. Neither did Shaw know the nature of Gabriel's sickness. "Shaw hates sickness," Gabriel wrote; "he would lose confidence in me."

Shaw waved away my second offering, Gabriel's letter. "Finish your tea first," he said, "then we'll talk."

I swallowed a big gulp of tea and burned my throat, and for a second my gaze, fixed on the electric heater in front of the fireplace with its imitation coal glowing dull red, became distorted. My throat really hurt. I poured some milk into my tea to cool it off, but my hand was positively shaking. Shaw tactfully looked away. Greater people than I had chickened out in front of him.

Finally, tea finished, he asked for Gabriel's letter. Gabriel presented the Atlas-Cantinflas-Mexican scheme in blazing words, admitting all the past mistakes. But now a new chapter in his adventurous life was to start.

"I must face facts from now on," Gabriel wrote. "I was dreaming too much and I am not a boy any more. I have to reorganize my whole life . . . give up sending two-page cables, phoning overseas and running around the world. I analyzed why all these happened: I was too restless, G. B. S., and greedy for success, but do not ever believe that I was greedy for money. I wanted success only because I wanted to be free, to earn my freedom and independence from Hollywood and from the dictatorship of British distributors . . ."

Shaw read on, slowly and carefully. He finished the letter but did not say anything. I fished into the manila envelope for the Atlas brochure containing the description of their holdings and financial status and plans for the future. Shaw skimmed through it.

"Do you know Mr. Floyd Odlum?" he asked.

"I've met him and his wife twice. She is Jacqueline Cochrane, the flier. I found him pleasant. I think he's of Irish origin."

That was the wrong thing to say; it brought back the bad taste of failure with the Irish dream. "Irish," Shaw repeated. "The Irish are a difficult race. A quarrelsome one and moody, too. You never know what they are going to do next. Maybe the American Irish learned to be different."

Then he promised to study the Odlum proposition, and put the brochure and Gabriel's letter aside. He gave me a meditative look. "You know it isn't right at all," he said. "It is none of my doing, but you and Gabby are too much separated. I have always told him he was not for marriage. He cannot comprehend a woman as she really is, and even worse, he doesn't care to comprehend her. And he cannot stand being tied. He has to be free. What are you doing with yourself alone?"

"I'm always busy with something, household and such. And I read a lot." I was ashamed to mention my writing. I was working on a story, and Gabriel had greatly encouraged me. But how could I talk about writing in the presence of George Bernard Shaw?

"Read? And what else?" he questioned. "Why don't you try to write?"

Had he sensed my thought or did he divine a secret talent in me? "Do you really think, G. B. S.," I stammered, "that I should write?"

"Why, every fool is writing nowadays," was his stimulating answer, "and you may have talent. Anyhow, something to occupy your mind. But why don't you go back to acting? You've been an actress. You were born for that. You have the face, the expression. You should play Lavinia in my *Androcles and the Lion*."

The part Gabriel wanted for Deborah Kerr! I couldn't help feeling lifted—me, the wife pushed back into the shadow, a weight around my husband's neck; and Bernard Shaw himself proposes that I play the lead in his play!

"I have an accent," I said. "And it would be impossible because I'm Gabriel's wife."

"Use another name. You commit a sin wasting yourself."

"But Gabriel doesn't want me to act any more."

"Then leave him."

"But I love him," I said with a sigh.

"To be in love is a ruinous attachment. It has done away with many, but one could leave it off."

"And he loves me, too. I think . . ."

"No doubt. At least that's what he thinks. The mistake you make is running after his whims. You take him and his tantrums too seriously. Maybe you take his love too seriously, too. Gabriel loves to play parts and he believes in them. He is a fully creative man and a creative man has to play with something all the time. You should let him have his way, but have yours as well and leave him a bit uncertain. That is the only way to hold his imagination. Besides, everyone has to have a personal interest of his own. If you don't do *now* what you have talent for, you will be very sorry." He stood up at this point. "And forget the household: any servant can take care of that. Use your energy and mind for greater things."

We were standing now face to face, his tall figure towering over me. I was wearing a simple black dress with a narrow but rather deep V in front. Shaw's eyes swept over my face. Then his eyes stopped at the point of the V. He pulled up one bushy eyebrow as he said:

"You are a remarkable woman. Awfully good looking. But you don't know your husband. You don't know him at all. But I know him. I know Gabby better than he knows himself. And I urge you to insist on accompanying him, after he gets back, when he goes to Rome."

The morning after my visit, Mrs. Laden called me. "I have to tell you that after you left, Mr. Shaw talked quite a bit about you," she said. "He liked you very much. And in the evening, he sat down to write a letter to Mr. Pascal."

The letter to Gabriel was dated October 27, 1949:

Dear Gabriel:

I have just seen Valerie, looking so well with her perfectly dressed classical head, that though it is against all my principles I told her that she is Lavinia to the life and ought to play her.

Spanish and Hungarian accents do not matter. American accents *do*. English accents are a drawback in *Androcles*.

Cantinflax [*sic*] is justified in refusing an engagement on approval, and standing on his reputation. I do the same myself as an author. But of course he will stand a dozen tests if you do not impose them on him.

The captain must not make his speeches to the Christians colloquially. He should rehearse them to a side drum beating a march rhythm.

After the collapses of Malta and Boston I have no confidence in the solvency of the Atlas Investment Corporation. But we can do no better; all the financial concerns are as likely to be bankrupt next year as I am myself. So Odlum can have the contract.

The accounts of your health are highly satisfactory. I look forward to seeing you in November on your way to Rome. Valerie must go with you, even if she has to set up a ripieno husband when you persist in working longer than from 10:30 to 16:30, which is quite enough.

G. B. S.

Mrs. Laden is enchanted with
her new nylons.

"You don't know your husband . . . but I know him," Shaw had said. At that time the sentence had skimmed over the surface of my mind like a toy paper boat. It is only now that the memory of it keeps coming back, only now when in my effort to understand the enigma of Gabriel I have begun to study Shaw himself and to realize that he had indeed known his "disciple" throughout.

No doubt there was something Mephistophelian in the author

of *The Devil's Disciple*. Not a malevolent demon though, but a mixture of Lucifer, the shining star of clear intellect, and of a jesting leprechaun who rebelled with laughter instead of hatred. There is a sketch of Bernard Shaw by William Cotton which brings out that sardonic Mephisto look in Shaw's appearance. Another sketch of his "Disciple," Gabriel, presents him too with the dark look of the Outcast. But while Shaw's portrait talks of a mocking defiance of Heaven, Gabriel's countenance bears a tragic yearning for it.

As with the master so with the pupil. The Devil and his Disciple shared many characteristics. They were both active rebels against bourgeois hypocrisy, and their morality was not of the accepted standards. In their youth they had both left school and jobs and had fled their countries and "family strangulation." They both sought escape from emotional ties and put their necks into the yoke of a legal marriage late in life. Shaw's words fit perfectly Gabriel's life and principles:

"If . . . a man is to attain consciousness of himself as a vessel of the *Zeitgeist* or will . . . he must pay the price of turning his back on the loaves and fishes, the duties, the ready-made logic, the systems and the creeds. He must do what he likes instead of doing what, on second-hand principles, he ought."

At first glance this seems to be the credo of the absolutely selfish, especially for those to whom duties are what Shaw called a "second-hand principle." But there is a profound paradox: this selfish creed can also be seen as absolute self-sacrifice in the call of a vocation. It is not easy to turn one's back on the "loaves and fishes," the security of mediocrity. Yet it is ruthlessly necessary for the development of a genius, be the genius an artist, a scientist, or a saint. This Shavian creed is embodied on one level in the artist, Dubedat, in *The Doctor's Dilemma,* and on another, higher level in the Saint in *Saint Joan*—which explains why those two plays were Gabriel's favorites.

Gabriel Pascal was perhaps the truest disciple Shaw ever had. He was unconsciously a Shavian from his early youth. Among his papers I found an unfinished sketch he had written called "My Credo":

"I always loved Eulenspiegel and had an admiration for the Piper. Only later did I discover that I am a mixture of both. I

like to make fun of the hypocrites and of the powerful and I like
to induce genuine children to run away from the boring medioc-
rities of life.

"Therefore, it is clear to me now that I was pre-destined to
meet Bernard Shaw and become his translator on the screen for
wider audiences. Shakespeare, Dante, Milton, Goldoni, Goethe,
and mostly Ibsen inspired me from youth, but the man whose
thinking I felt the nearest to mine was Bernard Shaw."

Gabriel wandered about "on the face of the earth" and
searched for expression as an "erring hobo" until he met Shaw.
"He encouraged me," Gabriel wrote, "and gave me back my faith
in myself, in my talent, in my artistic integrity and in my mission."

When the world was startled by Shaw's inexplicable choice of
an unknown, penniless Hungarian to produce his films, Gabriel's
explanation was, "I spoke his spirit."

I found quite significant the young Gabriel's attachment to Til
Eulenspiegel, that early Bernard Shaw and individualist of the
fourteenth century, who demonstrated through jokes the superi-
ority of an independent mind. But there was more than making
fun of hypocrites in Bernard Shaw and his faithful disciple Pascal: there was something Quixotic in both of them. While Shaw,
despite his idealism and his single-minded championing of the
causes he believed in, was saved from a Quixotic tragedy by his
level head and sense of humor, his disciple Gabriel was as tragic
as Cervantes' dreamer in conflict with the world and his own
soul. "In my whole life," he wrote, "I suffered superhumanly
from God burning in my soul."

Years later, his "mission" unfulfilled and his vision, that luminous "star of my destiny," still undefined, broken in body and
spirit, his Quixotic fantasies became even more real to him. From
his deathbed he was to write to Baba in India: "I remember centu-
ries ago in the brutal Renaissance period I was a gallant fencer
and fought for beauty, for truth, and died for the passion of a
woman. What a fool I was!" In another letter to Baba, ten days
before his death, he began to peel away one by one his imagined
identities: "I was a prince, I was a courtier, I was a poet, I was a
great adventurer and I was a great artist ... Maybe you hear a
frivolous remark from me in my dying pain, but you know that

thousands of years ago, I was a pixie and a faun and I was allowed to make fun of the gods."

Reading those lines later, I couldn't help thinking of Shaw's words about himself that his "strangeness" made him "all my life a sojourner on this planet rather than a native of it. Whether it be that I was born mad or a little too sane, my Kingdom was not of this world: I was at home only in the realm of my imagination, and at my ease only with the mighty deed. Therefore, I had become an actor, and created myself a fantastic personality . . . adaptable to various parts."

Shaw and Pascal playing with their masks. Or were those masks —every one of them—real?

After the success of *Pygmalion,* Gabriel forged a new and more befitting mask for himself—and G.P. was born. That public image put on the fat of pomposity with monogrammed, made-to-order shirts and underwear and with cigar boxes from Havana imprinted "specially selected for G. P." Shaw preferred this G.P. mask to that of the onetime self-supporting orphaned bastard, grown up into a hobo, about which Gabriel still liked to brag. Shaw therefore enjoyed cables like the one Gabriel sent to a Hollywood agent who had double-crossed him: "I give you my word of honor as a Hungarian Cavalry Officer and an English Farmer, you are the greatest crook unhung.—Gabriel Pascal."

As a consequence of an unhappy childhood, Shaw never learned how to show love and ended by being scornful of sentiment. Gabriel reacted differently to his own loveless childhood: he hungered for sentiment, sometimes mistaking it for real emotion. Searching for a father image, he poured his orphaned love on Shaw, who stood it remarkably well for a sentiment-hater. S. N. Behrman records in his book, *The Suspended Drawing Room,* the afternoon tea he had with Shaw and Gabriel at Ayot Saint Lawrence. "Shaw," Behrman writes, "looked at Pascal. I thought I saw an odd expression in his eyes; affectionate interest and also a certain puzzlement at finding himself so closely involved with this man."

I too noticed that "affectionate interest" in Shaw's eyes when, during my visit, he talked about Gabriel and told me: "You do not know your husband." He talked like a father, with a gentle disapproval of his favorite but incorrigible son. But when he went on to say that Gabriel "had to be free," was he rather re-membering his young self? Escaping women had become an art with Shaw, the most celebrated philanderer of his time. Many Shaw scholars, though, suspect him of being a great lover only on paper. He recognized sex as the manifestation of the "life-force," which, according to his belief, was God constantly creating Him-self. Sex, Shaw wrote, could cause a "celestial flood of emotion and exaltation," yet he felt a puritanical repulsion toward it. "In our sexual nature," he wrote, "we are torn by an irresistible at-traction and an overwhelming repugnance and disgust. We have two tyrannous physical passions: concupiscence and chastity." But Shaw himself "was never duped by sex, as a basis of permanent re-lationship."

"I should never have married at all," Shaw wrote at one time. His greatest passion was "for a higher life of the mind, for free-dom of the spirit," to which sexual attachment could only be a hindrance. And here I find the deepest similarity between Shaw and Pascal. In his relationship with women, Gabriel's behavior was as paradoxical as Shaw's. Like Shaw, he was highly susceptible to women and, like Shaw, he "never learned to accept the facts of flesh." As a young man, he fought off sexual desires by jumping into cold water. He felt that, as a searcher for God, he ought to seek deliverance from the flesh first. There was always the "monk" hidden in him and torturing him whenever he suc-cumbed to temptation. Perhaps this was why Gabriel, just like Shaw, preferred long-distance lovemaking: letter writing. Gabriel had a Madonna complex. In woman he searched for the *ewigweib-liche,* the redemptive female principle. He yearned for the pu-rity of a Mother-Lover, through whose understanding he would be relieved of his inner conflicts and, like Faust and Peer Gynt, would reach eternal salvation.

While the beloved was at a distance, inspiring his yearning let-ters, she grew away from the real person; she became a luminous vision, like Don Quixote's Dulcinea—until the shattering mo-ment of meeting. Then sex gained the upper hand and the face of the Madonna faded away. The guilt-ridden Gabriel and the free-dom-loving Gabriel would begin to talk about India and becom-ing a monk.

When, broken by the disappointments and intrigues of *Caesar and Cleopatra,* he had met me in Paris, Gabriel felt that I was the solution to his life. He was tired; he wanted peace and belonging. He called me his Solveig and only now, looking back, do I understand his letters to me: "The curse on me now will be untied through your love ... Only with you can I create again and open my wings and fly again ... I am like a monk who is leaving his monastery ... Throwing away my masks and jester's cap, with you I could be my real self."

Shaw must have known that once a philanderer always a philanderer, and maybe that is why he was insisting that I accompany Gabriel on his next trip to Rome.

There was little in the appearance of Shaw in his nineties to indicate a young dare-devil with flaming red beard. Talking to me earlier that afternoon, he looked like a venerable old prophet. I could not help thinking then that while some men turn into flabby eunuchs in their old age, Shaw kept his masculinity. I felt that he liked me and that old as he was, he noticed the woman in me. The thing that always struck me, during later visits, was his gallantry. He always started out by paying me a compliment. Then he was attentive: he wanted to know what occupied my mind. He was protective. Was I comfortable in that chair? Wasn't the drive to his place too long? Was the tea all right? When I left, he would always walk me out to the gate, advising safe driving on the winding country road. No, with George Bernard Shaw I wasn't a chummy "dear old girl" but I was Lavinia, and I was, as he teasingly called me sometimes, the "goddess Diana." I was a woman.

Shaw was serious when he offered me the part of Lavinia. His postcard came later:

> Professor Daniel Jones, University College, Gower St. W.C. 1, will correct your foreign accent.
>
> The Central School of Speech Training at the Albert Hall is also available; but a course there would be longer, and mixed up with a general theatrical training that you do not need.
>
> G. B. S.

Here was Shaw—Professor Higgins once more, out to transform a Hungarian accent into a proper British one. But I never went to Professor Daniel Jones and I think Shaw was disappointed in me.

Chapter 7

Au Revoir at
Ayot St. Lawrence

December 1st, 1949
Mr. George Bernard Shaw
Ayot St. Lawrence
Herts, England

My dear G. B. S.,

Cantinflas, his real name Mario Moreno, insisted that before I
go back to London and Rome I should come to Mexico to see
the possibilities of our future Bernard Shaw pictures here.

What I found here is not from this world. The studios are better equipped than any in England or even in Hollywood. Everything is wonderfully organized . . . I think I could make our pictures in the most economical way . . . The Cantinflas contract is
signed. Also I signed up Diego Rivera to be our art director.
He's already started on the sketches for Androcles. I think it is
our destiny to make our pictures here. The climate is wonderful.
I never felt so young and vigorous . . . but before I make any
more definite plans for further projects, I have to talk the whole
situation over with you. But please keep your mind open . . . You
will see the happiness in my eyes when I enter your room . . . I
am sending you my fondest thoughts from this paradise: the last
free country in the world.
Sempre tuo
Gabriel.

In Mexico, Gabriel became friendly with President Alemán. "I'll make a national cause out of the Bernard Shaw films here," he wrote to me in London. "I am playing my great Machiavellian game."

The London winter was dark and foggy. The lights in the apartment where Gabriel had never yet lived were always on. I had moved in six months earlier, and now I sensed suspicion in the eyes of the doormen, as if they thought Gabriel was a fictitious husband. Our friends tactfully stopped asking about him.

"What I am trying to do is not easy," he would write. "Be with me in your soul. If you love me and have trust in me I will have success, but if you vacillate or criticize, you are not harmonizing with me. Then I will fail. *Only your faith and love can hold me up:* this is the mystery of our strange partnership."

In one of his letters, he had sent me an old photo he had found of himself, a snapshot taken during World War I on the north Italian frontier. He couldn't have been more than nineteen. The yellowed picture showed him sitting in the sun on the terrace of a demolished building. He was stark naked but his lap was modestly covered by two dachshunds.

I put the picture on my night desk. The faded photograph made me nostalgic and one lonely night I wrote him: "How charming you are in your youth. You little, thin, naked Hussar. And those dogs of yours on your lap. My hands are almost itching for the touch of their silky, glossy-sleek dachshund skin.

"Would you for a second lift your horrid dogs from your lap? But of course I will look. How warm and good-smelling your skin must be from the sun. Your black hair and your strong round arms. What a dear, darling boy you must be. Life hasn't embittered you yet, you are still full of faith and dreams.

"But where was I then? Here my brown-legged boy is sitting ready for love—and I am not even born yet! Come, let us turn back time and let me wish: I wish to be a young Italian peasant girl at that moment. And now here we both are. You, alive, sitting in the sun, so naked. Watch now. Do you see me? I am coming up those stairs with swinging hips, bringing milk to you in a jug on my head. Now I hand the jug to you. Lifting it up by its two handles, you drink from it. I am giggling. You look up and laugh, the white milk running out of your mouth, down onto your brown skin. Desire is trembling in your eyes. My breasts tighten under the white peasant blouse—milk wants to develop in them from you. Look. The dogs jump off now and here you are in the nudity of Pan. Your hard mouth dashes on mine. You are tearing off the poor white blouse.

"Was it so? It would have been so if I had not been late for that appointment. I was to arrive only many years later at the Place Vendôme. Don't be angry that I was delayed a few minutes (on the clock of eternity they were only a few minutes), but I know that you are the slim, brown boy I should have met in the mountains of Italy.

"I've never told you yet that the white blouse I wore on our first meeting is packed away, never washed, as a memory. I never told you because when we are together my brown boy is the sedate, ever gloomy Mr. Pascal . . ."

The days went by. Gabriel was in New York working on the preliminary contracts with the Atlas Investment Corporation. I was worried and he knew it. He calmed me. "I trust Atlas," he wrote, "and don't worry. I have recovered my lost charm and have taken the bridle of our cart and am holding it strong. The two old horses know that I am the old Gabor again who wouldn't bend to anything or anybody except God and the Madonna. I am full of vigor, joy, creative desire: life is again a divine dream. The miracle is on its way. The Dutch in you cries out, 'Oh, he is dreaming again; then we are in for trouble!' Don't worry, don't, don't! I am flying cautiously, like an eagle, to build the fairytale nest for you."

As though stretched on a rack, I waited for the news from New York. Finally, it came: the Atlas deal was off.

Gabriel did not visit Shaw on his return; he could not face him. He only wrote that he was going to Rome to raise money for *Androcles*. But a warning came from Shaw, who was losing confidence: "I must take the Androcles affair into my own hands, it is *my* turn now."

Just about that time an offer came from the multimillionaire ex-president of Mexico, General Abelardo Rodríguez, who was willing to finance certain Shaw films in Mexico. Gabriel's answer to Shaw's "it is *my* turn now" conveyed the good news: "I am delighted that it is your 'turn now' and I'm confident that the change of wind will again save Orleans!" (Gabriel was referring to the miracle scene from *Saint Joan*.)

But the wind from Orleans blew stronger than ever from the wrong direction, and Shaw's "turn" was a devastating letter to Gabriel's Italian partners:

"Mr. Gabriel Pascal informs me that he is negotiating with you for a filming of my play *Androcles* in your studios. . . .

"Will you be good enough to let me know what arrangements you have discussed with Mr. Pascal, and what terms you expect from me. We must communicate with one another directly as Mr. Pascal, though a very distinguished artist, is not a man of business, and has no legal authority to deal with the matter. . . . Excuse my typewriting. The machine is out of order; and I am very old (93½) and not very dexterous."

It was the Holy Year in Rome and I was to join Gabriel there. He had surprised me by inviting Mother, too.

That time in Rome was the most unhappy experience of our marriage. When we arrived, I learned that Gabriel had reserved a double room for Mother and me; his room was at the other end of the long corridor. He excused himself: he was not on a pleasure trip. He had to work late into the night; business people were coming to see him; there would be phone calls; all that would disturb me. He added that he had asked us to Rome only to make us happy, but financially it was a great sacrifice for him. As always, he only wanted the best for us—and, as always, I misunderstood him.

He looked tense, even hostile. His face was pallid, his eyes puffy. Suddenly I felt compassion. How hard he struggled and how cruel life was to him. I told him that I understood, that he meant well. "Yet I can't help being confused and unhappy," I added. "We are so much apart. I want a real marriage, a marriage such as others have, a marriage in which one eats together, sleeps together, thinks together. I understand that all our unhappiness is caused by adversity but all this has gone on for years. Forgive me if at times I lose strength."

He flared at my words.

"Do you think that I don't sense all the time that you want to be free of me?" he demanded. "Why don't you leave me? Why aren't you sincere and say that you want a new life?"

I wanted to tell him I loved him but my tongue was tied. I wanted to reach out to him but my hands were stones. All I could do was tell him that I was ready to set him free if he wished.

"*You* are the one who wants to be free," he said, looking at me wildly. "Why this hypocrisy? Say it openly. I always knew that one day you would leave me—and you should. I'm no good for you. I have failed you."

I took Mother and my unhappiness to see ruins, museums, and all the churches. I could not help being touched by the endless caravans of the Holy Year pilgrims thronging the city, radiating such faith that for the first time in my life I realized that religion was a living thing and I wondered at the strength and unity of the Catholic Church.

We were still in Rome when a letter came from General Rodrí-guez's lawyer:

"It is a pleasure to answer your letter of January 19th, and to express to you my deep appreciation for the devotion you feel for our country and for your purposes of coming here to live among us and to work in a free country like Mexico.

"Our President, His Excellency Miguel Alemán, is quite satisfied of the possibility that you come to film the works of George Bernard Shaw, as you will see by the enclosed letter addressed to me . . ."

The letter ended with the proposal that Gabriel fly from Rome directly to Mexico to talk everything over with General Rodrí-guez, who was then reorganizing the film industry. President Alemán, at the same time, wrote to Bernard Shaw and instructed Ambassador O'Farril in the Mexican Embassy on Belgrave Square to get in touch with Mr. Shaw and give the necessary assurances.

Shaw thought it over, then wrote to Gabriel: "There is no time to consult with Belgrave Square. The Ambassador can do nothing. I enclose the agreements. With them in your pocket, you can arrange everything . . .

"We must take our chance as to security, and be content with the President's letter ... But the President lasts only until the next election or until he is assassinated; and his successor may be against the film business.

"However, we cannot do better."

Alone again in the South Street apartment, I developed a stubborn bronchitis. Finally I had to see a doctor, who prescribed some injections and pills.

His office wasn't far; I could walk to it through the edge of Hyde Park. One afternoon I became aware that it was spring: green and flowering spring, couples on benches, babies in carriages. My heart felt small as I realized my misery. Here I was alone in my youth: I had nobody to sit on the bench with, and no baby to love. I didn't even feel like a woman any more.

During the treatment, the doctor's hand seemed uncertain. He was a blondish young man with a weak chin. "What a lovely woman you are," he said, and his hand was shaking.

Next time I looked over my wardrobe carefully and realized I hadn't bought a dress in ages. The doctor asked me to the theater, then to dinner; I accepted. He phoned frequently and we met more and more often. I found myself waiting for his calls and buying spring hats. He merely represented hours when my loneliness and fear receded, but nonetheless I felt guilty. In vain I assured myself that I had the right to live and that Gabriel was neglecting me. If only I could stop loving him.

"We are created for each other and I know that even death cannot separate us," Gabriel wrote me, again making love by long distance. "We are paying dear for the ten Paris days but remember such days are not given without a reason ... maybe God joined our hands for a higher purpose." Everything was working out fine in Mexico, he added; General Rodríguez was ready to finance *The Devil's Disciple* as the first Shaw film, and, when Cantinflas was available, *Androcles and the Lion* would follow.

Then once more a thunderbolt from Ayot: "I conclude that the Mexican experiment had better be with *Blanco Posnet* ... in Spanish ... no English rights or players." Gabriel was frantic. He had just received the General's assurance that when the Shaw contracts arrived, "we will make the necessary formal arrangements" for the yearly production of the Shaw films in Mexico. But Shaw's withholding the English-speaking rights would make those films worthless for the world market. Gabriel's letter to Shaw blamed him for his many misfortunes: "Like Lazarus at the rich man's wedding, I was only sitting at the gate while parasites and third-rate talents made fantastic money ... because always at the moment I needed your cooperation you let me down ... I went to Tepeyac to the Shrine of the Madonna of Guadalupe and burned a big candle for you that She should illuminate your mind and not let you be unjust to me and I am sure She has contacted you already."

But it was I who was to be the earthly ambassador of the cause. Shaw was kind and polite, as always. I gathered all my courage and asked him about his intentions and what Gabriel should say to the General. He answered with an impatient wave of his hand.

"Gabby should do the first film as a tryout in Spanish. Then we shall see how serious those Mexicans are."

When I argued against that procedure, he gave me a reflective look. His eyes were tired; they had lost the sharpness and vitality which had been so noticeable at previous meetings. "Why do you worry your pretty head about business?" he asked. "Leave it to me and Gabriel."

"But I am worried," I told him. "Gabriel can't negotiate with the General's lawyers until he knows what is on your mind."

"Well," said Shaw, "I shall write him. But he should let me deal with *my* contract. And he should take care to arrange his own better than he did last time."

"But how can Gabriel make *any* contract until your intentions are clear?"

It was plain that Shaw wasn't listening. He leaned back in his armchair, his eyes on the opposite wall. "Gabby must get ready and do something fast for I won't keep long," he said in a barely audible voice. "Do you realize I am to die very soon?" I shook my head and he added impatiently, "I am dying. It's a peculiar sensation to be aware that perhaps tonight or tomorrow or in a few days all will be finished for me."

"You can live for many years yet."

He clung to my sentence and answered meditatively, "Yes, three more years perhaps, or four at most. But what's the use? It wouldn't make much difference. You can't possibly understand all this. Young people are unable to realize death. How can they know how it feels each day to be weaker, to be waiting for oblivion? It's worse than death itself."

Shaw was silent now, his eyes half-closed. I thought that he looked like the ancient dead tree, with its weather-worn, pale, wrinkled trunk, which stood by our farm road as the tombstone of its own vanished life. Shyly I broke the silence. "Gabriel loves you and I suppose he doesn't want to think of your death."

"Nonsense. Sentimental idiocy. He shouldn't mind me at all." Shaw seemed to be alert now and embarrassed by his momentary weakness. "Only the business is important: he wants to make money and so do I—though it is no use as the taxes are taking everything." He went into a long, complicated explanation to the effect that the more money he made the more taxes he paid and the poorer he became.

I listened patiently and then said, "I don't understand business at all. But I feel that if only business mattered, this world would be a very sad place. If there hadn't been anything else, then you yourself, G. B. S., wouldn't have written your plays in order to teach by making fun of social lies and false illusions. Instead, you would have been a banker."

His eyes ran over me smilingly. "Well, my child, you are a sentimentalist, too. Here you are, with all your assets. You should be an actress again. Instead, you are wasting yourself on him, throwing away your best years, while he is so busy with himself that he cannot even appreciate it. And you will never have security at his side. I am very uneasy about him."

Shaw promised to reconsider the matter of the English rights —which he did. But instead of airmailing the contract he dispatched it by ordinary mail. It took two months to arrive, only to get lost in Mexico City, for it had been sent to a by-then obsolete address of Gabriel's.

"On Monday Holy Week started and, in Mexico, all who are able flee the city," Gabriel wrote to Shaw. "I took advantage of this for a checkup at Mayo's. Doctor Buie is very satisfied with my condition . . ."

He was lying. He never told Shaw or me that new malignant tissues were found and that he needed radium treatment. Against his doctor's advice, he left Mayo's and flew to New York to meet with his lawyers and the lawyers of the General. He was then to fly back to Mexico City.

"It is Good Friday," Gabriel wrote me from New York, "and I am fasting and praying today for our salvation. I hope this is our last separation. I cannot bear life without you ... I arrived here from Mayo's in horrible pain and like a perished soul I lay in my hotel room in this infernal Babylon, tortured by lawyers ..."

General Rodríguez invited me to Mexico, and since Gabriel realized that he had to return to Mayo's for treatment, I was to meet him in Rochester and then fly with him to Mexico City.

Before leaving London, I called up the doctor. I told him that I was to join my husband and that this was goodbye. He was silent for a time. Then: "I always knew you belonged to him."

At the Rochester airport, Gabriel avoided my embrace. Later, as I sat silent in the car, he said: "There is a lie in your eyes." I felt the rosebud from the bouquet the doctor had sent me burning on the lapel of my suit.

For our few days' stay Mrs. Mayo gave us again our beloved cottage at Mayo-Wood Farm. As I entered, there were vases and vases of flowers—Gabriel's welcome to the place where we had been so happy. But now he did not reply to my thanks and went to unload the luggage. In the bathroom, I took the doctor's farewell letter, tore it to small pieces, and flushed it down the toilet.

A few days later, we were on the plane to Mexico—close again and trying to believe in our happiness. We landed in Mexico City late at night. Gabriel looked around for the General's car, which was supposed to meet us. There was no car and no message. "There must be some misunderstanding," Gabriel assured me.

But there wasn't. Gabriel never saw General Rodríguez again. A letter at the Del Prado Hotel informed us that, for the time being, the general had withdrawn from all business deals.

Even Gabriel lost his balance at this latest blow: "Everything I touch becomes ashes," he said. "Why? Why is all this happening to me?"

But as long as we were in Mexico, he decided to try to achieve his ends in another way. Ben Smith, "Sell 'Em Short Ben," an old friend, offered us his unoccupied apartment in a lovely modern house. I met Cantinflas again, and Dolores Del Río, Diego Rivera, and other figures of Mexico City's colorful society.

Gabriel was busy with new hopes and new negotiations, but every day it became more obvious that there was nothing for us in Mexico. How was he to confess the failure to Shaw, who had just written how much he dreaded "another fiasco"? How was he to tell Shaw that the paradise of the "fairytale land," the "last free country," had turned him out cold?

One day Gabriel tried to save a huge black ant from drowning in the shower. "He was like me," he said, "that desperate ant. He was running around in circles like a maniac, and though I opened the door for him, he couldn't see it. Maybe there is a door open for me somewhere and I can't see it either."

He grew more and more irritable. He moved into a separate bedroom, saying that he preferred to be alone. I lay awake at night, gazing at the stripes of light on the ceiling. Lately I often thought of the doctor, but I never mailed the letter I had written to him a few days earlier after a lunch with Cantinflas, when I had jokingly asked the comedian if it were true that in Mexico one could get a divorce within a week.

"Why don't you do it?" Gabriel said after we left Cantinflas. "Here is the great opportunity for both of us." His face was hostile. For the rest of the day, we did not speak. He knew well, I thought, that my question was not serious, yet he jumped at the idea of divorce. Perhaps with his coldness and unbearable moods he was actually using his "Machiavellian" method to force *me* to take the step.

I left the apartment and looked around the noisy, dirty Mexican streets, wondering what I was doing there. Then I went to the writing room in the Del Prado Hotel and wrote to the doctor, saying that I had missed him and maybe, after all, I cared for him. The envelope was halfway into the mailbox when I pulled it back.

The tension between us grew unbearable. After several small fires, it erupted. I burst out with all the things that had been accumulating in me over the years. He did not interrupt. "Tomorrow I'll pack and go back to England and let it be finished," I concluded.

In the morning, after a silent breakfast, Gabriel pulled a long letter from his dressing gown pocket. He said he had written it during the night and that he was going to read it to me "so you cannot interrupt me."

"Through the whole night," he read, the sheets trembling slightly in his hand, "I pondered, seeking a way to put an end to your feeling of terrible insecurity." At this point, he raised his voice accusingly. "When a woman takes away a man's faith in himself, everything is taken from him: his pride, his joy in the ability to make her happy. By feeling insecure, you show disbelief in me."

My eyes wandered over his face: his mouth tight in bitter lines, his hair disheveled. He was unshaven and he looked heavy, the open dressing gown bulky about him. But the old sensation of his being a living part of me came back.

"It is difficult to see into the depths of the human heart. You are a very normal, ideal woman and have a right to all the joys of life. But I—I have the dark, self-torturing character of Orestes, and lack practical knowledge of life. Can we live together? It is untrue that I wish to free myself from you; just the opposite. I feel that you have met somebody in England and you want to go and find happiness with him. Yet all this is illusion: one can't find real happiness outside of one's own soul."

He glanced up from the letter, then read on: "But if you wish, let us get a divorce. Yet, I ask you for one more chance: let us keep our divorce secret for six months and, during that time, let us try again together—without handcuffs. If these six months should prove that we can't live without each other, then let us get married again and forever. I would then be sure that you really meant it, that it isn't convenience or pity which holds you at my side."

He finished and looked into my face. His words had sounded like my own feelings: he wanted to be free, yet he held me back. The gall of yesterday was gone, but I knew it would return. There was no cure for us.

"There is no way out for us," I said aloud, after a silence. "There is no way out."

In the afternoon, we lit candles in the Cathedral.

Two weeks later, I returned to England on the *Queen Mary*. Gabriel was already in Rome to start the *Androcles* negotiations anew. Since the day we had lit the candles, one quarrel had followed another and our goodbye in New York was cool. On my part, this separation hurt less than previous ones and I welcomed my growing indifference, realizing at the same time that it was only a sort of numbness—the numbness of one tortured beyond the capacity to feel.

There were friends on the boat: Ben Goetz, the head of Metro in London, and Goldie, his wife; Jack Benny and his wife, Mary; Phil Harris and Alice Faye; Rochester and his wife. All of them sang "Happy Birthday" to me on June 12 and Gabriel's radiogram wished me happiness "with him or without him."

When the *Queen Mary* reached Southampton and the phone cables were connected, I called the doctor in London.

"I am sorry for my long silence," I wrote to Gabriel in Rome, "but I have been unable to write to you. As you asked me, I went to see Shaw yesterday."

Shaw had looked very weak. Again he expressed worry at the way things were going, saying that he did not expect to live long enough to see either Gabriel's next picture or the launching of the long-planned Shaw-Pascal Film Company. Gabriel, he grumbled, was proceeding as if he, Shaw, were going to be around for another half-century.

"Gabby," he declared, "*has* to make a successful picture without delay to save his career." Shaw said he would not renew another option on his plays until Gabriel had made *Androcles,* the filming of which was still in the planning stage. Again he insisted that I play Lavinia, adding that he had visualized a face like mine when he wrote the part. I demurred, saying that the film needed box office names. Shaw countered that his and Gabriel's names were sufficient.

"I am afraid," I wrote Gabriel in my account of the visit, "that G. B. S. is going to write you about this again. Well, I don't want to play Lavinia. If you finally start to work, we can't take any chances and you will need names . . . Thursday, I am going to see *The Cocktail Party* and, as you asked me, I will look up Rex Harrison backstage." Gabriel still wanted Rex to play the Emperor in *Androcles*.

My visit had not pacified Shaw. There was a new delay in *Androcles* and he wrote to Rome:

"A fiaschetto! Ugo Sola writes that you cannot have the studios until October.

"Meanwhile, you will have nothing to do but come back and slobber sentimentally over me, wasting your time and mine.

"It is exasperating."

Then another letter, on June 18, 1950:

"I have been uneasy about you lately. You are laying out your life as if I were sure to live another fifty years and putting all your eggs in that quite illusory basket, accordingly. It is extremely unlikely that I shall live another three years and not certain that I shall live another three days; and when I die, your connexion with me will have been a mere episode in your career. You will have half your life before you which you must fill up with new friendships and new interests ... never forget that dealing with very old people can be only transient ... look for a young Shaw; for though Shaws do not grow on gooseberry bushes, there are as many good fish in the sea as ever came out of it. Anyhow, you must live in your own generation, not in mine."

A postscript added: "Devotion to an old crock like me is sentimental folly."

Gabriel's answer that "you are young enough for me" and a present of fresh fruits from Italy to the old vegetarian made Shaw angry.

"Some tons of green figs just arrived from you," he wrote to Rome on July 3, 1950. "You must be perfectly mad. I do not eat green figs oftener than six times a year ... I object strongly to people sending me food as if I were a pet child in their care ... You say you are coming to England to SEE ME. I will *not* see you until you have given serious consideration to what I wrote to you about the future ... I will have no more of your damned sentiment on any terms. If you will not take care of your interests and think of your prospects when I am dead, I must do it for you. So stop sending the victuals and stay where you are. Don't force me to break with you for your own sake. Much as I value your art work, I don't want to ruin you. Above all, don't come back with a sack full of vegetables and oblige me to go all over this again."

Androcles was still uncertain when Gabriel returned to England. He missed Shaw's birthday on July 26. I went to Ayot in his place with a birthday cake with six candles on it, representing the six years remaining until his hundredth birthday.

"Gabriel has to make other films than mine," Shaw told me. "Apparently, he cannot raise the money for another Shaw film. I am not in vogue, so he should do other films or you will end up in the poorhouse."

We were flying now to Venice for the opening of the film festival; after that we were to fly to India as guests of the Maharaja of Jaipur. Gabriel had never forgotten his vision of a film about Mahatma Gandhi and had decided to accept Jaipur's invitation.

We had met the Maharaja and his beautiful wife, Ayesha, the Princess of Cooch Behar, in New York, at a party given by Mrs. Winston Guest for the Duke and Duchess of Windsor. At the party, Gabriel had talked about the Gandhi film with Jaipur, who expressed a great interest in the project and hinted at a possible partnership. A meeting in Delhi with Prime Minister Nehru was also arranged. We were to meet the Maharaja in Rome and then fly with him to India.

As always when new adventure lay ahead, Gabriel exuded magnetism. He wore his rakish smile and a flower in his buttonhole. He was now charming the stewardess by telling her fortune and assuring her of his gypsy clairvoyance.

"You never told *my* fortune," I complained, and put my palm in front of him.

He looked at both of my palms. Then he turned to me in utter astonishment: "There are millions in your hands," he said. "It seems that I am to leave you with millions. You remember the dream I wrote you about?"

He had dreamed, he had written recently from Rome, that he was dead and "floating in a pleasant way in a place between Heaven and Earth." He was explaining to the shadows around him how down below he was to produce the Bernard Shaw pictures and how he suffered with the financing problems and how he failed the Old Man. The shadows surrounded him, full of good will. "Don't worry," they said, "we will do it, we will help you because we like the Old Man. Financing doesn't mean a thing here. Let's go and start the ball rolling." Then, he wrote, I appeared "smiling triumphantly—but alive. You weren't a ghost. And you talked to me: 'You have the greatest success. You are making millions. Haven't I always told you that you handled things on earth the wrong way?'"

I smiled as I recalled the letter, which I thought was typical of Gabriel's vivid imagination and so never gave it a second thought. Little did I know that in a few years' time Gabriel was indeed to make "millions," perhaps, who knows, with the help of those good shadows. But the money would not be for him; he would be dead.

Venice was lively with the Film Festival. Gabriel had invited Jean Simmons and her sister to stay with us for a few days at the Hotel Excelsior on the Lido. We had a good time. Gabriel was irresistible. His impish mood manifested itself one night after a dinner party in Venice. It was midnight, and the lobby of the Danieli Hotel, where we were waiting for our vaporetto to take us back to the Lido, was filled with the rich and the famous. Two elderly gentlemen were relaxing quietly in armchairs nearby; they contrasted sharply with the rest of the crowd. Gabriel, pointing at the bald head of one of them, said, *"Lei, Signor, vede,* you have missed life, the whole beautiful show. You have never lived. Why?"

Surprised, the old man looked up, and, meeting Gabriel's friendly smile, answered, "Many of us have missed it."

Gabriel's voice was full of pity. "Yes, but you were on the wrong track altogether. Instead of being yourself, fully yourself, you lived for a dead world. You lived for books and you smell of their mould. You spent the divine gift of life on collecting rare manuscripts."

The old man looked surprised. "I have never had the pleasure of meeting you before."

The other man broke into the conversation, astonishment in his tone. "The Baron owns a famous library in Sicily. You must have heard about him."

"No, I haven't." Gabriel was swinging his cane. "But I am a magician. I feel things sometimes."

The old man called the Baron laughed now.

"You are a strange one," he said. "One seldom sees a face like yours. Who are *you?*"

"Vagabond, hobo, adventurer, a misbegotten faun." Gabriel was in his element; he adored talking about himself. "A good-for-nothing, who should have become a monk and a mystic but instead sold his soul to be a film producer."

"And she?" The Baron turned toward me with a smile. "The white Princess; is she your daughter?"

"She has the misfortune to be my wife." Once more Gabriel's voice was full of pity.

At the Bombay airport, Jaipur officials in large red turbans bowed to our Maharaja, touching his knees and garlanding him with flowers. Huge blue stars hung above us as we drove through the spicy air of the Malabar Hills to the palace of the Maharaja of Baroda, where we were to have dinner. Bombay had a prohibition law, so there were no drinks, and I, who almost never drank, was one avid thirst. What was more, according to the customs of the East, dinner was served about eleven at night. The irony of things: on my first day in India, the guest of two famous maharajas, I was never thirstier—or hungrier—in my life!

A bumpy four-hour ride through monsoon clouds in our host's private plane brought us to Jaipur State. Green jungles beneath us, then Jaipur City, a coral-pink ornament among ragged hills. As we left the plane, soldiers in white uniforms greeted His Highness with blasting trumpets. Our friend Jai was a real king here.

Rambagh Palace: domes and Moorish colonnades, wings and wings stretching out endlessly. Armies of silent servants in the cool, open corridors, their bare feet slapping softly on the marble floors. Cocktails under the colonnades with large electric fans beating the air. The slow rhythm of marble stairs leading down to the park. A fountain lit in vivid colors, a fiery jewel pinned on the darkness. Bells and gongs sighing from a hidden temple.

In the early hours of morning, a blood-curdling scream, then another answering from a distance. The scream rose again, followed by a chorus of cries. Gabriel sat up in bed. "India!" he said in a delighted voice. "India is awakening." The peacocks and the monkeys were having their morning get-togethers. Sunrise blazed on the curtains ... Once more I was awakened, this time by a clash of arms, the sonorous bellow of commands and the blast of trumpets: the changing of the guard. I felt sorry for all dwellers in kingly palaces; private citizens at least could sleep at dawn.

In the mornings, we cooled ourselves in the large swimming pool. Then we would go sightseeing. Jaipur City, with its lace-like raspberry-pink houses, is, I think, one of the most attractive cities in the world. The wide streets vibrate in colors: saris in red, yellow, green, and gold. The open shops of brassworkers tinkle. Fruit vendors balance heavy scales with ripe fruits.

Everywhere herds of ruminating cows with painted horns. A white-bearded *shaddu* with his begging bowl, the dark skin of his thin body as cracked as the crust of the dusty tree at his back. Peasants on bullock carts and saffron-robed monks on foot. A gypsy caravan with a bear cage and monkeys followed by a wedding crowd with a flower-crowned, dazzlingly garbed Mohammedan bridegroom going for his bride. Temples as monstrous as atavistic fear in the subconscious. A smiling Brahmin offering us sweetmeats and champa garlands.

Some evenings, we either played canasta at the Jaipur Polo Club or went to parties in the westernized homes of the fashionable suburbs, where only a remote cry reminded one now and then that the jungle was but a few miles distant.

At the beginning of September, the Maharaja's birthday was marked by lavish festivities. We guests would gather in the evenings on the Moorish portico of the City Palace where a long row of murals pictured the Jaipur kings. Small wells gurgled from the mosaic floors to cool the air. Comfortable sofas and easy chairs faced the park below. The descending lawns were parted by enormous fountains lit by floodlights.

At work in his office at Rambagh Palace the Maharaja dressed like any New Yorker on a very hot day. But for the festivities, he was a true Oriental prince: silk brocade coat, tight jodhpurs, heavy necklaces of precious stones, a huge diamond holding the spray of white egret feathers on his turban. The buttons of his coat were rubies.

"I'd like to be on hand when you lose a button," I told him.

I stood by a column of the portico. The breeze ruffled the light material of my sari. Down below, near the fountains, a military band played gay waltz tunes. From time to time, flames and smoke rising from the bottom of the park marked the sacrificial fires in the family temple of the goddess Kali, from which deep, thudding chants and gong-beats broke through the waltz melodies with a sensual rhythm. It seemed to me then as if India had opened up and was breathing about me like a night-blooming flower, intoxicating with dreams one could never utter. It was one of those moments when one feels life full and ripe and overflowing, when one is truly alive.

A shadow lurked under the column where I was standing. Eyes glared up in a red blaze—a hyena.

The Maharaja drove me back to Rambagh Palace in his open sports car, walked with me up to the guest wing, and bade me goodnight. Once inside, I locked the entrance door which led onto the open corridor. I was alone, for Gabriel, who had gone to Delhi to talk with Prime Minister Nehru about the Gandhi film, had been delayed because of bad weather. He had called me earlier in the day, for not only were there no planes but the monsoon floods had cut off all train transportation as well.

After locking the entrance, I made certain that the other doors of our suite were also locked. I don't know what I was afraid of in the well-guarded palace; I think I just wanted to lock India out.

I couldn't sleep for a long time. Outside, unseen lives hummed, stirred, sighed. India was gushing through the closed doors.

When I finally did sleep, it was only to be awakened by a startling knock. Frightened, I sat up in bed. Then the knocking became banging and a voice cried out in Hungarian, "Open up at once!" It was Gabriel, soaking wet. Pushing me aside without a word, he rushed into our bedroom and looked wildly around. When he saw nobody, he calmed down. Stuck in Delhi, he had become worried, thinking of me alone in a dream palace among the handsomest men in India, the Rajputs. He had rented a car with a chauffeur who, for good money, was willing to risk the monsoon floods.

*   *   *

Bombay again. In the lobby of the Taj Hotel, I noticed a Hindu in the colorless garb of the poorer classes following us to the elevator.

"Are you Mr. Gabriel Pascal?" he asked in fluent English. "I have been waiting for you at the command of Shri Meher Baba. He has come up from Poona to see you and is expecting you at seven o'clock tomorrow morning. I shall be here to fetch you."

When Gabriel returned after his meeting with Baba, he was sparkling. Merely being with Baba, he said, had given him back his vitality.

"Baba is going to the Himalayas, to be alone," Gabriel told me. "After that he'll start his 'fiery tour' through the country. How I would like to join him!" He looked at me. "You are the only woman I am able to love and stay married to. But if you ever leave me, I'll come back here to Baba and be a monk."

He talked on, recounting his morning's visit: "Baba used his alphabet board and called me his Phoenix again, and told me that I have been with him in several reincarnations. He promised me powers which I need for my great mission in the West. He prophesied that my career will rise high, higher than ever. I shall make many films and the Gandhi film will be a world sensation. He also said that the time is near when he will break his long silence and utter the 'word.'" Gabriel referred to the saving "word" which the silent master had promised years ago and for which all the disciples were waiting.

Our one-week stay in Bombay was drawing to its close. Gabriel had several meetings with Mahatma Gandhi's son, Devadas. We also met Mrs. Krishna Hutheesing, Nehru's younger sister.

Gabriel felt he had achieved his ends in India. The partnership with the Maharaja of Jaipur seemed to have been secured, and Mr. Birla, the greatest financier of India, was seriously interested. Also, Prime Minister Nehru had given his consent, which he confirmed later in a letter to Gabriel: "I feel . . . that you are the man who can produce something worthwhile. I was greatly interested in what you told me about this subject [the Gandhi film] and your whole approach to it."

We were still in Bombay when the shocking news of Bernard Shaw's injury came. He had fallen in his garden, fracturing his thigh, and had been taken to the hospital. Gabriel was very worried. He recalled that, at the time of his last visit, before leaving for our trip, he had had a presentiment that he would never again see Shaw alive. Shaw had told him that he "wanted to die." Mrs. Laden's reassuring cable that Mr. Shaw was comfortable relieved him somewhat, but remembering Shaw's parting words, he wrote him: "What is the use of your staying here longer if the world is no longer a joy for you? Your desire now is to go back to Nirvana where you can use your soul-power in the service of the entire Universe, instead of limiting it to this crazy little globe. It must be exciting to be about to go away on the greatest of all adventures, leaving behind the sufferings and the small illusions. But I do wish that you could find the desire again to stay with us a little longer . . ."

With these words ended the long letter exchange between Gabriel and Shaw.

By the middle of October I was back in London. We hadn't wasted much time in Rome. I had gone to Belgium with Gabriel's Italian partner and his wife on a wild-goose chase to raise money. Gabriel was trying to do the same thing in New York. "I cannot return empty-handed to the sickbed of Shaw," he wrote.

Shaw had developed complications and now, back in his own house, was weakening fast. Mrs. Laden urged Gabriel to hurry back. Near the end of October she telephoned me: "Mr. Shaw is asking for Mr. Pascal," she said. Her voice broke. "He is dying."

I immediately cabled my husband in New York and drove out myself to Ayot St. Lawrence on a gray autumn afternoon. When I reached Ayot I saw, as usual, none of the inhabitants of the old houses; many times, passing through this sleeping village, I had wondered if the people ever came outdoors. But further on, behind the green graveyard of the church, the road was black with cars. Around the usually abandoned red phone booth at the bend, reporters thronged like a dark cloud of vultures waiting for a death.

Mrs. Laden, pale, opened the door. For easier nursing, the downstairs dining room had been converted into a bedroom, where Shaw lay on a narrow, simple bed, facing the windows.

When I came in, he was lying on his back, covered to his chin, his knees pulled up. As I sat down beside him, he turned to me with a faint smile. There was a deep peace in his blue eyes. His mind seemed as clear as ever; only his voice was weak. He asked me about our trip to India and about Prime Minister Nehru, and when I told him that Gabriel was still in New York negotiating about *Androcles*, he asked:

"But when will he be back?"

"I hope soon," I answered.

"I assume it will be too late," he said slowly. "It won't be long now with me. I am dying finally." He spoke as though he were conveying good news.

"Oh, don't say that," I said.

My small wail angered him and strengthened his voice: "How much longer do you want me to lie here paralyzed and be watched like a monkey by those outside?"

Of course he knew about the reporters. I murmured, "I'm sorry."

He interrupted me impatiently. "Sorry for what? That an old man is dying? You shouldn't be sentimental about death. It's a good thing. Sentiments are a waste of time anyhow. They don't help."

"But compassion can help. It has power . . ." I didn't finish my sentence.

Shaw didn't answer and, after a silence, I got up to leave. As I did so, he turned his eyes toward me and smiled. Then he drew his hand from under the blanket to shake mine. His was as lifeless as a dead leaf. On a sudden impulse, I bent over and kissed his hand and then rested my warm cheek against its icy coldness. He did not take it away, even when my tears ran down on it. What did he feel when my tears wet his hand—he, who never admitted dropping a tear of sympathy for anyone, who had written, "Shaw neither gives nor takes such quarter?" Did my uncontrolled tears annoy him—or did they, in his nearness to death, comfort him? When I straightened up, he said in a soft voice, almost singing: "*Au revoir,* my dear, *au revoir.*"

His eyes looked beyond the window and the darkening garden. His smile was strange and detached. Then the chant came again: "*Au revoir, au revoir.*"

At the door, I turned back for a last look. I saw his nose, aquiline above the sunken pale cheeks, the white hair and the beard, and I heard again the tune, soft as a sigh, as if he were singing to himself: *"Au revoir, au revoir, au revoir."*

Gabriel was too late to see his great friend. He rushed back from New York with a suitcase full of vitamins from Paul de Kruif only to find that Shaw had died that same morning. He knelt in the deep silence of the room, then kissed the waxen face framed so peacefully by the white beard.

Only a handful of people attended Shaw's funeral at the Golders Green Crematorium: those who were close to him and the representatives of the Public Trustee of his estate.

A lone old lady stood outside the building. She had once been a suffragette. She stood there erect, holding high an old ragged flag, the flag of the suffragettes.

As if in a last salute to Shaw, the fierce fighter for all human rights, the wind flapped the faded flag against the gray November sky.

Chapter 8

My Fair Lady and the Sink-Eagle

BERNARD SHAW'S ashes were scattered in his garden. The Public Trustee took over the Shaw estate and recognized Gabriel's rights to certain Shaw plays.

After a few weeks in the South Street apartment Gabriel flew back to the United States to continue negotiations for *Androcles and the Lion*. A month later, I was rolling the carpets with camphor balls and covering the furniture. The huge trunks in the hall stood as symbols of high seas, adventure and a new life—all as a result of Gabriel's cable: "Deal with RKO signed."

His letter asked: "Will you give me another try? Maybe now I can fulfill my promise: to give you happiness and security. If you come, my true, loving heart is waiting for you, but not only my heart but my strong fist. No criticism. I am the boss." Wasn't he the boss always?

Mother and I crossed on the *Queen Mary* through icy gales. Three days on the Super Chief, then the white-washed Spanish station of Los Angeles; sunshine, palmtrees, bougainvilleas and Gabriel's tanned face and his smile. He was buoyant: "RKO is the happiest studio, the friendliest atmosphere, everybody loves me."

A drive down endless Sunset Boulevard; then the cool canyons of Beverly Hills, a steep road and a lovely house at the top. Large, elegantly furnished, it had a tennis court and an Olympic-size swimming pool and, at the door, two smiling Filipinos, a cook and a butler. Gabriel grinned happily at my surprise. I swallowed a comment about reckless spending. The house, once the hideaway of the eccentric billionaire Howard Hughes, had at an earlier time been occupied by another mystery man, Serge Rubinstein, who was to become the victim of an unsolved murder in New York.

The table on the terrace was lavishly set for a Sunday brunch and there were friends to meet me: Tim Durant, the great horseman, and his daughter, Marjorie; Gabriel's new publicity girl, Sharman Douglas, Ambassador Douglas' daughter; Laura Archera, once a concert violinist, now a film-cutter. Laura and I were to become fast friends.

When the guests left, I collapsed for a nap. I glanced sleepily around my beautiful new bedroom and took a deep breath of the California air; then I fell asleep to a choir of cicadas. Slowly awakening after hours of deep sleep, I felt like a child again, in my warm, soft bed on a Christmas morning, conscious only of something wonderful waiting for me. I delayed opening my eyes, trying to prolong the sweetness of expectation. "I'm happy." Suddenly I could characterize the emotion I was feeling. "I'm happy." The discovery amazed me, as the realization of sudden and miraculously regained health would amaze a sick person. For all those past years, I hadn't even been conscious of the lack of happiness.

In the coming weeks, Gabriel was a changed man. I wondered how we could ever have quarreled. He was preparing his film with dynamic energy. He was up at six, singing in his shower; then off to the studio. But soon his enthusiasm over "the happiest studio" began to change and the sharp lines of the wolf face reappeared. As usual he did not tell me much, but I gathered that there was a disagreement between him and the studio. He had hoped to meet RKO's owner, Howard Hughes, and talk things over, but the elusive billionaire was unreachable. Garboesque secrecy shrouded him; most of the studio executives had never met the man who signed their checks. But his shadow stretched over the RKO lot, and nothing could be done without his invisible okay.

Gabriel's first difficulty was the casting of the title role, Androcles. That part was the crux of the play, and he had had many discussions with Shaw about the type of actor who should play it. They both agreed that the hen-pecked, heroic little tailor was a Chaplinesque part. Cantinflas would have been perfect for it, but he was now unavailable. Gabriel approached his old friend Chaplin, but he was busy with his own film, *Limelight;* besides, RKO would never have agreed to him, for then, in the heyday of McCarthyism, he was under the cloud of suspicion as a Communist. That is also why Gabriel could not get his second choice, José Ferrer; though it was never proven, he too was suspected of being a Communist sympathizer. Then Gabriel thought of Harpo Marx, the silent Marx brother. The test he made was fabulous, but the studio said no. Finally, a fine young comedian, Alan Young, was signed for the part; but Gabriel knew it was a compromise. Alan Young, good actor though he was, was not the image of Androcles. Jean Simmons played Lavinia and her captain was Victor Mature. Ferrovius was played by Robert Newton. Poor Bob loved a drink or two, and that was to create many problems during shooting. Gabriel's original choice for the Emperor, Rex Harrison, was not available, but he succeeded in getting Maurice Evans, an old Shavian expert. Alan Mowbray, Reginald Gardiner, and Elsa Lanchester were also in the cast. Gabriel felt it was a lucky sign that he could secure his favorite cameraman, Harry Stradling, with whom he had worked on *Pygmalion.*

The frustrations were just beginning. Gabriel couldn't get the man he wanted as director, and the studio insisted on Chester Erskine, who had worked on the screenplay with Ken Englund. "Shaw would have thrown this in the ashcan," Gabriel said after reading the first scenes of their effort. He tried to work things out with the scenario writers, but time was limited and he had either to call off the film or start shooting.

When the cameras began to roll, it became obvious that he and the director did not see eye to eye. To overcome the rumors that "nobody can work with Pascal," Gabriel tried not to blow up, but he came home every day more and more disgusted.

"I should get rid of my director or quit," he would say. "He has the typical Hollywood conception of the whole thing and I should not compromise. I should call off the film. But how can I do that to you? I myself wouldn't mind being a hobo again."

Gabriel's office in the studio was once more loud with his fits of rage, and his yelling at his associates could be heard two blocks away. I wondered how Renato Sideli, his faithful assistant whom he brought over from England, could take those tantrums.

As Gabriel had a contract for two more pictures with Jean Simmons at RKO, we had decided to buy a house. We found one in the hills of Brentwood, near the ocean. Pure Spanish in style, it had fifteenth-century grilles and fixtures brought over from Spain by the silent film star, Milton Sills, who had built it. With it came three acres of beautifully landscaped ground, a large swimming pool and bathhouse. Gabriel was exultant. Never a lovelier place, never such trees and birds, such green lawns and flowers. We would live there forever.

An aging gardener also came with the place. He was a Dutchman named Fred, and the two of us were friends at first sight. I can still see his thin figure clad in tattered blue overalls, his overlarge glasses held up by the button of his nose, a faded, greasy hat on his head. He had a female pointer with a shiny black and white coat, called Lilli. That gave us two dogs, for we had recently fallen in love with a crazy, noisy Keeshond pup named Viking.

We were about to move into the new house when Gabriel showed me that "strong fist" he had warned me about before I arrived in California. We had been invited out. Usually, I was ready first, but that evening, my Italian friend Laura Archera was visiting me. Chatting in my bedroom, I forgot the time, and I was still undressed when Gabriel, showered, shaved, and dressed, appeared from his quarters. Seeing me still disheveled, he snorted at me. Laura's presence made him want to demonstrate that he was the man of the house; it also prompted me to abandon the never-answer-him-back policy which had worked miracles lately. Sitting at my dressing table and half-turned toward him, I haughtily said something designed to put him in his place and turned back to the mirror. As I did so, I became aware of a fast-approaching shadow. A slap cracked. My earring flew into a corner and I became slightly deaf in the right ear.

"I should have done that a long time ago to teach you who is wearing the pants in this house," Gabriel yelled. "If you dare open your mouth now you'll get another one."

Laura, the innocent cause of it all, sat frozen. Gabriel turned on her. "And you're a bitch, too, looking at me with such eyes, as if I had killed my wife! She's got only what she has long deserved! And I'll slap your face, too, if you don't stop staring at me that way! Oh, how I hate women."

Recovering my voice, I blew up. "Get out of here! Go alone to that party! I'm going to pack and leave you forever!"

He ran out, banging the door.

With the marks of his fingers burning on my right cheek, with half an earring and my chignon fallen over my shoulder, I sat demolished. I could hear him starting the car. The noise of the motor grew louder; the engine must have flooded. A sudden worry struck me: if he drove in a rage, he might kill himself. I slipped into my dress, fastened my hair, put back the earring and, followed by Laura, hurried down to the garage.

Gabriel was still trying to start the car. When he saw us approaching, he gave us the angry look of a trapped beast.

"I *am* going with you, and we'll drop Laura on our way," I said, getting in beside him. An inarticulate growl was the answer. I knew it for what it was, a shy expression of regret. He drove silently through Beverly Hills, but on Sunset Boulevard he cheered up.

"I think," he said with a grin, "I should have given you a slap on the other side of your face too. Then your color would be balanced." He turned to Laura. "You see, this is the way a man should handle a woman. From now on, I am going to beat her and make love to her—but no conversation!"

For our first dinner party our new house was festive with flowers and candles. The guests included Mr. and Mrs. Aldous Huxley, Clare Boothe Luce, Gerald Heard and Curt Freshel, an antivivisectionist and a friend of Shaw's. Laura Archera was also present. I was happy and proud of our new home. I didn't want to remember the premonition I had had on our first night there. I hadn't been able to sleep and had walked out on the small balcony of my bedroom. The garden below was lovely in the moonlight, the bird of paradise trees reaching above the Spanish tiles of the roof, casting deep shadows.

Our first real home, I thought, and no need for fear any more. Our life was in order now and the future bright. But inside me was an eerie voice: "Nothing is yours here . . . it will be taken, taken."

In the new house, we missed the occasional visits of George Sanders and Zsa Zsa Gabor. In Beverly Hills, we had been nearer to their house in Bel Air and handy for them to come to— separately after fights and together when all was well. Occasionally I would be startled by piano music from the downstairs living room. If I heard a bass voice singing a nostalgic Russian song, I knew that George had just slammed the door of their Bel Air house behind him and that soon Zsa Zsa would turn up crying that George was a brute and yet she could not help loving him. And she would show me all the marks of the fight with relish.

In the beginning we went to some Hollywood parties, but Gabriel preferred to stay home and read or play chess, if he could get a partner. Marlon Brando, a good player, came sometimes and the two of them would sit there staring at the chess board for what seemed to be hours, while Brando's Mexican girl friend and I yawned.

We did go to one big party, given by Tim Durant for the Chaplins. *Limelight* was finished and Charlie and Oona were going to Europe. A few days earlier we had seen the film at a private showing, and, carried away, I could not help sobbing. I felt silly when the lights went on, and was badly in need of a handkerchief. Embarrassed, I had to ask Chaplin, who was sitting next to me, for his. He not only obligingly gave me a handkerchief, but seemed pleased to see one of his audience dissolved in tears. I was relieved to notice that Chaplin was crying, too.

All Chaplin's friends were at the party, proving that those who liked him were not afraid to be close to a man persecuted by the FBI and harassed by the "patriotic" newspapers. The party was a Hawaiian luau, with lobsters cooking in a pit, Hawaiian hors d'oeuvres and drinks, and Hawaiian music beating in the night air in the red flame of torches. The setting aroused an atavistic desire to gyrate, to which Chaplin was the first to respond. Twirling and twisting in a wild rhythm, with vapor rising behind him from the lobster pit, he looked like a young man. Oona, decades younger, sat erect, watching the performance a bit disapprovingly, but with the tenderness of an old and wise mother. Chaplin was soon joined by Doris Duke and others, but though I was itching to dance, Gabriel's stern look stopped me. I used to love to gyrate at gay parties, but I knew Gabriel's dislike of any "display" on my part.

Gabriel's mysterious "brother" and his wife visited us unexpectedly in Hollywood, but I was never to learn the truth of his relationship with Gabriel, and I never asked. I sensed Gabriel's reluctance to talk. When we first met in Paris he had told me about the home he was taken from and the woman who took his first toy, that red drum, to give it to her own son. And now here was that "blond boy," grown into a skinny middle-aged man, and his wife, a plump, vivacious Italian Contessa. No two men could look more different than Gabriel and this "brother." The brother had done well with his life and was now a shipping magnate in Venezuela; he lived in great prosperity between his luxurious villa in Caracas and his home in Italy. He had come to the United States for a cure of his arthritis, and in the course of his trip he visited us. Gabriel was bitter about his "so-called brother," as he always referred to him, because though the brother had millions he hadn't helped Gabriel in the past.

They left and I didn't give them a second thought.

The lure of India, the message of Gandhi and his one "great mission"—to bring that message to the public—never let Gabriel rest. He was still working on *Androcles* at the studio, but his free moments were spent on the Gandhi film. His correspondence grew into an avalanche. He kept in touch with Prime Minister Nehru and his two sisters, Mrs. Pandit and Mrs. Krishna Hutheesing, and with the Minister of Health, the Princess Rajkumari Amrit-Kaur.

The Gandhi project attracted world interest and enthusiastic supporters, such as Howland H. Sargent, Assistant Secretary of State of the United States, and Chester Bowles, the American Ambassador to India. Ambassador Bowles wrote to Gabriel: "I believe you have a great opportunity to further the cause of Indo-

American friendship"; then he warned: "You are contemplating a complex and difficult task, one which could be fraught with all kinds of pitfalls."

How right he was: even the formation of an International Gandhi Film Committee—including Prime Minister Nehru, Albert Einstein, Aldous Huxley, Albert Schweitzer, James Michener, and, from the Ford Foundation, Paul Hoffman and Robert Hutchins—could not save the Gandhi project from intrigues. The rejection started in India, where there were attacks in the newspapers: how could Prime Minister Nehru ever have given permission to a "white producer from Hollywood" to do a picture about their Gandhi? But it was Gabriel's nature to challenge mountains and not be satisfied with the easy.

Casting the movie was no simple task. Prime Minister Nehru had said he was willing to have his part played by Charles Boyer, and, after a long correspondence and much diplomacy, Gabriel got permission to have the roles of Earl Mountbatten of Burma, the last Viceroy of India, and Lady Mountbatten played by Rex Harrison and Margaret Leighton. But the greatest problem seemed insoluble: who would play Gandhi? It was not just a question of physical resemblance; whoever played the part had to vibrate that blessedness, that *darshan,* which made even the scornful feel in Gandhi the presence of the indwelling Holy Spirit. Otherwise, Gabriel feared, the phenomenon of Gandhi could not be interpreted.

The numerous suggestions for the part of Gandhi included Alec Guinness and Yul Brynner, who were both photographed in a Gandhi mask. At one time Gabriel approached the Mahatma's saintly son, Manihal, who looked like his father. In a humble letter from South Africa, Manihal declined to play the role.

In India Gabriel had missed his meeting with Gandhi's famous pupil, Mihra Behn. She lived near the Kashmir border, working for the underprivileged, and was venerated as a holy woman. Born Madelaine Slade, daughter of a British Admiral, she had become a follower of Gandhi in her early youth. Gabriel thought of Greta Garbo for this part. The letter exchange between Mihra Behn and Gabriel grew into a deep spiritual friendship. Gabriel called her "sister," but they were never actually to meet.

Another problem was the script. Earlier Gabriel had bought

the screen rights of Vincent Sheean's book about Gandhi, *Lead, Kindly Light,* but for some reason neither Sheean nor his book seemed to be popular with the leading Indian politicians. Gabriel also had the permission of the Navijivan Trust to use Gandhi's autobiography, *The Story of My Experiment with Truth.* He engaged Gandhi's secretary, Pyerilal, to gather material and sent his friend Geza Herczeg, the writer, to India to work with him on the script.

The screenplay Herczeg presented on his return wasn't a workable script, and Gabriel thought of Aldous Huxley. We were invited to the Huxleys' for dinner, and I looked forward to meeting the writer whose works had always fascinated me, but whom at that point I had not yet met. I was to meet Gabriel, who was coming from the studio, at their house in Hollywood. I had some difficulty finding the street and the house. It was a modest building in a small garden, surrounded by similar houses, all of which looked like a crop of mushrooms that had grown out of the Hollywood flatland. I walked up to the door and rang the bell. The door was opened shortly, and in its dark frame stood the tall figure of Aldous Huxley. I was taken aback by his imposing appearance. His pale, noble face shone with intelligence. *"Ecce homo sapiens,"* I said to myself, as he stood there looking like the end-product of a successful evolutionary line.

The house was as dingy inside as outside. The sitting room was brightened by a marble bust of Maria Huxley. The living model soon came in with a platter of hors d'oeuvres from the kitchen. I liked Maria Huxley right away, yet strangely enough today nothing about her stands out in my memory except the peculiar way she used to signal their housekeeper in the kitchen for the next course. She would, without turning, reach back and knock rapidly on the kitchen door behind her chair.

The discussions with Huxley left Gabriel hesitant. "I'm afraid Aldous can't do a script of Gandhi," he told me. "He approaches spirituality like a scientist, with his mind and not with his heart. Just as his mysticism is more of a mental curiosity: it's a laboratory mysticism. He is cold and embarrassed by emotion. I don't think he understands that the dynamic force which moved Gandhi was his all-prevailing love."

In the end Huxley did not do the script. I lost track of the

Huxleys, and years later in New York I read that Maria Huxley had died. Poor Aldous, I thought, remembering how devoted he had been to her and how dependent he was on her. I don't recall how long after that it was when one day I was surprised by a call from my long-lost friend Laura Archera. She said she had just arrived in New York with her husband, and her husband was Aldous Huxley.

The great hope now was that the Ford Foundation, realizing the importance of Gandhi's message, especially in the face of the Communist threat in Asia, would undertake to finance the film. Paul Hoffman, then the head of the Foundation in Pasadena, and Robert Hutchins, who had just left the University of Chicago to join the Foundation, were all for the project. Gabriel met the board of directors and was asked to submit a budget. There were intimations that he could count on about $2 million from the Foundation.

The Gandhi film project had long ceased to be either a business venture or a vehicle to success for Gabriel. It was his vocation; he was possessed by it. "Gandhi," Gabriel would repeat, "was maybe the last grace sent us by God. We are at a crossroads: either we follow the Gandhian 'non-violence' or we perish by an atomic war."

Under Gandhi's influence, Gabriel had become a semi-vegetarian: that is, he would eat meat only when he couldn't avoid it. "I wish to be clean," he told me, "then I'll be more worthy to do the Gandhi film."

Gabriel's unformed desire to be a monk was brought to the surface by Gandhi's example. Like Gandhi, Gabriel too had been fighting against his sensuality since youth—but with less determination and success than Gandhi, who, in his early thirties, with his wife's consent, had given up the bodily part of their marriage. Earlier, too, Gabriel had often talked about our following in the footsteps of Francis and Clare of Assisi, in their celestial love. Little did we realize then that the path of the saints is dangerous for those unprepared for the heights and that there can be a morbid self-seeking pride in wrongly applied asceticism. Later he himself was to apprehend the mistake.

"Whoever denies the existence of his body will lose his spirit, too," he wrote two years later to a friend. ". . . Then came Gandhi and I believed that to make the life of Gandhi I had to live like Gandhi and be a faithful disciple of his. I completely stopped living a natural life. I was under that misapprehension and thus created an even greater abyss between me and Valerie."

I myself wasn't conscious of any danger then either. I was about to embark on the greatest adventure of the spirit: a search for God and my own soul. It all started with my reading about Gandhi. Earlier, I had listened to Gabriel's enthusiasm about him with a mixed feeling of boredom and downright worry: how could he waste his time with something so far-fetched and hardly profitable as a film about this man? Now I understood. Gandhi's life and his words pierced me with their truth. The question which had puzzled me when I read about Saint Francis came up again: what made an ordinary, rather vain, rather oversexed young man, at the beginning of a promising career, turn suddenly in another direction and end up as a Mahatma? It was not a one-day change into a Mahatma: it was a day-by-day victory over himself from the moment when he found love to be the answer to hatred and race prejudice.

I did not realize then that Gandhi had begun to change me, too. The St. Francis story had left a deep impression on me, but it was a story at times lost in a medieval naivete, somewhat disturbing to the modern mind. Gandhi, however, was a twentieth-century saint. Gandhi dared to practice what he preached and proved that it could be done: that moral principles could be applied not only individually, but in politics, and that one should not waver from truth, even against the interest of one's own party or nation.

My interest in Gandhi led me to study Hinduism and I ended up with the Vedanta. I don't think that anyone could have been more absorbed by a detective book than I was by those thoughts on God, the human soul, and eternity. I read and read with burning thirst and almost cried out with joy on finding ideas which, although they had never come to the surface of my mind, seemed to have been always known to me.

And now, everything suddenly opened up. In my excitement I

thought that I was reaching up to the Infinite. I did not realize
that I was merely savoring the joy of an intellectual discovery of
Truth: that between finding a knowledge about God and a real
unity with Him there was a tremendously cruel mountain to
climb. A mountain of self-annihilation where each rock under
foot would be a fragment of the ego one is shedding. One must die
for the self and then God can enter. You must die to live, said
Christ; you must be "poor in spirit," detached from the things of
the world which you should use "though not using them" and be
without desire and greed.

And I desired everything. Pleasures on an artistic and grand
scale. The enthronement of my own person in the fullness of life.
Renunciation of self struck me as an atrocity against my mind
and an ugly horror against my flesh. So I chased those disturbing
thoughts of detachment from my mind. It was so much more fascinating to sit around the blue pools of Beverly Hills and feel
oneself extremely elevated and above the ordinary crowd as one
pondered and talked about God.

It was Laura Archera who took Gabriel and me to the Vedanta
Society in Hollywood one Sunday. Gerald Heard lectured that
day. Afterward we wandered among the compound of buildings
and were introduced to the head of the Mission, Swami Prabhananda. The Vedanta Missions, I learned, had sprung up all over
the Western world and were under the direction of the Mother
Mission house in India, the Ramakrishna Mission. The religious
thought of the Vedanta is all-embracing, with "no location in
place or time," and "infinite, like the God it will preach"—the
sum total of the Truth in all religions, which has no place "for
persecution or intolerance . . . which will recognize divinity in
every man and woman."

The followers I met in the Hollywood Mission were all Americans, mostly from a Protestant background. Some of them took
the Vedantic way of complete renunciation and lived like monks
and nuns. The Mission had a retreat on an arid hilltop some distance from Los Angeles, and Swami Prabhananda took me there
one afternoon. We arrived at sunset at the simple building.
Among the wooden columns of its open portico, the breeze was
scented with the fragrance of sage bushes. The building stretched
long white arms and embraced a view of the setting sun and the

distant blue Pacific. The Swami of the monastery, in his saffron robe, greeted us, chanting a blessing, the palms of his hands touching as he bowed. His robe was blazing orange-red in the sunset, and Los Angeles, with its bustling freeways and smog and movie industry, seemed like a fast evaporating nightmare of *Maya*.

We all went to the chapel for an hour of prayer and meditation before dinner. The chapel was a small, round room, lit only by a few candles. We formed a circle and sat on the floor. I never, never knew how long an hour could be! After the Swami's intonation of prayer in English, silence followed; even the candlelights did not waver. I tried to think about God, but my thoughts soon scattered. I tried to say the Lord's Prayer, but could not keep my mind on the words beyond the first two sentences. I tried it again and again but soon even my scattered, worldly thoughts left me and I slumped into the stupor of a half-sleep. The Swami's voice awakened me. He said the concluding prayers and we filed out of the chapel to the simple dining room with long, wooden tables. Conversation started, and it was quite lively where Christopher Isherwood, a guest there for a retreat period, was sitting.

I continued with my spiritual reading and went occasionally to the Missions and talked to Swami Prabhananda, who was a very wise man. After a while, the pleasure of my books turned sour and once more I sensed a wall separating me from God, a wall the existence of which I had first realized while meditating in a chapel long ago in Switzerland. As strongly as I desired the world, I started to desire God, too. The longing I felt for Him was a longing of love exiled. Painful and sweet, it trembled through me —and then became still again. Once gone, it left a vague promise of some tremendous joy, but there seemed no way to recapture it.

And now I *wished* to pray. But not in the way I had done in the past, popping into a church with my thoughts only half there, but a real prayer in which God would touch me. But I had forgotten how to pray—perhaps I had never really known how. My childhood religiosity had covered me as superficially as my uncomfortable convent-school uniform, and I had shed the strict demands of the Catholic faith with that uniform. I had felt that I had outgrown both of them.

The desire to pray kept bothering me, and one evening, while I was reading my books, that desire became urgent. I got up and went out on the balcony. The black contours of the garden were sharply outlined against the starry sky. I guided my thoughts to the immensity of the Universe, the order and logic of it and the beauty of God. In half a second, my thoughts were scattered, as always. In India, the sages of Vedanta, when worshipping the Divine, contemplate the word *Om,* which signifies God-the-Absolute. "Om," I said, trying to embrace with my mind the Universe in the glory of God. "Om . . . Om." But there was only a silence in me. The word was unfamiliar, too. What if I call Him in my own tongue?

"*Isten,*" I said in Hungarian, forcing myself to concentrate. "*Isten,* God, I am sitting here in Your embrace, yet I don't feel You. Answer me, my God, come to me."

The dark wing of night overshadowed me. Everything was silent outside of me and inside. My heart was untouched. There was no answer.

"We have to give a party," Gabriel announced one day. Under the auspices of Frank Capra, the director, the film industry had invited the leading Indian film stars, directors, and producers to Hollywood. Because of the Gandhi film, it was only natural that we entertain them.

I engaged the most popular caterer in Hollywood, an amply proportioned Negro woman whom Gabriel promptly dubbed the Queen of Sheba. Knowing Gabriel's genius for messing up anything, I hoped I could keep him out of the whole affair.

On the morning of the party, Gabriel proclaimed at the breakfast table that to supplement the "stingy" menu I had ordered from the caterer, he was going to have our own help, a Hungarian couple, prepare a goulash dish. My voice was calm as I said: "You promised to keep out of this, didn't you? I can tell you that never in the one thousand years of Hungarian history has a Hungarian woman shared her kitchen without murder. The caterer and crew will be here at noon and they need the whole kitchen. I warn you that our cook was born in the middle of the paprika country. Even the Tartars and Turks wouldn't dare come near a woman from those parts."

"There will be goulash," said Gabriel. "And I want gallons of it. It's *my* party. I used to give kingly parties with hundreds of guests. I am a generous man, not a niggardly Dutch woman like yourself."

"There is going to be ..."

"I don't want to hear another word. I want goulash and I am the man here and you will do as *I* say. Don't dare look at me like that. And don't shrug your shoulders. Smile! And don't raise your voice—" His roar was echoed from beyond the dining room door. I realized that the echo came from our Hungarian couple, who were having their own division of opinion about something. I saw a pot flying through the kitchen window, hitting an orange tree and scattering the birds. Fred, the Dutch gardener, pulled his hat down and quickened his steps as he passed under the windows which, like so many megaphones, were broadcasting a Hungarian quartet.

At noon the caterer and her crew arrived in a caravan of station wagons. They crowded into the kitchen with their equipment, passing back and forth across the patio where the Hungarian butler had been demoted by his wife to chopping onions for the goulash. Half of his face was flaming red; his wife had scalded him with boiling milk during the morning's disagreement. Tears caused by the onions were dripping down his cheeks and his glances toward the kitchen window, through which the lines of his wife's plump figure were visible, betold homicide.

I was busy with the tent and the tables when the caterer, the Queen of Sheba, appeared like a heavy thundercloud and announced that she and her crew were leaving. She did not need to explain what had happened; I knew my Hungarians.

One hour later, my voice hoarse and every pore of my body perspiring, I had at last succeeded in assuring my cook that her goulash pots were not being thrown around but were being gently removed from the oven, that the kick she had received from Sheba was accidental, and that her husband had certainly misunderstood the Negro bartender who couldn't possibly have said "A fene egyen meg," since the bartender spoke only English and wasn't familiar with that popular Hungarian curse. Simultaneously, I managed to assure Sheba that the Hungarian couple had no race prejudice, that nobody in Hungary had, and that the only Negro ever to work in a Budapest hotel had been greatly honored and admired, even though it turned out that actually he was a bank-rupt Jewish merchant dyed black to look like a Moroccan waiter.

My peace negotiations had been constantly interrupted by phone calls from Gabriel's secretary at the studio announcing the additional guests Gabriel was inviting. When I protested that there wouldn't be enough food and seats, the secretary relayed Gabriel's reply to me: "Mr. Pascal says don't worry; there will be gallons of goulash and they can sit on . . . I am sorry, madame, I cannot repeat that."

I was hoping that Gabriel would be delayed at the studio until the party started, but I had just gotten out of the shower when I heard thunder below. He was home. Upon his arrival he had gone straight to the kitchen to "help." When I ran down barefoot in a dressing gown, I found Sheba's crew and the Hungarians in each other's hair and goulash flying everywhere. In the center of the kitchen, like two kingly beasts ready to spring, ruffled and blown up, the Queen of Sheba and Gabriel stood face to face. And goulash was dripping down on them from the ceiling.

When Sheba ordered her crew to pack and depart, only half an hour remained before the arrival of over two hundred guests. How I achieved an armistice and scraped the goulash together I do not know. It was a miracle born of desperation. The first guests arrived as I was scrambling into an evening dress and Gabriel was banging on my door, bellowing: "Aren't you ready yet? What were you doing the whole day? Why did I ever marry!"

One evening in the summer of 1951, less than a year after Bernard Shaw's death, Gabriel was bubbling over with a great idea. But as he was usually bubbling over with something new, I did not pay much attention. "You have nothing to worry about any more," he announced. "We are rich. I finally have the one coup of canasta and all the jokers in my hand. I have a million-dollar idea: I am going to turn *Pygmalion* into a musical."

My Fair Lady was born at that moment; but of course I didn't know it. I couldn't see the idea at all. My only role at that stage in *Lady's* history was to watch with anxiety as our savings were dissipated in the venture.

Gabriel made diplomatic approaches to the Shaw Trustee and

also began talks with Rodgers and Hammerstein. It soon became obvious that they were not convinced of the possibilities of the planned musical. Nor could Frank Loesser get excited. Cole Porter was a hope which Gabriel was very reluctant to give up, and he tried to persuade him time and again. But it was not until Gabriel met in New York with his old friend Lawrence Langner of the Theatre Guild that the ball began to roll.

Langner proposed the team of Alan Jay Lerner and Frederick Loewe. After a private showing of *Pygmalion,* they became enthusiastic. So did Langner and Theresa Helburn of the Guild. Negotiations started between the Guild, Gabriel, and the Shaw Trustee to find a way around the five-year license limit in Shaw's will, as the Trustee realized that no composer or financier could get involved in the project with such a time limit. A second problem was to sell the Shaw Trustee on Lerner and Loewe, for their hearts were set on Rodgers and Hammerstein.

Alan Lerner and Frederick Loewe came to our house in California on March 21, 1952. During lunch they seemed very eager to tackle the musical, provided Mary Martin would accept the role of Eliza Doolittle. Without her, they felt the musical would not stand up.

The lawyers and the Shaw Trustee finally found a way to change the five-year option clause, and the contract between Gabriel Pascal Enterprises and the Shaw estate was signed. Lerner and Loewe were only conditionally mentioned. The contract contained a clause which was to hang like the sword of Damocles over Gabriel's head: within six months he had to find a composer and a writer, but ones not less in stature than Rodgers and Hammerstein or Lerner and Loewe. But Rodgers and Hammerstein were now definitely out, and Lerner and Loewe still did not want to commit themselves without being assured of Mary Martin.

In the ensuing six months Gabriel and the Theatre Guild covered the entire field of writers and composers: Leonard Bernstein, Cole Porter, Betty Comden and Adolph Green, Gian-Carlo Menotti, and others. Then Gabriel received a letter from Lerner and Loewe in Honolulu, where they had gone to ruminate about the musical. They had written a few songs, but the more they thought about it the more they felt they could not write a verse without visualizing Mary Martin in the lead. Nothing remained then but to persuade her. She was then appearing in London in *South Pacific,* and Lawrence Langner and his wife, Armina, flew there to talk to her. It soon became clear that Mary did not think Eliza Doolittle was IT; also, there was her loyalty to Rodgers and Hammerstein, who were planning a new musical.

Lawrence Langner cabled the disheartening news to Gabriel, who then felt that he himself had to get into action. He phoned Langner in London that he had persuaded Lerner and Loewe to fly there and play some of their music for Mary; Langner must make a date with Mary right away. Then, as the Langners were going to Italy, Gabriel instructed Lawrence to go to Portofino and talk to Rex Harrison, "the only possible Professor Higgins."

Langner got tired of Gabriel's ordering everybody around and said so. He had not planned to go to Portofino, but to pacify Gabriel he called Rex long distance. The response was far from enthusiastic; Harrison was not interested and said he could not picture himself in a musical.

At this point Gabriel decided to leave *Androcles* in the cutting room and fly over himself, "to lay siege to Mary Martin in his own flamboyant manner," as Langner put it. As a starter, Gabriel decided to give a party in her honor.

"We were not too enthusiastic over the idea," said Langner, "but nothing could stop Gabby, who went at everything like a hurricane and swept all obstacles before him." Pascal the magician, Langner wrote, "simply waved the wand of his personality," and the party materialized in the stately mansion of a titled English lady. Gabriel took over the house and all the servants. Not satisfied with British food, he ordered a friend, a Viennese opera star famous for her cooking, to supervise the kitchen. She worked herself to death and the midnight buffet was fabulous, including as it did Indian curry dishes served Hindu style by the servants of the Jaipurs, who were among the guests. Langner learned that the Jaipurs were involved in Gabriel's financial hopes for the Gandhi film and remarked in his book: "I am not at all sure, in retrospect, that Gabby was not trying to kill two birds with one party."

But the bird Gabriel most wanted to catch had not so far appeared on the scene, though by now it was well past midnight and the party was in full swing, a sophisticated crowd of famous actors, artists, and aristocrats and beautiful women in beautiful gowns. Gabriel had even engaged a group of Hindu dancers to put Mary into a responsive mood. But there was still no sign of her. The curtain had long since fallen on *South Pacific* at the Drury Lane Theater, and she had had all the time and more to change into an evening dress. The supper had been eaten and the dances had been danced in the big ballroom "while poor Gabby wilted as he watched time go by"—and still no Mary Martin. The guests had begun to leave when at last there was a phone call: Mary Martin felt sick and could not come. This of course meant that she definitely was not interested in the *Pygmalion* musical; and Lerner and Loewe had to be persuaded that there must be some other Eliza somewhere.

With this "Machiavellian scheme" a flop, the accomplices—the Langners and Gabriel—stepped out into the cool air. Langner writes, "Gabby imbibed the mixture of petrol and oxygen fumes from the departing taxicabs and his spirit rose again. 'Lawrence,' he said, 'we shall not give up.'"

Back in New York the defeated team tried its best with Lerner and Loewe. They considered several Elizas. And on October 28, 1952, Lerner and Loewe reluctantly signed the contract to do the musical, "to be presented by the Theatre Guild in association with Gabriel Pascal."

A few weeks passed in colorful hope, Gabriel seeing us as millionaires; then once more *Pygmalion* proved itself to be the mocking fate in his life. Lerner and Loewe suddenly and unexpectedly broke their contract and backed out. Why? Were the rumors of a fight between them true, or was it because they could not tackle the musical without Mary Martin?

Mother was in Mexico waiting for her American visa and re-entry permit. It took long months before her case came up, and I drove across the border every week to visit her. She lived at first at a health farm run by a Hungarian professor; later I stayed with her in Tijuana, where I had taken her to be nearer the United States passport office. Gabriel drove down weekly to visit us.

One Sunday, Gabriel and I drove to nearby Rosarita Beach. Warm sun on our skins, Mexican food, guitar players in large sombreros. We were different that day. We became conscious of each other; we had the sensation of seeing each other as if in the close-range focus of a film camera. That Sunday, every movement, every word, seemed important. It was like falling in love once more.

At the hotel in Tijuana we were feverish and reached for each other and talked about the foolishness of the past. Through the half-open shutters the moon threw long shadows on our bed. We told each other: "Paris is back . . . the mirage of the Place Vendôme." We were in love.

"Please stay," I pleaded next morning. "Just one more day." I couldn't go with him, for I had an appointment with Mother at the Passport Office. But he said he could not stay, as Jerry Wald was waiting for him at Columbia Studios.

With tears, I looked at his car being swallowed up in the line of other cars crossing the border. Would I ever again be so happy with him?

When I finally returned home with Mother, I found a changed Gabriel. Jerry Wald and Columbia had not come through, and the *Pygmalion* musical wasn't moving at all. But the main trouble was with *Androcles and the Lion*. While Gabriel had been in England in pursuit of Mary Martin, Howard Hughes, feeling the film lacked sex interest, had proceeded to shoot additional scenes. Gabriel was shocked beyond words. What could he do now? Sue RKO? That, of course, would mean the termination of his contract with them for the two other films.

"Vestal virgins half-nude in a steambath," Gabriel told me, as we were sitting in the library after dinner. "That is Hollywood's idea of sex. They must think the American male is so tired and impotent that he has to have a vast exposure of female flesh to excite him."

"What will happen to us?" I asked, shivering.

"Don't worry," he assured me. "I've thought out everything. My whole soul is with the Gandhi film, but to survive until then, I have several irons in the fire." He would make films in Italy, "though business there is like children's play. Everybody pretends to be serious while exchanging imaginary money. But I love the life there. The fruit has aroma and the manure stinks real, not like here where a decent fly wouldn't even sit on it. We would be happier in Italy."

I was sitting on a mauve antique sofa that had been brought over from England. The heavy bronze lamps on the refectory table cast their light on the bookshelves and on the Piranesi etching on the wall. All this was my life, my home, my new roots. And Gabriel's suits hanging in the closets meant belonging, security, marriage. And now the gypsy caravan again?

"You have to realize," he told me, turning his head away, "that here we have nothing to look forward to. This is a world of shadows and of lies, dedicated to doping the human race with the products of bloodless sex-appeal. I cannot stand the vulgarity here any longer. All they do here is buy: they buy women, men, souls, talent, faith, honor—they put them into cans and pickle them. I am not their man. I never was. Shaw knew that. You know what I'm dreaming of doing? After I make *Gandhi,* and the three Shaw plays in Italy, and after we pocket the millions from the *Pygmalion* musical, I'll bow out of this masquerade. We'll buy a small boat and live on it. We'll sail slowly around the world, from harbor to harbor, and write, read, and dream."

"First Italy and now a boat," I said with a sigh.

"From my boyhood, I've always wanted to live on a boat," said Gabriel. "It means freedom." And his eyes gleamed as if he saw faraway horizons.

One Sunday we were invited to tea at Deborah Kerr's. Gabriel always remained very fond of his discovery, and now her two little daughters shared in his affection for her. The house above the cliffs of Santa Monica faced the Pacific and a purple sunset. The December day was cool. We drank good English tea beside the crackling fireplace. Melanie, the older child, was like a little flame herself: quick, bubbling, moving, chatting, wanting all the attention. Gabriel was enchanted with her and the two played games by themselves. They exchanged secret words. I heard Melanie ask him: "And what animal are you really . . . real really?"

"I am actually real really an eagle," Gabriel answered proudly, flapping his arms.

"And where do you live?" Melanie inquired, with wrinkled forehead.

"I live on mountain tops where there is always snow; sometimes, I sit on clouds and they take me wherever I wish. I can fly very high, higher than the stars."

"It's not true at all," Melanie interrupted. "You don't live there at all because you are a sink-eagle."

The strange word caught Deborah's ears. "What is a sink-eagle?" she asked.

Melanie put on a scientific expression. "A sink-eagle is an eagle who lives in the sink. A big, fat eagle who lives in the kitchen sink."

As we were driving home, Gabriel was pensive and his heavy eyes looked heavier. "The wisdom of children," he said. "How amazing they are. Indeed I am a sink-eagle, an eagle imprisoned in the kitchen sink—a free, proud bird once, now captive, domesticated and fat, eating the swill of the kitchen sink. A liar, a compromiser, who instead of going hungry satisfies his stomach with this vomit of film swindle, who isn't bold enough any more to fly the heights—he eats together with the pigs, but even fighting with them for the swill he isn't fast enough to get there. A nothing I am; a nothing among nothings: neither a saint nor a sinner any more ... a sink-eagle!"

The Woman of Shanghai

CHRISTMAS Eve, 1952. I had decorated the tree in the afternoon and placed it on a card table in the library. After Gabriel and I had lighted the wax candles with Mother looking on, I asked Fred, the old gardener, to join us. He came in his faded blue overalls, greasy hat in hand. The four of us stood around the tree, sang "Silent Night," stared at the tree a bit, then went our ways. There was no present for me. "From the *Pygmalion* musical," Gabriel said convincingly, "I'll buy you a diamond necklace—no, two diamond necklaces."

On the second day after Christmas, Gabriel called to me from the garden where he was dictating to his secretary.

"I need the small card table to work on," he said. "Where is it?"

"The Christmas tree is on it," I answered.

"Call Fred at once," he commanded, "and tell him to remove the tree and bring the table here."

"Can't you use another table? There are plenty of tables outside on the terrace." I was taken aback, as in the tradition of our country the Christmas tree is never taken down until after the feast of Epiphany. What hurt me most was that Gabriel knew I liked Christmas trees, and he also knew how much work I had put into decorating that one. "This is only the second day after Christmas," I reminded him.

He blew up. "Why do you always argue with me? Do at once what I tell you. Christmas is gone and I *hate* Christmas trees. It's all phony: it's hypocrisy. Go at once and call Fred!"

I didn't answer him. I withdrew to my room and sat there, numbed. How much longer can I take this? I asked myself, as I had so many times before—his unexpected moods, his shouting, his strange drive to destroy my joy?

Much later, when I left my room to make lunch, I noticed with a shock that the tree was not in the library corner. Broken ornaments littered the carpet. The tree lay on the grass outside, its decorations glittering in the sunlight. I stared at it. Suddenly it seemed to take on the appearance of an evil omen, a symbol of an assailed, broken home. I heard Gabriel's voice behind me, defensive and hostile: "I told you I needed *that* table."

I cried out uncontrollably, "There lies our last Christmas tree . . . our last Christmas . . . a terrible misfortune is coming."

We spent New Year's of 1953 in Tucson as guests of a well-known promoter interested in producing a Pirandello play in partnership with Gabriel. Then Gabriel left for New York to arrange for the New York opening of *Androcles and the Lion*. The lawsuit with RKO had been settled with the understanding that the scenes added by Howard Hughes would be removed from the film, and New York would see the same version which was then playing in Los Angeles. But Howard Hughes did not want anything more to do with Gabriel Pascal and Gabriel received a settlement, most of which went into that bottomless pit: payments of further installments for the musical rights to the future *My Fair Lady*.

Gabriel, away on a fund-raising trip, had missed the Los Angeles opening of *Androcles*. I went with our old friend, Tim Durant, the horseman. The press was there, of course, and many Hollywood importants. As the film went on, I began to perspire and shiver at the same time. I had no doubt that it would be ill-received and was going to be a disastrous flop.

The next day, I wrote to Gabriel: "Never did sorrow turn to

such joy. Yesterday, after the opening, I thought all was lost and Tim Durant slept through the whole thing and tried to comfort me afterward by saying that it wasn't so bad, but it would never make money ... I had nightmares all night long: those recurring dreams, searching for you at never-known places. I awakened crying and my body hurting. I was so afraid, so terribly afraid and alone. Then this morning your secretary called, and Irving Rubine called, all citing the wonderful write-ups from *every* Los Angeles paper! Then the phone began to ring and is still ringing with congratulations. My Heart, we are safe!"

In the afternoon of the day that *Androcles* was to open in New York, I was standing before the mirror in our room in the Plaza, trying on my evening gown, when Gabriel burst in.

"We are finished," he said. "RKO gave a press showing of the film about which I wasn't even told. And it was the Hughes version instead of the Los Angeles version. I'm ruined."

RKO apologized for the "mistake" of sending the old copy. But it made no difference that Gabriel's version was shown on opening night; the reviews were already in print. The small party Jean Dalrymple threw for us in her house on 55th Street was like a wake. Back in our hotel room, we sat up into the night, the early papers scattered on the floor around us, bloody with the slaughter of *Androcles* in the movie columns.

"This is the prelude to my end," Gabriel said. "Nobody will do business with me now, and I am too tired to fight on. Only God knows what will happen to us. I am happy that the Old Man isn't alive to see this. I couldn't fulfill my promise either to him or to you. I want to die."

"Let's not get discouraged."

His voice was toneless. "There is no hope without faith," he said slowly, "and I have lost faith in myself. Those critics are right: the film is bad—right or wrong version. I have no talent any more."

"You had to fight against terrible odds while you were making the film, and it had good write-ups in Hollywood," I said.

"No, everything was my fault," he sighed. "I compromised. I betrayed myself. My sin goes back years. I always felt I had a mission, that God sent me to this earth to work for His truth. But I made my art and my personal success my only aim and I didn't follow my vision to search for truth. I sold my soul, and kept on compromising. And I've been punished."

I tried to calm him: "Now there's the Gandhi film."

His face lit up. "Yes, Gandhi," he said, "if the Ford Foundation doesn't change its mind. Also, if they decide quickly. I'm living on borrowed time, and sometimes I have the feeling that there isn't much left."

That night, he slept clinging to me, as to a mother. Now and then he would shudder, move restlessly and cry out: "Where are you?"

"I'm here, holding you."

"Don't leave me," he said, in the lamenting voice of a little boy. "Now that we've found each other again, don't ever leave me . . . or I'll crash."

The same cry as years ago in Paris. "I'll never leave you," I said now, as I had said then.

Late in January I flew back to California. Gabriel was staying to work on the *Pygmalion* musical and other deals and to await the February 23 board meeting of the Ford Foundation, when a vote would be taken on financing the Gandhi film. At the airport we kissed, embracing desperately. I had no presentiment that this would be the last kiss for a long, long time.

Bad things never come singly. Mother needed an operation for which Gabriel had to borrow money, and Fred, the old gardener, was sick too. He had just returned from the hospital and was not allowed to work. Near exhaustion, I was nursing Mother, cooking, cleaning, gardening, and fixing up the house so we could rent it, which at that point seemed a faster solution than selling. We hoped that when things straightened out we could return to our home.

As the Ford Foundation board meeting approached, Gabriel had many conferences with Robert Hutchins and Bill Joyce, and things at the Foundation looked hopeful. Meanwhile, there were dealings with Jimmy Durante for the lead in a Rip Van Winkle film; the Pirandello negotiations were still in the air; and a TV series, to be made in Italy from some Shaw plays, was brewing. "One or the other will soon come through for us to live on," Gabriel wrote, "till the Gandhi film materializes." Then: "Leonard Bernstein, with a librettist, a choreographer, and Lawrence Langner, is attending a screening of *Pygmalion* this Friday afternoon. There is a legitimate hope that a contract will be signed soon."

Each day when the mailman came, greeted by the barking of Viking, the Keeshond, Fred would point at the thick, daily letter in my hand, and ask with a slight tremor in his voice, "When is Mr. Pascal coming home?" Fred knew that I was trying to rent the house and that then he would have to go. He could not work any longer and could not expect the tenants to give him board. But he had nothing to worry about for, as he had often told me, he was well off. He had an orchard of nut trees in the San Fernando Valley, and at Christmas he had proudly presented us with a large bag of his product. He also told me that he was looking forward to retirement.

"I'll build a house in my orchard in the Valley," Fred said. "It will be ready for my son and his family when they get back from Japan. They'll move in with me." (His son was a G.I. in Japan.) "You know," he would add, winking, "I've invested well on the stock market."

In the middle of February a special delivery letter came from New York. "For days, I was not able to tell you the news: Paul Hoffman has resigned from the Ford Foundation. He also made me understand that he has no influence on the intermediary Chairman ... He also made a remark from which I deduct that the new policy of the Foundation would be different from his regarding the Far East and, of course, *Gandhi* would come under that ..."

Gabriel was still hoping to have a talk with Henry Ford, whom we had met some years ago in Paris. Maybe *Gandhi* wasn't lost after all and the question of financing it would come up, as planned, at the February 23 board meeting. But the meeting with Henry Ford did not materialize, and *Gandhi* wasn't even mentioned on February 23. Gabriel now tried to interest UNESCO. "I am invited for dinner at the United Nations where, after the screening of *Pygmalion,* I am to make a speech." But of course UNESCO never had that kind of money, and backing for *Gandhi* had to be sought elsewhere.

Nothing went well on the *Pygmalion* musical front, either. If Gabriel and Lawrence Langner couldn't come up with a solution soon, Gabriel would either lose the rights or have to pay another large sum for further options. Leonard Bernstein was out of the picture; the musical, he felt, wasn't his cup of tea, and there was now no other possible composer on the scene. As a final blow, Lawrence Langner and the Theatre Guild gave up. Once more Gabriel was alone, as he had been in the past, with the *Pygmalion* contract in his pocket and nobody else believing that there were "millions in it." He was staying in his old hide-out, the New York Athletic Club on Central Park South. "Here, I pay $5 for my room and if at six o'clock in the bar I order an orange juice, I can get a sandwich for nothing," he wrote.

It was strange how his life kept repeating itself. His bumpy road had circled back to the Club, where he had found a haven twenty years earlier, after his career had collapsed in Germany. "Just like then," he wrote, "now again I have nothing and have to start from the beginning." But that was before Bernard Shaw and *Pygmalion* and he was twenty years younger. His health broke and he could not shake off a cold; his fever lingered for weeks. Always a believer in charlatans and horoscopes and fortune tellers, he now turned to the advice of a "Medical Astrologer," an elderly woman from New Jersey. She gave him some powders to get rid of his "body poisons," cast his horoscope, and assured him that, by the end of March, he would be "sitting on top of the world in more senses than one."

March came and a woman was combing New York in search of Gabriel Pascal, the film producer. Her voice coach, a Hungarian pianist who knew Pascal, had suggested him as the man who could help her with her career. The pianist had heard that Pascal was in New York, but did not know where he was staying. The woman had called all the luxury hotels with no result. But she was determined to find him, and find him she did.

She came from Shanghai. She was half Chinese and half Irish. A poor childhood behind her, she had been a night club performer and became a friend of the richest man in Shanghai, a Dutch banker known the world over. When the Communists came to power the banker was jailed, and only her efforts saved him from dying of hunger. Later, she succeeded in freeing him and together they escaped to the United States. By that time, they were married. They settled in New York in a Park Avenue apartment and bought a house in Riverdale. Most of his immense fortune had been left in China, but plenty remained, and she still had her fabulous jewelry. They soon became popular. She was exotically beautiful, and they entertained lavishly. Then the banker died, leaving his young widow to pursue her life's dream: to become an opera singer.

Much later I found among Gabriel's files some typewritten pages about the Woman which read like a press release. She must have given them to him when they first met. "Who is She?" the release begins, continuing, "in Shanghai she was nicknamed the 'Chinese Greta Garbo'—yet she is more than that . . . she is the true daughter of Lee-Tich-Kwei, one of the Eight Immortals, who always carried a gourd containing magic drugs." She does the same, the press release continues, as she cures people with her secret, magic drugs which she mixes into the food she is cooking: "She is a sorceress out of the east who can transport her guests with her magic food to seventh heaven." Besides that she is also "a great singer, a poet, and a financial wizard, a woman whose fiery dark eyes seem to peer into both past and future, penetrating into the invisible." A woman of great contradictions, she at times "rages with fire and screams in four octaves but she can also act with unlimited kindness." Her enemies should be afraid, as she is able "to destroy them with powerful thoughts." In her childhood her jewelry was make-believe but now she possesses "real diamonds, emeralds, rubies, and pearls," because she can always have what she really wants. "Who is this woman?" The question came again. And the answer: "She is a mystery."

And mystery she was. Any man with a Peer Gynt fantasy would find in her the Green Girl of the trolls.

Gabriel, of course, had no idea that he was the object of this woman's search. Despair was closing about him. He was still sick, and the powders of the New Jersey medical astrologer did not

seem to help. He was trying to keep from me the truth that the
"many irons in the fire" were falling one by one from his grasp.
Nothing remained but our belonging to each other: "I know I
have a mission on this earth which I have yet to fulfill and I also
know that my meeting with you was God's will, no matter how we
have kicked against marriage sometimes. If two such bitchy-na-
tured beings have clung together in so much hardship, it must
have been for a higher purpose. And I tell you now: until our
unity fills us with the greatest joy, we shall have no luck because
we do not deserve it . . ."

And again: "We should fall on our knees before the altar and
thank God that we met. You maybe have had enough of me? But
do not dream of another fairytale prince: you will be with me and
remain with me. So it is written . . ."

Later: "Today I know that there is no other fortress for us than
our loyalty, love and friendship, and if those ever cease the castle
in the air will collapse . . . We cannot wipe out that rendezvous in
Paris lest we pay with our blood for committing such a sin against
the Holy Spirit in us."

Maybe it was while he was writing those lines that the phone
rang in his room at the New York Athletic Club. The Woman of
Shanghai finally located him and invited him to dinner at her
Park Avenue apartment. He accepted the invitation; he loved
Chinese cooking.

The house where the cab stopped was just like all the other
apartment houses along the avenue, with a doorman and an elevator man. But when Gabriel rang the bell of his hostess's apartment and an old Chinese amah opened the door, he entered another world, a world of Oriental carvings, figurines, pagodas, and
lions painted on silk, and incense rising from bronze urns. The
woman, dressed in rich Cantonese silks, rose to greet him, her
jewels sparkling as she moved, graceful as a lean tigress.

Gabriel stared at her. "Purity and Prostitute," he wrote later in
his small notebook. "Shepherdess and Pirate's Wife. Small nose,
sharp eyes, thick lips. A woman . . ."

That night he did not return to the loneliness of his small, bare
room at the Club. On that night, as the Woman of Shanghai

wrote later, "We talked and loved the whole night through." And the mirrors of her living room reflected their love and even her Chinese *amah* and "the American cleaning fluids" could not erase the traces of that night from the silk upholstery of her couch.

I was busy that March. I showed our house to scores of people. On cool evenings I relaxed in the garden and old Fred came to sit with me, the two dogs, Lilli and Viking, at our feet. Fred would talk of his youth, of the mountains of Alaska, where he had gone to try his fortune, of the ragged gold prospectors and raging blizzards, of wild poker games when the air was heavy with smoke and sweat and alcohol; then of a young teacher who became his wife. She had been dead for many years. Then he would talk of their son. He was looking forward to living with the son and his family in the house he was going to build.

Fred talked about the "old boys" from Alaska. Some of them lived in Los Angeles. On his days off he used to play poker with them and return home dead drunk.

One day I found him balancing on top of the longest garden ladder, cutting the dry branches off a palm tree. I was angry with him; we had a new part-time gardener to do such jobs and the doctor had forbidden Fred to work. But he just laughed at me from the top of the ladder. "The new gardener," he snorted. "What the hell does he know?"

Evening came. Followed by the dogs, Fred came humming in from the garden. "Listen to that song," he said. "We used to sing it in Alaska. She used to like it, you know, that girl in Alaska . . . my wife." He winked and disappeared into the laundry room, which served also as his kitchen-dining room.

I sat down in the library to read. Some time later, I went to look for Fred. He wasn't in his room, but the lights were still on in the laundry. I looked through the window. His chair was empty, and a piece of lamb chop was still on his plate. "Funny," I thought, and started to open the door; but something heavy held it back. Fred was lying on the floor, dead. He was still warm and his eyes looked up astonished at the ceiling.

When I told the public administrator all I knew about Fred, he listened with a curious expression. "We have found his will," he said. "He left everything to a poor student boy who used to help him cut the grass here."

"Why would he cut off his own son?" I asked.

"He didn't have a son."

"But he had a wife in Alaska."

"We couldn't find any papers indicating that he had ever been married."

"He used to talk about them, his wife and his son. I remember the student; Fred said he looked like his son. Do you mean that the student is to have Fred's orchard and all the money he made on the stock market?"

The public administrator coughed. "Fred had no orchard," he said, "and as for the stock market—well, he left only a modest sum and asked for the cheapest funeral."

I remembered then Fred's daily question: "When is Mr. Pascal coming home?" He must have thought that Gabriel's homecoming would mean that things would take a turn for the better and we wouldn't rent the house. Fred had had nowhere to go.

Gabriel returned more and more often to the Park Avenue apartment. In that magic circle of escape, the humiliation and struggle of the past months evaporated. He felt young again in the immediacy of a new and strange experience—young, irresponsible, a dreamer and adventurer once more.

He was ensnared. In this sudden, crushing passion, his dual nature emerged. In the Woman of Shanghai he found the perfect match to the "other Gabriel," to his volcanic temperament, his impatient anger, his blind energy. His egomania, pride, and devouring ambition were reflected back from her. And in her he met his own subconscious self-hate and drive for self-destruction, as well as the other side of his own spiritualism: the search for the infinite through the occult. The Woman could interpret his dreams from ancient Chinese books and told him his future—which was to be great and was to be spent with her.

Daily he drank herb teas and ate food prepared with "life elixirs," believing that the Woman could cure cancer and many other ills. As a result of the cure, he experienced "prodigious sexual powers" and felt as if he were "flying." The Woman called him "the greatest lover of the century," "my Napoleon, my Alexander the Great, my Gabriel Pascal." About herself she later wrote that she was the "book of love" and that "God himself" had copyrighted that book for her and that anybody who ever made love to her could never again be satisfied with any other woman.

Gabriel's sex urge, so long suppressed by his worries and failures and by his "search for a higher self," was now liberated, flooding him with a new experience—and with guilt. On Good Friday, April 3, he wrote to me: "I went to Saint Patrick's today for the three hour service commemorating our Savior's Passion ... Kneeling there, I saw my iniquities. If only Christ would have mercy on me. If only you could forgive me. From me you have never had anything good. You have lived your young years with a sick, nervous maniac, running after dreams ..."

Night after night spent at the Park Avenue apartment: more guilt and more letters.

"Have faith in me. I'll solve all our problems and will be successful yet. Do not worry. I am holding the bridle fast and no matter how winding and steep this mountain road is on which our gypsy cart is thudding, rattling and shaking, a horde of hungry wolves after us, I shall bring this cart home and maybe somewhere, at the edge of the forest, there is yet a little hut waiting for us, for a new life and new love together."

Was he referring to Solveig's hut, waiting for the erring Peer?

Easter passed, and the house was still on the market. Difficulties were coming from every direction, Gabriel reported from New York. But, he wrote, "I am again a fiery arrow. I'll cut through everything. God help anybody who crosses my path ... All my past Gandhi-like meekness was rubbish. I am a fighter and not a saint and I will fight with all the talents God gave me to protect you from misery ... Only I want to hear from you: are you coming with me on this difficult road of mine with faith, love, and perhaps once more being in love? Tell me the *truth,* nothing but the truth, do not delude me or my fight is worthless."

I didn't understand the urgency of his question. What kind of an answer was he waiting for? I was his wife; what else could I do but follow him? Yet our marriage wasn't a marriage like others, and at times I felt cheated out of life. I was still too young. Maybe it was my fault. My mind went back to the very beginning of our life together.

"I know we had to meet," I wrote to him. "I had to cut through the Iron Curtain to be at our rendezvous in Paris ... Yet our love was never physical. Maybe it was more the wedding of our souls than ever it was of our bodies? I want to be completely honest with you and with myself: sex with you was always secondary for me. My love for you was and is more than sex. I am puzzled over this because I love your body. I love your skin, your smell; I love your hands, your hair. I love to kiss you and caress you. I feel a miraculous unity with you: as if your hands were my own and your body a continuation of mine. Everything which hurts you hurts me, and your wounds are my wounds. But this is not sex and it is more than being in love, because you are more important to me than I am for myself ... What is that tortuous chain which binds us together? Is it that we have always belonged and together we are destined to find our lost souls?"

How did my letter sound to him in the warm bed of the Woman of Park Avenue?

April 17, from New York:

"To your long, personal letter, I am not able to answer just now. You wrote beautifully and I understand it only too well. The nearer I seem to be to realization of the TV deals, the more the intrigue ..."

Intrigue it was. In *The Voice of Broadway* Dorothy Kilgallen wrote:

PASCAL UPSET OVER SALE OF SHAW'S TV RIGHTS
George Bernard Shaw still causes lively arguments, even though he's dead. Gabriel Pascal, who owns the film rights to Shaw's plays, is frantically upset over the sale of Shaw's TV rights to *Omnibus*. The skirmish may reach the courts, with Pascal claiming infringement.

April 22, New York:

"Only a miracle can save us now. I was so near to the realization of the TV deals ... the representatives of the Italian Company called in panic ... Apparently God is not sparing me from anything. His Hands are upon me. Where shall this slippery road take us?"

Cary Grant and his wife came to see the house. They loved it —but did not buy it. Mario Lanza came. He sang under the tall arocaria tree and said he loved the place. *"Domani,"* he said, he would come with his wife and children to buy it. I never heard from him again.

The house, with its terrible loneliness, lay upon me like a tombstone. There was no escape; even if it were sold the settling of the debts would not leave a penny. Bills were coming in every day; Gabriel owed money all over the place. And then, where to go?

On May 13, he finally wrote his answer to my "personal letter." The first sentences put me on guard about something which he hadn't the courage to tell me face to face.

"Twice before I tried to answer your letter. But it is not easy ... A long time has passed since we talked openly and I wish to talk to you as sincerely as I did once in Paris. How clearly I see now all the mistakes from the very beginning. It all started when your train rolled out from the Paris station. You went back to Hungary. We both knew then that it was wrong to part, yet you went. And as I looked after your disappearing train, something broke in me. I knew that you went back to Tibor. I realized then that you were still tied to him sexually, even though you said that you loved me ... And finally you admit now that you never felt a sexual passion toward me—not even then in Paris. And I perceive now, in a new light, that our unity in Paris, without that intoxication which you missed in our relationship, wasn't strong enough to make you jump off the train, even at the last minute ... And, sensing that sex with me did not fulfill you and you did not belong to me absolutely, I had no courage to tear you from the train. Yet that would have been the only honest thing to do —and after that, everything became an anti-climax."

"What does he mean?" I wondered. "What does he really want to say?"

"And today, due to a miraculous cure, I am absolutely healthy again and feel younger than twenty years ago ... and I know why you missed the sexual part of our relationship. We met just after

Caesar and Cleopatra, the time when my career was in danger and I was sick. I tell you this now because I do not want you to feel inferior because of the lack of sex feeling on your part. It was my fault and remained my fault all along: I was sick. My heart and soul rejoiced more than my body could."

There were tears in my eyes now. My poor, poor darling: how could he misunderstand me that much?

"There is no use in beautifying or making the bloody truth poetic: that the main cause of our unhappiness was that, however great and eternal our love, the chemistry did not work. We could never find that simple, primitive magnetism, that warm animal happiness of the flesh . . ."

I became icy inside. Did he have another woman? Would he otherwise distort my letter that much?

". . . and without that bodily happiness, there is no harmony, no success, no creation . . . I feel that you have sometimes tried that sensual fulfillment with other men. What else could I have done but draw my hurt male pride into myself and remain silent."

My suspicion was now almost confirmed: he was accusing me of disloyalty because he was disloyal himself.

"I could never give you anything but my miserable heart and you never understood its throbbing and longing, for I never had time to make you listen . . . I reach out for your hand now and I caress your hair, the most beautiful hair I ever caressed, and I tell you: you are free, and it is not necessary for you to continue to suffer with me because of our belonging in the spirit . . . I ask you again for the truth: are you going to stay with me . . . and not out of false pity. Answer me . . . The end has to be good because your heart is good and because my love for you never was a selfish passion but the purest desire to make you happy."

"No, I'm mistaken," I thought. "He wouldn't ask me to stay with him if he had another woman." I felt guilty now. I loved him, I loved him with my whole being; I had to talk to him.

I put in a call, but could not reach him at his room, even late at night, nor early the next morning. It was late afternoon the next day when I got him.

"How could you be such a child," I started breathlessly. "You didn't understand my letter."

"Thank you for calling," he interrupted. His voice was cold.

"We can't talk about these things over the phone. I'll be back soon. We have to decide without hysteria. I can't accomplish a thing here and the sooner I get to Italy, the better."

I sat staring at the telephone. What would happen now? Should I stay behind again? Did he want to get rid of me? I should never have married him, I thought. In his love, there was always a hidden hate. Bernard Shaw warned me not to sacrifice my life and talent for him. Why didn't I listen to Shaw? But then, I loved Gabriel.

Now I tried to think about that love. Was it always as living as it had been in the beginning? Hadn't it become a fixture, and hadn't reality passed it by? Did it *ever* have reality? Did I love him *now?* Had I loved him *then?* Weren't there only *moments* when I merged with his inner being, moments which lifted us out of a narrow existence into a larger moment, when our fused fingers seemed to touch constellations—but only to be alone again?

I tried to force myself to look into my own conscience to find an answer, but I slid away from my own searching look like a shadow on the wall. The days and weeks of my six years of marriage passed through my memory. Where had I been during those years? It seemed to me that most of the time I had been absent. I had imagined that I was giving up my career for Gabriel: and I had lost both. I couldn't concentrate on either. My intense grip on life had relaxed, and I was empty. Even the pain did not hurt as it used to. Where were the anguished tears after quarrels? Where was the yearning of those nights at the farm when I heard his returning steps turn toward his room and listened to his door creaking shut? Then I was alive; now I was dead. And I looked as a stranger might around the hall of our house with its waxed Spanish tiles and winding staircases. Had he and I ever lived here?

A casual friend asked me out to dinner. We decided on a restaurant at the beach. Driving through Santa Monica we passed an amusement park, and on a whim I suggested going in. There were throngs of people licking ice cream, sharp neon lights, the smell of hot dogs. Over the screams from the roller-coaster and the sharp reports from the shooting galleries I became aware of a constant, mechanical, horrible laughter. It was coming from a

dummy set on top of a building: a fat Chinese woman, dressed in
Oriental fashion, her black hair in a knot, her round face wrinkled with laughter. But her slit eyes did not laugh. They seemed
to be staring at me as she kept on laughing and bowing, beckon-
ing people to enter her Palace of Confusion.

"She looks so evil," I told my companion. The dummy bowed
toward me and laughed and laughed. "She's laughing at me." And
suddenly my fun was gone and I wanted to leave.

"Come on now," said my friend, and made me go in. Soon we
were lost, bumping into walls in the utter darkness. "Let's get out
of here," I said. But we couldn't get out. My friend's footsteps
suddenly died away. I groped about, seeking in vain for the opening he had passed through. Wherever I turned my fingers
touched damp, slippery walls. I was afraid. "How stupid," I
thought, trying to wave it away. "But I'm lost . . . I'll never get
out of here." And suddenly the labyrinth wasn't a cheap joke any
more; it was my life, caught in a blind alley.

It seemed to me that a long time passed before I heard my companion come back. I stretched out my hand and, after a few uncertain steps, I touched him. He grabbed my hand, drawing me
toward him. I felt the hard muscles of his arm and smelled his
manly smell and sensed the security of male strength. It was a
dizzy, fleeting moment, with no conscious effect on me; only later
did it stand out in my memory with a deep, irrevocable importance. For it was the moment when I finally turned away from Gabriel. Subconsciously, I had reached out for the security of another man. I wanted to be a woman again and enjoy a man's love.
I knew at that moment that Gabriel could never again fulfill that
desire.

That night I dreamed of Gabriel, seeing him in an embrace
with a woman. Then I *knew* with an absolute knowledge that he
had another woman.

Imogene Coca, the television star, rented the house for six
weeks, beginning June 15. I thought of taking Mother with me to
New York for those weeks, as I had no doubt that Gabriel
wouldn't or couldn't take me to Italy.

When I was last in New York I had seen a lot of Pauline. She had changed from the gay, happy woman I had met in London into a deeply disturbed one. Her marriage had broken up. She had taken a studio apartment on the West Side and had escaped into painting. She wrote to me now that she was going to Europe and that I could have her apartment for the six weeks. The trouble between Gabriel and me did not surprise her; hadn't she gone through the same experience with him herself years ago? I accepted her offer of the apartment.

Gabriel came back to California for a few days to dissolve the remains of the Hollywood venture and then to return to New York en route to Italy. I met him at the airport. In the past, I used to wait for him at the gate; now I waited in the terminal building. We exchanged a light kiss and busied ourselves with the luggage. As I drove home, I forced myself to talk.

"What are your plans?"

"Well, you know, Italy . . ."

I hesitated for a moment, then: "And I?" I glanced at him out of the corner of my eye. His face was motionless as he said: "Maybe later I can take you over there." He stopped. Then I began to talk, but it was as if someone else spoke the short, cruel sentences. No use for us to pretend, I said, let's face it; it is all over. I couldn't wait for him endlessly, and I was sure he didn't want me to wait for him any longer. I wanted to live, finally, and try my own career.

I talked on and on. My words sounded as if they were coming from a wound-up machine. The only thing I wanted was to hurt him and to hurt myself. He sat motionless, which irked me more and more. In a matter-of-fact, businesslike tone I asked: "What agent should I go to? Who would be best for my career?" He was silent. I gritted my teeth. "Wouldn't I look better with short hair?" He loved my long hair and used to say that I would be allowed to cut it only when I ceased to love him.

"Do what you like," he answered hoarsely.

The days passed in taut silence. I hardly saw him. I was getting the house ready for Imogene Coca and was also packing Gabriel's belongings, which he was to ship to Europe.

On Saturday, unexpectedly, he joined me as I sat by the pool.

He lay down some distance from me. "What shall I live on until I can stand on my own feet?" I asked.

"I can't give you much now, but I'll send you some money soon." I looked at his tanned body, the familiar lines of his neck, his black hair, graying a bit; and once again there was that mixture of pain and hatred.

We sank into silence. Those three acres of Eden around us, and the white villa we used to call home mocked us now as, like a cursed Adam and Eve, we lay on the grass.

After a long pause, he said: "Now, finally, we are free."

"Yes, we are free." I felt him looking at me. I smiled and stretched out on the grass. A thousand little knots of hate and pain inside me were struggling to break open, but my voice was controlled when I changed the subject. "You wrote me about some 'miracle cure.' What kind of cure? Beware of charlatans."

His face became masklike, and he didn't look at me. "Oh, I met somebody in New York, a woman. Actually, I was trying to sell our house to her. I showed her the photos and she wanted it very much, but she found the price too high."

I remembered faintly that in one of his long-distance calls he had mentioned a rich widow who was interested in the house.

"Well," he continued, "she cured me with some miraculous elixirs and herbs. She said that my glands were half dead and that caused my tiredness and loss of vigor. The herbs gave me a peculiar uplift. I never felt anything like that before—like a young man again. I am a new man now."

"And who is she?"

He hesitated. "She . . . she is a very extraordinary person. She has great occult powers, too . . . I had a strange experience. A very strange one . . ." His eyes looked far off.

There was a long silence. Could *she* be the other woman? "Are you in love with her?" I asked.

"Love, no. Love is something else." He was still avoiding my eyes. "I have no inner connection in my soul with her at all but . . ." Viking interrupted with fierce barking as Gabriel's agent, Bill Shiffrin, appeared in the driveway. The moment was gone; Gabriel never finished what he had wanted to say.

Bill Shiffrin had come to sell a story. Gabriel could film it cheaply in Europe. "It's a great love story," Bill said, his eyes shining with the eagerness of a salesman. "It's about a breaking marriage and, at the end, the mystical reunion of the couple."

The separating couple, Bill related, find themselves through a car accident in a strange valley at the foot of a mysterious mountain. Their fate brings them to a weird old man and a weird old house. And it seems to them that they are dead, killed in the accident, and that there, in that house, they leave time behind to enter eternity. But then they have to return from the valley of the magic mountain, the valley of death, to their old lives. They have learned their lesson and now have a new chance to fulfill the promise they once had vowed to each other.

"It's called *Promise*," Bill added, "from Mildred Cram, you know. She wrote that best-seller *Forever*."

The name and the title hit on a memory: the autumn forest of Fontainbleau, the time when Gabriel and I first met. Hand in hand we had walked on the yellow leaves, shuddering with love. Gabriel had talked about Mildred Cram's book, *Forever*, saying that our love was like that story—forever. And now, in these last days together, the name of Mildred Cram came up again.

"Isn't it strange," I said to Gabriel after Bill Shiffrin left, "as if a circle had been closed now: our lives together between the covers of two books, *Forever* and *Promise*."

He did not answer, but picked up the manuscript and went into the house.

That evening we cooked dinner together in our old way, and that somehow brought us closer. We talked of commonplace things and went upstairs to our separate bedrooms.

Our last night together, under the same roof. Tomorrow he would be off. I felt I had to talk to him; I had to tell him, before it was too late. I changed into a light, golden dressing gown, made from a sari, and went to our connecting door.

"Can I come in?" I asked. He was reading in bed. The bed was a large, antique piece, framed by steps. I sat on the steps. I could talk only about practical matters. His eyes, dark and sad, never left my face.

"How beautiful you are," he interrupted. "I have never seen you so beautiful and so remote, like a vision of Helen of Troy. I want to remember you always like this."

I returned to my room. The words I couldn't speak were choking me. I couldn't sleep. It is not true, I thought again and again, that we have become strangers to one another and that tomorrow he is leaving forever.

I heard my door opening, and his footsteps. He hesitated. In the pale light coming through the windows I could see him standing motionless. Then he took a deep breath and started toward my bed. Very quietly, he sat down on the edge. I didn't move. Cautiously, not touching me, he lay down beside me. We lay silent, rigid, side by side. Why didn't I stretch out my hand? Why didn't I talk? I was to ask myself these questions over and over in the coming years.

After a long time he got up and, as noiselessly as he had come, he left.

PART THREE

Chapter 4

The Labyrinth

Gabriel,

Your plane had left and I stood there nails pressed into my palms so that I would not scream aloud in my pain it was always terrible when you left many times I stood at airports but now it was different I went back to the car pulled up the top of it and finally I could cry I cannot go to bed I cannot sleep I have to write to you now tomorrow I would not be able to write this way any more and I have to tell you now how it hurt driving back on the same road on which I have driven you out to the airport and now I was passing alone by the Church we had passed together where you said: 'Now it's only five minutes to the airport' where are those last five minutes when you were still with me? I was driving back blind with tears and I was crying aloud then I saw clearly your blue pajamas which you napped in this afternoon and for no reason there was a picture of the room in the Ritz Hotel you were coming in the door with two hatboxes smiling and said 'Bébé Bérard should paint you in the nude wearing these hats' I don't want to remember God have mercy on me this past week wasn't true at all . . . you were my life and now you will never return to me I wanted to talk to you I wanted to tell you but I was paralyzed oh this terrible dark house your abandoned room the bed as you left it after your nap the water is still flowing in your bathroom the only sound of life in this dead silence you had forgotten as usual to turn off the faucet and now you will never turn that faucet again the sound of the flowing water the continuation of your presence without your presence I cannot turn it off I want to hear it and it hurts why does it hurt me that much and you are not hurt you never loved me and I am glad because I don't want you to suffer as I am suffering tomorrow will be better it will pass don't think of me be free go be free and I thank you that you were thank you for the ten days in Paris thank you for Mumford's Farm thank you for life because with you I was alive and now back to the nightmares searching for you endlessly in my dreams in never seen streets strange writing you this letter on this desk the only piece of furniture I took out of Hungary the same desk on which from Tibor's house I wrote to you every night for eight months and now I am writing the last love letter to you how could it all end this way then I thought you will be the father of my children I don't want to think now I want to survive to be strong and you have to be strong too you have not yet finished your work here God be with you I put you in His hands and pray that He would never allow you to be thrown to the mercy of others save you from worries sickness from loneliness and from second-rate hotel rooms from traveling second-class from second-rate food from shabby clothing oh God cure me lift this torture and grant that we meet again in another life never part my soul from yours please take care of yourself and try to lose weight your tummy is too big and don't overwork when shall I see you again when shall I?

Valerie.

New York. A different New York from the one I had been in on brief visits with my husband: an indifferent New York this was, with my small self pressed into a crowded loneliness among hard-faced, inhuman-looking strangers.

Mother was just as frightened as I, but at least we had Pauline's apartment, a small bubble of protection, at the Hotel des Artistes. It was good to awaken in the mornings to the only natural noise in the city: neighing from the stables opposite, and the clatter of horses' hooves as the animals started out for a gallop in Central Park.

Gabriel was in London. A modest check came with his letter: "I'll send more as soon as I can ... I would never forsake you, all I am fighting for is your security." He never mentioned my farewell letter, but later I found it among his papers, the ink smeared with my tears, the lines running berserk without punctuation.

I was confused. I didn't know why I had dragged Mother and myself here. All I was hanging on to was an intuition that somehow New York would bring a solution, that somewhere a new life was waiting for me.

The heat was suffocating, a gray, steaming blanket over the city, and Pauline's duplex with its huge studio windows facing south was a two-story oven. In the afternoons, we escaped to Central Park and sat on benches into the evening, looking at the playing field where children threw balls lazily into the smog. I stared at the staggered line of the skyscrapers—monstrous towers like the many temples of Lucifer, painted evil red by the setting dirt-veiled sun. I was frightened. I was so frightened that the muscles of my spine contracted and sweat broke out all over me.

Gabriel's letters helped. His slanting handwriting came almost daily with news of his business developments and assurances that he would help me once he could. Everything had been his fault in the past, he wrote, but maybe my seven years with him weren't a total loss, for "with all my fantasies, sins, and sorrows you still have to admit I was a genuine guy." Never did I dream that on the other side of Central Park lived a woman who waited just as anxiously for my husband's handwriting as I did.

The Woman of Shanghai was bewildered by her lover's enigmatic behavior. He had changed since his return from California. He had little time for her during his last week in New York and he did not let her come to the airport to say goodbye, even though, as she complained, "inside in your heart and mind" he knew that he would not come back. And if he really loved her, why couldn't she go with him? Because he had to work? She of-

fered him $20,000 for their "enjoyment" and a rest together. But
Gabriel "turned it down"; worse, he was now writing long, criti-
cal letters to her, to the woman who had given him back his
health only so that he could open his eyes wide and clear "to see
the faults of that lonely woman in New York." And she, who had
rejoiced "in finding Ideal Genius Gabriel Pascal as beacon and
consort," was now abandoned.

Red roses were cabled to Park Avenue in appeasement, with an
invitation to spend a weekend in London. All she was good for
was a weekend? She was hurt.

Gabriel had only one desire now: to be left alone. He did not
want a new entanglement with a new mistress. He wanted to be
free to "follow the vision." "Alone I want to be and alone I want
to stay," he wrote me from a jet en route to Milan, but he signed
the letter "still your Greenhaired Son." But he wanted to be free
without letting me go:

"Just now, we are flying over the Mont Blanc, leaving Geneva
behind where, on doctor's orders, I made love to you for four
days and nights to cure your gall-bladder. Remember, my poor
Heart? But what is Mont Blanc to me when my spirit is already
on Mount Everest. Before I left London I wired to Colonel Hunt,
the leader of the Mount Everest expedition, that I am ready to fly
to him at once with a cameraman and make the Mount Everest
film, even if I have to climb up with him. The hell with Shaw
and his plays. I want life, I want to create, I want to laugh. I am
from the race of Prometheus and not of those film worms . . . If
he takes my offer we could be out of the waters and all those
crawling insects of Hollywood and New York would shit all over
themselves with jealousy and would be drowned in their shit, the
dirty Judases. And you will be proud yet that you have been my
wife—just do not piss into your pants there in New York. I'll
make you yet a millionairess!"

Oh, my God, I thought, here we go again. Now Mount Everest.
Always the impossible, always the unreachable.

"Here we are landing in Milan. These new jet planes are fabulous. I shall yet fly to the moon, too . . . Tonight I'll dine at the

Villa d'Este, alone, as a happy bachelor, and will drink for your health and for my ex-mother-in-law's health. I am not mad at her any more, the old witch. The matrimonial pretensions over, I wouldn't mind to take you back as a mistress—where can I find a more beautiful one? I promise, you would be astonished. No Gandhian nonsense any more and no monkish dreams. My penis is already prancing when I think of your last letter promising me to be brave and saying that when you are a famous actress I can have a key to your apartment . . . Here is my adored Italy where I can be gay and true, the hell with the hypocrisy of England and America."

Four letters from four women awaited Gabriel at the Principe di Savoia Hotel in Milan. The two from New York, curiously, bore the same date: one was from the Woman on Park Avenue, the other from me. There were also letters from Pauline and Hedwig Brugge.

Gabriel's friendship with Hedwig, his first love from his hungry days in Berlin, had survived all his other love affairs. They corresponded regularly and Gabriel all through the decades had helped the desolate, sick woman financially. Now Hedwig was welcoming *mein Gaborjunge,* as she still called him, to Europe, jubilant over his great plans: "You have mastered life, you mastered being on earth . . . You indeed are a Phoenix, never conquered, but always reborn from ashes . . . and I followed you and still follow you forever."

Pauline wrote in Hungarian: "I have lived with you and loved you," and for years she could not forget him. "You lived in my soul like an Ideal"; yet all along she knew that there was something amiss with him, "something did not jibe with you; you were not a whole being, not *eine Einrichkeit . . .*" He was like a comet, and women "are destroyed by such a dazzling, shining being." And a woman wants to be all to a man like that, "not just sex, but Mother, Sister, Friend, Pupil—a woman will be all these to a Fiery Being like you—but she ends up alone." This had been her fate and "is Valerie's fate now."

The Woman of Shanghai wrote that she had been sick ever

since he had left her. She could not eat because of her love and longing for him. He had taken her heart and soul away and her body could be "charged" only by him.

My letter described a Long Island weekend where I had been very unhappy: "Your shadow follows me wherever I go. When shall I stop loving you?"

Putting the letters like so many dried flower petals from past summers into his files, did Gabriel think of himself as the Pied Piper? Did he sometimes see himself in the mirror—stocky, with a paunch, a lion's head under a mane of black hair—and wonder why women attached themselves to him even against their better judgment? Was it because of the illusion that he could imbue with a mesmeric power, that he possessed the secret which could give meaning to life, and that he could see miracles where nobody else saw them? And that he alone could play the magic flute of Pan and the Pied Piper, and the woman who heard it could never forget it?

Things did not move for me in New York. Mr. Martin Jurow, from the William Morris Agency, thought that I could make it, but summer was a bad time; I should try in September. Could I get rid of the house that fast, after Imogene Coca moved out in the middle of August? It was doubtful. Meanwhile, I got myself a job in Jean Dalrymple's office; I answered phone calls and tried to learn to type. The latter brought cheers from Gabriel. If only I had learned to type earlier, I could have helped him with his work and maybe we wouldn't have grown away from each other.

"But like everything else, that was my fault, too," he wrote. "I was your Pygmalion, and I should have formed you to be my helpmate." He did not mention Mount Everest any more, and his "adored Italy" was now a "land of crooks," as his business dealings were not going as he had hoped. Then came the refrain of all his letters: "I am alone and wish to stay alone." And a mystifying remark: "Since I left you, I have fought off the most dangerous temptations: to sell myself, my soul, body, and freedom. Needless to say, that remained only temptation." A rich woman, I thought. But who?

Eventually, I heard. Gabriel was being seen all over Rome in the company of a beautiful Frenchwoman. My reaction surprised me. I had that sickening feeling of oncoming nausea. Why did I believe him when he said he was "completely alone"? How could he still dupe me? It must be the same woman from this spring in New York, the "strange experience."

The Frenchwoman had been the fiancée of a friend of his, who had jilted her, and Gabriel, because of his good heart, was trying to comfort her now in Montecatini. His explanation arrived in the same mail with an envelope from the Bank of America, containing his check, which had bounced. And there he was, traveling and staying in an expensive hotel with his woman. I wrote him, calling him a monster of selfishness and a liar. By accusing him, I felt I was demeaning myself, yet I derived a cruel satisfaction from my words.

Like a hair-thin root of a newborn plant anchoring to clods of earth, I began to be attached to a group of new friends. Soon I was dating. The Jaipurs arrived for a short stay and took me to parties. New York was losing its fearsome appearance. Gabriel did not welcome the changed tone of my letters. "Success with men," he wrote somewhat sourly, "never made a woman happy yet. Of course, all they want is to go to bed with you. Do not become the victim of New York. And I do not need the confirmation of those idiotic New York males about your beauty: neither they nor yourself ever dreamt the beauty you could become if you followed my vision of yourself."

A Milan financing group was interested in the two scenarios Gabriel had offered them for consideration. One of them was *The Promise,* but now Bill Shiffrin wasn't sure if he could still get the rights. "I should have read the scenario then in Los Angeles," Gabriel wrote, "but I was insane and so hurt that all I could do was run ... My punishment had already started: never did I feel so lonely. I am tired and sad. Words are worthless and deeds weigh the balance of the scales against me. Like Peer Gynt, I am standing at the crossroads and poor Solveig is crying somewhere far away."

And indeed he was at the crossroads. One of the roads could

lead back to me through the film of *The Promise,* as I was to find out soon. After a brief silence three letters from Italy burst into my life. On a Monday, Gabriel wrote: "I am afraid that our love, which was the most painful and torturous bond in my entire life, will never cease ... I talked about separation only because I thought that we could find each other once more if we cleared our minds of that idiotic lie: marriage ... I repeatedly wrote to you about an experience which happened to me while I was alone in New York this spring but that has nothing to do with pure love and true belonging." The idea of another woman, he continued, could never be a solution for him: "My problems lie deeper and maybe they are insoluble in this incarnation ... I did not run away from you but from my masks ... If I am to avoid perishing in the Hollywood idiocy and in the Broadway crookedness and *find my way back to myself,* I have to be alone. It is not easy to impose this way of life on myself."

Tuesday, he informed me that Bill Shiffrin had finally confirmed the sale of the rights to *The Promise* and that I should get in touch with Mercedes de Acosta, the writer and close friend of Greta Garbo, who would convince Greta that this film could be her comeback. "And this will be your comeback too, because I need you badly to help me with this picture. You will get a salary in your capacity as an assistant to the producer ... I want you to come as soon as possible and if you had read the script you would now understand the double significance of my making this picture."

I did understand. I remembered the strange connection between the two Mildred Cram books and our lives, and my bitter remark about the circle of our lives together being closed between the covers of those two books, *Forever* and *Promise.* In the story, the breaking marriage is saved. Now the film could bring us together once more to fulfill *our* promise, the promise we vowed at Saint Etienne in Paris.

On Wednesday: "If you are sincere to me and to yourself in saying that you still love me, why don't you place Mother with the Hungarian nuns in New Jersey, get rid of the house at any price, and come back to me for another try for half a year, or a year, or as long as you can take me. I am longing for you, for purity and peace with you, and it is better for me to die than to live another way. Answer me now: can you come back, forgetting and forgiving or do you really want us to part forever?"

Then a cable on July 27: "*Il sogno di Parigi non è ancora morto ... Potremo salvarlo.*"

The dream of Paris is not yet dead. We can save it. Could it be saved? I felt as if I were sitting on a roller coaster. To go back to him and start all over again, the fights, bitter words, hostile moods, unexpected attacks, and that silence, that terrible silence ... back to be mesmerized again, to have the last drop of myself wrung out again. To go back to be shaken day and night by his restless energies, to the insecurity of a wandering life, to the gypsy caravan. No, I shouldn't be sidetracked, but concentrate all my energies on building a new life.

Yet I missed him, my life had no meaning without him. To cover up my indecision, I launched an attack: how and why this sudden change? He had been so jubilant to be alone. And what about that "strange experience"? What about his hostile behavior in Los Angeles, then the Frenchwoman? I had to know the whole truth.

He did not change "from one day to another," Gabriel defended himself. He had to be alone to clear his mind and now that that was done, he wanted me back. The experience in New York was something very "deep" which shook him with an "elementary force," but he could talk about it only if we found each other once more.

"I am not a liar, or cheater, or deceiver. I am clean. I never rolled in human dirt. I kept my body and soul clean ... Isn't it our duty to save the dream which we turned into such bitter reality and the vision we put to such shame? Where shall I run, in which corner of the earth shall I hide to end my pain?"

I had to answer. I cabled the same three words which had been my answer to him six years earlier from Hungary: "I love you." But what a difference. Then, with those words, I had put my life into his hands. Now they meant that though I still loved him, my bitterness, distrust and insecurity were not resolved, and I wasn't sure any more.

Peer Gynt at the crossroads. One road could lead back to me, but what about the other? The Milan group was considering a second film, a story of two young lovers who wandered one night to an open-air performance of the opera *Turandot*. The film would include a short sequence from the opera and Gabriel could not help thinking that there was never a more perfect protagonist for the cruel, beautiful Princess than his Chinese friend—whom he had promised to help with her career. He hadn't written to her for more than a month, thus evoking a flood of sad and accusing letters from her. There was the possibility of a part, Gabriel finally wrote to Park Avenue.

In the middle of August I was back in Los Angeles. The negotiations with the Milan bankers looked good, but so far Gabriel had no money to bring me over to Italy.

"I want to live, I want to laugh, I am not used up yet," he wrote. "Only with you can I laugh and be happy that I am alive, but only in my style, according to *my* dreams. It is a pity that you never knew my dreams, they never really interested you. Just the same, you never saw the male in me. Yet it is here with its strength, magnetism and male goodness—if you come with the right approach. Maybe my approach toward you was a wrong one, too . . . But, please do understand: the only way to bear with me is to take *my* rhythm, *my* tempo, and only if you accept those can you enjoy me. It is a waste of time to criticize me and try to change me. In my shit there is more spirit than in certain people's brains. I know my values and I know my faults, and do not want anything from anybody which doesn't come from the heart and I'd rather starve than go back to lies. I am a man again. Here I am standing, my Vally, waiting for you with open arms, with a true, exorcised and clarified brain and rock-hard penis . . . Here I am waiting for you as a lover, as a friend, as anything you want, only let me forget that ugly word: HUSBAND. All the meanness, all the lies started with that word. With a lover, neither you nor I would have dared to be so unjust and cruel. Embracing you with infinite love and all the joy of my heart—Gábor."

"Your voice was chilly over the phone," Gabriel complained to me from London. "And in your last letter, you seemed to be reluctant to give up your new freedom." He was in London to raise money by selling his rights to the *Pygmalion* musical to a New York promoter. He was offered $100,000 in cash; "and that would enable us to get out from this impasse and start a new life together."

It was now toward the end of August. Impatient with the slow Milan bankers, Gabriel had gone to Munich. Together with Wolfgang Reinhardt, the son of his old friend, Max Reinhardt, he started the *Deutsche Pascal Film,* intending to combine the Italian interest with German financing. But he did not want us to live in Munich. "If you sell the house, sell it unfurnished. I found a place near Rome which we can have for almost nothing. You can ship the furniture from San Pedro on an Italian boat quite reasonably ... Life could be yet majestically beautiful. I will yet prove it to you with a love infinite ..."

One more letter, dated August 28, from Zurich: "You have never yet answered straight: are you coming back? About myself and that strange experience, only if I see you can I talk ... Now I am only interested in one thing: to work and, if you return, to find my peace with you. I have to finish now. I have to run after my phantoms."

Early in September, Bill Shiffrin called to say he had to talk with me. I knew it was about *The Promise.* When he arrived, I sat down with him at the pool and offered him a drink.

"Gabby was supposed to send me $25,000 for the option rights weeks ago," Shiffrin started in right away. "I can't keep the offer open much longer. Where is he anyhow?"

It was then that the mailman came with a special delivery. Bill looked curiously at the Italian airmail stamps on the letter and I said: "Yes, it's from him."

"Why don't you read it?" he asked eagerly. "Maybe it says something about the deal."

Reluctantly, as I would have preferred to open the letter in privacy, I tore off the side of the envelope. The first sentence made my heart jump. "I was waiting to answer you, hoping that, in the last moment, something would come through, but I have to tell you the truth: everything failed ... I was not able to raise the money for *The Promise.*"

With Shiffrin's eyes on me, I exercised heroic self-control.

"Any news?" he asked.

"I don't know yet." I had to read on. The film business in Italy was in a few hands and he did not belong to the "Club," Gabriel wrote; and Munich was a provincial town, dealing in pennies, and, even if he was finally to realize his plans there, he would not have any money for a long while.

The lines began to waver in front of my eyes and I had to re-read the sentence: "I am afraid we must part our ways for a longer time, for only alone can I emerge from this tragedy . . . I wish to disappear into nothingness, enough of this senseless comedy: holding onto a façade which never has been true . . ."

I couldn't go on. I looked up from the letter, dazed, and my eyes met Bill Shiffrin's. I was vaguely astonished that he was still sitting there holding his drink, while I felt as if I had fallen through space and time. He did not ask any more questions, swallowed his drink and left in haste.

I continued reading up to a sentence which hit me: "I have a sad way out, but this would separate us completely and irrevocably and also it would not help you . . ." What did he mean? What *could* he mean? A woman, and a woman with money? But only a few days ago, on August 28, he had written about our reunion, and this letter was dated September 1. He could not possibly have gotten that seriously involved with someone in a few days. The woman must have been in his life all along. I read on: ". . . but probably you really wish to be free and try your own life, since with me you lived in slavery . . . how sad your life was with me I can see only now . . . Finally, I had to stop and look back and see that in my mad race I have left only shambles behind and made everybody unhappy who ever had the misfortune to be connected with me . . . I would like to tell you many things, but I cannot now. God bless, my Heart, and forgive me that I was not able to do a better job."

He must be innocent, I thought, he wouldn't write this way if he weren't. I would give my life for his success. I pictured him alone and forsaken in Rome; if only I could go at once to him, take his hand, talk to him. But I couldn't; I had no money.

Once again I looked at the date on the envelope: "Roma, Settembre 1, 1953."

*   *   *

Years later I found in Gabriel's files a copy of a cable dated: "Roma, Settembre 1, 1953." It was addressed to the Woman on Park Avenue:

"Overjoyed by your last cable . . . Open your wings, we will fly high."

Chapter 2

The Curse of Ahasuerus

A Cadillac, a chauffeur, twenty trunks filled with Cantonese silk dresses, dried Chinese herbs and elixirs, and a large red cat landed at Genoa with the Woman of Shanghai on Sunday, September 20, 1953. Gabriel was waiting at the dock.

They drove to Venice, where Gabriel had gone to meet Mike Todd and talk with him about *Gandhi*. Irene Selznick was there, too, with an offer for the *Pygmalion* musical. "Wait for my news from Venice," Gabriel's letter said. The news came, but it was not good: both prospects had petered out.

The Cadillac moved on to the Villa Ibsen at Siusi. Gabriel had an old option for a film of *Peer Gynt* and now he had an appointment with Tankred Ibsen, the grandson of the dramatist. Gabriel had always felt close to the character of Peer Gynt, the self-seeker, who lost his identity by selling his soul to the troll way of life. Peer's final question: "Where was I, as myself, as the whole man, the true man?" and the Button-Molder's answer: "Yourself you never have been at all!" were the themes of Gabriel's own search for identity. At that time I was too far away even to touch on Gabriel's problems or to understand the depth of his sufferings. Only much later, after studying *Peer Gynt* as a possible key to the puzzle of Gabriel, did I realize how symbolic it was that he would think of filming it at the time when he was breaking away from me, his imagined Solveig, to start a new illusion with the Green Girl, Anitra.

After Siusi a mad race began: Munich, Salzburg, Rome, Munich again, then Hamburg, trying to raise money, to sell his dreams. He ran, and the Woman ran with him. His cocksure letters were like the shouts of a man in a lost battle. To a business friend in New York: "I am more worried about you than you are about me, because God gave me this fantastic power of action, and when I believe in something, the mountains move, the rivers stop . . ."

It was in Venice that Gabriel asked for the first loan from the Woman of Shanghai, sure that he could return it soon. He couldn't. Then came a second loan, followed by others. They weren't large amounts and he carefully noted them in his small date book: a few hundred dollars here and there. Then his debts began to grow. In the past, Gabriel never thought much of money, giving and taking it cheerfully. But he had never borrowed from a woman, especially from a woman whose lover he was. He was ashamed and the Woman disappointed. Nothing she had hoped for had happened. The question of her career never even came up. The man she had followed had no time or energy for her and there was only one thing on his mind: to save his own career. She was being used, she felt. Fights began between them. And next to the account of debts in his notebook Gabriel scribbled in Hungarian: "That face in the mirror is not me any more."

The Woman was left behind in Rome while Gabriel flew to Munich, and her thoughts were sobering ones: "Suddenly, I found myself alone in a hotel room," she wrote to him. What was she doing, she asked herself, in a strange room, in a strange town, in a strange land? All she had come for was love. But "where is love?" she wrote. Could she yet nurse him back to his old self with her herbs? And then "maybe your eyes will not look so far away?"

After Gabriel returned to Rome, the berserk run around Europe with the Woman began again. His debts to her were mounting, but he was still doing his best to keep up the "façade." He stayed at the best hotels. Monogrammed pure silk shirts were still being made to order for him by the dozen at Turnbull and Asser on Jermyn Street in London, and the Duke of Windsor's tailor was still busy making his suits. In one of the last letters I received from him, he wrote: "Remember, when the illusion of my power is no more in the heads of people, I will not be able to get the smallest help from my so-called best friends."

That illusion was fast dying. Every day there were bitter scenes and accusations with his Woman. But luck must be waiting somewhere, at the roulette table of his destiny. Feverishly, he put newer and newer plans on the *rouge et noir. Candida,* to be filmed with Maria Schell in Munich; *The Doctor's Dilemma,* financed by a Lichtenstein group; once more dealings with the Mexican President, Miguel Alemán, for *Blanco Posnet* in Mexico City; then David Lean and *Man and Superman;* a new buyer for the *Pygmalion* musical; a disappointing negotiation with Otto Preminger . . . And the game was never bigger: his "soul and integrity" were at stake. He *had* to pay the Woman back and he *had* to send money to his wife.

He had a date with Baba in India for February 1—if he could make it. In those dark days he hung on to the faith that Baba had the power to help him not only spiritually but with the Gandhi film.

He collapsed on his return to Rome. The doctor diagnosed the sickness as food poisoning. Gabriel lay in bed with a high fever, his body swollen and red. Then, after a long, long time, he wrote to me, but never mailed the letter. The beginning and the end of it are missing:

". . . only one who suffered so superhumanly. Only at the moment of realizing that my pain is a necessity for my life realization it suddenly stopped hurting me and the heavens opened to me and I saw the Great Truth as I knew it once instinctively when I was a boy . . . 'Pascal' is dead, but Gabriel the Phoenix will arise from the ashes. Send your kind thoughts, my dear Vally, toward his flight."

A week later, he was in London, alone. He had forced himself to get up and go there for a meeting with Sir Alexander Korda. Earlier he had offered Korda partnership in the *Pygmalion* musical. Now, entering the Piccadilly offices of London Films, did he think of the strange similarity to events twenty years earlier? Then, with Shaw's *Pygmalion* contract in his pocket, he had gone to Korda in the Denham Studios. Korda had turned him down and, lacking carfare, Gabriel had had to walk back to London. Now again he had nothing and Korda everything, including a knighthood.

"This is the greatest property ever offered to you," Gabriel said, facing Korda in his elegant office. "The *Pygmalion* musical cannot be anything but a tremendous hit, and the film of it will hit the jackpot. It will guarantee a sure income for you over the next ten to fifteen years."

Cold sweat on his upper lip, he tried to conceal the trembling of his hands as he fished for documents in his portfolio. He still had fever, but he talked in his old, dynamic way. But his words seemed to fall back, defeated, against Korda's stony coldness.

"Then here is the *Gandhi* film." Gabriel was not giving up; he put letters from Prime Minister Nehru and others on the desk. "This film would bring you prestige, would give you an opportunity to help the world with the most important message of today: non-violence. It would bring money to you and *peace* to me."

Korda turned down both propositions, and London became the most bitter station of Gabriel's humiliation. He was received with indifference while the city resounded with the names of people who had been nobodies when he was at the top. The fog in the streets already had the bite of winter. Those cold streets held up a mirror of memories. They reflected back the portrait of the Gabriel Pascal of old, with his imperious walk, his arrogance, his impish laughter. It was not easy for the graying man with his sick, heavy body to face that magical Gabriel Pascal from the past—the one who had made headlines, the friend of George Bernard Shaw, the petted "Gabby" of London Society. And he was frightened: was there any future for him?

And there in the lone terror of the night he cried out to Baba in India:

My dearest Baba,
     Whatever you may be, Saint or Demon, Servant or Commander of secret forces, answer me now.

Our Lord had fourteen Stations of the Calvary, then He was crucified and resurrected. Why then must I, a dirty nothing, a piece of imagination of my own, a phantom, an unexplainable contradiction of God and the Devil, go on suffering?

Five days ago, I had food poisoning and I was close to passing away from that grotesque earthly form of mine—then I was saved again to continue this senseless masquerade, this pretentious playing of a human being which I am not, a genius which I am not, a criminal which I am not. Where did my devilish mistake start, when did I sell my soul for faces, for imaginary values; where was the border of honesty, when did I leave behind that simple peasant boy *I*, the boy who was lying in the fields dreaming with open eyes? Then there was yet a divine mission in my dreams: I heard divine voices and listened to divine inspirations. Where was the border when I began to listen to the Devil, to err on this earth in the strange fright of my soul? What was the purpose of all this? Answer me.

How can a human body go through all these upheavals of passion and disillusion and never lose hope and never lose faith? Baba, I am not from Hell. Even the best motor-car stops if its driver is mad and abusing its engine until it explodes somewhere in an abyss, finishing its aimless running against pitiless rocks. Why then must I go on? Is there a divine plan? If you are a Servant, a Messenger of the Great Universal Spirit, answer me now . . . I left my wife . . . and now I am to leave a Chinese girl whom I met six months ago. She aroused the maddest passion in me, but is fighting against my spirit . . . she is very rich and as you know I am poor . . . but I do not want to make another grave mistake—the time is getting short for me to find and to tell about truth. Is this my mission? But why the suffering, the frustration? Do you know the answer or are you just pretending and searching as desperately as I am for the right road? But you must know, after so many years of silence and meditation, you *must* know the great, the simple Divine Answer. Answer me, whoever you are, answer me: the first of February is so far away.

Distraught, I sat surrounded by my luggage at a West Side hotel in New York. The noise, the smell, the language of the place nauseated me. But it was cheap. I was to stay there with Mother until I could have Pauline's apartment back while she went to Nevada for her divorce. The California house had been rented for six months from November 1.

Since October there had been a strange silence from Gabriel—only a few cables from a bewildering variety of places. What was he doing, planning? Why didn't he write?

As I began to unpack my suitcases, the phone rang. It was Gabriel.

He was in London, he said, and all alone. He emphasized the "alone."

"Why didn't you write in all this time?" I burst out. "How could you forsake me this way? It's criminal."

"I am not a criminal." His voice faltered. "There isn't a moment when I am not worried about you. I have no money."

"But writing doesn't cost money, neither does sincerity."

"I've written you many letters," he said weakly, "but I couldn't mail them." Then he told me that he had been dangerously sick, some kind of poisoning: "I nearly died . . . I wish I could have died."

I felt the danger signal of pity and returning love. "Where are you now?"

"I'm staying at Claridge's."

My pity evaporated. I nearly laughed at myself. Claridge's! Poor starving Gabriel. I bet he wouldn't be having two eggs for dinner, like me.

"I want a divorce!" The cry broke out of me in a shrill voice which didn't sound like mine.

Pauline left for Nevada, and I moved into her apartment. Mother was living in New Jersey, in a convent run by Hungarian nuns. I wanted to get a job, and thought of modeling. An agency arranged an appointment at the studio of a fashion photographer. At the studio, girls were waiting, obviously for the same reason—a noisy lot, pretty and common, full of vigor and youthful hunger for life. Suddenly, I felt old. I remembered myself in Hungary, fighting my way up to star billing, my name in neon lights above the cinemas of Budapest, my photos on sale in the stores, distinguished men as my beaux, the horror of the war, the marriage to Tibor . . . then Gabriel and life among the elite of the world. And now—was I to begin all over again? But I had lost that enthusiasm, that hungry, pushing faith. What was I doing here among these girls?

I got up and left.

A dinner party with friends at the Colony Restaurant. In the course of conversation, my neighbor at the table said: "Oh, I know Gabby Pascal very well. I saw him this autumn in the Tyrol. He was having dinner with a Chinese lady, the widow of a banker friend of mine from Shanghai."

The walls of the Colony moved in. So he *was* with a woman. When and where had he met her? Who was she? Was she the "sad way out"? And why did he lie to me that he was alone? I felt an almost physical pain but it was not jealousy—rather the shame of being fooled while I was still trying to believe him.

For days, I was shattered and unable to face the town. Then two letters arrived from California. In the first, I was advised to pay taxes of $965 on the house at once; in the other, I was informed that my tenants had simply moved out. Five months remained of their lease and to catch up with them would mean a long lawsuit. The house was empty again and the mortgage and now the tax had to be paid.

That night I developed a fever, awakening in the morning with an excruciating pain in my back. For two days, I lay without desire to live. Discovering that I was ill, a friend sent a doctor around. The doctor, Joe Kuh, was a young man full of faith and enthusiasm, who made up his mind to cure me. He also nosed about my apartment, apparently under the impression—a correct one—that I wasn't eating. He came each day, attacking my well-developed kidney infection with a needle. His faith made me want to live, whereupon my worries returned. Since Gabriel's last letter from London in November I hadn't heard from him. I no longer knew where he was. I had to write to his English lawyer. It was humiliating to ask a lawyer for my husband's address and to tell him about my dire situation, but I had to get in touch with Gabriel at once.

On Monday, December 7, 1953, the lawyer replied that he himself didn't know where his client was. The same mail brought a letter from Gabriel, dated December 5 and mailed from the Lisbon airport. What was he doing there?

"I have written many letters to you, but never sent them," Gabriel wrote. "I have been through the most tragic, humiliating and sad three months of my life. I have tried everything. Like a cursed Ahasuerus, I ran through all Europe: Salzburg, Munich, Frankfurt, Hamburg, Paris, London, and again Munich, Rome, Madrid, and I am in Lisbon now. It will be decided here whether I go direct to India or whether it will be possible to come back to you in New York for a few days . . . I would like to put everything in order and leave a sum of money for you—and only this duty of mine has kept me from going to India . . . Why has all this happened to you and to me? If only once more I could look up to the sky with clear eyes and step before the presence of God and find out where my sinful soul lost its balance. I was never so sad in my life and this is right because I must be punished. For all our mistakes we have to pay: with money, blood, sweat or even with the eternal life of our souls . . . At the latest, you will hear from me in two weeks ·.. I have been very sick, too. It isn't easy for such a miserable being as I have become to be freed from this Calvary. Forgive me all the bitter hours with so little joy which you have spent with me. I always think of you with love."

I was still under the influence of the letter when Dr. Kuh arrived. He was rolling out his instruments on the dresser when the telephone rang at my bedside.

"Yes?" I said.

"It's me."

The room swayed. It was Gabriel! Gabriel in New York!

"I . . . I will explain," he was saying in a hoarse voice. "Don't ask questions. Hear me out calmly . . . I have just arrived from Portugal."

"Come at once." I felt relief, convinced somehow that everything would be all right now that he was in town.

"I can't come now. You have to understand."

"Understand what?" I knew then that something was wrong.

"I am in a trap. I am in a woman's trap." His voice was frantic. "I cannot say anything now. The only reason I came back was to help you. But you must leave me alone; otherwise we are in great trouble."

"I don't understand what you're talking about," I told him. "I just don't understand. I'm sick. I'm alone. The tenants moved out of the house, and the tax . . ."

"I know," he interrupted me. "Don't repeat it, please. This morning I received a letter from my English lawyer with your letter to him enclosed. How did you dare to write to him in such a way . . . as if I were a criminal, forsaking you?"

Stunned, I thought of the English lawyer's letter, which I had received only that morning, and in which he had denied knowing Gabriel's whereabouts. Yet he had forwarded my letter to Gabriel in New York! Obviously, Gabriel himself had instructed him not to tell me he was to be here. In his own Lisbon letter, mailed only two days before, he was vague about his plans, although at that time he must have been getting ready to fly to New York. That letter which had touched me so—even that was a lie. Probably he wouldn't even have called me if it hadn't been for the lawyer's warning note.

"Where are you staying?" I felt seasick.

"I can't tell you anything. I will call you again in an hour's time." And he put down the receiver.

"Excuse the delay." The doctor turned to me. "But I broke my syringe."

I stared at him. I had forgotten that he was there. His words triggered a convulsion. I let myself go, perhaps subconsciously seeking someone to cling to. The doctor could only look at me in bewilderment as I sobbed.

The cab traveled north on Central Park West into one of the park roads leading to the East Side. Gabriel had picked me up on the corner opposite 67th Street and Central Park West. I still didn't know where he was staying. During the past week, he had called me a few times. His words were short and cold.

I couldn't see him clearly in the dim light of the cab. "You cut your hair," he said. His voice was thick.

I said, "Please understand that I don't want anything from you and there is no necessity for hiding, not even if you are living in the very 'trap' of your woman. I will not have you watched and sue for non-support and adultery, or make scenes. I am simply not interested in your doings. The only reason I talk to you at all is because of the house."

The cab stopped in front of a small Hungarian restaurant. He must have been sure that nobody would see us there. Only when we were seated did our eyes meet. His sickly appearance shocked me—not so much his outer appearance as something behind it. His open and self-assured expression, his proud, kingly posture—these had vanished. The man sitting there seemed like the lifeless, outside shell of Gabriel Pascal, as if his soul had left him.

He was rude to the waiter, and when his food came he didn't touch it. Then he said, "Since we parted, I have tried out three women and I am not in love with you any more." His words were pronounced with animosity. "Nor am I in love with anybody else. I have other worries."

I didn't answer. I didn't ask. I didn't want to hear anything.

In the days that followed he would phone me from time to time and we would talk of nothing. He said he was staying at the New York Athletic Club. Finally I could stand it no longer; I *had* to talk to him, to beg for the truth. I called him at the Club around midnight. He wasn't there; nor was he back at one or at two or even at five in the morning. I left messages but was ashamed to say that "Mrs. Pascal had called," so I used my maiden name.

He returned my calls the next day. He had had a late meeting. I said I had not asked where he had been. And why did I call him? Nothing important any more, I said.

Finally, there was news from the real-estate agent in California. Again I called Gabriel and he said he would come over to discuss the offer. I served tea in front of the fireplace. And there he sat, avoiding my eyes: the husband turned stranger. Then the phone rang: a man who had been trying to date me. An impulse to show Gabriel how little he mattered now turned my "How are you?" into a love song. My caller asked if I would finally dine with him.

"When? Why not tonight? How wonderful!" I cooed. "Oh, wherever you like. I've missed you, too." My would-be dinner partner seemed to lose his voice at the other end in his surprise at my suddenly changed behavior.

When I sat down and reached for my cup, Gabriel's silence made me look up. I noticed that his face had become distorted with restraint, and suddenly a tear ran down to the collar of his suit. Quickly, as if I had observed nothing, I said, "I'll fix some more tea."

In the kitchen I felt weak. Never before had I seen him cry, and that silent tear was the saddest thing I had ever experienced. When I returned with the teapot, we were both more composed. Soon he got up to leave. At the door, I reached for his hand. He took it; then shyly he embraced me and kissed me lightly on the cheek.

The usual excitement was in the air as Christmas approached. In a shop window on East 57th Street I caught sight of a necktie that Gabriel would like. I bought it because of his tear.

It had started to drizzle when, in the drab twilight, I cut through the square in front of the Plaza Hotel to walk up Central Park South toward my hotel. It occurred to me to leave the tie in its Christmas box for Gabriel at the New York Athletic Club. When I reached the Club I hesitated by the entrance. Through the glass I could see a tall Christmas tree scattering light over the hall inside, and I reached the lowest point of my inner darkness. Was it only last Christmas that we had had a home together and had stood around a tree, humming carols?

"Can I help you?" The doorman's voice scattered my thoughts. I suddenly felt ashamed, shook my head, and went away.

We met again. Having tea with me in Pauline's apartment, he seemed to be easing up. I felt he wanted to talk, to tell me everything, but he couldn't. Finally, he made some obscure remarks that his affair "with the Woman" was about to be over. I listened without saying anything; then, when he was about to leave, I gave him the necktie. He was touched. "I'll always treasure it," he said. And indeed he did, wearing it forever in his final rest.

"*Introibo ad altare Dei . . .*" The white-haired old priest began the Midnight Mass at Christmas. Outside, among tall pine trees, the winter wind howled. The windows of the chapel trembled. The candle flames swayed. Black, kneeling shadows: the nuns. The peace of the convent in the country where I went to spend Christmas with my mother closed me in.

"Send forth Thy light and Thy Truth," the priest was praying at the foot of the altar. "I am lost," I was telling God. "Do you hear me? Help me, help Gabriel and me out of our darkness. Give us light. Oh, God, let me find you!" Suddenly, a sentence I had read that day in the nuns' library came into my mind: "Thou wouldst not have sought Me had I not already been seeking thee." Was I not searching for Him through books and thoughts? Yet He did not answer. But if that sentence were true, then He would answer! As in my childhood, I was suddenly overwhelmed with a sweet longing, as if a joyous call rose in me, like the tremulous tune on the shepherd's flute in the thin mountain air, a nostalgic note rising and vanishing away. A tune so eternally known, so heartbreakingly happy as if He were calling.

Before I had left for the convent, Gabriel, once again not feeling well, had flown to the Mayo Clinic. Somebody loaned him the money to go, he said. He called me from Rochester; then came a letter struggling for words: "For a long time I haven't felt as near to you as tonight over the phone. I wrote you from the plane but I couldn't mail it. You are the only one who doesn't want anything from me but sincerity. But I cannot. To tell you everything, we would need months or years, until finally cured of each other, we could talk as friends talk . . ."

When he returned from the Clinic he called me at the convent. There was no longer any danger of cancer, he said. I was elated by this news, only to be cast down by his next words. Before he left for Mayo's he had promised to break a previous engagement in order to spend New Year's Eve with me. Now he said he couldn't.

I felt again the agonizing shame of the deceived one. I had believed him when he said that the affair was finished. Now it was plain that he was going to spend New Year's Eve with *her*.

The next day, he called again. "I'm free for New Year's Eve." His voice was cheerful.

"I'm sorry," I told him coldly, "but it's too late. I've accepted another invitation." What lie, I wondered, had he told the other woman?

He was silent for a while, then: "Let's meet before New Year's Eve, in the afternoon," adding, "I have to see you." Reluctantly I said yes.

On the last afternoon of 1953 we had tea at Gabriel's Club. He was wearing the necktie I had given him. After tea, he hailed a cab, directing it to Saint Patrick's Cathedral. "In church," he said, "I would like to say goodbye to this year which has parted us and pray that God will lead us out of this confusion."

Inside the cathedral we knelt side by side at the altar of Mary, as we had knelt at Saint Etienne in Paris that first time. There was no pain in me now. Paris was another life. I wasn't praying. The dull clamor of the streets reached me through the walls, speaking of life outside, a new life in which I would forget my sad, long sickness. And Gabriel, kneeling at my side, was as remote as Paris. You can't hurt me any more, I thought.

He stood up and stepped to the candle rack. Was he going to light "our candles"? He was. For the sake of style, I thought, so as to close the verse with the rhyme with which it started in Paris. His hand, receding from the candle rack, touched mine but our two hands, which once had clung together, abruptly pulled apart.

"I am disgusted with you," I said two weeks later as we faced each other in Pauline's apartment. I was standing among my suitcases, ready to fly back to California where I was to arrange matters concerning the house. Gabriel had asked me to give him my last money in England, the thousand pounds which remained in my account (he had borrowed another thousand earlier). "Your money is frozen in England anyhow," he argued, "and it would save me; I have a debt there I have to settle at once." He had brought along a document, which he had signed, for the equivalent of my English pounds in American dollars which I was to get from one of his projected deals—if and when it materialized. In a few months, by April, he would have money, he said. And to prove his words, he drew contracts, documents and letters from his portfolio. It seemed to me, as he talked, that his sentences flew like proud birds from his mouth and fluttered around the room, only to fall with broken wings. He himself did not believe in his hopes any more.

"You know that you left me in misery," I finally told him. "But what is worse, you lied to me, you were insincere with me. You also know that since your return you haven't given me a penny and all my savings are gone. And now you have the gall to ask for the last money I have on this earth. I don't even hate you; I just despise you."

He stood astounded. Then with trembling hands he gathered the papers he had laid out for me and put them back in his portfolio. He took my plane ticket out of it and put it on the table.

"I'll give you the check," I said suddenly.

He shot me a stricken look. He mumbled "no," and said that I was right not to trust him: he was a finished man.

I signed the check and pushed it into his hand.

We left the apartment together. A limousine sent by a beau of mine was waiting downstairs to take me to the airport. I offered Gabriel a lift; somewhat reluctantly he accepted, for it was a bitter cold day and there was no cab in sight. He stopped the car on Park Avenue near 62nd Street. I looked back at him from the rear window. He was standing there on the curb, in the grayness of the street, the freezing wind tearing at his light spring coat. He disappeared and I began to cry. How would I know that he had stopped the car in front of the apartment house where the Woman of Shanghai lived?

Already in Europe the Woman had sensed that she was wrestling for Gabriel with something greater than he was. Who, or what, was it? God or Baba or his own stubborn drive for "perfection"? Why would he feel that their love was sinful? And why did he want to go to Baba in India? She feared Baba. Though she believed that she herself possessed occult powers, the Indian Perfect Master threatened to be a more powerful wizard.

Since their return to New York, their relationship had worsened. Gabriel was unable to assist her in her career; she lost valuable time with him and the repayment of her loans seemed each day more doubtful. The "millions in *Pygmalion*" and other assets were empty talk and the only tangible thing Gabriel had was that house in California with its antiques and paintings, but a wife attached to it as well.

Gabriel felt guilty toward the Woman to whom he had promised so much and given nothing. The Park Avenue apartment ceased to be the haven of last spring. He wanted to get away, but,

as she reminded him, he owed her money. He answered her re-
proaches with outbursts of anger, which were matched by her
own. Yet they could not let each other go. He became sick again
and was convinced that "illness was put upon me as punishment
for not abandoning a sinful life," as he wrote to his "Sister"
Mirha Behn in India.

The date to pay a new installment to the Shaw Trustee for the
extension of the *Pygmalion* musical rights was fast approaching.
Gabriel was moving everything for a loan, but he couldn't raise a
penny. Only one day was left and one door open. That evening,
he went to the Park Avenue apartment. The Woman said that it
was too late now for her to sell some securities, so next morning
they went together to the Provident Pawn Shop. There she
pawned some jewelry and loaned $7,500 to Gabriel, who cabled it
right away to England.

"You remember," he wrote to a London friend, "when you
asked me what would happen if the date came to pay the Shaw
Trustee and I told you: I will pay . . . pay even if I have to sell
my eternal soul for it. Well, I sold more than my soul: I sold my
honor."

Gabriel's date to meet Baba in India had been changed to February 24. On February 25—Baba's birthday—Gabriel was to start
with him on a pilgrimage. But the hope of getting to India grew
dimmer, for once again he could not raise any money. He was now
offering all his assets, including the *Pygmalion* musical rights,
"which alone are worth a million," to different promoters for
$100,000—with the exception of the rights to *Gandhi,* the film he
was to do "dead or alive." But nobody was interested.

In the past when Gabriel had been in New York, one of Baba's
American pupils worked as his secretary. He was a jobless actor
named Harold who had approached Gabriel, hoping to further
his career through the connection. He was stocky and ruddy-
faced, a mixture of unctuous servility, arrogant ignorance, and
undigested spiritual ideas. He was friendly with another devoted
follower of Baba, a middle-aged, well-to-do lady named Margaret
Scott.

Born in the Midwest of a German family, Margaret Scott had been a lonely child. Pretty, with long red-blond pigtails and large blue eyes, she was a dreamer—a quality she would never lose on the long road which was to take her from the Midwest to the Orient. She always remained the pigtailed girl, and her whole life was one long waiting for a "miracle." She was always sure that the miracle would be there on some future day, hanging suspended like a golden ball on a Christmas tree. Many times she dreamed that she had found the miracle, only to awaken disillusioned. As the years went by, her awakenings became more and more violent; but she would once again close her eyes tight and continue to dream.

Then came a time when she wanted to dream without awakening. One night, aboard a freighter somewhere in the warm seas of the Far East, she attempted to find in death the miracle she could not find in life. In the few minutes between life and suicide she met a silent stranger on the deck. He was a Hindu with a beautiful face. He was wearing snow-white garments and had long, black hair, a beard, and a mustache. His eyes were large and fiery. She thought she had seen a vision of Jesus Christ. The stranger was Shri Meher Baba. He pulled her back from the rail, and from then on Margaret began to dream her new dream. Her life became centered around Baba.

In New York she often heard Baba's followers speak of his favorite disciple, Gabriel Pascal, Baba's "Phoenix." Margaret, of course, was more than curious to meet him, but so far she had never had an opportunity. Then one day, Harold, Baba's pupil, approached her to arrange a meeting. Harold wanted to help. He knew of Gabriel's desperate attempts to raise money for the trip to meet Baba on February 24 and surely the devoted Mrs. Scott would advance the required sum.

Margaret Scott did not know the reason for Gabriel's visit; she was expecting some spiritual revelations from Baba's favorite disciple. The man Harold introduced looked like nothing she had imagined. He appeared sickly, his ankles swollen, his eyes confused. Almost immediately after Harold left, he told Mrs. Scott the reason for his visit: he wanted a loan.

Margaret could not cover up her disappointment. Being a rich woman, she hated to be used, especially that spontaneously and openly. There was a long, embarrassed silence. Gabriel, humiliated, got up to leave. Their eyes met. They recognized each other: two miracle seekers.

"If I cannot go to Baba in time, there is only suicide for me," he burst out.

Suicide. Margaret shuddered. She knew what he was talking about. She motioned him to sit down. After that, everything happened fast: that confession bottled up in Gabriel so long broke out in a wild deluge. He told of his inner split and how he, a man proud of his integrity, honor, talent, and career, had lost everything, even his God. His story twined about his broken marriage, his business failures, his maddening passion for the Woman of Shanghai, that passion which was the death of his "higher self." He confessed that he was hopelessly trapped by his debts to her. Was there still a way out? "Only Baba would know," he ended his story. Baba had the *Answer*.

Margaret sat spellbound. "As he talked," she remembered later, "it seemed to me that his face began to change. It smoothed, as if with every word he said, lines of suffering and sickness peeled off. Yes, his face became translucent, that is the word: translucent, like an Angel's. The evil disappeared and he looked like the Archangel Gabriel. A flaming, beautiful Angel. His eyes grew larger and larger and I could not see anything but those eyes. I was lost in them, as their depth reflected the stars of the Universe ... and at that moment, I *knew* who he had been ... but I cannot tell. I cannot yet tell."

When Margaret promised the round-trip ticket to India, Gabriel said a "beautiful and symbolic thing," she remembered, blushing and sighing. "He said that sometime earlier he had taken a vow: if God was to help him out of the mess he was in, he would never touch a woman again, but would devote his remaining time to searching for the Truth. He said he had always wanted to be a monk and now he would be one. There is a divine connection," Margaret was to assure me later.

During the weekend of February 20, in a hotel in Hyde Park, New York, Gabriel told the Woman of Shanghai that three days later he was to take off for India, that their relationship had to change to one of pure friendship, and that he would be back in April with "plenty of money" to repay his debt to her.

Her anger was volcanic. He could not walk out on her like that, after having used and abused her, taken her money—and her jewelry still in the pawnshop.

It was sometime after that scene—and after Gabriel had held fast to his vow against a new temptation—that he had the dream.

"I dreamed that I awakened," he related to Margaret, "and I saw a sword suspended above my bed with its sharp end pointing at me. It looked like an ancient weapon, with burning-red rubies on its ivory handle. It was really more a vision, it was so vivid. Then slowly, the sword disappeared. When I really awakened, I wondered what that dream had meant. Did it signify my initiation into a new life? Was it the sword of the spirit? What do you think?"

Margaret blushed with excitement. Here she was in the middle of the most fascinating story ever. Shyly, she took out of her handbag a box containing an old-fashioned amethyst ring.

"I *know* what your dream meant," she said, "but I cannot tell you yet. Just take this ring to Baba and ask him my question: 'Is he the *one?*' If he nods his head, bring me back the ring and I'll tell you what your dream meant and who you were in another life."

Gabriel was too busy with his own thoughts to catch the significance of her blushing words or the ring and, somewhat absent-mindedly, he promised to give it to Baba.

On the morning of February 22, Gabriel, with Margaret and Harold, went to the air terminal and bought his round trip ticket to India. He was to leave on February 23. Afterward all three of them got into a cab which Gabriel directed to the Woman of Shanghai's apartment house, where Gabriel got out; Margaret and Harold continued on in the cab.

Gabriel spent only a short time in the apartment, as it was still before lunch time when he appeared in his lawyer's office on Madison Avenue. Even though it was a holiday, the lawyer, Irving Margulies, had gone to his office because Gabriel intended to leave the following day. They discussed the Gandhi film contracts and other business matters. But Gabriel never asked his lawyer's advice about two vital documents which were to be in the hands of the Woman of Shanghai before the end of that day. One was a carefully worded, businesslike letter, typewritten and obviously dictated to someone, maybe Harold. It presented a gift of a percentage of the producer's share of the future *Pygmalion* musical to his "loyal executive secretary," the Woman of Shanghai. No doubt it was designed to calm her worry over the loans.

At six o'clock that evening he returned to her apartment to give her the letter and to say goodbye to her. But when he left much later, the letter wasn't the only thing he left behind. There was also a short note, scribbled on New York Athletic Club stationery:

> This is my will: if I should die on this my trip to India, you are my sole heiress. Signed the 22 February, 1954
> Gabriel Pascal
> in New York City.

It was addressed to the Woman of Shanghai and was witnessed by two Chinese signatures.

Eight months later, when the Woman of Shanghai offered that will to be probated, she was questioned about the circumstances. She said that on the night of February 22, Gabriel, her fiancé, had had dinner at her place. He expressed again his wish, as he had so often in the past, to write his last will, making her his beneficiary. That night, being worried about his trip to India and the possibility of his death, Gabriel told her that he was "not properly divorced yet" and, because her jewelry was still in the pawnshop and he owed her money too, he wanted to write a will. She said that she had protested and assured him she did not want anything from him.

All this was overheard by the chauffeur. "The chauffeur knows everything," she said. "On the trip to Italy he was with us all the time." Although the chauffeur was dismissed from his job after the European trip, he still did occasional work for her and that night had stayed late in the apartment to pack some suitcases. Gabriel turned the chauffeur down as a witness for the will because, the Woman said, he did not want a servant as a witness. But in the end the illiterate Chinese cook, an old woman who did not speak any English, was one of the witnesses; the other was a young Chinese girl who spoke both Chinese and English and who did some secretarial work for the Woman of Shanghai. This girl lived quite far away and they had to wait a long time for her to get there. When she finally appeared, the story went, Gabriel sat down at the dining room table and explained to the witnesses that he was going to write a will on behalf of the Woman of Shanghai. Then he wrote his one-sentence "if" will. "All I know," the Woman of Shanghai said in court, "is the man made me a will; he loved me, and I loved him. He had nothing; I gave him all my time and love."

What could Gabriel have said about that night of February 22, when he seemingly forgot that he had a wife still living in the house that was his only tangible asset and which he willed away to a rich woman? The dead cannot be questioned even though sometimes they talk. There remained a letter, written on a later date, to Baba: "I am cured of all my illnesses which attacked me after the 22nd of February . . . also a Chinese lady, who pesters me with her so-called goodness, tried to aggravate me. She was the person I nearly killed on the night of the 22nd of February, when you saved me from dirty flesh . . ."

The next morning, February 23, Gabriel canceled his trip to India.

On February 25, Baba's birthday, the pilgrimage in India commenced without the favorite disciple. But even without going to India, Gabriel told Margaret Scott, he was liberated on February 22. "Baba performed the miracle," Margaret said, "and saved Gabriel from his fleshly desires forever." It was through her sacrifice—buying the tickets to India—that Baba had worked; of this Margaret was convinced. Yes, she said, beaming at the memory, "it was through me that Gabriel was saved and was able to sever all connections with that Chinese woman."

On February 25, Margaret sent a birthday card—for Baba's birthday—to Gabriel. On it was a picture of a pigtailed blonde girl sitting in a swing—"the child I was," Margaret wrote on the card and congratulated Gabriel on his own "New Birth, which had taken place in your soul."

And thus Margaret Scott's last, greatest, and most intricately woven dream began.

*   *   *

When the tenants in the California house broke their lease, I thought it was a disaster. Actually, it turned out to be a blessing. The house was now available for sale, and, in the middle of February, General Omar Bradley bought it. Only in retrospect was I to realize that it was a miracle sent to me at the right time, for the sale solved my financial problem for the time being. Had it not occurred when it did, I would have been forced to spend the summer in California, trying to get rid of the house, and I wouldn't have been at Gabriel's side when he most needed me.

When he called me from New York on February 18, I did not tell him about the sale. I wanted the escrow to go through first and the money to be safe in the bank. I didn't trust him any more. On the phone he sounded elated. In a few days, he was to leave for India. A follower of Baba had loaned him the money. His health had been very bad lately, he said. I was worried about him and asked him to call me before he went. Soon he phoned again: "I'm not going after all," he announced. "Maybe later. *Gandhi* has to wait. I have no right to go before I put my affairs in order with you. I'm coming to Los Angeles."

I was relieved that he was not going to India, but I wasn't happy at all about his coming to California. I didn't want to see him, at least not for a while. I was determined to go through with the divorce, even though at one point he had asked me to wait another year. From the way he talked, I realized it was not the hope to save our marriage which had prompted him; rather he was afraid to be vulnerable.

It was midnight on March 1 when my phone rang. Gabriel was calling from the lobby of the Beverly Wilshire Hotel, where he had arrived to find no room available. He sounded worn out.

I was exhausted beyond my strength by the hurried packing to have the house ready for the Bradleys. To get up now, to fix up Gabriel's room, and then to face him in the middle of the night was too much. But after a sleepless half hour, I called him back. He was still in the lobby. "Come over here; you cannot sit there the whole night." His answer was unfriendly. No, he would not come, but he would call me about our meeting.

A week passed before I saw him. Whatever he had secretly hoped for from that meeting did not come through. He soon left and I broke out into hysterical sobs.

*   *   *

Three days later we signed the divorce settlement. I was stubborn. Against my lawyer's advice, I waived all my rights to my husband's assets, including the *Pygmalion* musical rights and the other Shaw rights. I settled for the modest amount which remained from the sale of the house after everything was paid off.

Gabriel came to the house to meet my lawyer and sign the papers. When he read the settlement, he looked relieved: he was off the alimony hook. I had no idea that with that settlement I had opened the door for the Woman of Shanghai to claim Gabriel's whole estate.

After we both signed the settlement, the lawyer left and we sat on the terrace. A gust of wind clapped the hard leaves of the bird of paradise tree together. It sounded as if the trees were talking in a fast, running chatter. But we were silent. When Gabriel suddenly began to talk, I was startled. "I saw my drum clearly just now," he said, in an astonished voice. "It was almost like a vision for a second, in front of my eyes."

I knew what he was talking about: that red toy drum which, in his boyhood, had been taken away from him and given to his new "brother."

"It was bright red," he continued, without looking at me, "such a happy, living red like the rubies on the handle of the sword I dreamed about the other night."

"What sword?" I didn't want to talk about the drum. I didn't want to fall for the Greenhaired Boy again, for the little orphan from the Transylvanian mountains from whom the toys were taken all his life—even this big, white house here. I had had enough of all that.

"I dreamed one night," Gabriel answered, "that I awakened and saw a sword suspended in the darkness above me. A strange light was emanating from it. I reached up for it. What do you suppose that meant?"

"Why should a dream mean anything?" I asked. "You remember that I always saw you as a fallen angel? The sword might mean that you are about to get back your old inspiration and your fighting spirit."

"Strangely," he said, "the very night when I made a certain vow was the night that I had that dream."

"All this talk about dreams is an idle pastime," I said, with a sudden misgiving and a desire to end the discussion. "One has to concentrate on the daylight. By the way, what happened to your mysterious woman?"

"It was the saddest and most humiliating experience of my life . . ." He interrupted himself, then added, "I don't blame her, though—it was my fault." He withdrew like a snail into his house; his face seemed impenetrable.

It was dusk when the taxi stopped outside the gate to take him to the airport. At the door he suddenly grabbed me and kissed me, parting my lips forcefully with his tongue. It was a strange kiss. It lacked passion, even love: it was like an angry bite.

Chapter 3

The Cords of
the Nether World

IN New York, the spring was full of the promise of a new life. I didn't want to think about Gabriel. He had paid back all he owed to the Woman of Park Avenue, partly from the money left from the sale of the house, partly from a new loan from Margaret Scott.

"The Chinese Woman," Margaret Scott told me later, "did not want her money back: that debt was her last hold on him. But Gabriel repaid her anyhow and therefore it was I who saved him forever from her."

The Woman of Shanghai refused to accept that her affair with Gabriel was over. While he was in California her letters, telegrams, and phone calls, like long, persuasive arms, had reached after him. Gabriel answered that he thanked her for her love but he wanted to stay alone.

Since he was then planning to leave for England, the Woman asked him for a "last goodbye" together in Florida. He agreed to take her to Palm Beach for a few days, provided that she realized he was now "Abelard the monk," castrated forever, not physically but by his vow to God. "And I kept my vow," he reported to Margaret Scott.

Back from Florida, he had to postpone his reservation at the Connaught Hotel in London and write to Wolfgang Reinhardt in

Munich that he was delayed by a sudden sickness. He did not know what was wrong with him but a strange weakness that grew worse from day to day made his steps unsteady. For the time being he had to be satisfied to work on his several projects from his room on the nineteenth floor of the New York Athletic Club. He engaged a young writer, Vernon Brooks, as his assistant. The first thing Brooks had to do when he started to work for Gabriel in April was to copy two letters of recommendation—one to Sol Hurok and one to Billy Rose—that Gabriel had written for the Woman of Shanghai. She was gifted, the letters said, as a writer and a singer; also, she could cure with Chinese herbs.

The Florida goodbye had not turned out to be a gentle ending. Subsequently, the Woman's letters came every day to the Club, clamoring for an explanation for his changed attitude.

Gabriel spoke quite a bit about her to Vernon Brooks, who was aware of all the letters and phone calls. "Pascal's attitude toward her," Brooks later said, "was quite clear and unequivocal. It did not change nor was it ambivalent. He wanted to break off relations with her, but since he did not want to offend her, he hoped to accomplish this by his departure for England."

But time and again he had to postpone his trip. He was getting weaker. "Apparently this illness," he wrote to an old friend in England, "is nothing else than the breaking out of all the poisoning, physical and spiritual, which has happened to me in this last year . . . But if you believe in God, He gives a helping hand, even to the worst sinner. In the last moment, the Madonna takes you by the hand, like a little boy, and she leads you to the altar of God to kneel down and ask forgiveness. And forgiveness is given at once. So here I lie, a poor sinner, who made a farce of his divine inheritance . . ."

To atone for his sins, Gabriel was fasting. "He fasted for almost three months," Vernon Brooks said, "eating very little solid food. This, he said, was the right way to rid one's body of poisons—not only the poisons of disease, but of an evil relationship."

Gabriel called me in April; he wanted me to meet a lady who had been very good to him, a Mrs. Margaret Scott; we would dine at Lüchow's, then go to the circus. I said I had another date. "You cancel your date," he commanded. But later he called to say that he could not make it: he was sick. Days passed and I didn't hear from him. I told myself that now he was as remote as if he were living on some distant galaxy and not a few blocks away on Central Park South.

He finally called and mentioned that his feet were swollen. He also said that he was fasting. Why? I asked. For his purification, he answered. His body and soul were poisoned. I don't want to hear, I don't want to talk to him, I thought; the sooner he goes to England, the better. If only he could get well and go.

The zebra-skin upholstery of El Morocco is cool against my skin. I am told that I am lovely and that I am loved. I am not the left-behind, humiliated woman any more ... A friend said: "Now you are living, you're no longer a vegetable planted in a lovely garden in California. You're a woman again."

Yes, but where was I going? What was I going to do?

A weekend with friends on a Long Island estate. I got up early in the morning and went for a walk. The woods were still gray, but the branches, like outstretched arms, rocked their new buds in the slight breeze. I noticed a flowering tree. It was overwhelmingly beautiful as it stood amid the grayness. I could not explain what suddenly happened to me; it was as if I fell into a trance, as if some inside eyes opened and, for an instant, I was touched by the beauty of God. In the future, this indescribable feeling was to return at times. It was like second eyesight. I was suffused with humility and love. He for Whom I yearned seemed nearer. The words of *Te Deum Laudamus* came to my lips. I sang the hymn, half-forgotten since my schooldays. My voice sounded off key. "My Lord, You made my voice, now You have to listen to it."

When I started back to the house, the Nearness left me, leaving a wounded happiness. And I thought: "My God, You have been baiting me for a long time, and now You are about to catch me. I feel You are pulling the lines tighter and my mouth is full with the sweetness of Your bait ... But, please, not yet, not yet ... give me more time, more time to swim in freedom ..."

One Sunday Gabriel unexpectedly visited me in my new apartment on East 72nd Street. The apartment was in a brownstone and I had furnished it with the few things I had kept from the

California house; the rest of the antiques and paintings were waiting now to be auctioned at the Parke-Bernet Galleries. Gabriel looked thinner, his skin was yellowish and his steps heavy, as if he had difficulty walking. I had the feeling he had come because he wanted to talk, but he couldn't. I was glad; I didn't want to talk any more. It was too late to talk.

"Valerie's eyes were so cold, ice cold," Gabriel told Pauline on the phone that evening. Divorced and heartbroken, Pauline still lived in her studio apartment, painting and painting to take her mind off the misery of being left alone. Gabriel talked with her often in those days, but he never mentioned the existence of the Woman of Shanghai to her.

Gabriel hated me now for my gay new life, for the men around me and for my seeming indifference to our separation. I had betrayed him, he felt; I had never been his Solveig and what he loved in me was his own illusion.

His letters went to friends: "I will be in England in a few weeks, alone, because I have divorced Valerie . . . it was a sad experience. She nearly wrecked my life . . ."

To Blanche Patch, Bernard Shaw's old secretary: "It will interest you also that I am separated from Valerie and a happy bachelor again. Poor GBS would have been happy to know that I have freed myself from the old witch mother and her daughter, the water nymph."

To his old comrade, Lord Grantley: "I do not know if I wrote you earlier that I am a happy bachelor again . . . I divorced Valerie and I am free again and wiser. You cannot make from a Hungarian mixture of a peasant girl and an aristocrat a humble wife for a crazy hobo. So the seven-year-itch is over; I am calm now and you will see your old hobo in the most agreeable form in England by the end of this month."

But Gabriel was a conniving Peer Gynt when he wrote to his Venezuelan millionaire "brother," who had loaned him $10,000 on promissory notes. The notes were long overdue and the brother was getting nasty about them. How could he pay him back, Gabriel countered, when he had been robbed of all he had in a settlement by his ruthless wife? But it was worthwhile, whatever it cost him, to get his freedom back: "I don't blame Valerie. I knew how she was. I only blame myself for going that far with her ... it was not vanity or sex attachment, but pure humanity not to leave her in that horrible Hungary."

The Woman of Shanghai was puzzled and she was suffering: why had she lost her lover? Why did Gabriel say that their love was not real because it wasn't a "pure" love, but only sex? And now, she complained, he was even accusing her of being the cause of his suffering.

"You are mistaken," Gabriel answered. "I am not suffering for you, for any woman or any human being. My whole struggle, physical and spiritual, with all the demons is to get back my integrity which I lost about twelve months ago."

It was twelve months ago that they had met and loved. Was he saying now, she angrily demanded, that he had lost his integrity then? The truth was that he had lost his integrity when he had gone back to Los Angeles "to divorce" and came back a changed man: "You lost your youthful spirit, you lost your soul there and still you have not found it," she wrote. "You were fooled" for seven years "by your wise Hungarian."

"I agree with you in one part completely," Gabriel answered. "You are right that I lost my youthful spirit in Los Angeles. You are right that I lost my boyish genius. So I don't know what the hell you want from me. I have nothing to give and nothing to take. You confessed yourself that our love finished a long time ago. Our friendship is on a very shaky, unethical cloud in the air, so why can't you leave me alone."

She was not the type ever to accept defeat. Her letters and phone calls continued to besiege "Abelard the monk" hiding behind the "no women" boundaries of his club. Most of the time, Vernon Brooks observed, Gabriel tore up her daily letters, but some of their correspondence remained in the files to bear eloquent witness against her future claim as his fiancée on Gabriel's estate.

Gabriel gave orders to the club switchboard operator not to put through the Woman's calls. Those calls were heated accusations, her voice screaming across the wire, and Brooks said the sick man could not take such arguments any longer. She then tried to befriend Brooks, who, feeling it would be improper to "discuss Mr. Pascal" without his knowledge, declined her invitations. By then she suspected witchcraft. Gabriel was under the influence of Margaret Scott. It was she who had destroyed their love, who tried to get him away from her, first by buying the tickets to India and then by loaning Gabriel money to repay his debts to her. To get to the heart of the matter she cabled Baba in India.

Even though Baba's answer was vague, the contact was made to counteract Margaret's influence over Gabriel. He was still fasting and the Woman of Shanghai offered her soups, promising to cook them without her herbs and elixirs, which Gabriel suspected were poisonous. As she insisted, Gabriel had no heart to turn her down. He sent Vernon Brooks to the Park Avenue apartment to pick up the food. But he never touched it. He usually asked Brooks to give it to the help or flush it down the toilet. But one afternoon, Brooks said, "He ate one bite of some meat and immediately became sick." After that Gabriel refused the food and Brooks stopped going to the Park Avenue apartment.

Besides his problems with his two women—one, the Chinese Woman, pursuing him and one, me, rejecting him—Gabriel was fighting for his health and for his work. His letters embraced the world of films and finance from Europe to India. His mind was never so brilliant, his letters never more precise. And his luck in business was turning. He obtained the rights to the Kalman operetta *Countess Maritza* with $25,000 lent him by the theatrical promoter Rita Allan. The film was to be made in Munich, with Wolfgang Reinhardt and the Deutsche Pascal Films. There were dollars now for Shaw's *Candida*. Wolfgang Reinhardt's source, "that Viennese miller, shoemaker or archbishop or whatever he is you dug up," was coming across with the marks. Then: "I have a production arrangement for next year for Irwin Shaw's superior book *The Young Lions* . . . to be done together with the German version." But, he continued, "I need two or three weeks' rest in Baden-Baden before I can do anything. I am weak . . . a prisoner of this Club room, but sometimes a prison becomes also a dear place to you, like Reading was to Oscar Wilde. I was not able to write a single ballad, but I threw away the *schladen:* I am not involved with anybody, everything is clear cut, straight, no more pretensions, no illusions . . ."

Gabriel was to fly first to London to meet with the Shaw Trustee, then to Hamburg for a deal, and also to pick up Hedwig Brugge. After decades, Hedwig and he had met in Munich the past September. He had paid for her trip and expenses so that she could fulfill her dearest wish: to see her "Gaborjünge" once more. It was a short meeting, as Gabriel had to rush back to Rome, but it had given new strength and happiness to the sick old woman.

"I can be in Hamburg the first week in June," he wrote to Hedwig, "then I can drive you to Baden-Baden to a nice coffee-klatsch. Don't worry about your finances; I'll be able now to straighten them out, and don't worry about me either; I am to play now the last scene of the Third Act and this will be the most beautiful drama of my life. I'll call it *The Tale of a Faun*, because that is what I was all the time: a faun playing a human being."

Now more than ever Gabriel felt it was his special mission to do the Gandhi film. All others were trifles, ways to get money to live on while he prepared for his life task. He was getting sicker every day, but with tremendous self-discipline he dictated hour after hour, leaving behind a thick file of Gandhi correspondence. Once more, he got together with Aldous Huxley to work out a scenario for the picture.

Then suddenly he felt a bit better and was arranging for his trip and bidding friends goodbye. "The end of next week, if God gives me strength, I am flying to England," he wrote to Barbara Hutton, his friend from the early 30s. She too was sick then, physically and from a deep disappointment. "I am sorry you are suffering . . . I was suffering too, only supernatural forces pulled me through; apparently, I still have a mission so they do not want me to die such a shameful death in a Club room."

And to "Dicky," Lord Grantley, who himself lay near death in London: "We both balance precariously on the edge of Hades and it would be better if we took a big jump away from the Kingdom of Darkness . . . Life is really beautiful . . . you, who enjoyed it like a connoisseur, and I, who enjoyed it like a savage . . ."

No, he did not want to die. A free life, new adventures lay ahead. "You know," he wrote to Wolfgang Reinhardt in Germany, "I am only happy if I can be like Til Eulenspiegel and sing on the roadsides. No possessions, no responsibilities. That's not my business. My business is to entertain, and inspire and enlighten through entertaining ... Here in America, I was always a stranger, out of rhythm; a caricature. The Americans are a great and wonderful people, but I was too old to learn their ways, adopt their mannerisms; I was among them like Peer Gynt among the Trolls ..."

June 1, to the Managing Director of the Connaught Hotel, London: "Postpone reservation. Will definitely arrive on June 13th.—Gabriel Pascal."

June 1, to Brenners Park-Hotel, Baden-Baden: "Postpone reservations another week. Definitely in Baden-Baden on the 17th of June.—Gabriel Pascal."

As a candle flares up suddenly before the flame goes out, Gabriel's improvement was brief. He felt worse than ever. He was back to dictating letters in bed. The news came from London that Sir Alexander Korda had obtained the rights for *Arms and the Man* from the Shaw Trustee. Gabriel took the news with the calm of a man who, deep in his heart, knows that all this does not matter any more. With a generous gesture, he offered Sir Alexander Shaw's original dialogue, written years ago for Gabriel when *he* had planned to film *Arms and the Man*. "Dear Alex," he wrote to his old rival and compatriot, "I offer this material because of my admiration for Larry [Sir Laurence Olivier] as Sergius and to you, as a gift from a 'hobo' Hungarian to a 'Lord' Hungarian. Maybe this material means very little to you. For me once it meant the whole world."

My lawyer advised me that in the first part of June my divorce case would come up in California. I phoned Gabriel that I was flying to Los Angeles on the evening of June 9. He said that he himself was to leave soon for London. Neither of us proposed a farewell meeting. Then Gabriel remarked that he was thinking of spending a weekend in Saratoga before taking off for Europe. I wished him a good trip.

"Mr. Pascal told me one afternoon," Vernon Brooks later remembered, "that he was going to Saratoga Springs because his doctor thought it would be good for him, and that the Chinese lady wanted to accompany him. He had decided to let her go along because it would be his farewell to her before he left for Europe, and he thought it would be a gesture she would appreciate."

The surprised Vernon Brooks understood Gabriel's change of attitude only later, from a letter he dictated to Baba. Ever since she had cabled Baba and received his answer, Gabriel wrote, the Woman of Shanghai had been a different person. She was not trying any more to pretend to an "intimate relationship with me" and, even more, she was urging him not to put off his trip to India any longer and saying that "her only desire and dream is that I reach you." She had sent a telegram on June 4, Gabriel's birthday, that she was "rejoicing in your truth search." That apparently was the reason Gabriel agreed to let her go with him to Saratoga Springs. They left on June 6, a Saturday, and planned to return on Tuesday.

Monday morning Brooks went as usual to the Club to attend to Gabriel's mail. To his great surprise, the room wasn't empty. There was Gabriel, lying in his bed.

"I couldn't stand it for another day," he said to Brooks, and that was the only remark he ever made about that weekend.

June 8, to Mr. Rudolph Richard, Managing Director of the Connaught Hotel, London: "Once again, I have to postpone. I will definitely leave New York on Wednesday, June 16th.— Gabriel Pascal."

June 8, to Baden-Baden: "Postpone reservation for another week.—Pascal."

I was getting ready for my flight to California when Gabriel called me unexpectedly. He said that he had postponed his trip to

Europe for another week, but he did not tell me why. He did not tell me that he couldn't even walk any more without the help of Vernon Brooks. He said he had called me because I had to meet Mrs. Margaret Scott before I left. I told him I was very busy and I had no reason to meet Mrs. Scott.

Sometime later, my doorbell rang. A lean, serious-looking young man stood there, introducing himself as Vernon Brooks. He brought me some books which I was to give to Charles Boyer in Hollywood—Prime Minister Nehru's books, autographed by him. (Boyer was to play Nehru in the Gandhi film.) Then Brooks gave me an urgent note from Gabriel saying that Mrs. Scott was waiting for me and he would be grateful if I would go to her. I told Brooks that I would.

When Gabriel called Margaret Scott earlier, he had asked her to see me. "I want you to look into Valerie's eyes," Gabriel said to her, "and then answer my one-million-dollar question: What kind of a woman is she really? And do you think that she has ever loved me?"

Margaret was more than curious to meet me. By then her whole life spiraled about Gabriel and the future was a golden cloud of eternity in a holy triangle: Baba, Gabriel, and herself. She must have imagined me as some kind of Hollywood temptress and was visibly shocked when she opened the door. "My," she said, 'you look like my own daughter."

I was there only a short time when the phone rang. From Margaret's short answer—"Yes, she is here"—I concluded it was Gabriel. Margaret knew that I was leaving that same evening for California. I told her, rather reluctantly, that I did not think there was anything else to do but to go ahead with the divorce, and that Gabriel himself had always wanted to be free. Margaret nodded, her eyes intent: "Yes, he has to be free for Baba."

I had hardly left when Gabriel phoned again. He asked Margaret's feeling about me and asked her to write down every word I said. I do not know what form my words took, strained as they were through Margaret's passion for Baba and Gabriel, nor, on the other hand, what interpretation Gabriel gave to them. But a letter went to Baba: "Here I have to confess my many temptations. My ex-wife tried to play herself back into my graces, but sweet Margaret Scott very energetically told her that I have visions other than women, so she definitely gave me my freedom yesterday ... I will clear this battlefield on the 16th of this month. I will stay one day in London, then go to Baden-Baden ... will get healthy and be, by the end of August, in India, in your arms—your always faithful Phoenix."

But when Vernon Brooks was gone and the daily work was done, the night descended ... the fearful nights of loneliness, the unsharable loneliness of the dying. On those nights he would call up Margaret Scott, and they would talk until the dawn was gray over the towers of New York. He would talk about his childhood and about the young man in the uniform of the Austro-Hungarian monarchy. Then it would be daylight again and Vernon Brooks would come. Gabriel asked him to put up, in his room, the picture of himself taken at the time when he was thin, with his young face and large eyes staring out from behind the stiff collar of his Hussar uniform.

It was on one of those mornings that his doctor, Arnold Hutschnecker, the author of *The Will to Live,* found him lying in bed with a strange expression. "Now I know," Gabriel told him, "that I am dying."

And he told him about his dream: "I was in a void somewhere. Thick gray fog was rolling about me. I was terribly frightened. I looked about myself and realized that I was standing at the foot of a tremendous, throne like platform, the top of which was lost in the fog. There was a gray twilight. Suddenly, a voice broke through the fog, thundering above me: 'The name of Gabriel Pascal is removed from the living.' I knew I was doomed forever. Then the voice softened into clemency and light burst through the fog. The voice said: 'But you shall not die but will be born again and you will have a new name.' And there my dream ended."

A letter to Hedwig Brugge: "Everything is postponed once more: Monday, I must go to the Roosevelt Hospital; it seems my liver is attacked. I have to stay at least for one week of examinations. But my spirit is clear. I have never seen with such crystal clarity the reason for my coming to this earth, for the sufferings since my boyhood. Now I see why I had to go through all the sins, false luxury, pretensions, loveless wives, useless sweethearts, all the Don Juanesque comedy of a typical farce character. I shiver when I think of Grabbe ... almost as if he created me in his dramatic mind, in his *Don Juan und Faust*. But his solution lacked the grace of salvation ... Do not worry about me, Hedwig; superior forces are praying for the saving of my soul ..."

Chapter 4

~~~~~~~~

"I Have Loved, O Lord, the Beauty of Your House..."

I was trembling as I stepped out of the Los Angeles courtroom where the interlocutory divorce decree had been granted. A year from this date, I wouldn't be Gabriel's wife any more. As my lawyer pushed the door open for me, flashing bulbs and television cameras attacked me. I was jammed into a corner by the press.

My lawyer had made a mistake. Earlier he had told me, "We've been switched to another judge, and he's difficult. 'Mental cruelty' won't do with him. Didn't you mention that Mr. Pascal was involved with some woman in Europe?"

I was reluctant to drag our name through the mud, but the lawyer insisted that if I didn't use the "other woman" story, he could not guarantee the case. He also assured me that there was no sign of the press outside. "Gabriel is in England by now," I thought, "and I have to go through with this"; so I agreed. My worst fears were realized: the "other woman" story made the afternoon headlines and the television news.

I sat ashamed in my hotel room, wondering how I could have been so idiotic. Maybe the English papers would take the news and Gabriel would read it in London. The bell captain knocked on my door with a special delivery letter from Gabriel, dated two days earlier in New York. So he had never left! "Things with me have gone from bad to worse and I must go tomorrow to Roosevelt Hospital." The lines were shaky, hardly readable. "My Heart," he called me in his old way, "I am to start on a difficult road now from which there is no returning . . . and leave social life: it is syphilis."

I flew back to New York and called Roosevelt Hospital. Vernon Brooks answered, but Gabriel took over. "I was afraid you'd stay and try your luck there," he said. His voice was weak, but he sounded happy. "I'm so relieved," he continued. "This morning, a priest came; his name is Father Francis. I'm sure Saint Francis must have sent him. And suddenly I knew that I wasn't at peace with my soul and with God, so after all these years, I went to confession and had Holy Communion. And as I was just now lying here with that wonderful feeling of peace, you called."

I wanted to go to the hospital immediately.

"No, not yet," he said reluctantly. "I'll call you when you can come. But please bring my rosary."

His rosary. In the old days, he used to carry it in his pocket: it meant to him that he had a Mother, Mary. Last June, when I was wandering about his room after our "forever goodbye" at the Los Angeles airport, something cracked under my feet. On the dark red Bokhara rug lay his rosary; it had dropped from his pocket and he had run off without it.

I called the hospital every day and received the same answer from the nurse or Vernon Brooks: "No change. He's doing fine." A few times, Gabriel talked with me. When he was a bit stronger, he said, he would call for me.

A week passed. On Sunday, I went to bed early. Some hours later, I awakened shuddering. I switched on the light and got up, but my legs could hardly carry me to the kitchen for a drink of water. I can still see the dream: a room in the dusk. I was lying on a bed covered with a sheet. A figure in a whitish dress was standing at the foot of the bed. Steel hands seemed to grip my throat; I couldn't breathe; a suffocating burden pressed against my chest. I wanted to cry out for help, but couldn't. An icy flood seemed to rise about me, drawing nearer and nearer to my heart. "Help! Help!" I was finally able to cry; but the white figure remained motionless. Then I understood that there was no help for me, for I was dying. I saw myself in my agony, my brown, awkward hands, twisted in pain, grasping the sheet. But they weren't *my* hands, they were Gabriel's! It was his body, and he was dying —but I was dying too: we were dying in the same person. I screamed and awakened.

It was good now to stand in the bright light in the kitchen and drink water. It was good to look out the window and hold onto the existence of a Yellow Cab cruising through the street. It was only a dream, I kept reassuring myself; but tomorrow I would have to talk with Gabriel's doctor.

The wait in the doctor's office seemed an eternity. Finally I was facing him. He told me the words my mind refused to accept: "The poor man is dying. Cancer of the liver . . . it's hard to tell you how much longer . . ."

Gabriel was lying on his back in the bed, looking amazingly young with that translucent expression of his other self, the archangel; his eyes unnaturally large, very dark, and shining. He tried to raise himself when he saw me, but fell back. He smiled. I couldn't say anything. We only looked at each other and we knew that whatever had happened, we had always belonged to each other.

"Mr. Pascal wanted to be handsome for you. He had a shave this morning," someone said. Turning, I saw a nurse standing at the foot of the bed. The room, the white figure of the nurse, and Gabriel, covered with a sheet: my dream.

Margaret Scott stood in the corner with Vernon Brooks.

"I called for you," Gabriel began, "because I want to fly with you and Margaret to the Mayo Clinic. You are still my wife for one more year under California law, and only you have the right to take me out of here. I don't want to stay here . . . I'll die here," he said, a wild look of fear coming into his eyes.

When I went to talk to the doctor, he said that Gabriel shouldn't be flown. "Mayo's can't help him," he said. "Nobody can help him." And it wasn't true that he needed my intervention in order to leave the hospital. "Mr. Pascal can leave us," the doctor said, "any time he wishes. But of course I hope you realize that he would die on his way to Mayo's."

Later, I often thought that Gabriel's proposed trip was a subterfuge to get me to the hospital. He didn't want to hurt Margaret Scott's feelings; she had not only canceled a planned trip to South Africa on account of his illness, but had also taken a room in a hotel near the hospital. Moreover, she had spent every minute of the previous week at his bedside. Gabriel must have sensed that she would resent my being there. I often wonder if he knew that, unconfessed even to herself, Margaret Scott was passionately in love with him. But I am sure that it was consideration for her that had previously prompted him to keep me away from the hospital. Now he knew he was dying and wanted me at his side. Anyhow, he never again mentioned Mayo's.

Margaret Scott and I stayed in Gabriel's room till late evening. "I have to talk to you," she said when we left the hospital together. She took me to her hotel, the Henry Hudson, nearby, and we sat down in the deserted lobby. Margaret bent forward with an eager expression, watching my face, the lamp behind her wide-brimmed, blue straw hat projecting an eerie halo around her white hair. "Well," she began with gravity, "I don't know what to do about the Chinese Woman. She keeps calling."

The Chinese Woman! I knew at once who she must be—the "mystery woman," the Chinese Woman from the Tyrol. Could it be that her home was right here in New York? The taste of past bitterness came back to my mouth.

Margaret Scott was saying that Gabriel had instructed Brooks and the nurse not to let the Chinese Woman into the hospital, and had even refused to talk to her on the phone.

"Why doesn't he want to see her?" I asked, controlling my voice.

"Why?" said Margaret. "Well, my dear, that is a long, long story." She began with February 18, the day she had first met Gabriel, and it was long past midnight when she finished and sat wiping the perspiration from her face with a piece of Kleenex. It was suffocatingly hot in the lobby.

"I still don't know what to do about her. Maybe she should be let in. I'm sorry for her, especially because now she seems to be converted by Baba . . ." She was silent for a second, then I saw a sudden flash of fear in her eyes. "You know, she hates me. She thinks that I hypnotized Gabriel. She also knows that I loaned him the money to repay her. And she is out for me."

"That's ridiculous," I said.

Margaret moistened her lips, then grabbed my hand. "Well," she said, "Gabriel is afraid of her. Deadly afraid. You can laugh if you wish, but I've lived for twenty-odd years in the Far East . . ." Her voice trailed off. "Don't you know what I'm talking about?" she continued. "Well, I'll tell you: black magic. She has great occult powers, and Gabriel knows it. He could break her power only through Baba. And whom she hates, she can destroy."

Next morning I awakened from a deep sleep with the feeling that something was terribly wrong. I remembered: Gabriel was dying. I looked at my suntanned legs and thought that one day they would be white bones somewhere; and the thought, strangely, comforted me. What was happening to Gabriel now was the lot of all of us.

Soon I was walking through Central Park to the hospital. For the second time that day the awareness of death arose in me, but this time it was quite different. This time it came suddenly and it shook the everyday world under my feet. It was an insight into the timeless immensity beyond and ahead of my minute existence. The skyscrapers seemed just as pathetic in that moment as the people rushing by. Was it possible that only a few days ago I was bothered about what kind of dress to wear? And that I had planned my summer more carefully than my eternal life? This revelation of death was like a mirror in an amusement park, reflecting me and my aspirations distorted into a caricature. My anxiety, my sleepless nights, my wish to be famous and successful again. I took a deep breath, as if a heavy burden had been lifted: I felt free.

Margaret Scott was already sitting next to Gabriel's bed. He seemed weaker, but he gave me a happy smile. At lunch I went with Margaret for a bite in the hospital cafeteria. She talked about Baba—rapturously and with credulity, undisturbed by logic. She believed in Baba's divinity and in her own role as a chosen one. Though she was an intelligent woman with a sense of humor, the moment she touched spiritual realms she flew into a world of fantasy.

She talked on and on about Gabriel and Baba, beaming with

an exuberant happiness, at times giggling like a young girl. Later, when I knew her better, I noticed how quickly she could fall from those happy moods into utter despair and crying fits. It was as if the protective blinds of her fantasies had been lifted and, for one unbearable moment, she saw reality.

I was worried about her. How would she take Gabriel's death? And I was worried about her loans to him. There was more than the first loan that had paid off the debt to the Woman of Shanghai, for Margaret had also loaned the money for the second installment on the *Pygmalion* musical rights, and now she was paying the hospital bills. Gabriel's last letter to me said that it was a "question of honor" for his affairs with Margaret Scott to be in order. But he was dying bankrupt, and, even though he had given her power of attorney to deduct all her loans from the sale of our antiques and paintings at the Parke-Bernet Galleries, I knew that the moment he died all his creditors would jump at those only tangible assets.

Margaret smiled at my worry. "Oh, Baba will take care of it," she said, "and Gabriel will not die. I have given all I could to Gabriel, and it was as if I had given it to Baba. And you will see a miracle yet!"

Going back to Gabriel's room I saw again two men waiting outside in the corridor. I came to identify them as the Tall and Short Hungarians. The Tall One professed an old friendship with Gabriel, but it turned out later he was the emissary of the Woman of Shanghai. The Short Hungarian was a theatrical agent who had been involved in Gabriel's projects during the last few months and was also a friend of the Chinese Woman. Now I noticed that he again held papers in his hand for Gabriel to sign. Both men seemed extremely anxious to get into the room, but Gabriel had told me not to admit them.

Gabriel was sinking rapidly and was refusing food. "The only thing he has asked for," the nurse said, "is some chicken soup. Why don't you bring some cans of it?"

"He hates canned food," I said.

The nurse shrugged. "He won't know the difference any more."

I was not going to cheat Gabriel on what could very well be his last meal. I went home and made some good chicken soup. I remembered the chicken soup I made for him after his operation at the Mayo Clinic, when he had said: "The first food I eat should be my wife's."

When I returned, Margaret Scott and Vernon Brooks were in the room. Gabriel lifted himself with difficulty and smelled my soup. "How wonderful," he said, "thank you. But where are the plates, *our* plates?"

I understood. He was telling me that he was coming home to me and he wanted to eat the dinner, his last one, from *our* plates. I went back to the apartment for china and silverware and a beautiful tablecloth. Back at the hospital, I set the table, Gabriel's eyes never leaving me. He looked contented and happy. He took a spoonful of the soup and a bite of the meat. Our eyes met. His told me that he knew he was going to die. His gaze grew tender; he stroked my hair, my face. His eyes said that he recognized me again as the girl of the Place Vendôme, then, slowly, he turned them away. He caught sight of a pair of pigeons on the window sill. One of them took off, circling heavily against the shimmering hot summer sky.

"This was the best soup of my life," Gabriel said, turning back to me, "but give the rest to Brooks. I don't exist any more."

He was giving up possession of the world he had grasped for like a noisy child, snatching with open hands colored glass baubles, dropping one as he reached for another. I don't exist any more—nobody existed more fully than he did in the many contradictory Gabriels, but now, in the simple, terrible truth of death, he was finally himself.

A few more days and he is dead, facing the Judge. The thought terrified me. I never before thought of God as the Judge. But at this moment I knew that one has to answer, that one will be judged by the most terrible witness of all—oneself—as in the blinding sanctity of God one sees oneself falling short of the likeness of Christ. O God, forgive him, I wanted to pray, but I couldn't.

I was in the rectory of the Paulist Fathers, opposite the hospital, waiting for Father Francis X. Diskin, the "Father Francis"

Gabriel had mentioned. Seated in the bare reception room, I wondered why I had come. It was not my first visit. Earlier in the week, I had brought Margaret Scott. She was upset by Father Francis' daily visits to the hospital and was shocked to learn that Gabriel was receiving Holy Communion every morning. She held that Gabriel was a disciple of Baba, that the "backward superstitions" and "rituals" of a "dogmatic" religion could only deprive his soul of its eternal freedom, which could be reached only through Baba. And she wanted to prevent the priest's coming.

Margaret was raised in a Protestant family, with severe prejudices against the Catholic Church, so I had asked her to come with me to visit Father Diskin and see for herself that he wasn't the Devil. "Come for Gabriel's sake," I had pleaded with her. That always proved to be the magic sentence.

Somehow, Father Diskin struck the right chord with her. Not only was she soon at ease, but shortly she was telling him in detail about Baba. Thus the ice was broken; from then on, she ceased to give dark looks to visiting priests.

But on this day I came to the rectory alone. It was sticky and hot, and I had a splitting headache. "Why am I sitting here?" I asked myself. All the same, a strange power kept me nailed to the chair. Soon, Father Diskin entered, and his calm, cool kindness encouraged me. He expressed his happiness that Gabriel had returned to his Church and told me that he had already received Extreme Unction. Then he added that I should be on guard lest Gabriel be confused by Margaret's dissertations about Baba. "He should die firm in his faith," he said, "untroubled by contradictions."

I didn't feel like staying, nor did I feel like going. Suddenly I began talking nervously. I too, I told the priest, had been raised a Catholic. I too had lost my faith. I described my doubts, my futile searchings. Father Diskin listened patiently. When I stood up to leave, he said: "Because you are seeking God earnestly, He will show you the way."

"If only I could pray now," I said, "pray for Gabriel. How can I pray? I feel numb inside."

"Ask the Blessed Mother for help," the priest said. "Go down on your knees and try to pray. Cling to God and He will answer."

Crossing the narrow street back to the hospital, I frowned.

Kneel down—those formalities which I could never abide! What difference did it make? One could pray lying on one's back. Yes, if one *could* pray, but I *couldn't!*

In the brightly waxed corridor near Gabriel's room I spotted Margaret deep in conversation with the Tall Hungarian. Seeing him, I again wondered vaguely about his concern; he was only a superficial acquaintance of Gabriel's. On this day he told me that he knew Gabriel did not want to be disturbed by visitors, but the Woman of Shanghai had received a cable from Baba, and she *must* give that cable personally to Gabriel.

I thought about the Woman of Shanghai for the first time since Margaret had talked to me about her, and the bitter taste returned to my mouth. But Gabriel was dying; I had to overcome my emotions; I felt I had to forgive so he would be forgiven. That woman loved him, just as I loved him; she should see him before he died. I realized that the cable from Baba was a subterfuge. Gabriel certainly would like to see such a cable, she must have figured, and Baba was Margaret's master too; therefore, Margaret shouldn't object to her visit. I felt sorry for the Woman of Shanghai. I asked the Tall Hungarian for her telephone number and went to the booth in the waiting room.

A woman's voice with an Oriental accent answered. When, after identifying myself, I asked for her by name, there was a chilly pause, then the reply that she herself was on the line. I wasn't discouraged by her tone. My hurt came from Gabriel, and my account with Gabriel was settled. After all, I should have nothing against her: she was a stranger to me. I talked in a friendly manner and she warmed up.

"Tell him, please, that I have to see him," she pleaded.

I promised to do so.

"Is that woman, that Margaret Scott, there?" she asked in a harsh voice.

"Yes, she is here. But you are mistaken. Believe me, she is a wonderful person."

"Is she?" She laughed. "She took Gabriel away from me. She is killing him."

Confounded, I put the receiver down. I wanted to get her to

the hospital but I couldn't ask Margaret to stay away during the visit. And what if she were to come every day? The two were certain to meet and it would be terrible to have tension, or perhaps even a scene, at Gabriel's deathbed. With all my good intentions about overcoming my feelings, I had to admit that the thought of her coming every day was more than unpleasant.

"Where have you been so long?" Gabriel asked plaintively when I sat down at his side. I took his hand and his face lit up again with that smile to which I cannot give any other adjective than "beatific." I had already decided to bring up the matter of the Woman of Shanghai, but only after I had spoken to Margaret. I closed my eyes and leaned back in the chair. I was tired.

"My God . . . oh, my God, how beautiful," I heard Gabriel say. I looked up. He was lying on his back, his eyes wide open, not focusing, yet seeming to behold something marvelous. His voice was full of wonder. "I see it now . . . I understand . . . the miracle of life . . . how good it is to be alive." He spoke in broken words, but it did not sound like a goodbye to life; it had the ring of a jubilant greeting of some never-seen new wonder.

The nurse hustled in. The Woman of Shanghai had called again and asked me to call her back right away. Gabriel's expression changed. I realized he had heard the nurse.

"Is she here?" he asked.

I had to tell him I had spoken to her. "She's waiting on the phone," I continued. "Why don't you want to see her?"

He avoided my eyes. "Tell her that she can come now." He looked up and continued eagerly, "Yes, yes, she should come. I *do* want to see her."

I felt for a second as if an old wound had opened inside of me.

Margaret and the Tall Hungarian were still in the corridor. The Hungarian had produced a copy of Baba's cable and Margaret was studying it. "Baba's messages," she said, "always have several divine meanings and only the initiated ones can grasp them all."

I told them what had happened, adding, "Look here, Margaret, she thinks that you are responsible for Gabriel's breaking off with her. When she comes, there will be a lot of hatred around Gabriel's deathbed. In this very cable, Baba is warning against that by saying that all jealousy and hate should cease. I think it's up to you now to make peace. I know you never did anything against her, but she thinks you did. You can dissolve all her hostility by going now with him"—I pointed to the Tall Hungarian—"to her apartment, and you yourself can bring her here. She'll be touched by your friendliness, and she'll respond."

"Me! Go to her?" Margaret was aghast. "I have no reason to put myself in such a humiliating position." Her hands trembled as she reread Baba's message, but then her face changed. "Yes, I see now. You are right. I shall go. My sacrifices will bring love and love can make miracles. You will yet see the miracle: Gabriel will live and this hospital will go down in history as the place of Baba's greatest manifestation."

Beaming, Margaret left with the Tall Hungarian and I returned to Gabriel.

I took his hand and buried my face in his palm. In the past, in those rare moments when we were fully conscious of our love, I had relinquished myself in him and he in me and our unity was so strong that we felt each other's thoughts. And now, at his deathbed, as I shut my mind to any thought but him, my body took over the part of his incapacitated one, acting out his unspoken wishes.

He drew me to his chest, embracing me with one arm. "My dear Heart," he said. "You are still the one who always knows best."

Time passed and I started to worry. What if arguments had broken out between Margaret and the Chinese Woman? I went out into the corridor just as three figures emerged from the elevator at the far end. Between Margaret and the Tall Hungarian walked a dark-haired woman wearing a light blue dress cut in Chinese fashion, and bedecked with jewelry. Hurrying to greet them, on a sudden impulse I embraced the dark-haired woman, telling her how impatiently Gabriel was waiting for her. Then I took her into the room, motioning Margaret to come out with me and leave them alone. But Gabriel stopped us.

"I don't want you two to go," he said. "Sit down, all of you."

The Woman of Shanghai took the chair at his bedside. The dream seemed to be coming true: compassion was conquering jealousy. If the three of us could really forgive and love, maybe, as

Margaret had predicted, there would be a miracle. At that moment, I almost believed in it.

I tried to start a conversation, but my effort met with silence. Since I was concentrating all my attention on the Woman of Shanghai, I didn't notice Margaret's expression, nor could I see, in the darkness of the room, that she was holding back a cry.

The silence stretched into minutes. Then Gabriel lifted his hand with a wave, saying firmly but gently to the Woman of Shanghai: "Now you *must* go."

"Why can't *I* stay with him and you can?" In the corridor she grasped my hand and her long, red nails went deep into my flesh. I understood her hurt. I walked her to the elevator, promising to call if Gabriel wanted to see her again. She seemed so broken and so childishly soft. I did not know then that I had lost her good will forever, nor did I know that her visit would be brought up in court to strengthen her case in the trial over the will.

When the elevator door closed behind her I was relieved. That gave me a bad conscience. Was I still jealous? If so, I had not really forgiven fully, and there could be a miracle only if love overcame hate.

Margaret also was gone—to have a bite to eat, I assumed. When later there was still no sign of her, I went to look for her. Across the hall from Gabriel's room there was an empty room that we used for short rests. I found Margaret there, on the floor, crying hysterically. "Oh, that woman, that Chinese woman is the devil," she sobbed. "And he is a liar. She has killed him and it serves him right."

On the way to the hospital, Margaret had learned that the Woman of Shanghai had accompanied Gabriel to Saratoga Springs on June 6. "He didn't want *me* to go with him—he lied to me, *to me* who has sacrificed so much for him," Margaret screamed. "He lied to me and to Baba and he will die for this. And he will never be free again. No more miracle . . . I'm going . . . I never want to see him again." She was incoherent. Jumping up, she ran to the wall, knocking herself against it again and again.

It took all my power to calm her. I knew that she did not want to leave, but if she stayed, I told her, there must be no words, no tears, no shadow on her face in Gabriel's presence. "You've told me several times that you loved Gabriel selflessly, with a divine love. Prove it, then," I told her. And she stayed.

The following morning, I found Gabriel changed. The beatific smile and the brilliance of the eyes were gone. His legs were bluish, cold, and swollen. As I sat there next to his bed, I thought again that in a few days he would face God and eternity. Had he achieved what he had been put on earth for, or was his life a waste? If he had failed, how much was it my fault? I had had seven years with him; how had I used them? Hadn't he said to me: "Please, help me to better myself!" Had I upheld him with my faith?

Be honest for once in your life, I said to myself. Is he the only one to blame for the Woman of Shanghai? And for the separation? Remember your icy voice that June morning when you drove him home from the Los Angeles airport. If there had been love in you that morning, everything might have happened differently. Perhaps he would have opened up and poured out all his misery, humiliation, and temptation while he was alone in New York. But you didn't have one good word for him. And later, when he wrote you and asked you to follow him to Italy, his letter cried for love and understanding. But your self-love was greater than your love for him and you vacillated. If my heart had been pure and had turned to God, answering only and always with love, I could have helped him. His sin, therefore, is my sin too.

It is too late now, I thought, the deeds are done, the words are spoken and all that remains is the judgment.

If only I could pray. "Go into your center," I had read somewhere. But where was my center? I had read so many books about so many different religions, but they had left my heart empty and my mind in chaos. I had no faith to turn to. After all those books, I was unable to do what a child can do: talk to God in prayer.

I became aware that Gabriel was looking at me.

"How and where can I find God?" The question broke out of me. "Do you know what I mean?"

He nodded.

"Can I ever find God on Park Avenue?" The question referred to a conversation between us long ago, when I had told him that

I wanted both God and my desires. Without my realizing it, the question exposed the reason why I couldn't find God: I was still not willing to pay the price for faith. I still wanted my sins. I didn't know it then, but one can of course find God on Park Avenue as well as anywhere else, if one is seeking God and not oneself.

Gabriel fully understood the duplicity of my question. "No, no!" he almost shouted. "Don't ever try that. Never do as I did."

I felt a desperate need for a decision. "What should I do?" I asked him. "Should I go to India? To Mihra Behn?"

"No, not yet," he said, his words hardly audible.

"What should I do? Where is the truth, what is the truth?"

He was silent for a while; then he said slowly, "Only a few more days and I shall know the truth," he said. "And I will tell it to you. I promise, I will tell it to you." He closed his eyes.

Saturday was a confused day, when all the devils of distraction were let loose. The trouble started when Pauline called to announce that she was coming to the hospital right away. Gabriel told me to tell her not to come until he asked for her. Pauline sounded hostile. "I *am* coming," she said, and put down the receiver. She did not tell me that the two Hungarians and the Woman of Shanghai had gotten hold of her with the tale that everybody was being kept away because Baba's High Priestess, Margaret Scott, was conducting some kind of Black Mass in the room and that I too was under her influence. Pauline, uneasy, wanted to see what was going on.

Margaret was very quiet that day. When Pauline swept into the room, she took Margaret's chair and, sitting there, held Gabriel's hands. Finally Margaret lost control and threw herself, weeping, on Gabriel. Pauline pulled her off and a scene ensued. I begged them to leave the room. Pauline was hurt, but we parted as friends. At the end of the corridor, I saw the two Hungarians, who joined Pauline as she walked toward the elevator.

I had hardly succeeded in calming Margaret when I was called to the phone. "Did he ask for me?" The Woman of Shanghai's voice was pleading. "And did you tell him that I would like to see him just once more? And please, please tell him that my love for him was a pure love."

I told Gabriel that the Woman wanted to see him one more time.

"No," he said, "I want to rest. I want only silence. To rest in silence."

"Do you want me to go, too?" I asked. "Wouldn't you rest better?"

"Only with you can I rest," he answered.

Early Sunday morning I entered his room. His eyes were turned toward the ceiling and he was alone, the loneliness of the dying pulled about him like an impenetrable screen. When he saw me, recognition lit up his face, which more and more had come to resemble a skull. With a heartbreaking effort, he tried to lift his fleshless arm toward me.

"You. Is this really you? Oh, my God, finally you are found. I have found you again. I dreamed that I had lost you. I just cannot believe it is you, that I have found you."

I bent over him and his arms closed about me.

"Yes, this is you . . . you, really you." He was fighting for air as he talked. "I have never lost you, then. It was only a bad dream."

"Yes, it was only a bad dream," I said, my face pressing against his. His embrace, icy cold through my light summer dress, grew so tight that I could hardly breathe. I felt his tears on my face, mingling with mine.

"Don't ever leave me," he pleaded.

"I'll never leave you," I replied.

At three o'clock the next morning, after a short rest at home, I returned to the hospital. I was wearing the same white blouse I had worn when I first met Gabriel in Paris. I wanted to wear it at our last meeting on this earth.

Margaret, who had sat with him while I rested, looked very tired under the rim of her hat. As I came in she stood up to leave and, at the door, she told me, "I cannot bear his struggle. I won't come any more. This body isn't Gabriel any more. You stay with him till it is all over. This is your place now. You were his wife. I only loved his spirit and his spirit is gone."

The new day was breaking. The morning nurse took over, but, after checking Gabriel, she tactfully withdrew. The minutes grew into hours. He would be lucid for seconds, then in slumber again, his eyes half-open, a grayish film spread over them. He wasn't fighting death any longer; he was ready to go. I was trying to repress an overwhelming stupor. I can't sleep now, I told myself; I must pray, concentrate on him, help him through. I shook myself awake. He started to moan in his pain, then, recognizing me, he cried out, "Oh, my God, God . . . help."

"Don't be afraid, don't. God loves you."

He gripped my outstretched hand. Father Diskin's words came back: kneel down and ask the Blessed Mother for help. I knelt down telling myself it was only a formality, and hoping that the nurse wouldn't come in and find me like this, I began to pray aloud: "Hail Mary, full of grace . . ."

The result was miraculous, as if an electric shock had run through Gabriel's body. His eyes opened wide, he stopped moaning, and, though with difficulty, he clasped his hands in prayer and smiled at me happily, as if I had finally discovered what he was waiting for.

"Pray for us sinners now and at the hour of our death."

"Pray . . . at the hour of death." He struggled with the words.

Then I said the Lord's Prayer, imploring God. But I didn't feel Him; there was no answer.

"Pray . . . pray," moaned Gabriel.

But I can't, I thought. My voice falls into an emptiness. Why isn't He answering? What should I do? And my inner voice said: "You know so well what to do, you selfish, frivolous woman. Your cry to Me is a lie because you are trying to put through an unfair deal: to get Me without giving yourself. Remember what your husband wrote you once: 'Everything is in your hands: the salvation, the miracle, or the damnation.' And now his frightened soul is clinging to your heart and you don't help him."

It was true. I had to decide to change my life, my amusing new life. If only I could believe. "But you do believe," that inner voice argued. "Except you are afraid of the price you have to pay for a living faith."

Gabriel's eyes never left my face and his expression told me that he knew what was going on inside him. A few more hours and all would be over for him, a few more hours during which I might help him; still, I fought against the final step.

"God," I prayed aloud, "have mercy on him, don't judge him by our mistakes. We sinned; we were in love with fame and success. Running after them, we forgot You and lost ourselves. But he always longed for You. He searched for You. He fought with himself to reach You."

"Yes, yes, I did," Gabriel breathed heavily.

"Remember that he could not hate; he never willfully hurt any living being. Come to us, Lord."

"Yes, come to us," Gabriel cried.

At that moment, I felt a power in me. Suddenly everything seemed simple. "I have made my decision," I said. "I will change my life. Have mercy on his soul and I promise I will change. Give him Your mercy. He cannot finish his work on earth to serve You, so let me do it for him. O Lord, put his sins on me, let me suffer for them here on earth and let his soul go free."

Suddenly I felt that I had been heard, that God was with us.

"He is here, do you feel Him?" I said to Gabriel. "Don't be afraid any more, just say to Him 'I love you,' because you do love Him. And I made an offering: instead of you it will be me. All the good I do will be your merit; every prayer I say, you will say it."

The nurse came in. "Are you going to stay with him now," she asked, "or have your lunch?"

"I'm not hungry," I answered. She didn't leave, but motioned me to the door.

"It's none of my business," she said in a whisper, "but I like you. And my advice is that you should get in touch with your lawyer at once. I've heard certain things, and I suspect this lady, Mrs. Scott, is after his money. I heard her saying, 'All that is mine is yours and all that is yours is mine.' Speak to your lawyer at once. He"—and she pointed toward the bed—"is no more, and don't forget life will go on and need is a cruel thing. Don't be soft now."

I did not reply. After all, why should I tell her that the truth was just the opposite? She left and I went back to Gabriel.

"Pray," he said.

"Our Father, Who art in Heaven," I started. But something was wrong; something had gone out of me. I tried to recapture those wonderful earlier moments, but my words had a dull echo. Gabriel's clasped hands fell apart. "No, no good," he muttered, while I went on with the prayer.

The feeling that God had forsaken me persisted; and He had forsaken me, I realized, because I had lied. By my silence I had agreed with the nurse that Margaret was after Gabriel's money. I had impugned Margaret's character by failing to correct the nurse. I was still playing the part of the elegant Mrs. Pascal, the wife of the famous producer. Not for anything would I admit that Gabriel was utterly broke and that Margaret's loan was paying for the hospital and for that very nurse. And all this after I had offered myself to God.

"I am dying. Help. Pray." Gabriel was gasping.

I had to do something at once. I rushed to the phone to call Margaret and apologize. Of course, I couldn't tell her who had said what; I would simply say that I had listened to gossip without correcting it and ask her forgiveness.

Someone was in the phone booth, so I sat down on a sofa. Out here life was flowing normally. Opposite me, two women were chatting. One of them was wearing a nicely cut linen dress, just what I would have liked for myself. Her bracelets jingled as she opened a heavy gold compact and powdered her face. Farther on, some young nurses were giggling, following with their eyes a tall, good-looking doctor who strolled along the corridor, a stethoscope dangling from the pocket of his white coat. At that moment, the idea of apologizing to Margaret seemed silly. What could I say to her anyhow? Only to be out of here! To be somewhere on a beach in the sunshine and forget death.

I hurried back to the sickroom and sat down by Gabriel's bed, reaching for his hand. He pushed me away. "No, no," he murmured.

"Someone was talking on the phone," I said.

He turned his face away from me, groaning.

"I'll go back. I'll go." The booth was empty now and Margaret answered at once. I don't think she understood much of my stammering. "Dearest," she told me, "I'd forgive you if you had put a knife in me. Go back and pray. I will do the same here."

Triumphantly I said to Gabriel: "Everything is all right now." And I knelt down. But again it was no use; there was only emptiness.

"What a hypocrite you are," I told myself. "You thought you could escape easily with Margaret." I have to correct the nurse and tell her the truth, I thought, but she will think I am mad.

"O God," I was sighing, "how can I humiliate myself that much?" But again, Gabriel's eyes were begging for help—for prayer. Unless I tell the truth God won't come back to me.

When the nurse returned, I took her to a far corner of the room. She heard me out, astonished.

"Well, I only wanted your good," she said. "How could I know? But I can tell you one thing: I have seen many people die, but never have I had such a strange case. Something around here. Something about him and you—it makes me shiver inside. They usually die so that you hardly notice them. But here—well, forget it. You are young." She patted my hand affectionately and went out of the room.

I knelt again and now I could pray. He smiled happily as he prayed with me. After a time, he stretched out his right hand and placed it on mine. His voice was clear and strong.

"My dear, dear, little Heart." Those were his last words to me. After that, falling into a semi-coma, he called constantly for God.

As darkness came on, he became quiet. We were alone. They had all gone: Margaret, Pauline, the two Hungarians, and the Woman of Shanghai, like actors leaving the stage when the curtain is about to fall.

The nurse touched my shoulder. "Have a rest, here at his side." She pulled an armchair close to the bed, placed a pillow under my head and propped my legs up on another chair.

"Try to sleep," she said. "I'll be out in the corridor until the night nurse comes, in case you need me."

I reached out for Gabriel's hand, and his fingers closed weakly about mine. They were frighteningly cold. A restless sleep overtook me. I awakened as the chair was pulled from under my feet. "Sorry," the night nurse said. "I didn't see that your feet were on the chair. Anyhow," she continued, "you have no place here. You are blocking my way to the bed. He may die any minute. Sit over there in the corner."

"This is my place," I retorted. "You can't help him any more; you should sit in the corner or leave me alone with him as the other nurse did."

"I am the nurse and my place is here." She settled down in the corner and began to knit, accompanying her work with a low murmur.

I have to pray, I thought. He should not die unaided by my conscious love and concentration. But the nurse and her murmuring disturbed me. And I felt her hostility.

"Nurse," I called over to her in a low voice. "I understand your duty, but this might be his last hour, and for you it is all the same if you sit outside."

"You should go out and not me. You have nothing to do here. I will report the case to the doctor."

She jumped up, gathering her knitting into a large bag.

"You have no love in your heart," I declared.

"What do you know about my heart?" She ran out. After a while, she was back again, under the lamp, her fingers busy on a long gray roll of knitting. In the tiny circle of light, her face seemed to have been carved in stone; her white cap was like the tiara of a cruel archaic goddess—one of the Parcae, I thought, knitting and cutting the threads of lives. Her murmur grew unbearable. An eerie fear came over me, as if evil were around. If he died now, in this very dark moment, unaided by my prayer and faith—Oh, God, why have You left me? What wrong have I done now? Of course, I was angry at the nurse; I almost hated her.

"Nurse," I called. "Forgive my hurting you by saying that there is no love in you." I held out my hand.

She straightened up in surprise, then took my hand. "Let's pray together," I said.

We knelt down, and her deep voice chimed like a church bell as she said: "Our Father, Who art in Heaven . . ."

When she returned to her chair, I remained on my knees, my clasped hands above Gabriel's. "My God, stay with us now and take Gabriel into Your eternal embrace." I fell silent, the words left me, all I felt was love.

As I knelt there in wordless prayer, something inside me began to flutter. I began to tremble with something like fear, but a fear which I had never before experienced: an awesome fear, yet without evil, full of an exalted joy over something which I felt approaching me, something terrible and immense.

It drew nearer. A complete awareness of my own nothingness. The fear grew. My Lord, I am not worthy. I felt smaller than a grain of dust, confronted with that Approach. What sweetness in my nothingness, what joy in His immensity . . .

I felt that Something entered into me; and at that moment, my heart seemed to be breaking. It was as if I had caught fire. I was burning, but with a physical sensation of a real fire, not a symbolic one. My mind, not yet quite extinguished, raised questions, but I pushed them back; I did not want to know, lest that Something leave me. After that, my reason faded away. I was no more; I was absorbed. The fire grew, burning violently; my whole being was burning.

In retrospect I remembered that all the time I knew where I was. I could feel a dull pain in my knee: I could see the design of the wallpaper in the semi-darkness of the room; but beyond the wall and on it and around me was an unbearable marvel of beauty which I did not see, but felt.

The joy was unbearable. The fire grew vast. Consuming, violent joy—I was burning to ashes. I could not endure more. O Lord, I do not want to die . . . I cannot take more.

Slowly the fire began to be extinguished. Intellect fought its way back. The senses returned. The room emerged from the fog.

I said to Gabriel, "The Lord was here." His eyes were open and on me. And suddenly I knew: he must have gone through the same purifying flames. Then I remembered what he had promised me. "A few more days," he had said, "and I will know the Truth; then I will tell it to you." And by the grace of God this was so. The fire of His love and forgiveness manifested itself physically to me, because He knew my weakness and my doubts, and He knew that I had to be given something which I could never dismiss from my mind.

I got up and sat back in the armchair. I wanted to stay awake, but I fell into a deep sleep.

"Oh . . . Oh . . . Oh," I heard, and saw the gray dawn through my half-opened eyes. The groan became a scream. My heavy lids opened to see a half-nude yellowish body tossing in the light. I remembered that it was Gabriel and he was dying. I jumped up. The nurse had stepped to the bed, touching his pulse. "Probably an hour or so," she whispered.

I knelt down again at his side, praying. The sun was rising: a clear, blue morning. A gentle breeze blew through the open window. Then the burning red on the housetops blended into gold-yellow as the sun rose higher. The nurse bent over Gabriel, then motioned to me: the moment was here. With my whole strength, I started to say aloud: "I believe in God, the Father Almighty . . ."

His mouth was sucking for air, his right hand moving forward slowly on the pillow, as if reaching for something. Then he said clearly: "My God . . . of course." Then silence.

The fight was over. He was free. I looked through the window to the cloudless sky. I saw a column of white smoke rising straight from a chimney like a burnt offering and then becoming one with the sky.

PART FOUR

Chapter 1

The Trial

THERE was tranquility and peace at the convent in New Jersey where I went after Gabriel's death. Early Masses in the chapel, swimming in the tree-framed lake, long walks.

I felt weightless in a never-experienced joy—as if I was accompanying Gabriel in his flight to freedom. I remembered his letter of last summer from Ischia: "Soon I will be a spirit again, a nameless, faceless, laughing spirit."

And now everything is far away, left behind, and unreal. There is only God. His presence is all around me. I am inebriated. The landscape is transformed as if a veil is lifted and I see beyond the surface into the depth of reality. Everything is unbelievably beautiful. My eyesight cleansed, I see shimmering, intense colors; the air around me is vibrating and alive and forms delight me. Blades of grass, clods of earth seemed to be magnified: animated and intensely important, tiny flower heads standing out with the authority of their existence. Two turquoise-gold dragonflies like laughter upon the ripples of the lake. A tall, flowering weed stops my walk, swaying in the sunshine, a perfect miracle. Its small white flowers grow in dimension as if the weed is burning now in white flames and all the glory of God, the chorus of cherubims and seraphims are singing on it.

And it seems to me as if He is whispering to me in an even, delightful voice. Everything now is simple and just, everything that was an unconnected, cruel jumble before. I am not alone any more. His burning love connects me with everything.

And I say to Him: "How great is Your Kingdom. If only I knew all the words of every language so that I could praise You in all. If only I could love You in all. If I could be so beautiful, pure, and perfect, that collapsing in Your presence, I would be worthy to utter Your name."

And He says to me: "When you pray to Me, *I* pray in you, and when you marvel at My creation, looking through your eyes, *I* marvel at Myself. Loving you, I love Myself, and loving Me, you love yourself and in Me all that is."

"My Lover, Tremendous one, crush me in Your arms and melt me away in Your embrace. Naked I want to be, naked of thoughts, of ties, naked of memories, naked of my flesh, and naked of my *I*."

And the Lover kissed.

"Have you ever heard that name?" Gabriel's lawyer, Irwin Margulies, asked me. He had mentioned the name of the Woman of Shanghai. "She has a will from Gabriel, naming her as his sole beneficiary, and she's about to probate it."

The words of the Woman of Shanghai came back to me. After Gabriel's death I had paid a visit to her Park Avenue apartment with a large gift-wrapped box from Margaret Scott. Before sailing for South Africa, Margaret had bought three lovely identical summer handbags from Saks Fifth Avenue—for Pauline, the Woman of Shanghai, and me. They were meant to be tokens of the love for Gabriel which united the three of us, and Margaret had asked me to deliver them personally.

Strangely, I felt no pain or hate or even discomfort as I sat in the apartment where my husband once made love to the woman opposite me. She was friendly. I assured her that I had put her red roses and her poem into Gabriel's coffin, as she could not bear to come to the funeral parlor.

When I gave her Margaret's present, her mood suddenly changed. She threw the box down and tore up her letter. Her voice trembled with hate: "That Scott woman was the one who killed him. She ruined our love with all that Baba hogwash."

I kept silent as she turned toward me with a hostile expression. "Gabriel loved me," she said. "I was the only woman he ever loved, who could satisfy him. I gave him everything, I gave him love and he gave me everything he had."

"He gave me everything he had." Those were the words I remembered now as I listened to Margulies repeating the nineteen words of the will: *"This is my will: if I should die on this my trip to India, you are my sole heiress."*

For days those nineteen words were like nineteen nails hammered into my brain. Could that will have been his true will even on February 22? But what made him write it? I realized that the answer lay in the story Margaret Scott had told me that sultry night at the Henry Hudson Hotel. Gabriel had to write the will on the eve of his leaving for India. Therefore, I felt it was my duty to oppose probation. I was in a position to do so as my divorce had never become final and I was his legal widow.

There was another claimant for Gabriel's estate: the Venezuelan millionaire "brother." "You can't fight him too," my lawyer said. "The Chinese woman has a strong chance to win, as the court favors testacy against intestacy. We'd better unite fronts with the brother."

The whole thing was rather academic, I thought; Gabriel had nothing when he died. But apparently I was alone in this opinion; others seemed to think there was still quite a bit in those Shaw rights.

The story broke in the newspapers. *Time* wrote that Gabriel Pascal left everything "to his great and good friend ... wealthy and exotic Irish-Chinese widow of a Dutch banker" and added: "Big plum in Pascal's estate: sole movie rights to six plays of George Bernard Shaw—properties which could easily gross millions of dollars." Other write-ups made it appear that having divorced my husband just before he died and pocketed a settlement, I now sought to upset the will and deprive his fiancée.

The darkness of those days. I had thought that nothing could ever hurt me again, as I was immersed in the all-forgiving love of

God. But now I felt forsaken by Him. I was crushed into a loneliness more terrible than ever before. I belonged nowhere. I cut myself away from my former life. But the doors of Heaven too were closed to me now. And there weren't even memories left to be cherished: my years with Gabriel were overshadowed by the Woman of Shanghai. And the future? What should I do? There was the worry of the daily bread in a strange city. Nothing remained to me but my faith; stripped naked of any comfort, I clung to it like one who is shipwrecked.

I was still putting off the final step of my return to the Church: taking the Sacraments. Those events after my return from the convent disturbed me so deeply that I felt I wasn't ready, much less worthy. At least, that was my excuse for my reluctance.

It was already October when I finally went to see Father Diskin. I was seated in the same barren reception room where I had first met him. He heard me out patiently. Though he did not try to influence me, I surprised myself by saying that, after all, maybe I should go to confession. I chose the Thursday of the following week.

As that Thursday drew nearer, such darkness descended upon me that I began to doubt. The thought of returning to the Church and its rigid discipline seemed like returning to a joyless prison. I could love God free from any established form of Church. At the same time, I knew too well that, if a religion were only a certain form of philosophy for me, it would never give me the strength to battle against my faults and sins. But to be a practicing Catholic again seemed to be too great a price to pay.

Wednesday evening, nevertheless, I went through the list of my trespasses; then the devil got loose in me. Why go tomorrow? Why take the consequences of that final step? It was true enough, I told myself, that I had promised God and the passing soul of Gabriel that I would mend my ways. But did that mean a return to the Church? And hadn't he, Gabriel, betrayed me? Had *he* kept his promise to be my protector when he wrote that will in order to save his own skin? Why then should I go on being his victim, even after his death? Also, how could I ever imagine that my promise could help his soul? That actually was a very vain thought; it was pride. Besides, everybody for himself—my sacrifice could never pay *his* debts. Here I was, a nobody, an empty, useless, lonely self. Why had I turned away from my former life, just when it had begun to develop into something lovely? But maybe it wasn't too late. On the other hand, if I go to that confession tomorrow, there is no way back. My torment grew.

"O God, You Who have left me since the convent, give back my faith. Or let me go to Hell without bothering me constantly with Yourself. Take me or leave me. But . . . oh, take me." I went down on my knees, gazing into the darkness. Then, suddenly, I felt the *will* rising in me. It was strong, cold, without pity. I said to myself that, even if there was to be complete oblivion after death, I must choose the way of my promise. Even if the fire which I had experienced at Gabriel's deathbed was nothing but self-delusion, that promise binds me. I have no other way.

After my confession I knelt in the Church. On the aisle where Gabriel's coffin had traveled a few months ago, now school children were walking toward the altar, reciting the Rosary. It was the Feast of the Holy Rosary. The priest had told me in the confessional: "You must be especially patronized by Our Lady as today is the feast of her Rosary."

The Rosary. Gabriel had asked me back to him with the words, "Bring my rosary." And my return to the Church had to happen on the Feast of the Rosary.

I had joined the Legion of Mary, a society of lay people, at Saint Paul's Parish. In pairs we walked the streets of New York's slums, visiting families.

Our meetings were held once a week in the Rectory, opposite the entrance of the Roosevelt Hospital, and on those nights I used to wait for the bus next to that awning under which Gabriel had walked into the hospital to die.

The battles within myself were not over. I remember distinctly a rainy day when I was pulling a grocery cart on Third Avenue and feeling sorry for myself. I went to a faraway market to save money and I thought of the rich woman and the rich "brother" claiming my husband's estate. The temptation rose again: to get away from all, forget Gabriel, the Woman of Shanghai, and the brother, and go back to my life where I had left it before I had gone to the hospital. What had I achieved by my change? Instead of fighting to be on top again, I was now fighting for obscure, small jobs for less pay in a week than what I used to give my cooks. I sank among the nameless crowd, elbowing at the rush-hour subway stations. Why am I trying to reach for something beyond my capacity? Why am I trying to cut off my natural desires? Am I not mistaken? And if I am, what a tragically irrevocable mistake! To be a saint? I wasn't made to be one. The very thought of becoming a saint, I said to myself, is the same old vanity again. Top billing. But let me face it; I am no heroine; I am mediocre; I was mediocre in my sins, and now I am converted into a mediocre betterness. I was and am always a coward: never either-or. If I weren't a coward, I would go back to my happy sins, or if I weren't a coward, I would become a saint. No; no heroine, no saint, just elbowing among the faceless crowd on the spiritual subway stations.

"Why all my confusions, all my doubts?" "What is the truth *for me?* Where to go, what to do? Anyhow what do You want from me?" I asked God. Or did I ask myself?

"There is no other way," it seemed to me the answer came, "than to find yourself through your doubts and sufferings and worries and when you have found yourself, you will find the way. You are mediocre, you said. It is true you are no Joan of Arc. You were not intended to be one. That your name will not shine among the great saints, and that your capacities are average, that is how I willed you to be. Why don't you embrace, with all humility, your cross: the cross of being average? Crucify your great vanity on it. You can be a nameless saint, an unknown one, a saint of dull duties and even days. You can start right here and now. Today, as so many days, you were bitter about the Woman of Shanghai. Fighting for your truth is right, but the fight has to be detached from hate. And isn't she also My child and your sister? Isn't she the heiress of My Kingdom, if she so chooses? Her share isn't less than yours in My love. And I say to you, until you can pray 'Father forgive,' you are not Mine."

*   *   *

"The deceased, Gabriel Pascal, died on July 6, 1954." The trial over the will opened in Surrogate Court before Judge Frankenthaler at ten o'clock on the morning of November 16, 1955. It was almost dark outside from heavy thunderclouds. Distant rumbling grew into loud thunder, as if the sky were protesting against the words of Mr. Stephens, the lawyer for the Woman of Shanghai, who was now introducing her case.

The Woman sat opposite me, surrounded by a large group of her friends. The Tall Hungarian was behind her, leaning forward from time to time and whispering in her ear. He avoided looking in my direction. So did Harold, Baba's pupil and Gabriel's one-time secretary, who apparently came to be a witness in the Woman of Shanghai's behalf. Outside in the corridor the newspaper reporters and photographers waited.

By this time, the "miracle" Gabriel and Margaret Scott had so firmly believed in was beginning to work. A year earlier Alan Jay Lerner and Frederick Loewe had approached the Shaw Trustee for the *Pygmalion* musical rights. The Trustee acknowledged the rights of the Pascal estate in the property on the basis that, because of the changes Gabriel had made in *Pygmalion* for the film version, he had been co-author with Shaw. The Pascal estate was therefore to share the royalties with the Shaw estate.

Because of the rumors of the possible success of *My Fair Lady*, as the *Pygmalion* musical was to be called, the value of the Pascal estate was constantly growing in the imagination of the writers of newspaper articles; they now estimated it at "over $100,000."

The Woman of Shanghai was confident of her victory. The court in Albany, in ordering a trial, accepted her arguments that a broader interpretation might be given to the conditional will. At the trial she would have the opportunity to prove her assertion that she had been Pascal's "fiancée, benefactor, and companion for a long period of time," and that Pascal had actually been separated from his wife for "several years." The fact that I had entered a divorce suit and had waived my rights in a property settlement was strongly in her favor. She had also argued that Pascal had not canceled his trip to India but only *postponed* it and that therefore he actually died in New York City on his way to India.

But there were possible witnesses against the Woman's claim to be "the natural object of Pascal's bounty," and one was Margaret

Scott. She had been thunderstruck when she learned of the will. Her first reaction was a deluge of letters from South Africa, saying that she was ready to fly back at any time to testify to all she knew of Gabriel's relationship with the Woman of Shanghai.

Nor did Margaret consider me a rightful contestant for Gabriel's estate. She, Margaret, was his only true "trustee," she wrote, because of his "symbolic" act in giving her power of attorney to act in his absence at the auction of our furnishings and to deduct her loans from the proceeds of the sale.

"All that is mine was his," she wrote, "and therefore all that was his is mine, and all of that belongs to Baba." She had given those loans to Gabriel, she wrote, with the understanding that they were to bear fruit for Baba's "great cause."

Then, in the summer of 1955, Margaret suddenly returned from South Africa and moved into the Robert Fulton Hotel. "Inner instructions" had made her come back, she explained: she was to unveil the dark mystery which had killed Gabriel. She played her detective role with great relish, weaving a confused and intricate fable about herself, Gabriel, and Baba. The Woman of Shanghai appeared in it, sometimes as a villain, at other times as the lost soul whom she, Margaret, ought to save. She was more than ever convinced and fearful of the Chinese Woman's occult powers.

But Margaret's sudden return was also prompted by her decision to claim her rights, based on that power of attorney. She explained to the lawyer about the "millions" which Gabriel's properties, if placed in Baba's hands, would bring to all for a good cause. Margaret's faith in the millions hidden somewhere in Gabriel's estate never wavered. "You'll see," she said. "The miracle Gabriel foretold is coming. He was a master spirit. He knew." That discussion took place before anybody had any inkling about the future of *My Fair Lady*.

Margaret became more and more involved in her fable, but as she collided with the cold reality of the lawyer's office, where she was only a creditor among the many other creditors, her violent reactions increased. She would call me or come to see me and have crying fits, and it would take me quite a while to calm her.

Some time before the trial, Margaret phoned me between four and five in the morning. "I am going to be destroyed by black magic." Her voice was hoarse and shaky. A few minutes earlier, she said, she had received a phone call from the Chinese Woman.

Later there was another call in the curious hour between four and five in the morning. Margaret became frantic with fear and asked my lawyer for advice. Since the pre-trial examinations were going on, my lawyer asked the Woman of Shanghai if she knew Mrs. Margaret Scott and if she had telephoned her.

"*She* tried to get hold of *me*," she answered. "I do not want to speak to her. I don't speak to her. She called me from the Robert Fulton Hotel at five o'clock in the morning one month ago. She asked me to help her. I refused to talk to her. She is very nervous."

"Didn't *you* call her and tell her to lay off this case?" the lawyer asked.

"No. *She* asked *me* to lay off this case," the Woman of Shanghai insisted.

"Did you threaten that . . ." my lawyer began, only to be interrupted by the objections of the Woman's lawyer.

As the date of the trial itself neared, Margaret became ambiguous. She showed me a letter from India, instructing her to get in touch with the Woman of Shanghai. "But I'm afraid of her," she said, and her eyes darkened with fear.

Then one day she said she had thought it over: she did not want to testify at the trial. "Don't forget," she added, "that Baba teaches love and forgiveness and I should not be involved in anything of the World."

"But if you're subpoenaed," I pointed out, "you have to tell the truth about Gabriel's relationship with the Chinese Woman. And don't you think it's false not to help what you feel is true?"

"There are times," she answered with solemnity, "and I can prove it to you, when a lie could become a divine truth."

I soon understood what she meant by that. She had received a letter from Baba's sister in India, telling her to stand by the Chinese Woman at the trial. The Woman of Shanghai had befriended some people from the New York Baba group and now she was exchanging letters with Baba's sister.

"Is that what you meant by a 'divine' lie?" I asked Margaret.

Face to face with me, she lost her assurance. "What can I do?" she said. "Tell me what to do. I cannot go against Baba's wishes.

He is my Master, who directs my life to a higher consciousness where lie and truth are different from those on your level of consciousness." She took a deep breath and continued: "You have to realize that Baba is an *Avatar* who has to be obeyed blindly. But if I am questioned at the trial and tell the truth, I am not helping her. On the other hand, Baba is right in saying that I am the only one who can dissolve her hatred and save her soul. So I *have* to help her. Oh, why can't I have peace with Gabriel and Baba; why did I have to get involved in the human and the personal again? All I want are my lovely, beautiful dreams."

The Woman of Shanghai's lawyer approached with an offer of a settlement: the estate to be divided equally between her, the brother, and myself. My lawyers put tremendous pressure on me to accept the settlement. I refused to agree and was whisked down to Surrogate's Court to appear in the chambers of Judge Frankenthaler, where I still held out. "I don't want a third of the estate or any money at all," I said. "I am only fighting for what I consider to be the truth." I added that if I had thought that the will was indeed my husband's wish I would not have fought against it in the first place.

Margaret had also begged me to settle. She said she knew that the Chinese Woman did not want those hidden "millions" in Gabriel's estate, but only wanted vindication and to prove that Gabriel had loved her. If the case was settled, she would give her share to "Baba's cause."

One Sunday about a week before the trial, Margaret came to see me. I asked her what she had decided about testifying for me and whether she would also tell about my reconciliation with Gabriel.

Her face became red and she burst out, "He was never reconciled with you and never wanted to be. That part of his life was finished when he entered into a higher plane with Baba and me. I've been sorry for you all this time because I like you, but I have to put you straight: I was the *only* one who belonged to him. I belonged to him on a divine level. And then you came back and took *my* place in the hospital. You hurt me, you just don't know how you hurt me by that."

Her thin mouth was trembling. It was my fault, she said, that Gabriel died, I who stopped Baba's miracle: though Gabriel had been in the clutches of dark, destroying powers, Baba still could have saved him. But I had called in the Catholic priest and made Gabriel return to his Church and thus lose his faith in Baba.

"You pushed him back to a *personal* level and thus forced his soul back to further reincarnations," Margaret went on accusingly. "But I loved him with a pure, impersonal love, and my love was touched only in the hospital with a personal love: but not like your love which was an earthly matter, already dissolved. No, my love became the beautiful fusion of the impersonal-personal which is but the highest *divine* love. And now I have to tell you the truth: *I* am his fiancée. *I* am his spouse in a spiritual marriage in Baba. *I am his sole heiress.* Wouldn't I have been a fool to give him all that money if it weren't so?"

She sat there, agitated, the dreamy haze gone from her blue eyes; they were round and angry, like a ruffled mother hen's. "You two are fighting for his inheritance and here I am, nowhere," she cried. "I gave him all I had and all he had *is* mine and *he* is mine, or if it isn't so then he was a thief and a scoundrel!"

She got up to leave but at the door, as if she was suddenly sorry for me, she turned back. "One day you will understand," she said, "but now you have to remember that I was initiated into the greatest mysteries and I have the highest knowledge of God."

That was the last time I saw her.

My lawyer did not subpoena Margaret, but Vernon Brooks, another witness who could have endangered my opponents' claim, sat in court not far from me.

While Gabriel was alive the Woman of Shanghai had tried to befriend Vernon Brooks, but he had kept himself aloof. After the lawsuit started and other attempts to talk to Brooks had failed, she had written him, saying that she had received an anonymous telephone call warning her that certain letters of hers were in Brooks' hands. Were they copies of letters already found among Pascal's papers, or were they some other ones? Brooks had assured her that he had no letters in his possession.

She was worried about her letters all along. On the day of Gabriel's death, she had called up Vernon Brooks. "Please," she pleaded, "go to his room in the club and get my letters. They are silly letters and I don't want anybody to see them."

Brooks found the room already sealed when he got there. And now those letters, together with copies of Gabriel's letters to her, were to be introduced in evidence against her claim of being the woman Gabriel wanted to marry and to whom he had left everything he had.

At that time, anonymous phone calls were playing quite a part. I had received a number of threats and so had Vernon Brooks, who had been warned to keep away from the trial.

It was quite dark now outside. The storm had reached its height and rain was pouring over the courthouse windows. Mr. Stephens, my opponent's lawyer, was reading from a paper, his voice overpowered by the thunder: "At the time of his death, he resided at the New York Athletic Club. He died at the Roosevelt Hospital . . ."

I saw him die, I thought. Among all those who came to claim, to argue, to witness, to judge, I am the only one who shared his death.

"He left surviving him a widow, Valerie Pascal, who at that time had been separated from him . . ." The monotonous monologue went on.

It was like being an onlooker at a drama in which I had played a leading part. The character actors came and went. Yt Kan, the old, illiterate Chinese cook, sat on the witness stand, small and dark in her black dress and with her severe knot of hair, answering through an interpreter. Then Miss Huang, the Woman of Shanghai's secretary, who had been the other witness to the will. Then Harold, Gabriel's ex-secretary, finally playing his first important part. Indeed he would have made a good actor, I thought. He enjoyed the spotlight. His answers flew eagerly, loquaciously, notwithstanding the warning to answer only yes or no. When questioned about Baba he answered in the ringing voice of a revivalist preacher: "Shri Meher Baba . . . who in India is regarded as a spiritually perfect master, whose function is to bring men closer to God." No, he is not comparable to Mahatma Gandhi, Harold answered a further question. "Baba's followers relegate him to a position higher than Gandhi." He and the Tall Hungarian both testified for the Woman of Shanghai that Pascal had only *postponed* his trip to India, and that there was a deep relationship between him and her. Also, the testimony went on, Pascal had asked her to come to the hospital when he was dying, and the Tall Hungarian went to fetch her.

When the witnesses had been heard the three lawyers presented their arguments.

Judge Frankenthaler remarked that the trial was set to hear testimony supporting the validity of the Chinese Woman's claim. But, the Judge asked, "What testimony is there to show that the will is a valid will, as opposed to the definitely conditional language used by the deceased? There is no question that the deceased intended to take a trip. The question is, what did he mean in his will? You say that the reference to the trip was an inducement."

"That is right, sir," said Stephens, the Chinese Woman's lawyer.

"Not a condition of its taking effect," asserted the Judge.

"That is correct, sir."

"The language is capable of other construction." The Surrogate threw back the ball. "What has been shown to indicate that there should be the other construction? . . . he wrote it in his own language, in his own words: 'If I should die on this my trip.'"

"He also said, your Honor, 'This is my will,'" argued Mr. Stephens.

Yes, the Surrogate agreed, but—what was his will? "If I should die on this my trip to India, you are my sole heiress." Then the Surrogate added, "He had four months after that to make a different will, if he wanted to."

But Pascal had given that will to the woman to whom he was close, who had been kind to him, who also had loaned him money. Would he then, under such circumstances, argued Mr. Stephens, give her something like a lottery ticket: that if he died on this trip, she would inherit, and if he did not die on this trip, she would not?

"Or," answered the Surrogate, "was he saying, 'I am merely

going to make a provision for my present trip because I can't tell what will happen. When I come back, then I will give consideration to something else and I will take this up a little more carefully.' . . . Is it not possible that he regarded this as a sort of emergency will, just to cover this trip?"

"I don't believe that that was the intention," said Mr. Stephens. "If I might quote a little poem. The child in the poem says, 'If I should die before I wake'; that doesn't mean that the child is saying 'God take care of me while I am asleep. When I am awake, I will take care of myself.' There was a general intention."

"He was just covering the immediate period and intending to make another prayer the following day," suggested the Surrogate. A ripple of laughter ran through the newsmen.

"The law favors testacy as against intestacy," Mr. Stephens tried.

"But only if the testator intended that there should be testacy," answered the judge.

Mr. Stephens tried another angle: the will should be given a broader interpretation because it was "unartfully drawn." Gabriel Pascal was a foreigner and also a show-business man used to spectacular language and not accustomed to tight legal language. He really did not know enough English to feel the difference in words.

Mr. Garrel, my lawyer, refuted him quickly: Pascal was the man whom George Bernard Shaw, a great master of the English language, had picked as the sole interpreter of his plays. Furthermore, Pascal was a businessman, an independent producer who had to deal with contracts written in English. The will of February 22 was actually very carefully worded by a man who knew very well the language he was using.

The morning newspapers covered the trial in headlines. On the second day the letters of the Woman of Shanghai were introduced into evidence over the desperate objections of her lawyer. Mr. Garrel called Vernon Brooks to the witness stand. His questions on the relationship between Gabriel and the Woman of Shanghai brought forth a deluge of objections from her lawyer, but the judge accepted Garrel's argument offering Brooks' testimony because of the claim "that the proponent was the natural object of Pascal's bounty and that this will was not intended to be conditional." Brooks' testimony proved to be shattering to that claim.

Stephens now brought out his big gun: he told of the divorce and the property settlement, putting me on the witness stand to admit that I had waived all my rights. Therefore, he argued, the will should be accepted as the true wish of the deceased.

Garrel answered that there was no final divorce, that I was the widow, and that there had been a "deathbed reconciliation." And he called Vernon Brooks once more to the stand.

Brooks testified that Pascal asked him to get in touch with me and to tell me to bring his rosary to the hospital. "Mrs. Pascal was at his bedside constantly," Brooks continued. "Whenever I would go into the room she was generally sitting in a chair beside his bed, holding his hand, talking to him. She actually ate in the hospital room with him on one occasion, when he had even asked her to bring their own china and silverware for the meal."

"Was the relationship friendly or unfriendly?" my lawyer asked.

"The relationship was decidedly more than friendly," Brooks answered.

Mr. Stephens argued that the testimony did not establish a legal reconciliation.

"I will concede," said Mr. Garrel, "that the principle is that a reconciliation must include co-habitation, but I will contend that that applies only to those situations where there is a possibility of co-habitation, which was not possible here, and under these circumstances."

"You contend that, under the circumstances here, it was a final reconciliation?" asked the judge.

"Yes," Mr. Garrel replied.

PASCAL'S "IFFY" WILL IS NOW UP TO THE SURROGATE, ran the headlines the next day. And in the gossip columns: "Bombshell in the much-publicized 'will case' ... Pascal did not intend to marry Manchu Princess ... contesting estate with his widow ...."

Months passed while I waited for the decision of the Surrogate. I was calm. I had done what I had to do; the rest was no longer in my power. But I was greatly astonished that after all the publicity about the trial there was no word from Margaret. Her silence was very much unlike her, especially after that last meeting when she had left in anger, only to make up over the telephone later.

In February I came down with flu and was in bed feeling miserable. Late one evening, my phone rang. My "hello" was answered by a voice which sounded insane or in a trance—an evil voice.

"Margaret Scott is dead!" the voice shrieked. "And you are the next one. Now you shall die!"

While I held the receiver, numb, the voice repeated the sentence at the same pitch and word for word, as if it were a recording. Then I hung up.

Margaret Scott was indeed dead; the voice was well informed. On the morning of February 25—Baba's birthday—her body was found lying on the roof of the inside court of the Robert Fulton Hotel. Two years earlier to the day Gabriel had planned to arrive in India on Margaret's round-trip ticket; and two years earlier, Margaret had sent him a birthday card and congratulated him on his "new Birth"—his liberation from his passion for the Woman of Shanghai.

I found out from an old friend of hers who lived in the same hotel that about the time of the trial she had left for Florida, where she stayed in the house of Arthur Ford, a renowned medium. Before leaving for Florida, the friend said, Margaret behaved very curiously. She seemed to be deadly frightened of something; she had burned up all her papers and even taken another name. On her return to New York she acted even more disturbed. Nobody knew that she was back. She did not want to contact even the Baba group. She had registered in the hotel under that other name and kept talking of being destroyed by some dark powers. She had developed a frightful-looking carbuncle on her neck and had finally decided to go to the hospital on February 25, Baba's birthday, to have it removed.

On the night of February 24, she went to bed early and her old friend gave her a sedative, prescribed by the doctor. She had asked the friend to open the window for her, as she wanted fresh air and always slept with open windows.

Between four and five in the morning, the hour which Margaret most feared, the night clerk of the hotel heard a terrifying crushing sound. Margaret had fallen out of her eighth-floor window.

The police listed her death as an accident.

My Fair Lady opened on Broadway on March 15, 1956. Opening night was a benefit with black ties, evening gowns, and those tense last moments before the curtain goes up to unveil a success or failure. From my seat, I could see Frederick Loewe, vibrant with excitement, shaking hands; further away was the lean figure of Alan Jay Lerner.

I read and reread the small print in the program: "Adapted from George Bernard Shaw's *Pygmalion,* produced on the screen by Gabriel Pascal." These lines entwining the two names had the brevity of a tombstone. And in a way it was a tombstone, a small memorial to a strange friendship of two dead men, and buried under it, forgotten, lay the struggles and victory, and then the defeat, of the man without whom *My Fair Lady* would not be opening here tonight.

The rest was to be the history of one of the greatest Broadway successes. The musical played for years in New York and all over the world. Five million dollars were paid for the film rights, and millions from its royalties poured into the coffers of the Shaw estate. Pascal had been right when, after obtaining the option for *Pygmalion,* he told Shaw: "I will make you rich and even more famous than you are now." And if Shaw were alive today, he would be winking delightedly: "Am I not, as I always have told you about myself, the most brilliant businessman? That half a crown deal with Pascal which made millions."

How in Gabriel's life everything always moved in connected and repeated circles! The first *Pygmalion* had made a fortune— but for others; and so did the second one. Gabriel died bankrupt, borrowing money even for the comfort of his deathbed. And now his estate was to increase over the years to well over the mark of $2 million.

A month after the opening of *My Fair Lady* the decision of the Surrogate's Court on the will of February 22, 1954, was handed down. The Woman of Shanghai lost her case. She appealed, but she lost again.

Gabriel's estate was to be divided equally between the brother and me, and Judge Frankenthaler appointed me as its administratrix.

Margaret Scott's estate was repaid, and the money went to her daughter.

Hedwig Brugge died before I had the money to help her, which I knew Gabriel wanted me to do. Her last letter came shortly after his death:

"I have been Gabriel's standard-bearer from my early youth till the end . . . I never let go of his standard. I held it high in wind and sunshine, high and bright . . . but what good did it do him? None at all. Useless and senseless, I wasted my life. Yet, it was a divine privilege to love him."

Yes, it was a divine privilege to love him.

Valerie Pascal was born in Budapest and educated at the Ursuline Convent there. As a girl she loved to write stories and, even more, to act in school plays. Against her family's wishes she determined to become an actress, and, after training at the Royal Academy of Dramatic Art, she was an immediate and brilliant success, both on the stage and in the movies. Her career was interrupted when the war reached Hungary in 1944, and it was with hopes of resuming it that she overcame all the obstacles a Communist bureaucracy could put in her way and went to Paris to make a screen test for Gabriel Pascal, the famed Hungarian-born film producer. What happened as a result of their meeting is the story told by this book.

Mrs. Pascal began to work on her husband's biography shortly after he died, writing first in Hungarian, then, as her mastery of the language increased, in English. It was a difficult and emotionally exhausting task, one she put aside several times, only to take it up again. The chance discovery a few years ago of the Shaw-Pascal correspondence provided the impetus that helped her to finish the manuscript.

Valerie Pascal is now the wife of George Delacorte, the philanthropist and publisher, and lives in New York.

0-595-33772-4

Printed in the United States
26645LVS00002B/76-195

9 780595 337729